KHAJA QUTUBUDDIN

Logic Testing and Design for Testability

MIT Press Series in Computer Systems
Herb Schwetman, editor

Metamodeling: A Study of Approximations in Queueing Models,
by Subhash Chandra Agrawal, 1985

Logic Testing and Design for Testability,
by Hideo Fujiwara, 1985

Logic Testing and Design for Testability

Hideo Fujiwara

The MIT Press
Cambridge, Massachusetts
London, England

Second Printing, 1990

This book was set in Times New Roman by Asco Trade Typesetting Ltd., Hong Kong and printed and bound by Halliday Lithograph in the United States of America

Library of Congress Cataloging in Publication Data

Fujiwara, Hideo.
Logic testing and design for testability.
(MIT Press series in computer systems)
Bibliography: p.
Includes index.
1. Logic circuits—Testing. I. Title. II. Series.
TK7868.L6F85 1985 621.3815'37 85-84
ISBN 0-262-06096-5

Contents

Series Foreword

This series is devoted to all aspects of computer systems. This means that subjects ranging from circuit components and microprocessors to architecture to supercomputers and systems programming will be appropriate. Analysis of systems will be important as well. System theories are developing, theories that permit deeper understandings of complex interrelationships and their effects on performance, reliability, and usefulness.

We expect to offer books that not only develop new material but also describe projects and systems. In addition to understanding concepts, we need to benefit from the decision making that goes into actual development projects; selection from among alternatives can be crucial to success. We are soliciting contributions in which several aspects of systems are classified and compared. A better understanding of both the similarities and the differences found in systems is needed.

It is an exciting time in the area of computer systems. New technologies mean that architectures that were at one time interesting but infeasible are now feasible. Better software engineering means that we can consider several software alternatives, instead of "more of the same old thing," in terms of operating systems and system software. Faster and cheaper communications mean that intercomponent distances are less important. We hope that this series contributes to this excitement in the area of computer systems by chronicling past achievements and publicizing new concepts. The format allows publication of lengthy presentations that are of interest to a select readership.

Herb Schwetman

Preface

With the great and growing use of computers (especially microcomputers) in many aspects of society, it is evident that the computers must perform more and more reliably. The reliability of a computer depends much on testing—that is, the determination whether circuits have been manufactured properly and behave correctly. However, because of the rapidly increasing circuit density in large-scale-integration and very-large-scale-integration technology, testing is getting much more difficult. One approach to alleviating this problem is embodied in "design for testability" techniques, by which extra circuitry is added to a circuit or a chip to reduce the complexity of testing. In the past, design problems were approached with the idea of minimizing the complexity of the hardware. Testing was considered only after the design of a circuit had been completed. Recently, however, design for testability has attracted interest in connection with LSI and VLSI designs, because the cost of hardware has been decreasing while the cost of testing has been increasing. There is now a growing interest in design for testability with the increasing use of VLSI circuits.

This book is intended to provide insight into the theory and practice of logic testing and design for testability. The book is divided into two parts. Part I deals with logic testing and part II with design for testability. Although an attempt is made to include topics of general importance, many important techniques associated with logic testing and design for testability are also dealt with. Related topics include test generation, fault simulation, complexity of testing, design techniques to minimize the cost of test application and test generation, scan design, compact testing, built-in testing, and various design techniques for self-testable systems.

The book may be used as a text for a graduate-level course in electrical engineering or computer science. It should also be helpful to computer designers, logic designers, and test designers who want a better understanding of the principles of logic testing and design for testability and who may apply the techniques to their designs. Researchers who may be interested in going deeper into the study of logic testing and design for testability will also find the book useful.

I wish to express deep gratitude to H. Ozaki of Osaka University and K. Kinoshita of Hiroshima University for their encouragement and support for this work. I am heavily indebted to various persons for discussions, suggestions, and criticisms. I am especially grateful to S. Toida of Old Dominion University, V. K. Agarwal of McGill University, T. Sasao of Osaka University, Y. Takamatsu of Saga University, and A. Yamada, S. Funatsu, and T. Shimono of NEC Corporation.

Hideo Fujiwara

Logic Testing and Design for Testability

I LOGIC TESTING

1 Introduction to Logic Testing

The development of computers has been stimulated greatly by integrated-circuit technology. Circuit density has increased dramatically, and the cost of devices has decreased as their performance has improved. With these developments, reliability has become increasingly important. However, with the advent of very-large-scale integration (VLSI), testing has come up against a wall of "intractability" and is at a standstill. Since the gate density of VLSI circuits is increasing much more rapidly than the number of access terminals, the ability to generate test patterns and to process fault simulations is deteriorating. The difficulty can be reduced by the development of faster and more efficient algorithms for test-pattern generation or by the use of design techniques to enhance testability.

1.1 Logic Circuits

Logic circuits are constructed by interconnecting elements called *gates* whose inputs and outputs represent only the values denoted by 0 and 1. Some common gates are AND, OR, NOT, NAND, NOR, and EOR (Exclusive-OR); their symbols are shown in figure 1.1. The output of each gate can be represented by a logic function or a Boolean function of the inputs. The terms *logic* and *Boolean* are often used to denote the same meaning. A logic function can be specified by a truth table, a Karnaugh map, or a set of cubes. Figure 1.2 demonstrates these three forms. The Boolean (logic) operations $\cdot$, $+$, and $\bar{\ }$ correspond to AND, OR, and NOT, respectively.

The output z of an AND gate with inputs x_1 and x_2 is 1 if and only if both of its inputs are 1 simultaneously, and can be expressed as

$$z = x_1 \cdot x_2.$$

The output z of an OR gate with inputs x_1 and x_2 is 1 if and only if any of its inputs are 1, and can be expressed as

$$z = x_1 + x_2.$$

The output z of a NOT gate or an inverter with input x is 1 if and only if its input is 0, and can be expressed as

$$z = \bar{x}.$$

The output z of a NAND gate with inputs x_1 and x_2 is 1 if and only if any of its inputs are 0, and can be expressed as

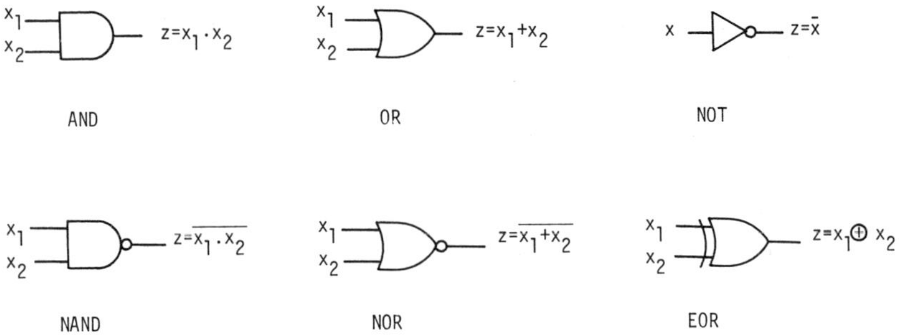

Figure 1.1
Symbols for gates

x_1	x_2	x_3	f
0	0	0	0
0	0	1	0
0	1	0	0
0	1	1	1
1	0	0	1
1	0	1	1
1	1	0	1
1	1	1	0

(a) Truth table

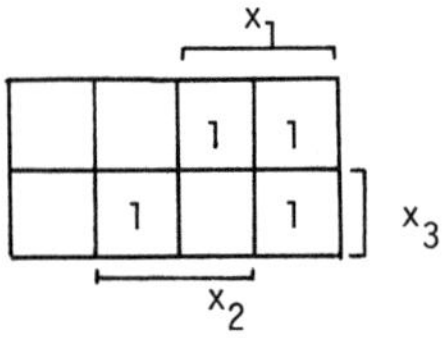

(b) Karnaugh map

x_1	x_2	x_3
1	0	-
1	-	0
0	1	1

(c) A set of cubes

Figure 1.2
Representations for a logic function

$$z = \overline{x_1 \cdot x_2} = \bar{x}_1 + \bar{x}_2.$$

The output z of a NOR gate with inputs x_1 and x_2 is 1 if and only if both of its inputs are 0, and can be expressed as

$$z = \overline{x_1 + x_2} = \bar{x}_1 \cdot \bar{x}_2.$$

The output z of an EOR gate with inputs x_1 and x_2 is 1 if and only if its input are not simultaneously equal, and can be expressed as

$$z = \bar{x}_1 x_2 + x_1 \bar{x}_2 = x_1 \oplus x_2.$$

Logic circuits can be categorized as *combinational* or *sequential*. A combinational (logic) circuit consists of an interconnected set of gates with no feedback loops. (A feedback loop is a directed path from the output of some gate G to an input of gate G.) The output values of a combinational circuit at a given time depend only on the present inputs. Hence, each output can be specified by a logic function of its input variables. A block diagram for combinational circuits is shown in figure 1.3, where $x_1, \ldots, x_n$ are the inputs and $z_1, \ldots, z_m$ are the outputs.

A sequential (logic) circuit contains feedback loops. The output values at a given time depend not only on the present inputs but also on inputs applied previously. The history of previous inputs is summarized in the *state* of the circuit. Figure 1.4 shows a block diagram for sequential circuits. A sequential circuit consists of two sections: a combinational circuit and a memory circuit. The circuit of figure 1.4 has n primary inputs $x_1, \ldots, x_n$; m primary outputs $z_1, \ldots, z_m$; p feedback inputs $y_1, \ldots, y_p$; and p feedback outputs $Y_1, \ldots, Y_p$. $Y_1, \ldots, Y_p$ are also inputs to the memory, and $y_1, \ldots, y_p$ are outputs of the memory. The *present state* of the circuit is represented by the variables $y_1, \ldots, y_p$, and the *next state* is determined by $Y_1, \ldots, Y_p$.

The mathematical model of a sequential circuit is called a *sequential machine* or a *finite-state machine*. A sequential machine M is characterized by the following:

a finite set S of states,
a finite set I of input symbols,
a finite set O of output symbols,
a mapping N of $S \times I$ into S (called the *next-state function*), and
a mapping Z of $S \times I$ into O (called the *output function*).

The sequential machine M is expressed by the 5-tuple (S, I, O, N, Z).

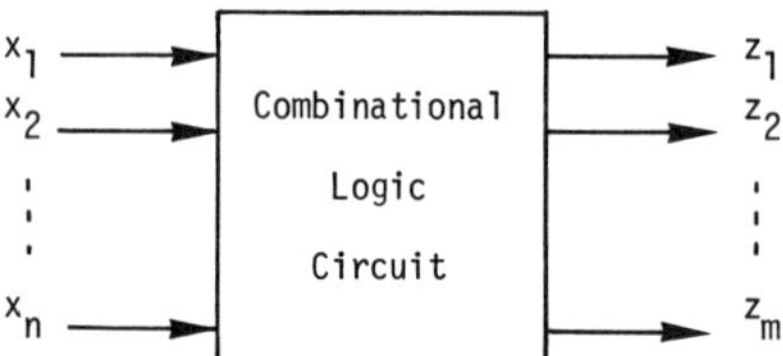

Figure 1.3
Block diagram of combinational logic circuits

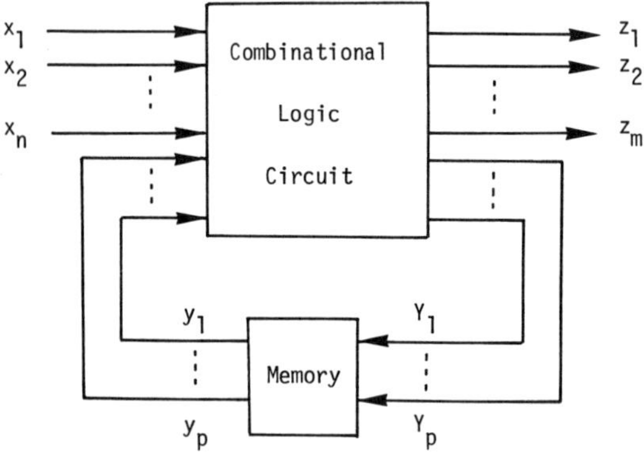

Figure 1.4
Block diagram of sequential logic circuits

A sequential machine can be conveniently represented either in tabular form by a *state table* (*flow table*) or in graph form by a *state diagram*. A state table, as illustrated in figure 1.5(a), lists the present states as row headings and the input symbols (also called input values or input states) as column headings. The entry in row S_i and column I_j represents the next state $N(S_i, I_j)$ and the output $Z(S_i, I_j)$. The machine shown in figure 1.5(a) has four states (labeled 1, 2, 3, 4) and a binary input and output. Figure 1.5(b) shows the state diagram corresponding to the table of figure 1.5(a). A state diagram is a directed graph whose nodes correspond to states of the machine and whose arcs correspond to state transitions. Each arc is labeled with the input value separated by a slash from the output value associated with the transition.

Sequential circuits are categorized as either *synchronous* or *asynchronous*, depending upon whether or not the behavior of the circuit is clocked at

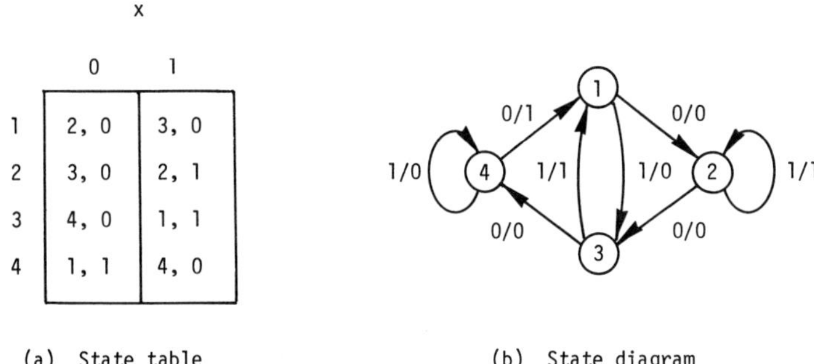

	x = 0	x = 1
1	2, 0	3, 0
2	3, 0	2, 1
3	4, 0	1, 1
4	1, 1	4, 0

Figure 1.5
Representations for a sequential machine

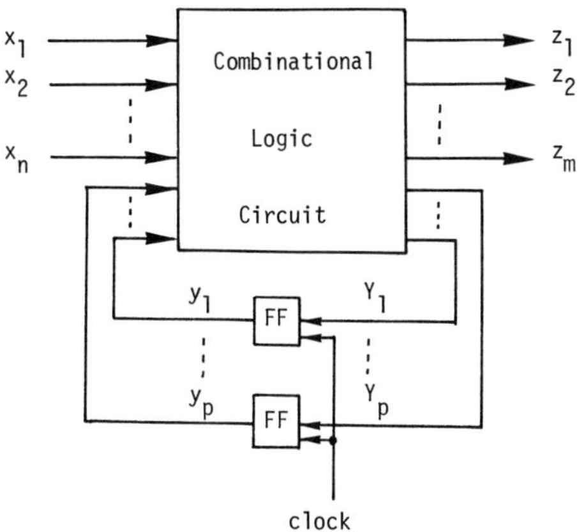

Figure 1.6
Block diagram for a synchronous sequential logic circuit

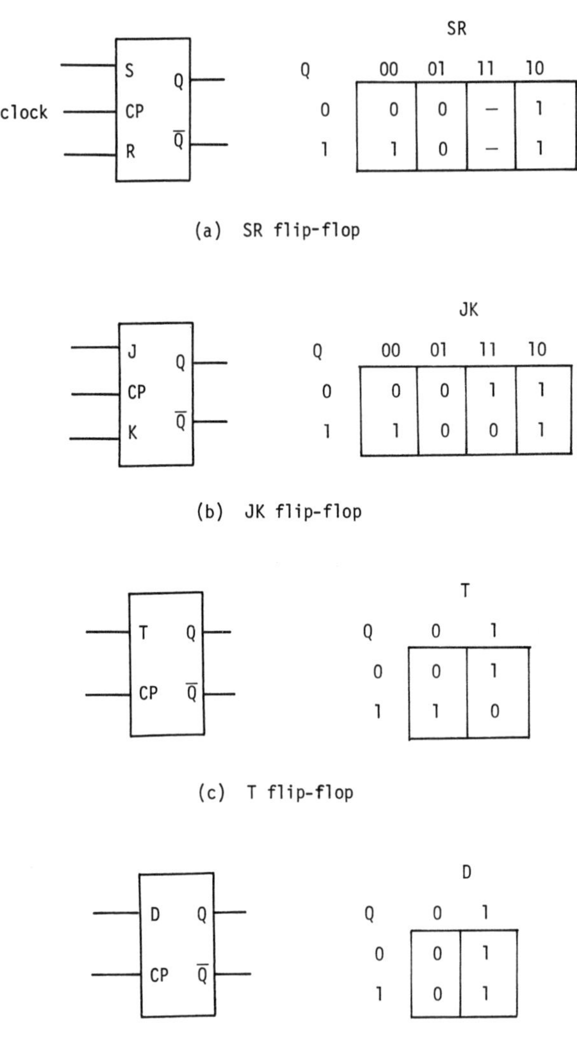

Figure 1.7
Representations for flip-flops

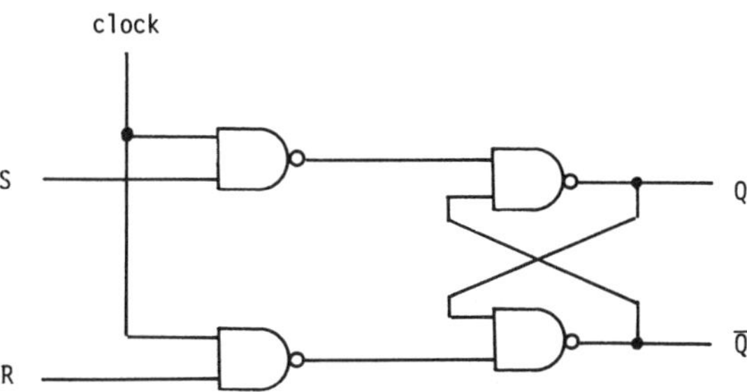

Figure 1.8
Realization of the SR flip-flop

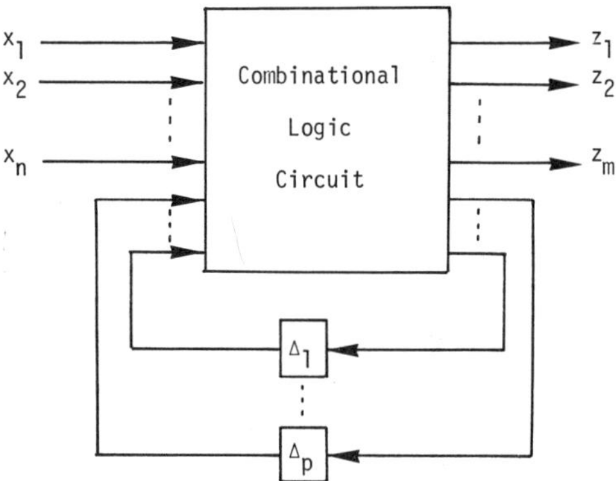

Figure 1.9
Block diagram for asynchronous sequential logic circuit

discrete instants of time. The operation of synchronous sequential circuits is controlled by a synchronizing pulse signal called a *clock pulse* or simply a *clock*. The clock is usually applied to the memory portion of the circuit. Figure 1.6 is a block diagram for synchronous circuits. A series of bistable memory elements called *clocked flip-flops* (FF) are used in synchronous circuits. The most popular memory elements are the D (Delay), T (Trigger), SR (Set-Reset), and JK flip-flops shown in figure 1.7. Figure 1.8 shows a realization of the SR flip-flop. Other flip-flops can be similarly constructed from cross-coupled NAND or NOR gates.

The behavior of an asynchronous circuit is not synchronized; it is unclocked. Each feedback line is assumed to have a finite, positive, pure delay, as is shown in figure 1.9. Proper operation of such an asynchronous circuit requires the following conditions.

- Because of delays, a combinational circuit may produce a transient error or spike, called a *hazard.* Such an error, if applied to the input of an unclocked flip-flop or latch, may result in a permanent incorrect state. Hence the combinational logic portion of the circuit should be designed to be hazard-free.

- The inputs are constrained so as to change only when the memory elements are all in *stable* conditions ($y_i = Y_i$ for all i). This is called the *fundamental mode operation.*

- A situation whereby more than one state variable must change in the course of a transition is called a *race* condition. If correct behavior of the circuit depends upon the outcome of the race, then it is called a *critical race.* To ensure that the operation of the circuit is not affected by transients, the critical race should be avoided by making the proper state assignment.

1.2 Fault Modeling

Logic gates are realized by transistors, which are classified into bipolar transistors and metal oxide semiconductor field-effect transistors (MOSFET, or simply MOS). The logic families based on bipolar transistors are transistor-transistor logic (TTL), emitter-coupled logic (ECL), and so forth. Some logic families based on MOSFET are p-channel MOSFET (p-MOS), n-channel MOSFET (n-MOS), and complementary MOSFET (CMOS). Although ECL and TTL are important for high-speed applications, their integration sizes are limited by the heat generated by their heavy power consumption and by large gate sizes. In contrast, the MOS logic families are well suited for LSI or VLSI, because larger integrations can be obtained with them than with bipolar logic families. Most LSI and VLSI circuits of today are implemented by MOS. However, the increasing use of MOS technology for LSI and VLSI circuits has introduced new testing problems, as will be seen later in this chapter.

A *fault* of a circuit is a physical defect of one or more components. Faults can be classified as logical or parametric. A *logical fault* is one that causes the logic function of a circuit element or an input signal to be changed to some other logic function; a *parametric fault* alters the magnitude of a circuit parameter, causing a change in some factor such as circuit speed, current, or voltage.

Circuit malfunctions associated with timing are due mainly to circuit

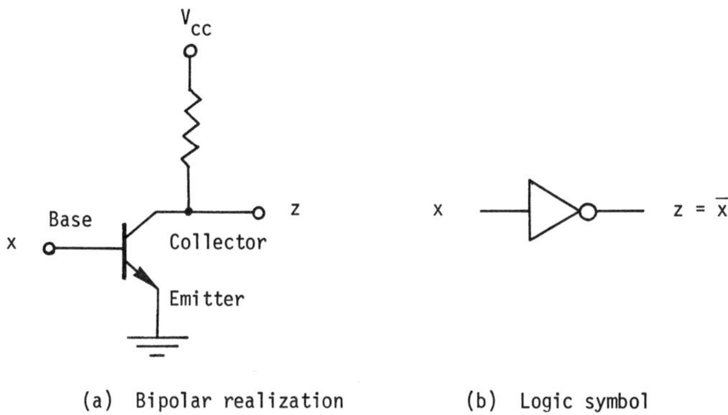

Figure 1.10
Inverter

delays. Those faults that relate to circuit delays such as slow gates are called *delay faults.* Usually, delay faults only affect the timing operation of the circuit, which may cause hazards or critical races.

Faults that are present in some intervals of time and absent in others are *intermittent faults.* Faults that are always present and do not occur, disappear, or change their nature during testing are called *permanent faults* or *solid faults.* Although many intermittent faults eventually become solid, the early detection of intermittent faults is very important to the reliable operation of the circuit. However, there are no reliable means of detecting their occurrence, since such a fault may disappear when a test is applied. In this book, we will consider mainly logical and solid faults.

Figure 1.10 shows an n-p-n transistor implementing an inverter. When the input x is a high voltage, the output z is a low voltage; when x is a low voltage, z is a high voltage. An open collector or base of the transistor would cause the output z to be permanently high, i.e., stuck at 1 (s-a-1). On the other hand, a short circuit between the collector and the emitter would cause z to be permanently low, i.e., stuck at 0 (s-a-0). These faults are called *stuck-at faults.*

Faults in which two lines are shorted are called *bridging faults.* The technology used will determine what effect the bridging will have. Generally, either high or low will dominate. If two output lines are shorted and low dominates, both are replaced by the AND gate of the two lines, as shown in figure 1.11. This effect is the same as the Wired-AND usually used in TTL gates. (Figure 1.12 shows the Wired-AND logic used in TTL gates.)

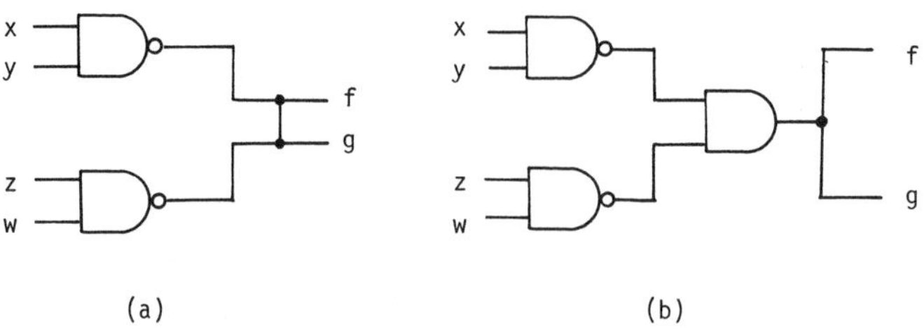

Figure 1.11
AND-type bridging fault

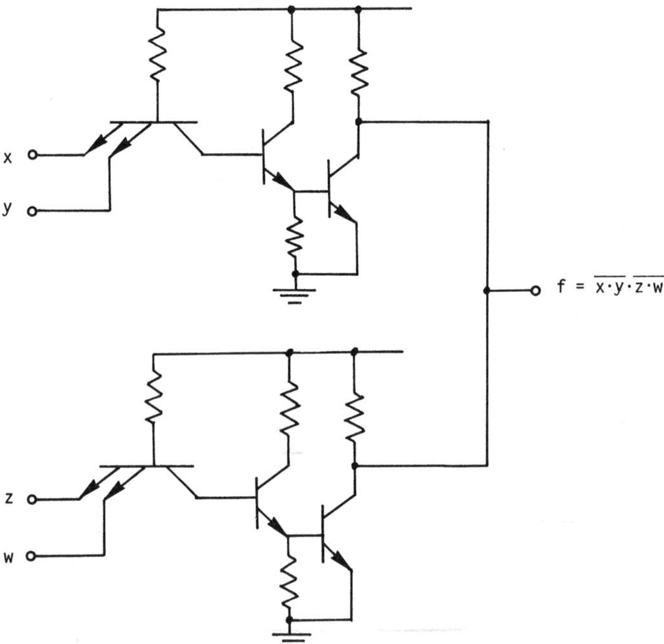

Figure 1.12
Wired-AND used in TTL gates

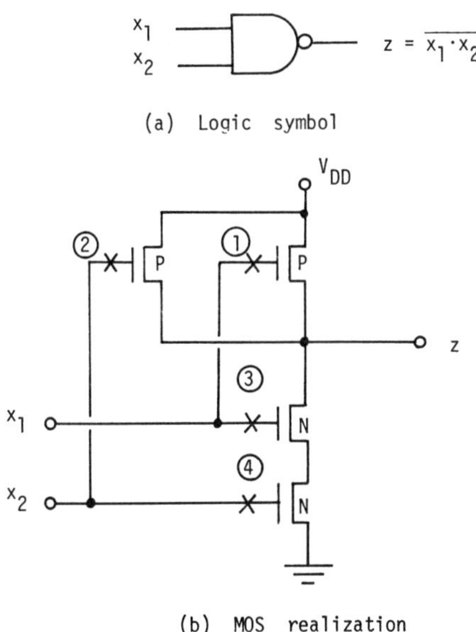

Figure 1.13
CMOS two-input NAND gate

If high dominates, both of the lines are replaced by the OR gate of the two lines. The ECL gate has the feature that the OR of the outputs can be realized simply by tying together these outputs. Hence, in logic circuits implemented by ECL gates, bridging faults cause the affected signals to be ORed.

For most practical purposes, logical faults are successfully modeled by stuck-at faults or bridging faults. However, not all faults can be modeled by these classical faults. This is illustrated by the following examples. Figure 1.13 shows a CMOS two-input NAND gate with p-MOS and n-MOS FETs. The output z is a low voltage if and only if both inputs x_1 and x_2 are high. In figure 1.13, four possible open faults (numbered 1 through 4) are indicated. The first fault, numbered 1, is caused by an open, or missing, p-channel x_1-input pull-up transistor. Under this fault, when the input x_1 is low and the input x_2 is high, the output z becomes an undesired, high-impedance state and retains the logic value of the previous output state. The length of time the state is retained, however, is determined by the leakage current at the node. (Table 1.1 is the truth table for the two-input CMOS NAND gate for both the fault-free condition and the three faulted

Table 1.1
Truth table for CMOS NAND gate

x_1	x_2	z normal	z open at ①	z open at ②	z open at ③ or ④
0	0	1	1	1	1
0	1	1	Previous state	1	1
1	0	1	1	Previous state	1
1	1	0	0	0	Previous state

conditions.) Consequently, these open faults cause combinational circuits to become *sequential*, and thus they cannot be modeled as classical (e.g., stuck-at) faults.

Crosspoint faults in programmable logic arrays (PLAs) also cannot be modeled by the classical faults. Figure 1.14(a) shows an implementation of a PLA in MOS technology. PLAs usually realize two-level AND-OR logic circuits. Figure 1.14(b) shows the two-level AND-OR logic circuit equivalent to the PLA of figure 1.14(a). A PLA inherently has a device (a diode or a transistor) at every crosspoint in the arrays, even if it may not be used. The connection of each device is programmed to realize the desired logic. A crosspoint fault can be caused in a PLA by an extra or a missing device. Although most of the crosspoint faults can be modeled by stuck-at faults, there still exist some crosspoint faults that cannot be modeled by stuck-at faults.

Consider an extra device at the crosspoint A shown in figure 1.14(a). In the absence of a fault, the output realizes the logic function

$$z = x_1 x_2 + \bar{x}_1 \bar{x}_2 x_3.$$

If a transistor appears at A, the first product term $x_1 x_2$ will shrink to $x_1 x_2 x_3$. Hence, the faulted function will be

$$z = x_1 x_2 x_3 + \bar{x}_1 \bar{x}_2 x_3.$$

This function cannot be caused by any stuck-at fault in the equivalent AND-OR logic circuit of figure 1.14(b).

1.3 Testing Problems

To ensure the proper operation of a system, we must be able to detect a fault when one has occurred and to locate it or isolate it to a specific

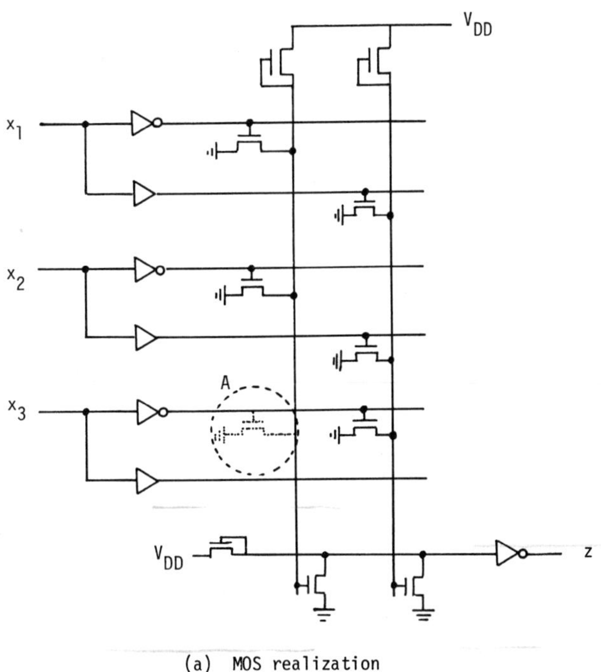

(a) MOS realization

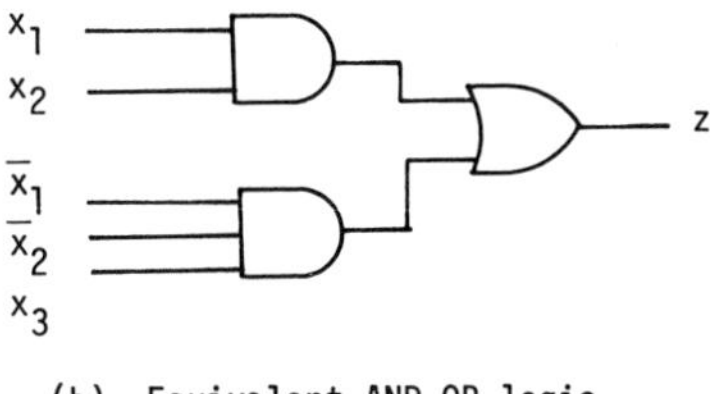

(b) Equivalent AND-OR logic

Figure 1.14
Programmable logic array

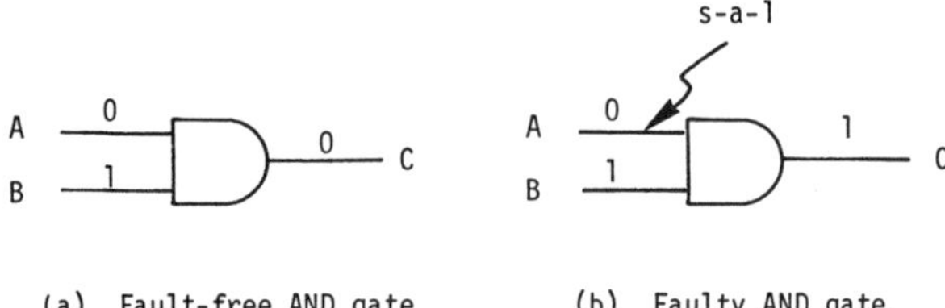

Figure 1.15
Test for stuck-at fault

component—preferably an easily replaceable one. The former procedure is called *fault detection*, and the latter is called *fault location*, *fault isolation*, or *fault diagnosis*. These tasks are accomplished with tests. A *test* is a procedure to detect and/or locate faults. Tests are categorized as fault-detection tests or fault diagnostic tests. A fault-detection test tells only whether a circuit is faulty or fault-free; it tells nothing about the identity of a fault if one is present. A fault diagnostic test provides the location and the type of a fault and other information. The quantity of information provided is called the *diagnostic resolution* of the test; a fault-detection test is a fault diagnostic test of zero diagnostic resolution.

Logic circuits are tested by applying a sequence of input patterns that produce erroneous responses when faults are present and then comparing the responses with the correct (expected) ones. Such an input pattern used in testing is called a *test pattern*. In general, a test for a logic circuit consists of many test patterns. They are referred to as a *test set* or a *test sequence*. The latter term, which means a series of test patterns, is used if the test patterns must be applied in a specific order. Test patterns, together with the output responses, are sometimes called *test data*.

Figure 1.15(a) shows a fault-free AND gate. Figure 1.15(b) shows a faulty AND gate in which input A is stuck-at-1. The input pattern applied to the fault-free AND gate has an output value of 0. In contrast, the output value of the faulty AND gate is 1, since the stuck-at-1 fault on A creates the erroneous response. There is a definite difference between the faulty gate and the fault-free gate. Therefore, the pattern 01 shown in figure 1.15 is a test pattern for the A s-a-1 fault.

If there exists only one fault in a circuit, it is called a *single fault*. If there exist two or more faults at the same time, then the set of faults is called a *multiple fault*. For a circuit with k lines, there are at most $2k$ possible single

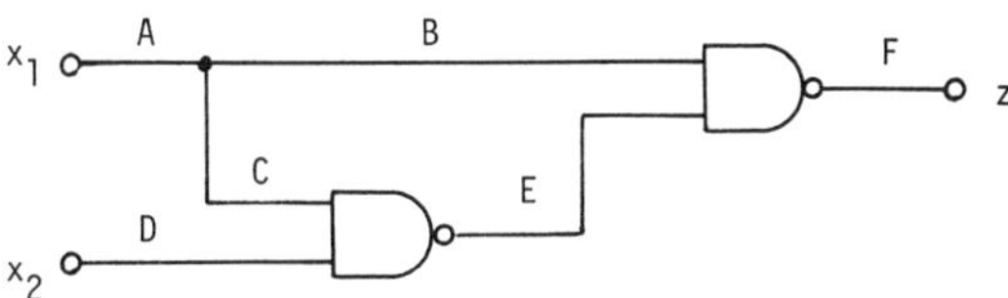

Figure 1.16

Table 1.2
All single stuck faults

x_1	x_2	z	A/0	B/0	C/0	D/0	E/0	F/0	A/1	B/1	C/1	D/1	E/1	F/1
0	0	1	1	1	1	1	1	0	0	0	1	1	1	1
0	1	1	1	1	1	1	1	0	1	0	1	1	1	1
1	0	0	1	1	0	0	1	0	0	0	0	1	0	1
1	1	1	1	1	0	0	1	0	1	1	1	1	0	1

stuck-at faults. For multiple faults, the number of possible faults increases dramatically to $3^k - 1$, since any line may be fault-free, s-a-0, or s-a-1. A circuit with 100 lines would contain approximately 5×10^{47} faults. This would be far too many faults to assume, and hence testing for multiple faults would be impractical. However, for most approaches the model of a single stuck-at fault has proved to provide the best practical basis. For example, every complete single-fault-detection test set in any internal fanout-free combinational circuit is known to cover at least 98 percent of all multiple faults made up of six or fewer faults (Agarwal and Fung 1981).

Since several different faults often may cause a circuit to malfunction in precisely the same way, it is convenient to group these *equivalent faults* (or *indistinguishable faults*) into equivalence classes. In the circuit shown in figure 1.16, there are six signal lines (nets); hence, there are at most twelve possible single stuck-at faults. Table 1.2 illustrates a truth table with columns listing all possible single stuck-at faults and rows indicating all input patterns, where a line A stuck-at-0 fault, for example, is denoted as A/0. As can be seen from table 1.2, the malfunctions caused by A/0, B/0, E/0, D/1, and F/1 are all the same, so they are grouped together in a fault

equivalence class. Similarly, C/0, D/0, and E/1 are grouped together, as shown in table 1.3. A fault is called *redundant* if its presence causes no malfunction. In other words, the output function of a circuit with a redun-

Table 1.3
Fault equivalence classes

f_0	z (fault-free), C/1
f_1	A/0, B/0, E/0, D/1, F/1
f_2	C/0, D/0, E/1
f_3	F/0
f_4	A/1
f_5	B/1

Table 1.4
Fault table for representative faults

x_1	x_2	f_1	f_2	f_3	f_4	f_5
0	0			x	x	x
0	1			x		x
1	0	x				
1	1		x	x		

dant fault is exactly the same as that of the fault-free circuit. In the circuit of figure 1.16, fault C/1 is redundant, as table 1.3 shows.

In fault detection and location, only the faults that are picked out as *representative faults* from each fault equivalence class need be considered, since any two equivalent faults are indistinguishable from input-output behavior only. Table 1.4, which is a *fault table* for five representative faults of table 1.3, indicates precisely which test pattern will detect each fault. Finding a fault-detection test set is simply a matter of defining a set of rows, each indicating a test pattern, so that each column indicating a fault class may have an "x" in one of the rows. For this example we obtain $\{00, 10, 11\}$ as a fault-detection test set. A fault diagnostic test set is obtained by defining a set of rows so that no pair of column patterns corresponding to the rows may be the same. From table 1.4 we have $\{00, 01, 10, 11\}$ as the diagnostic test set.

The testing of logic circuits is performed in two main stages: generating test patterns for a circuit under test (the *test generation* stage) and applying the test patterns to the circuit (the *test application* stage). Thus, the generation of test patterns is important; however, it is very difficult for large (e.g.

LSI and VLSI) circuits, so most of the effort of the past 20 years in this field went into research and development on efficient and economical test-generation procedures.

The quality of a test (a set or a sequence of test patterns) depends much on the fault coverage as well as the size or length of the test. The *fault coverage* (or *test coverage*) of a test is the fraction of faults that can be detected or located within the circuit under test. The fault coverage of a given test is determined by a process called *fault simulation*, in which every given test patterns is applied to a fault-free circuit and to each of the given faulty circuits, each circuit behavior is simulated, and each circuit response is analyzed to find what faults are detected by the test pattern. Fault simulation is also used to produce *fault dictionaries*, in which the information needed to identify a faulty element or component is gathered.

Summary

The test-generation process includes fault modeling and reduction, test-pattern generation, fault simulation, fault-coverage evaluation, and the production of a fault dictionary. The first step consists of developing a fault dictionary for the circuit (that is, modeling the faults that are assumed) and reducing the number of faults in terms of the fault equivalence relation. Usually, the "single stuck-at fault" model is adopted, and the fault dictionary is generated directly from the logic-circuit description by arranging the distinguishable faults for each gate in tabular form. Next, test patterns are generated to test for the set of faults listed in the fault dictionary. The test patterns are then simulated against the faulted circuits in the fault dictionary, and the fault coverage is evaluated from the results of the fault simulation (which include lists of tested and untested faults). If the fault coverage is inadequate, then the process of test-pattern generation and fault simulation is repeated for the untested faults until an adequate fault coverage is achieved. Finally, the fault dictionary is completed by specifying enough information to detect and locate the faults.

To be practical and cost-effective, the above test-generation process is generally automated in the form of a collection of application software. In particular, the test-pattern generation and the fault simulation should interact effectively to give a high level of fault coverage at a low computation cost. The application of LSI and VLSI requires more efficient *automatic test generation* (ATG) systems.

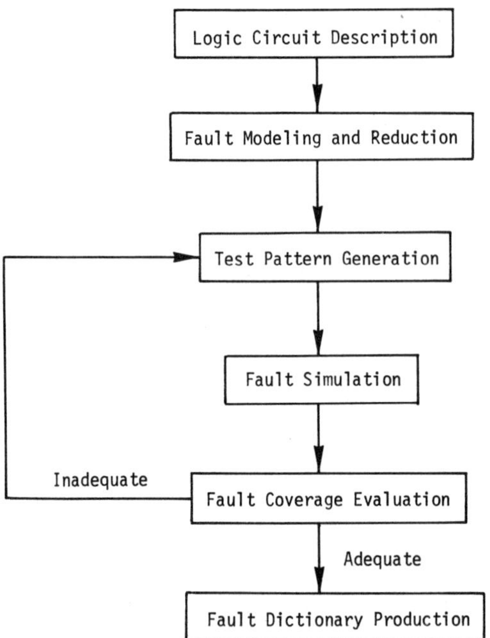

Figure 1.17
Procedure for test generation

1.4 Testing Schemes

Logic testing is performed in various stages, including factory testing of chips, boards, and systems and field testing of boards and systems during periodic maintenance and repair. Usually, fault detection comes first. If it is determined that a fault is present, fault diagnosis is then used to isolate the faulty node or component for repair. In the testing of LSI and VLSI chips it is not necessary to locate faulty gates, since the entire chip must be discarded if any output value is faulty. However, fault diagnosis is required in the testing of boards and systems, and diagnosis at the system level is very important in factory testing and in field maintenance. After a fault has been isolated at the system level, components or individual modules are replaced until a repair is accomplished.

Testing approaches are distinguished by the techniques used to generate and process test data, and can be divided into two categories: on-line and off-line. *On-line testing* is executed during system run time, concurrent with normal computer operation. Data patterns from normal computation serve as test patterns, and a failure caused by some fault can be detected by built-in monitoring circuits. Since testing and normal computation can proceed concurrently, on-line testing is also called *concurrent* testing and is effective against intermittent faults. *Off-line* testing is executed when the system under test is off line. In off-line testing, specific test patterns are usually provided; data patterns from normal computation cannot serve as test patterns.

Testing approaches are also divided into external testing and built-in testing. In *external testing* the test equipment is external to the system under test; that is, test patterns are applied by the external tester and the responses are then evaluated. In *built-in testing* the test equipment is built into the system under test. As described below, on-line testing uses built-in monitoring circuits to detect a failure caused by some intermittent or solid fault, and thus it belongs to the category of built-in testing. Off-line testing encompasses both types of testing schemes, external and built-in.

On-line testing schemes are usually implemented by *redundancy techniques*: information redundancy and hardware redundancy. Information-redundancy approaches include such popular coding schemes as parity, cyclic redundancy checks, and error-correcting codes; hardware-redundancy techniques include self-checking circuits at the gate level, duplication at the module level, and replicated computers at the system level.

The most widely used linear codes are odd and even parity check codes for single-bit fault detection and Hamming codes for multiple-bit fault detection. In those error-detecting codes, one or more redundant bits are simply appended to detect errors. For example, consider a combinational circuit with n inputs and m outputs. If only $k < 2^m$ output values can occur during normal operation, the occurrence of any of $2^m - k$ unallowable values indicates a malfunction caused by a fault in the circuit. The output values that do occur are called *code words*, and unallowable output values are called *noncode words*. Error-detecting codes are usually used to design hardware that can automatically detect errors in the circuit (figure 1.18).

Self-checking circuits are those circuits in which the occurrence of a fault can be recognized only by observing the outputs of the circuit. An important subclass of self-checking circuits is *totally self-checking circuits*, defined as follows. A circuit is *fault-secure* for a set of faults F if, for any fault in F and any allowable code input, the output is a noncode word or the correct

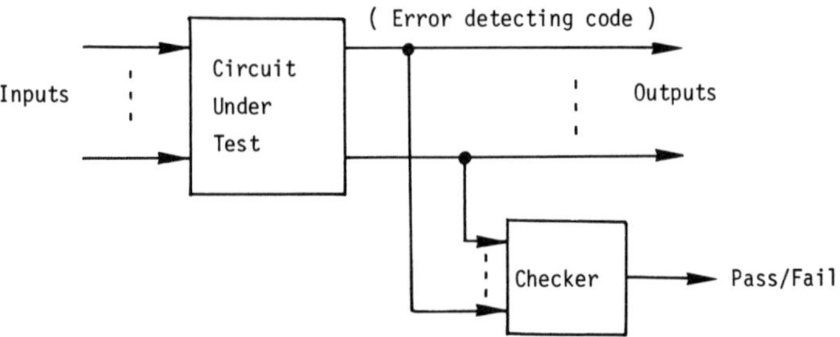

Figure 1.18
On-line testing using information redundancy

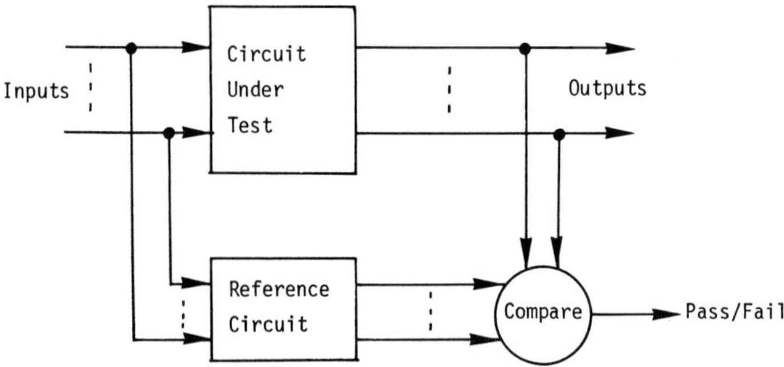

Figure 1.19
On-line testing using hardware redundancy

code word, never an incorrect code word. In other words, the output of the faulty circuit cannot be a code word and, at the same time, be different from the correct output. Thus, as long as the output is a code word, it can safely be assumed to be correct. On the other hand, a circuit is *self-testing* for a set of faults F if, for any fault f in F, there exists an allowable code input that detects f (i.e., the resulting output is a noncode word). In other words, the input set contains at least one test for every fault in the prescribed set. A totally self-checking circuit is both fault-secure and self-testing for all faults under consideration. Hence, a totally self-checking circuit can guarantee that any fault in the circuit cannot cause an error in the output without detection of the fault.

One of the most effective approaches to on-line testing using hardware redundancy is *dual redundancy*; that is, straightforward duplication of the resource being tested. Figure 1.19 shows this duplication scheme for built-in

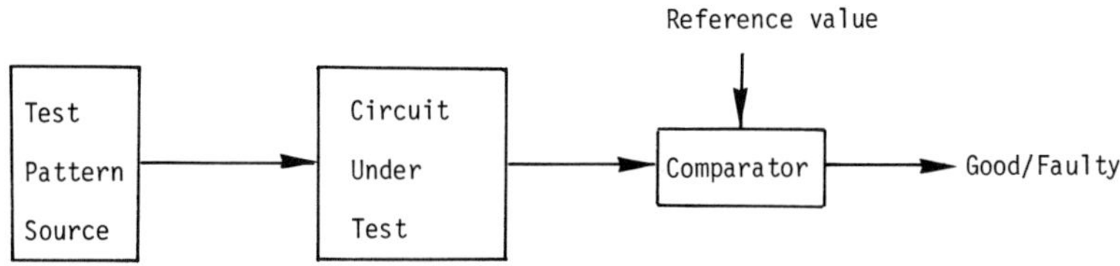

Figure 1.20
General testing scheme

testing. Although full duplication is the upper bound on hardware redundancy for fault detection and thus requires more hardware than other hardware-redundancy approaches, the duplication scheme can easily be adopted at any part of the computer system and at any level within the computer hierarchy.

In the external-testing approaches, the circuit under test (CUT) is tested with *automatic test equipment* (ATE) in which a sequence of test patterns are applied to the CUT and the responses of the CUT are compared against reference values (correct responses). Figure 1.20 shows the general scheme of testing. Test patterns and reference values are produced by either software-based or hardware-based methods. In the software-based scheme, test patterns and correct responses are generated in advance and stored in memory. Test patterns are produced either manually, by a design or test engineer, or automatically, by test-generation programs. In contrast, both test patterns and reference values can be produced each time a CUT is tested by hardware-implemented algorithms. In these hardware-based schemes, test patterns are usually generated randomly or pseudorandomly and simultaneously applied to the CUT and a known good circuit, called a *gold circuit*. The output responses of the CUT are then compared with those of the gold circuit. This type of testing method (figure 1.21) is called *random testing*, and in contrast the former software-based testing is called *deterministic testing*. Deterministic testing requires costly or time-consuming test generation and memory to store huge amounts of test data, where as random testing eliminates the cost and the time requirement of generating or storing test data. However, random testing has disadvantages: The need for a gold circuit may be bothersome, and the reliability of the gold circuit is not guaranteed. Synchronization of the two circuits and fault coverage of random test patterns may also cause problems.

In the above-mentioned testing schemes, the total responses are com-

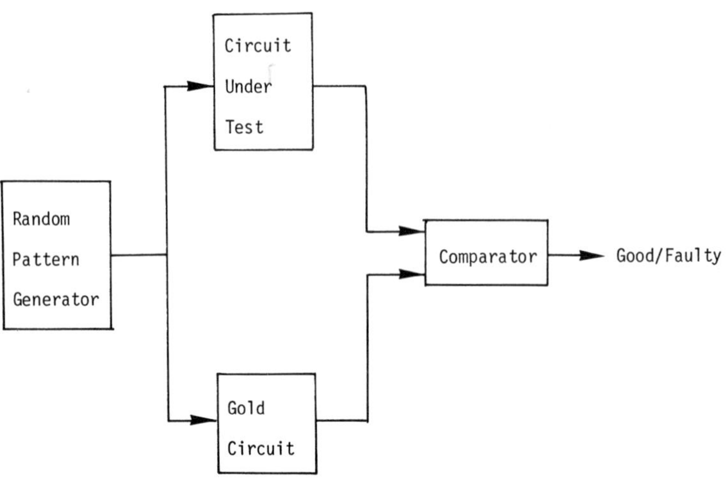

Figure 1.21
Random testing

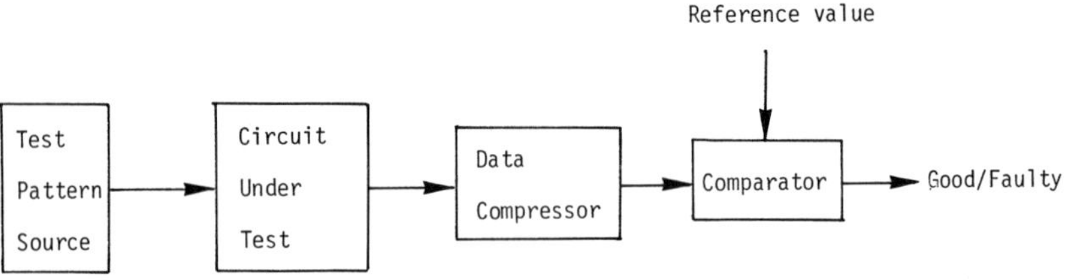

Figure 1.22
Compact testing

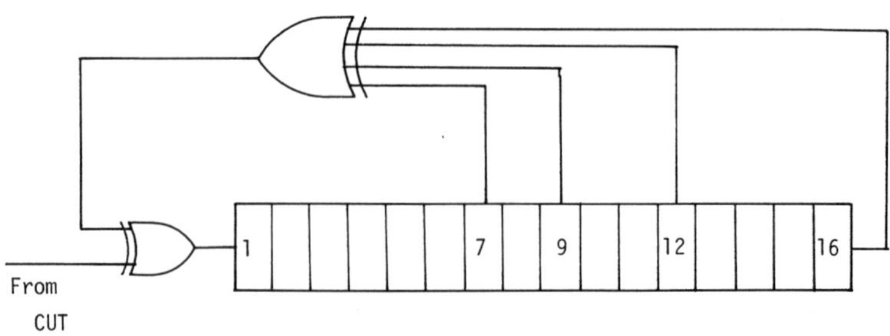

Figure 1.23
A 16-bit linear feedback shift register (Frohwerk 1977). © Copyright 1977 Hewlett-Packard Company. Reproduced with permission.

pared with the correct reference values, which are usually high volumes. This difficulty of analysis and storage of huge amounts of response data can be avoided through an approach called *compact testing*, in which, rather than the total responses, compressed response data are used for comparison. Figure 1.22 shows the general scheme for compact testing. The model of figure 1.22 allows wide variations in the methods for test-pattern generation and data compression. In a global sense, compact testing methods may be classified as either deterministic or random in connection with the techniques used to generate test patterns. The data compressor can be implemented with simple circuitry, such as counters and linear-feedback shift registers. Since compact testing requires little test equipment, it is suited for built-in testing. A widely used method of compact testing is *signature analysis*, which compresses the output response through a 16-bit linear feedback shift register whose contents are called the *signature*. Figure 1.23 shows a 16-bit linear-feedback shift register.

2 Test Generation

In this chapter we consider the problem of test generation and examine several algorithms for the computation of tests. In the first four sections, we restrict our attention to test generation for combinational circuits. In the last section, we consider the problem of generating tests for sequential circuits.

Many algorithms for test generation have been proposed over the years. Most of those approaches were of more theoretical than practical significance and consequently have not been put to practical use. Only a few approaches are of practical use. The most widely used algorithm is the D-algorithm (Roth 1966). This is a complete algorithm in the sense that it will generate a test for any logical fault if such a test exists. However, it has been pointed out that the D-algorithm is inefficient in generating tests for circuits with many EOR gates. To improve this defect of the D-algorithm, another test-generation algorithm called PODEM (Path-Oriented DEcision Making) was proposed (Goel 1981a). However, a fanout-oriented test-generation algorithm (called FAN) has recently been developed (Fujiwara and Shimono 1983a,b) that generates tests much more efficiently than the D-algorithm or PODEM. These three algorithms are described in detail below.

The generation of tests is usually much more difficult for sequential circuits than for combinational ones. This is due mainly to the poor controllability and observability of sequential logic. However, the controllability and observability of sequential circuits—that is, their testability—can be raised to the level of combinational ones by some techniques known as "design for testability." Those techniques allow tests for sequential circuits to be reduced to tests of the same sort that are used for combinational circuits. Hence, if we assume that sequential circuits under tests are always implemented by those design techniques, it is sufficient to develop efficient test-generation algorithms only for combinational circuits. For this reason, this chapter emphasizes test-generation algorithms for combinational circuits and treats those for sequential circuits only briefly.

2.1 Boolean Difference

Each output of a combinational logic circuit realizes a logic (Boolean) function. Let $F(x_1, x_2, \ldots, x_n)$ be a logic function of the input Boolean variables $x_1, x_2, \ldots, x_n$. The *Boolean difference* of $F(\mathbf{X})$ with respect to an input x_i is defined as

$$F(x_1,\ldots,x_i,\ldots,x_n) \oplus F(x_1,\ldots,\bar{x}_i,\ldots,x_n)$$

and is denoted by

$$\frac{dF(\mathbf{X})}{dx_i}.$$

It can also be represented as

$$\frac{dF(\mathbf{X})}{dx_i} = F_i(0) \oplus F_i(1)$$

where

$$F_i(0) = F(x_1,\ldots,x_{i-1},0,x_{i+1},\ldots,x_n),$$

$$F_i(1) = F(x_1,\ldots,x_{i-1},1,x_{i+1},\ldots,x_n).$$

In general, a logic function is composed of some component functions using logic operations, such as complement, product, and sum. Thus, the formulas that express the Boolean difference of those operations in terms of the Boolean differences of the component functions are useful in calculating the Boolean difference. On the basis of the definition of the Boolean difference, those formulas can be derived as follows:

$$\frac{d\overline{F(\mathbf{X})}}{dx_i} = \frac{dF(\mathbf{X})}{dx_i}, \tag{1}$$

$$\frac{dF(\mathbf{X})}{dx_i} = \frac{dF(\mathbf{X})}{d\bar{x}_i}, \tag{2}$$

$$\frac{d}{dx_i}\frac{dF(\mathbf{X})}{dx_j} = \frac{d}{dx_j}\frac{dF(\mathbf{X})}{dx_i}, \tag{3}$$

$$\frac{d[F(\mathbf{X})G(\mathbf{X})]}{dx_i} = F(\mathbf{X})\frac{dG(\mathbf{X})}{dx_i} \oplus G(\mathbf{X})\frac{dF(\mathbf{X})}{dx_i} \oplus \frac{dF(\mathbf{X})}{dx_i}\frac{dG(\mathbf{X})}{dx_i}, \tag{4}$$

$$\frac{d[F(\mathbf{X})+G(\mathbf{X})]}{dx_i} = \overline{F(\mathbf{X})}\frac{dG(\mathbf{X})}{dx_i} \oplus \overline{G(\mathbf{X})}\frac{dF(\mathbf{X})}{dx_i} \oplus \frac{dF(\mathbf{X})}{dx_i}\frac{dG(\mathbf{X})}{dx_i}, \tag{5}$$

$$\frac{d[F(\mathbf{X}) \oplus G(\mathbf{X})]}{dx_i} = \frac{dF(\mathbf{X})}{dx_i} \oplus \frac{dG(\mathbf{X})}{dx_i}. \tag{6}$$

Example 2.1 Consider the circuit shown in figure 2.1. The output is $F(\mathbf{X}) = x_1x_2 + \bar{x}_2x_3$. From the definition of the Boolean difference,

$$\frac{dF}{dx_1} = F_1(0) \oplus F_1(1)$$

$$= \bar{x}_2 x_3 \oplus (x_2 + \bar{x}_2 x_3)$$

$$= \overline{\bar{x}_2 x_3}(x_2 + \bar{x}_2 x_3) \oplus \bar{x}_2 x_3 \overline{(x_2 + \bar{x}_2 x_3)}$$

$$= x_2.$$

Using Boolean algebra,

$$\frac{dF}{dx_1} = \frac{d(G_1 + G_2)}{dx_1} \qquad [G_1 = x_1 x_2 \text{ and } G_2 = \bar{x}_2 x_3]$$

$$= \bar{G}_1 \frac{dG_2}{dx_1} \oplus \bar{G}_2 \frac{dG_1}{dx_1} \oplus \frac{dG_1}{dx_1}\frac{dG_2}{dx_1} \qquad \text{[by eq. 5]}$$

$$= \bar{G}_2 \frac{dG_1}{dx_1} \qquad \left[\text{since } \frac{dG_2}{dx_1} = 0\right]$$

$$= (x_2 + \bar{x}_3)\left(x_1 \frac{dx_2}{dx_1} \oplus x_2 \frac{dx_1}{dx_1} \oplus \frac{dx_1}{dx_1}\frac{dx_2}{dx_1}\right) \qquad \text{[by eq. 4]}$$

$$= (x_2 + \bar{x}_3) \cdot x_2 \qquad \left[\text{since } \frac{dx_1}{dx_1} = 1 \text{ and } \frac{dx_2}{dx_1} = 0\right]$$

$$= x_2.$$

Consider $F(x_1, \ldots, x_n)$ as an output function of a combinational circuit. Let α be a fault in which input x_i is s-a-0. The function realized by the faulty circuit is

$$F_\alpha(x_1, x_2, \ldots, x_n) = F(x_1, \ldots, x_{i-1}, 0, x_{i+1}, \ldots, x_n)$$
$$= F_i(0).$$

The test pattern that detects the fault α is an input combination or vector $\mathbf{X}$ that satisfies

$$F(\mathbf{X}) \oplus F_\alpha(\mathbf{X}) = 1.$$

Using some arithmetic, we obtain

$$F(\mathbf{X}) \oplus F_\alpha(\mathbf{X}) = (\bar{x}_i F_i(0) \oplus x_i F_i(1)) \oplus F_i(0)$$
$$= \bar{x}_i F_i(0) \oplus x_i F_i(1) \oplus (\bar{x}_i \oplus x_i) F_i(0)$$

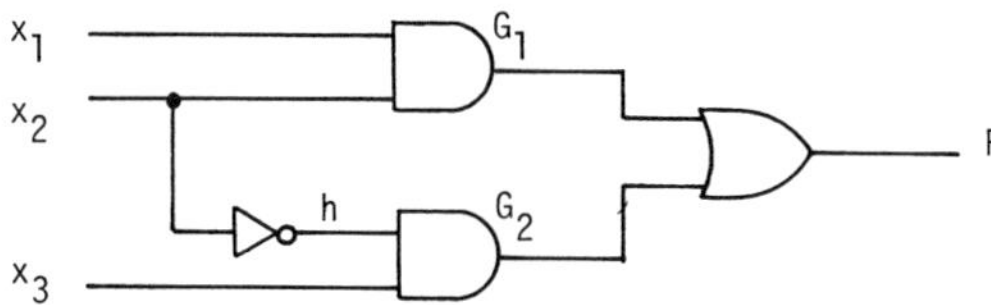

Figure 2.1

$$= \bar{x}_i F_i(0) \oplus \bar{x}_i F_i(0) \oplus x_i F_i(1) \oplus x_i F_i(0)$$

$$= x_i(F_i(1) \oplus F_i(0))$$

$$= x_i \frac{dF(\mathbf{X})}{dx_i}.$$

Thus the set of all tests that detect the fault x_i s-a-0 is

$$\left\{\mathbf{X}; x_i \frac{dF(\mathbf{X})}{dx_i} = 1\right\}$$

and is defined by the Boolean expression

$$x_i \cdot \frac{dF}{dx_i}.$$

This expression implies that $x_i = 1$ and $dF/dx_i = 1$. Since $x_i = 1$, then x_i applies the opposite value on the faulty input. The factor dF/dx_i ensures that this erroneous signal affects the value of F. Similarly, the set of all tests that detect the fault x_i s-a-1 is defined by the Boolean expression

$$\bar{x}_i \cdot \frac{dF}{dx_i}.$$

Example 2.2 Consider the circuit of figure 2.1. The output is $F(\mathbf{X}) = x_1 x_2 + \bar{x}_2 x_3$. The set of tests that detect the fault x_1 s-a-0 is calculated as follows:

$$\frac{dF}{dx_1} = F_1(0) \oplus F_1(1)$$

$$= \bar{x}_2 x_3 \oplus (x_2 \oplus \bar{x}_2 x_3)$$

$$= x_2.$$

Thus, the set of all tests that detect this fault is defined by the Boolean expression

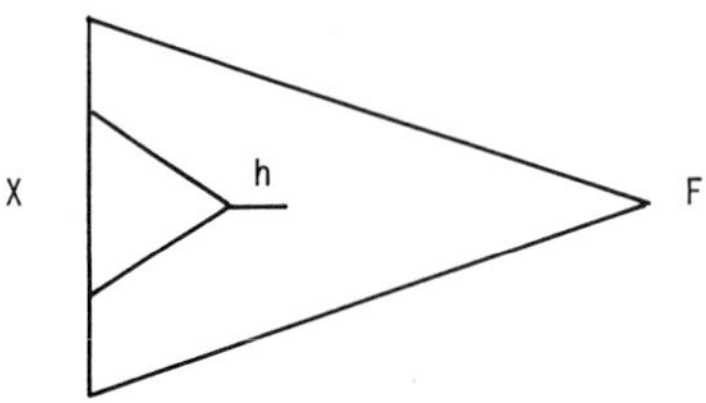

Figure 2.2
Internal signal line

$$x_1 \frac{dF(\mathbf{X})}{dx_1} = x_1 x_2.$$

This means that the fault x_1 s-a-0 causes an erroneous signal x_1 and this erroneous signal affects the output value of F only if $x_1 x_2 = 1$, that is, only if $x_1 = 1$ and $x_2 = 1$.

In general, faults can exist not only on external or primary inputs but also on signal lines that are internal to the circuit. The Boolean difference can also be used to derive tests for stuck-at faults on internal signal lines. For the circuit of figure 2.2, let $F(\mathbf{X})$ be the output function of the circuit and let h be an internal signal line. We can express h as a function of $\mathbf{X}$: $h(\mathbf{X})$. We can express the output function F as a function of $\mathbf{X}$ and h by considering h as an input. Let this function be F^*; that is,

$$F^*(\mathbf{X}, h) = F(\mathbf{X}).$$

To detect the fault h s-a-0, it is necessary to propagate the opposite value 1 to h and to propagate the difference of normal and erroneous signal values to the output of the circuit. Thus, the set of all tests that detect the fault h s-a-0 is defined by the Boolean expression

$$h(\mathbf{X}) \cdot \frac{dF^*(\mathbf{X}, h)}{dh}.$$

Similarly, the set of all tests that detect the fault h s-a-1 is defined by the Boolean expression

$$\overline{h(\mathbf{X})} \cdot \frac{dF^*(\mathbf{X}, h)}{dh}.$$

Example 2.3 For the circuit of figure 2.1, consider the fault h s-a-1, where h is an input of G_2. The output function

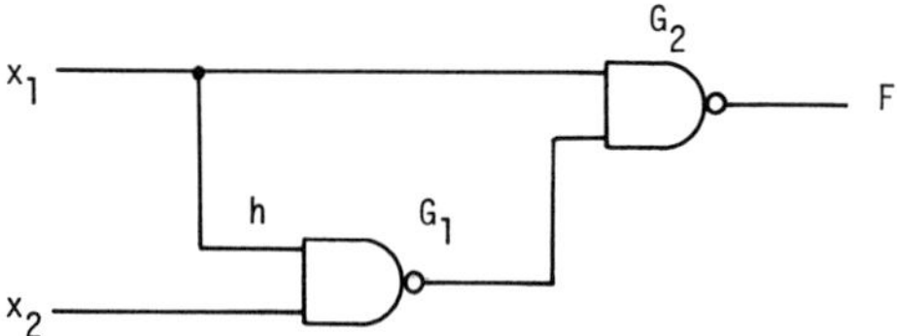

Figure 2.3

$F(\mathbf{X}) = x_1x_2 + \bar{x}_2x_3$

will be expressed as a function of x_1, x_2, x_3 and h:

$F^*(\mathbf{X}, h) = x_1x_2 + hx_3$

where $h(\mathbf{X}) = \bar{x}_2$. Thus, we have

$$\frac{dF^*(\mathbf{X}, h)}{dh} = x_1x_2 \oplus (x_1x_2 + x_3)$$

$$= (\bar{x}_1 + \bar{x}_2)x_3.$$

The set of all tests that detect the fault h s-a-1 is defined by the Boolean expression

$$\overline{h(\mathbf{X})} \cdot \frac{dF^*(\mathbf{X}, h)}{dh} = x_2(\bar{x}_1 + \bar{x}_2)x_3$$

$$= \bar{x}_1x_2x_3.$$

Hence, the fault h s-a-1 is detected if and only if $x_1 = 0$ and $x_2 = x_3 = 1$.

Example 2.4 Consider the circuit of figure 2.3. The output is $F(\mathbf{X}) = \bar{x}_1 + x_1x_2 = \bar{x}_1 + x_2$. Compute the set of all tests that detect the fault h s-a-1, where h is an input of G_1 as shown in figure 2.3. F can be expressed as a function F^* of $\mathbf{X}$ and h:

$F^*(\mathbf{X}, h) = \bar{x}_1 + hx_2,$

where $h(\mathbf{X}) = x_1$. Thus,

$$\frac{dF^*(\mathbf{X}, h)}{dh} = \bar{x}_1 \oplus (\bar{x}_1 + x_2)$$

$$= x_1x_2.$$

The set of all tests that detect the fault h s-a-1 is defined by Boolean expression

$$\overline{h(\mathbf{X})} \cdot \frac{dF^*(\mathbf{X}, h)}{dh} = \bar{x}_1 x_1 x_2$$

$$= 0.$$

This means that no test patterns exist for the fault h s-a-1; that is, the fault h s-a-1 is redundant.

The effect of two faults at the input of a logic circuit on its output can be analyzed by defining the double Boolean difference as

$$\frac{dF(\mathbf{X})}{d(x_i x_j)} = F(x_1, \ldots, x_i, \ldots, x_j, \ldots, x_n) \oplus F(x_1, \ldots, \bar{x}_i, \ldots, \bar{x}_j, \ldots, x_n).$$

Thus, test generation for multiple stuck-at faults can be generalized by using multiple Boolean differences (Ku and Masson 1975).

The test-generation method using the Boolean difference was developed by Sellers et al. (1968a). The Boolean-difference approach can be characterized as algebraic in that it manipulates circuit equations to generate tests. Several other algebraic test-generation methods have been developed. These include the propositional method of Poage (1963), the equivalent normal form of Armstrong (1966), the cause-effect equation of Bossen and Hong (1971), the SPOOF procedure of Clegg (1973), and the structure description function of Kinoshita et al. (1980).

These approaches all generate equations for a fault-free circuit and manipulate those equations to generate tests. However, in general, it is a difficult task to manipulate algebraic equations. For large circuits, a great amount of algebraic manipulation may be required to derive tests for a given fault. Moreover, because these algebraic methods generate *all* the tests for a given fault, they have the disadvantage of requiring a large quantity of time and memory, which may make them impractical for large circuits.

2.2 The D-Algorithm

There are other test-generation methods that use the topological gate-level description of a circuit instead of manipulating Boolean equations. Those

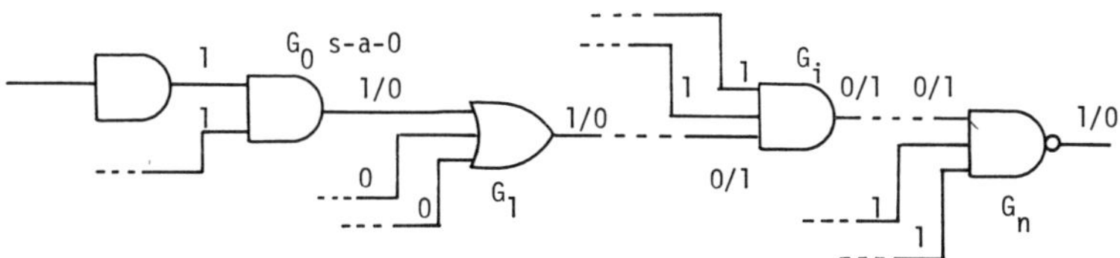

Figure 2.4
Single-path sensitization

methods all involve path sensitization and signal propagation using a backtracking mechanism.

One-dimensional path sensitization or *single-path sensitization* is one of the simplest approaches to test generation. The basic idea of the method is to select a path from the site of the fault, say gate G_0, through a sequence G_1, ..., G_n of gates leading to an output of the circuit. First, inputs of G_0 are specified so as to generate the opposite value of the faulty value (0 for s-a-1 and 1 for s-a-0) at the site of the fault. Then, the inputs to $G_1, \ldots, G_n$ are determined so as to propagate the fault signal along this path to the primary output of the circuit. The technique for doing so is illustrated in figure 2.4. All inputs to G_i except an input on the path are set to 1 for an AND/NAND gate and 0 for an OR/NOR gate. In this figure, the symbol 0/1 represents a signal that has value 0 in the normal or good circuit and 1 in the faulty circuit, and 1/0 represents a symbol that has value 1 in the normal circuit and 0 in the faulty circuit. This process is called the *forward-trace* or *error-propagation* phase of the method. The path is called a *sensitized path.* Finally, we must find a primary input pattern that will realize all the necessary gate input values. This is done by tracing backward from the inputs of $G_0, \ldots, G_n$ to the primary inputs of the circuit. This process is called the *backward-trace* or *line-justification* phase of the method.

Example 2.5 For the circuit of figure 2.5, in order for the fault x_1 s-a-0 to be detected, x_1 must be 1 and the error signal must be propagated along some path. We have a choice of propagating the error signal to the output z_1 via a path through G_1, G_5 and G_7 or through G_1, G_4, G_6, and G_7. To propagate through G_1 requires that x_2 be 1. To propagate through G_5 and G_7 requires the output of G_3 to be 1 and the output of G_6 to be 0. This implies that the output of G_2 must be 0, and thus $x_3 = 0$ or $x_4 = 0$. Consequently, we have two tests: $x_1 x_2 \bar{x}_3$ and $x_1 x_2 \bar{x}_4$. In these tests a difference between normal

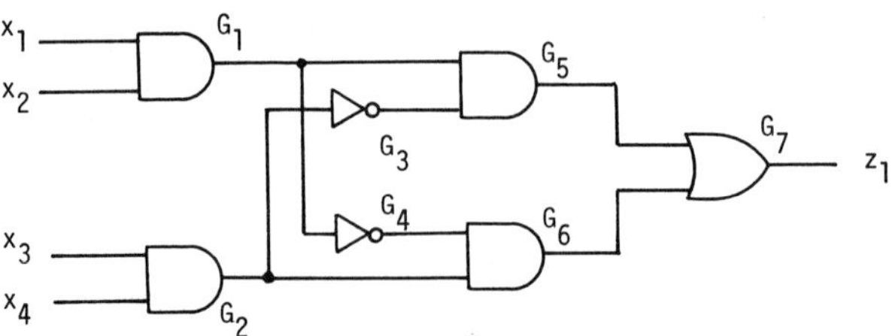

Figure 2.5

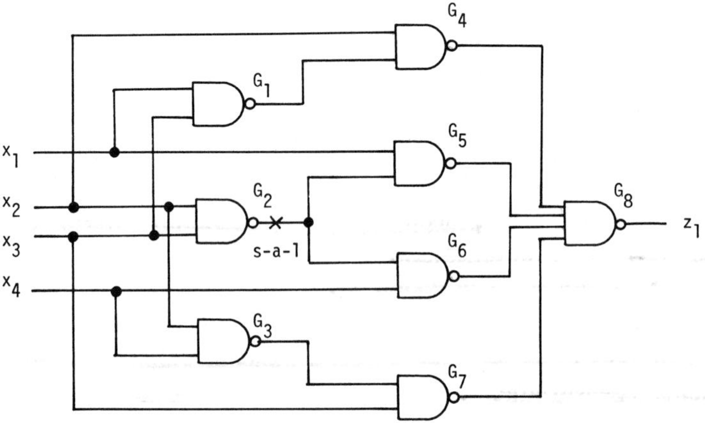

Figure 2.6

and faulty signals propagates along the path $x_1 G_1 G_5 G_7 z_1$, and hence this path is a sensitized path.

The single-path sensitization method has a fatal flaw. In general, there can exist testable faults in a circuit for which it is impossible to generate tests if only one path is allowed to be sensitized at a time. A simple example was reported by Schneider (1967). The circuit is shown in figure 2.6, and the fault in question is G_2 output s-a-1. To generate the value 0 at the output of G_2 requires the input $x_2 = x_3 = 1$. Any single path from G_2 to z_1 must pass through G_5 or G_6. If only a single path through G_5 and G_8 is selected to be sensitized, it requires $x_1 = 1$ and $G_4 = G_6 = G_7 = 1$. Furthermore, $G_6 = 1$ requires $x_4 = 0$. However, $x_2 = x_3 = 1$ and $x_4 = 0$ implies $G_7 = 0$, which is an inconsistency. By symmetry of the circuit, another sensitization along

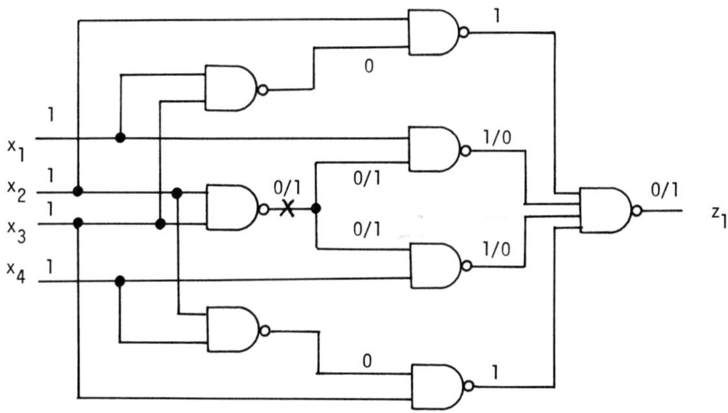

Figure 2.7
Multiple-path sensitization

path $G_6 G_8$ must also fail. This inconsistency seems to imply that the fault cannot be detected. However, the input pattern $x_1 = x_2 = x_3 = x_4 = 1$ provides a test for the fault in question. Figure 2.7 shows the behavior of both normal and faulty circuits for this input. In this figure, we notice that the effect of the fault has been propagated simultaneously along two paths. The single-path sensitization method failed to derive the test because it allowed only one path to be sensitized at a time. Therefore, in order to guarantee finding a test for a fault if one exists, we must consider the sensitization of all possible paths from the site of the fault to the circuit outputs simultaneously. This multiple-path sensitization approach, called the *D-algorithm,* was first formulated by Roth (1966; see also Roth et al. 1967). The D-algorithm is formalized in terms of a cubical algebra called the *D-calculus.* Before describing the algorithm, I will introduce three types of cubes and the D-calculus.

For a gate G which realizes the logic function f, the singular cover of G is a set of the prime implicants of f and $\bar{f}$. Each prime implicant of the singular cover is called a *singular cube*. For example, consider the two-input AND gate shown in figure 2.8. The prime implicant of f is $x_1 x_2$, and the prime implicants of $\bar{f}$ are $\bar{x}_1$ and $\bar{x}_2$. Thus, the singular cover of the AND gate is that shown in figure 2.8.

A *primitive D-cube of a fault* (pdcf) is used to express tests for a fault in terms of the input and output lines of the faulty gate. As an example,

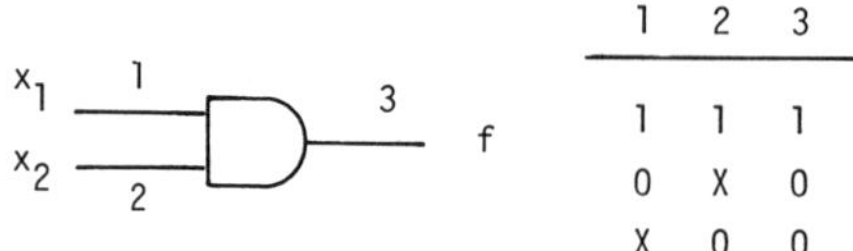

Figure 2.8
A two-input AND gate and its singular cover

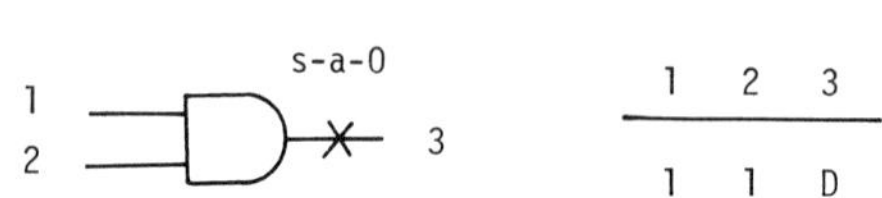

Figure 2.9
A fault and its primitive D-cube

consider the AND gate with an output s-a-0 fault shown in figure 2.9. To test the fault it is necessary to set 1 on the output line, and thus lines 1 and 2 must be forced to value 1. Then line 3 will have value 0 if the fault is present and value 1 if it is absent. Hence, the corresponding primitive D-cube of the fault is

1	2	3
1	1	D

where D means value 1 in the normal circuit and value 0 in the faulty circuit. Similarly, $\bar{D}$ will be used to represent a signal that has the value 0 in the normal circuit and 1 in the faulty circuit. Note that all appearances of D in a cube are constrained to take the same value. Thus, the cube $D0\bar{D}$ represents the two cubes 001 and 100. On the contrary, the symbol X indicates "don't care" and may take the values 0 and 1 independent of other values. Thus, the cube $X0X$ represents the four values 000, 001, 100, and 101.

The primitive D-cubes of a fault are constructed by intersecting pairs of singular cubes from the singular covers of the faulty and fault-free gates. Let the singular cubes for which the output of the fault-free gate is 1 (0) be denoted by α_1 (α_0). Let the singular cubes for which the output of the faulty gate is 1 (0) be denoted by β_1 (β_0). The primitive D-cubes of the fault that result in output D can be obtained by intersecting the inputs of each cube in α_1 with those for each cube in β_0. Similarly, the primitive D-cubes of the fault resulting in output $\bar{D}$ can be obtained by intersecting cubes in α_0 and β_1.

(a) AND gate: inputs 1, 2; output 3

(b)

1	2	3	
1	1	1	α_1
0	X	0	α_0
X	0	0	

(c)

1	2	3	
1	X	1	β_1
X	1	1	
0	0	0	β_0

(d)

1	2	3	
0	1	$\bar{D}$	$\alpha_0 \cap \beta_1$
1	0	$\bar{D}$	

Figure 2.10
A fault and its primitive D-cubes

Example 2.6 Suppose there is a fault that transforms an AND gate into an OR gate. The singular covers of the fault-free and faulty gates are shown in figure 2.10. By intersecting each pair of cubes from α_1 and β_0, and α_0 and β_1, we obtain the primitive D-cubes of the fault as shown in figure 2.10(d). The first cube is derived by intersecting the inputs of the first cubes of α_0 and β_1 and placing $\bar{D}$ at the output. The second cube is obtained similarly from the second cubes of α_0 and β_1. The intersection of the inputs of α_1 and β_0 is empty.

For the purpose of generating tests for faults that can be detected by primary outputs of the circuit, there are *propagation D-cubes* of a gate, which specify the minimal input conditions to the gate that are required to propagate an error signal on an input (or inputs) to the output of that gate. Roth (1966) calls these cubes "primitive D-cubes of a logical block." Propagation D-cubes can be derived from the singular cover as follows. For each pair of cubes in the singular cover that have different output values, intersect them by the following rules:

$0 \cap 0 = 0 \cap \mathrm{X} = \mathrm{X} \cap 0 = 0,$

$1 \cap 1 = 1 \cap \mathrm{X} = \mathrm{X} \cap 1 = 1,$

$\mathrm{X} \cap \mathrm{X} = \mathrm{X},$

$1 \cap 0 = \mathrm{D}, \quad 0 \cap 1 = \bar{\mathrm{D}}.$

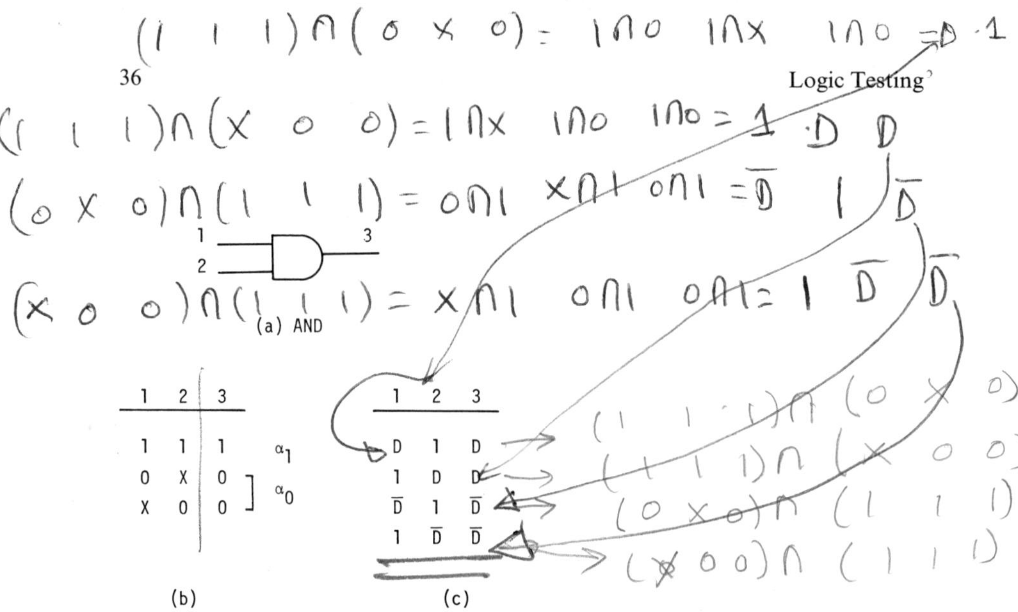

Figure 2.11
A two-input AND gate and its singular cover and propagation D-cubes

The propagation D-cubes for a two-input AND gate are given in figure 2.11(c). The D-cube $D1D$ represents the two cubes 111 in the normal circuit and 010 in the faulty circuit. Thus, the D-cube specifies an input condition to propagate an error signal on line 1 through the gate to line 3.

Propagation D-cubes for multiple input errors can be obtained similarly. For example, consider the propagation of double error signals on input lines 1 and 2 of the AND gate in figure 2.11. When both lines 1 and 2 have value 1 in the normal circuit and 0 in the faulty circuit, output line 3 will take 1 in the normal circuit and 0 in the faulty circuit. Thus, the propagation D-cube becomes

1	2	3
D	D	D

This D-cube can be obtained by intersecting the cubes 111 and 000, just as is done for single-error propagation D-cubes. Similarly, by intersecting 000 with 111 we obtain

1	2	3
$\bar{D}$	$\bar{D}$	$\bar{D}$

Table 2.1
Coordinate D-intersection

$\cap$	0	1	x	D	$\bar{D}$
0	0	$\emptyset$	0	ψ	ψ
1	$\emptyset$	1	1	ψ	ψ
x	0	1	x	D	$\bar{D}$
D	ψ	ψ	D	D	ψ
$\bar{D}$	ψ	ψ	$\bar{D}$	ψ	$\bar{D}$

$\emptyset$ = empty, ψ = undefined

For a three-input AND gate, we obtain the following multiple D-cubes:

1	2	3	4
D	D	1	D
D	1	D	D
1	D	D	D
D	D	D	D
$\bar{D}$	$\bar{D}$	1	$\bar{D}$
$\bar{D}$	1	$\bar{D}$	$\bar{D}$
1	$\bar{D}$	$\bar{D}$	$\bar{D}$
$\bar{D}$	$\bar{D}$	$\bar{D}$	$\bar{D}$

Let α and β be two D-cubes. The *D-intersection* $\alpha \cap \beta$ is defined using the coordinate D-intersection in table 2.1 and the following rules:

$\alpha \cap \beta = \emptyset$ (empty) if any coordinate intersection is $\emptyset$.

$\alpha \cap \beta = \psi$ (undefined) if any coordinate intersection is ψ.

$\alpha \cap \beta$ = the cube formed from the respective coordinate intersections if neither 1 nor 2 holds.

For example,

$0XD1X \cap X\bar{D}D11 = 0\bar{D}D11$,

$0XD1X \cap 10DXX = \emptyset$,

$0XD1X \cap 00\bar{D}\bar{D}X = \psi$.

The D-intersection is used to generate a sensitized path. For example, consider the circuit of figure 2.12. To generate a sensitized path from line 1

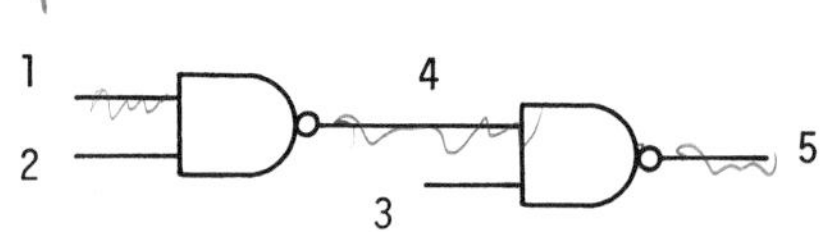

Figure 2.12

to line 5, we D-intersect the relevant propagation D-cubes for the two NAND gates as follows:

$$\frac{1 \quad 2 \quad 3 \quad 4 \quad 5}{D \quad 1 \quad X \quad \bar{D} \quad X} \cap \frac{1 \quad 2 \quad 3 \quad 4 \quad 5}{X \quad X \quad 1 \quad \bar{D} \quad D} = \frac{1 \quad 2 \quad 3 \quad 4 \quad 5}{D \quad 1 \quad 1 \quad \bar{D} \quad D}$$

This cube represents a test sensitizing a path from line 1 to line 5.

Now we can specify the D-algorithm, since the necessary preliminaries have been defined. The flowchart of the D-algorithm is given in figure 2.13. Each box in the flowchart will be explained in the following.

We begin by initializing a test cube to be completely unspecified. We label this test cube 0 (tc^0). Then, we select a primitive D-cube of the fault in question. For example, consider the circuit of figure 2.14 and the line 6 s-a-1 fault. The primitive D-cube of the fault is

2	3	6
1	1	$\bar{D}$

Usually a choice exists, since more than one primitive D-cube of the fault exist. For example, for the line 6 s-a-0 fault we have two primitive D-cubes:

2	3	6
0	X	D
X	0	D

In such a case we select a cube arbitrarily, but we may need during the execution of the algorithm to return and consider another possible choice. This is called *backtracking*. Backtracking may have to be iterated until all choices have been considered.

In box 3 of figure 2.13 the selected D-cube is D-intersected with the test cube tc^0. In our example, the D-intersection of tc^0 with the primitive D-cube of the line 6 s-a-1 fault is

2	3	6
1	1	$\bar{D}$

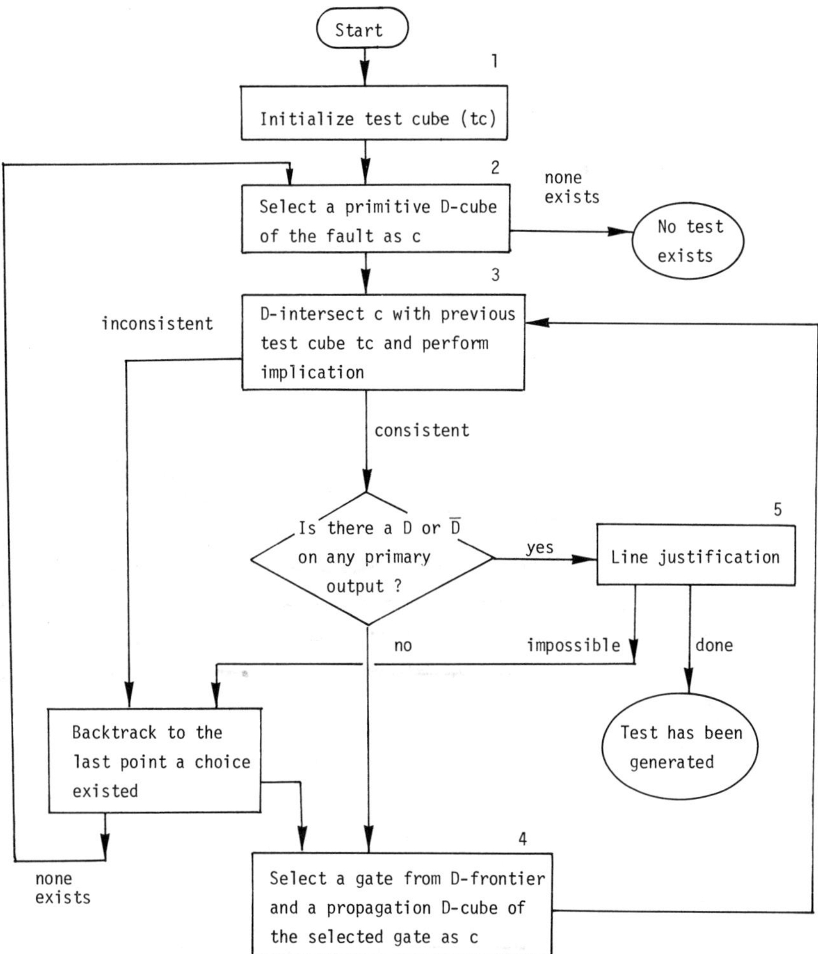

Figure 2.13
Flowchart for D-algorithm

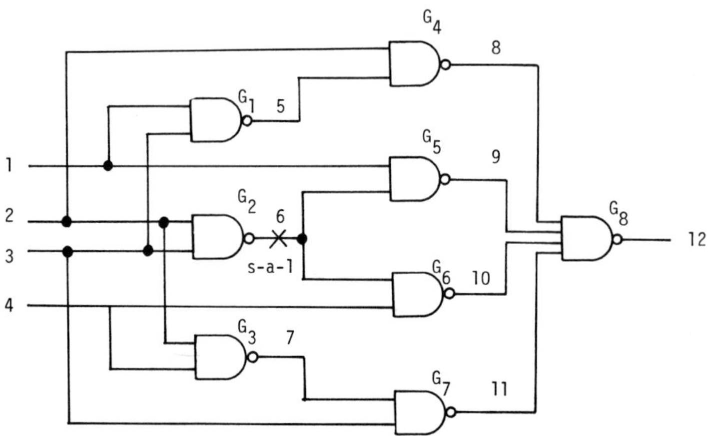

Figure 2.14

Next, the *implication* is performed. The implication procedure is to specify all gates, inputs, and outputs that will be determined uniquely or implied by other line values in the current test cube. These implied line values can be determined by intersecting the test cube with the singular cubes for the associated gate. For example, for an AND gate, if one input has value 0 and the output is unspecified, then the output of the AND gate will be specified to be 0. If the output value is 1 but all inputs are unspecified, then all input values will be implied to be 1. As a complicated case, the output of an AND gate is implied to be D ($\bar{D}$) if some input(s) is (are) D ($\bar{D}$) and all other inputs are 1. Moreover, if one input value is D and another input value is $\bar{D}$, the output is implied to be 0.

An *inconsistency* occurs when the value implied on a line is different from the value that has already been specified on the line. If an inconsistency occurs, we must backtrack to the last point at which a choice existed, reset all lines to their values at this point, and start again with the next choice.

The implication operation completely traces such signal determination both forward and backward through the circuit. If the faulty signal D or $\bar{D}$ has been propagated to a primary output, then *line justification* (called *consistency operation* in Roth 1966) will be performed. This process will be explained later.

In box 3 of figure 2.13, the process of propagating the faulty signal D or $\bar{D}$ is performed one step further toward primary output. This process is called

D-drive. The set of all gates whose output values are unspecified but whose input has some signal D or $\bar{D}$ is called the *D-frontier*. For our example, the D-frontier of the test cube tc^0 is $\{G_5, G_6\}$. D-drive first selects a gate in the D-frontier. Then D-intersection of the current test cube with a propagation D-cube of the selected gate is performed. For our example, suppose we select gate G_5 in the D-frontier and a propagation D-cube

	1	6	9
pdc^1 =	1	$\bar{D}$	D

The D-intersection of tc^0 with the propagation D-cube is as follows.

	1	2	3	4	5	6	7	8	9	10	11	12
tc^0 =	X	1	1	X	X	$\bar{D}$	X	X	X	X	X	X
pdc^1 =	1					$\bar{D}$			D			
$tc^1 = tc^0 \cap pdc^1$ =	1	1	1	X	X	$\bar{D}$	X	X	D	X	X	X

If such D-intersection is impossible with all the propagation D-cubes of the selected gate, a new gate in the D-frontier is selected. If D-intersection cannot be accomplished for any gate in the D-frontier, we backtrack to the last point at which a choice existed, reset all line to their values at that point, and begin with the next choice.

After D-drive, implication for the new test cube is performed. For our example, the D-intersection of tc^1 with a singular cube (sc) of gate G_1 is

	1	2	3	4	5	6	7	8	9	10	11	12
tc^1 =	1	1	1	X	X	$\bar{D}$	X	X	D	X	X	X
sc^1 =	1		1		0							
$tc^2 = tc^1 \cap sc^1$ =	1	1	1	X	0	$\bar{D}$	X	X	D	X	X	X

Moreover, by D-intersecting tc^2 with a singular cube of gate G_4 we obtain

	1	2	3	4	5	6	7	8	9	10	11	12
sc^2 =		X			0			1				
$tc^3 = tc^2 \cap sc^2$ =	1	1	1	X	0	$\bar{D}$	X	1	D	X	X	X

At this point, the D-frontier of tc^3 is $\{G_6, G_8\}$. Suppose we select G_8 to execute the D-drive. The D-intersection of tc^3 with a propagation D-cube of G_8 is

	1	2	3	4	5	6	7	8	9	10	11	12
$\mathrm{pdc}^2 =$								1	D	1	1	$\bar{D}$
$\mathrm{tc}^4 = \mathrm{tc}^3 \cap \mathrm{pdc}^2 =$	1	1	1	X	0	$\bar{D}$	X	1	D	1	1	$\bar{D}$

The implications for this test cube proceed as follows: The value 1 on line 11 forces value 0 on line 7 since line 3 is fixed at value 1, and the value 1 on line 10 forces value 0 on line 4 since line 6 is currently value $\bar{D}$. When gate G_3 is examined for implications it is found to be inconsistent; the NAND gate cannot have an input value 0 and an output value 0 simultaneously.

Hence, we backtrack to the last point at which a choice existed. In this case, we reset the text cube to tc^3, whose D-frontier is $\{G_6, G_8\}$. Since we selected G_8 last time, this time we select G_6. The D-intersection of tc^3 with a propagation D-cube of G_6 is

	1	2	3	4	5	6	7	8	9	10	11	12
$\mathrm{tc}^3 =$	1	1	1	X	0	$\bar{D}$	X	1	D	X	X	X
$\mathrm{pdc}^3 =$				1		$\bar{D}$				D		
$\mathrm{tc}^4 = \mathrm{tc}^3 \cap \mathrm{pdc}^3 =$	1	1	1	1	0	$\bar{D}$	X	1	D	D	X	X

This implication for tc^4 is as follows: the ones on lines 2 and 4 imply value 0 on line 7, which implies value 1 on line 11. At this point, lines 9 ad 10 are D, and lines 8 and 11 are 0, thereby forcing value $\bar{D}$ on the primary output line 12. Thus we have

	1	2	3	4	5	6	7	8	9	10	11	12
$\mathrm{tc}^5 =$	1	1	1	1	0	$\bar{D}$	0	1	D	D	1	$\bar{D}$

Since the faulty signal $\bar{D}$ has reached the primary output, the line justification (consistency operation) would normally be started. The execution of D-drive and implication may result in specifying the output of a gate G but leaving the inputs of G unspecified. This type of output line is called an *unjustified line*. It is necessary to specify input values so as to produce the specified output values. This process is called *line justification* or *consistency operation* in box 5 of figure 2.13. Figure 2.15 is the flowchart of the line-justification procedure. For our example, however, in the test cube tc^5 all gates with outputs 0 or 1 have their signals already accounted for by their inputs. Thus, tc^5 is a test for the fault in question, line 6 s-a-1. The test pattern is $T = 1111$.

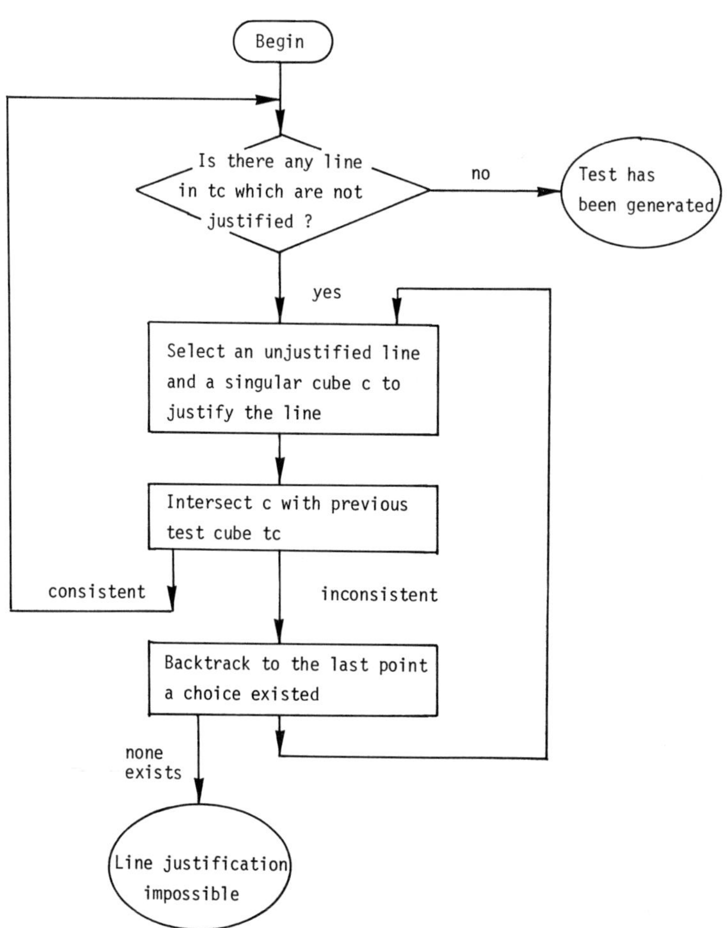

Figure 2.15
Line justification (consistency operation)

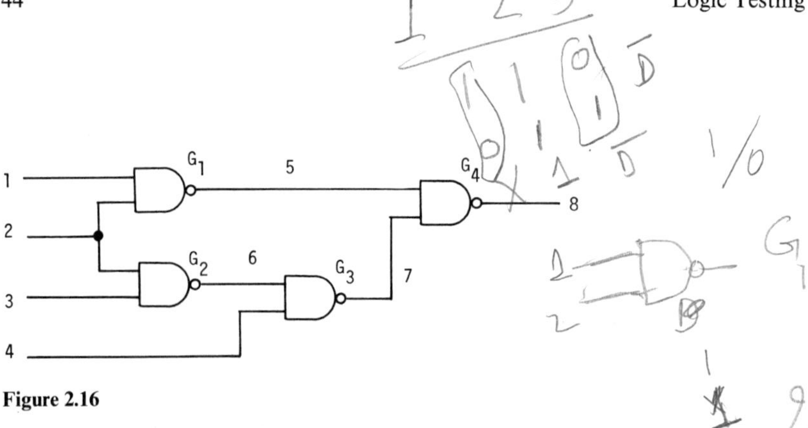

Figure 2.16

As an illustration of line justification, consider the line 1 s-a-0 fault for the circuit in figure 2.16. After D-drive we obtain the test cube

	1	2	3	4	5	6	7	8
$tc^1 =$	D	1	X	X	$\bar{D}$	X	1	D

In this test cube, line 7 is unjustified. The singular cover of gate G_3 is

4	6	7
0	X	1
X	0	1
1	1	0

Suppose that we select the second singular cube and intersect it with tc^1 to justify line 7. The D-intersection is

	1	2	3	4	5	6	7	8
$tc^1 =$	D	1	X	X	$\bar{D}$	X	1	D
$sc^2 =$				X		0	1	
$tc^2 = tc^1 \cap sc^2 =$	D	1	X	X	$\bar{D}$	0	1	D

At this point, line 6 becomes an unjustified line. Thus, the D-intersection of tc^2 with a singular cube of gate G_2 must be performed as follows:

	1	2	3	4	5	6	7	8
$tc^2 =$	D	1	X	X	$\bar{D}$	0	1	D
$sc^3 =$		1	1			0		
$tc^3 = tc^2 \cap sc^3 =$	D	1	1	X	$\bar{D}$	0	1	D

Since all lines in tc^3 are justified, the test generation for the line 1 s-a-0 is completed.

there is more than one choice available at each decision node. Through an implicit enumeration process, all alternatives at each decision node are examined until a test is found. Thus, we can see intuitively that the D-algorithm will derive a test for any logical fault if such a test exists. This has been proved by Roth (1966).

In the D-algorithm the computation of a test for a fault proceeds in two stages: first the D-drive from the site of the fault to the primary output, then consistency or line justification backward to the primary inputs. Roth (1980) extended the original D-algorithm by mixing D-drive and line-justification processes. In that algorithm, at each stage the D-frontier (gates with an X on their output and a D or a $\bar{D}$ on their inputs) and the *C-frontier* (gates whose output line is unjustified) are computed. A gate is said to be "on the frontier" if it is on the D-frontier or the C-frontier. At each step, the gate on the frontier is selected, whether on the D-frontier or the C-frontier, that has the smallest distance. (The distance of a gate on the D-frontier is measured in terms of the number of gates to the primary outputs. Similarly, the distance of a gate on the C-frontier is measured in terms of the number of gates to the primary inputs.) In the original D-algorithm, first each gate is selected from the D-frontier to D-drive, and then after the faulty signal D or $\bar{D}$ has reached the primary output each gate from the C-frontier is chosen successively to perform the consistency operation. Hence, this algorithm mixing the D-frontier and the C-frontier is an extended version of the D-algorithm.

There is another variation of the D-algorithm. The D-algorithm uses a calculus based on five values: 0, 1, D, $\bar{D}$, and X. Cha et al. (1978) reported another test-generation algorithm for combinational circuits using nine values: 0, 1, D, $\bar{D}$, $0/D$, $0/\bar{D}$, $1/D$, $1/\bar{D}$, and X. Here, a/b ($a = 0$ or 1; $b = D$ or $\bar{D}$) means that the value of the line is not completely specified yet and can be a or b.

Akers (1976) presented a test-generation algorithm using a 16-value calculus. Takamatsu et al. (1983) extended the nine-value algorithm of Cha et al. to an algorithm using ten values: 0, 1, D, $\bar{D}$, $0/D$, $0/\bar{D}$, $1/D$, $1/\bar{D}$, X, and $D/\bar{D}$.

2.3 The PODEM Algorithm

A test-generation algorithm called the PODEM (Path Oriented DEcision Making) algorithm was reported by Goel (1981a) and shown to be more

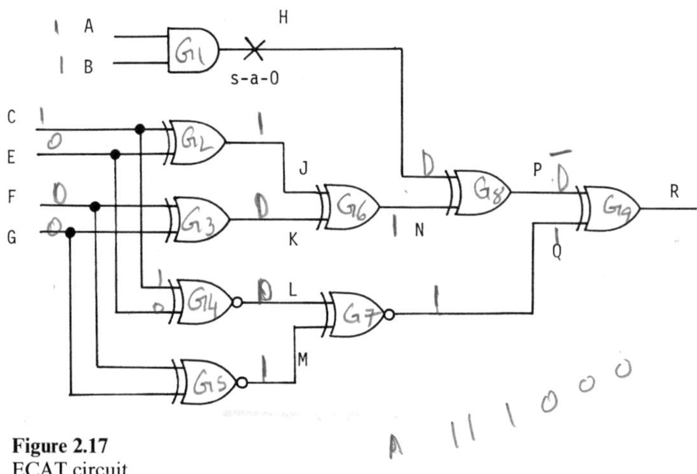

Figure 2.17
ECAT circuit

efficient than the D-algorithm. The D-algorithm has been pointed out to be ineffective for the class of combinational circuits used to implement error-correction-and-translation (ECAT) functions. ECAT-type circuits are characterized by consisting of some number of EOR trees with reconvergence.

Consider figure 2.17, which shows an ECAT circuit. For the fault H s-a-0, the D-algorithm may go through the following steps. First, the primitive D-cube of the fault is chosen. In this case, $A = B = 1$ and $H = D$. To propagate the faulty signal to the primary output R, D-drive operations are performed by D-intersecting the test cube with the propagation D-cubes of gates along the path. After D-drive, $N = 1$, $P = \bar{D}$, $Q = 1$, and $R = D$ may be obtained. Next, the D-algorithm begins to justify lines N and Q. However, since lines N and Q realize the complementary functions with each other, no justification is possible for the concurrent assignment $N = 1$ and $Q = 1$. Thus, the D-algorithm must enumerate input values exhaustively until the absence of the justification will be confirmed. In this enumeration process, the D-algorithm creates a decision tree and examines all alternatives at each decision node, as shown in figure 2.18. In this figure, the D-algorithm backtracks tediously many times until it reaches the assignment $N = 1$ and $Q = 0$.

In the D-algorithm, since the assignment of values is allowed to internal lines, more than one choice is available at each internal line or gate and

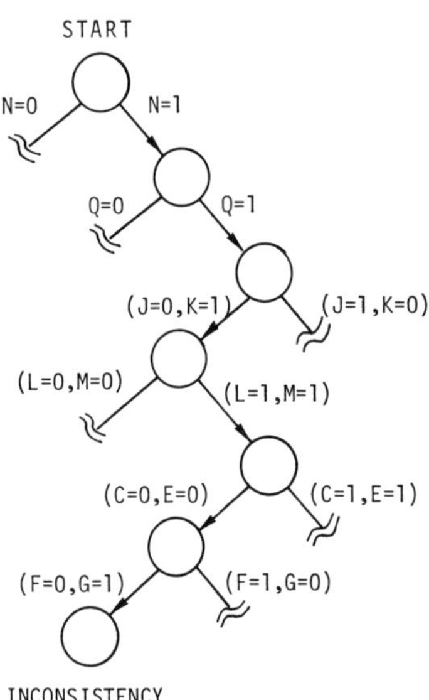

Figure 2.18
Decision tree in D-algorithm

backtracking could occur at each gate. In contrast, the PODEM algorithm allows assigning values only to primary inputs. The values assigned to primary inputs are then propagated toward internal lines by the implication. Thus, in the PODEM algorithm, backtracking can occur only at the primary inputs. The PODEM algorithm examines all possible primary input patterns implicitly but exhaustively as tests for a given fault. Of course, the examination of primary input patterns is terminated as soon as a test is found. If it is determined that no primary input pattern can be a test, the fault is undetectable or redundant. Figure 2.19 is the flowchart of the PODEM algorithm.

For the H s-a-0 fault of the circuit in figure 2.17, the PODEM algorithm is carried out as follows. First, a binary value is assigned to an unassigned primary input in order to provide a faulty signal at the site of the fault. (The procedure for determining a primary input and a value to be assigned will be described later.) Suppose we assign $A = 1$. Next, we determine the implications of all primary inputs. The implication is identical to the forward implication process in the D-algorithm. Since assignments occur

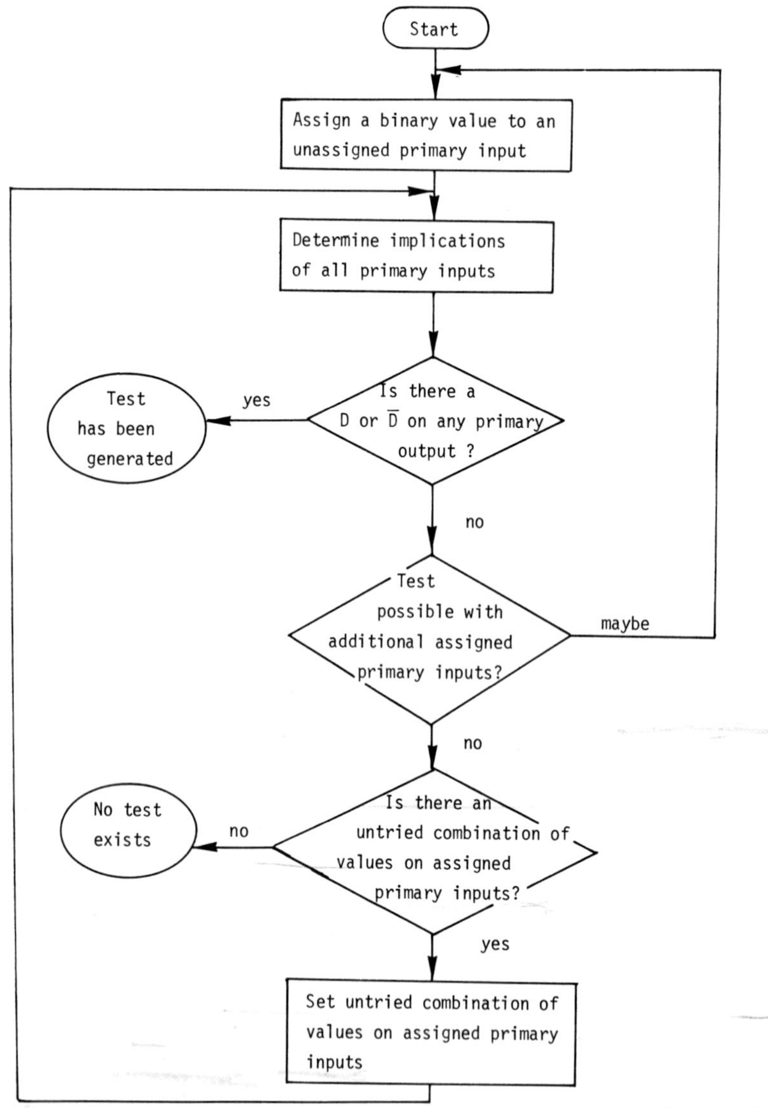

Figure 2.19
Flowchart for PODEM algorithm (from Goel 1981a; © 1981 IEEE)

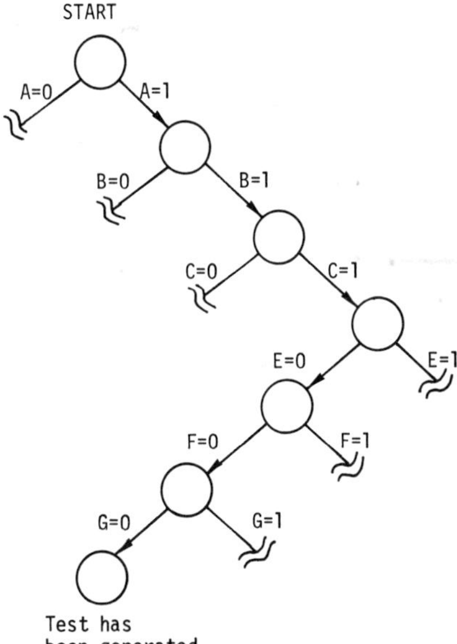

Figure 2.20
Decision tree in PODEM algorithm

only at the primary inputs, we need not consider the backward implication. For our example, since $A = 1$ causes no implication, we again choose a primary input B and assign $B = 1$ to provide a faulty signal. Then, $A = 1$ and $B = 1$ imply $H = D$.

Once the faulty signal has been provided, the objective is to propagate a D or a $\bar{D}$ one level of gate closer to a primary output than before. For our example, to propagate the value D on H to P we assign $C = 1$, which is followed by the assignment $E = 0$. At this point, $C = 1$ and $E = 0$ imply $J = 1$ and $L = 0$. Continuing the assignment and implication, we have $F = 0$ and $G = 0$. At this point, the implications of primary inputs force $K = 0$, $M = 1$, $N = 1$, and $Q = 0$. Moreover, $H = D$ and $N = 1$ imply $P = \bar{D}$, and $P = \bar{D}$ and $Q = 0$ imply $R = \bar{D}$. This completes the generation of a test for the fault H s-a-0.

In these processes, the PODEM algorithm creates a decision tree as shown in figure 2.20. The decision tree is an ordered list of nodes with each node identifying a current assignment of either a 0 or a 1 to one primary input, and the ordering reflects the sequence in which the current assignments were made. The decision tree can be implemented as a LIFO (last in first out) stack. The above-mentioned example suggests that the PODEM algorithm is more efficient than the D-algorithm for ECAT-type circuits. While the D-algorithm backtracks many times to generate a test for the fault H s-a-0, as shown in figure 2.18, the PODEM algorithm generates the test without backtracking.

The process of choosing a primary input and a logic value for initial assignment is performed in two steps:

(1) An initial objective is determined. An *objective* is defined by a pair (v, s) where v is a logic value 0 or 1 (called the *objective value*) and s is an *objective line* (the line at which the objective value is desired). If a faulty signal D or $\bar{D}$ has not yet appeared at the site of the fault, the initial objective is directed toward providing the faulty signal on the associated line. For an s-a-0 (s-a-1) fault on line L, the objective line is L and the objective value is 1 (0). If a faulty signal has already been provided, the initial objective is directed toward propagating a D or $\bar{D}$ to a primary output. In this case, PODEM uses a look-ahead technique called *X-path check*: It checks whether there is any path from a gate in the D-frontier to a primary output such that all lines along the path are at X. In the case when there exists no D-frontier with such a path, backtracking occurs.

(2) Given the initial objective, a primary input and a logic value are chosen such that the chosen logic value assigned to the chosen primary input has a good likelihood of helping to meet the initial objective. This process is called *backtrace* by Goel (1981a). The flowchart of the backtrace procedure is shown in figure 2.21. The backtrace procedure searches a path from the objective line backward to a primary input. During the process, the next objective is chosen from the current objective by the following heuristics: When the current objective value is such that it can be obtained by setting any one input of the gate to a *controlling state* (for example, 0 for an AND/NAND gate or 1 for an OR/NOR gate), we choose the input that can be most easily set. When the current objective value can be obtained only by setting all inputs of the gate to a *noncontrolling state* (for example, 1 for an AND/NAND gate or 0 for an OR/NOR gate), we choose the input that is hardest to set, since an early determination of the inability to set the chosen input will save the time that would be wasted in attempting to set the remaining inputs of the gate. In these heuristics (i.e., the choice of the "easiest to control" input or the "hardest to control" input), several mea-

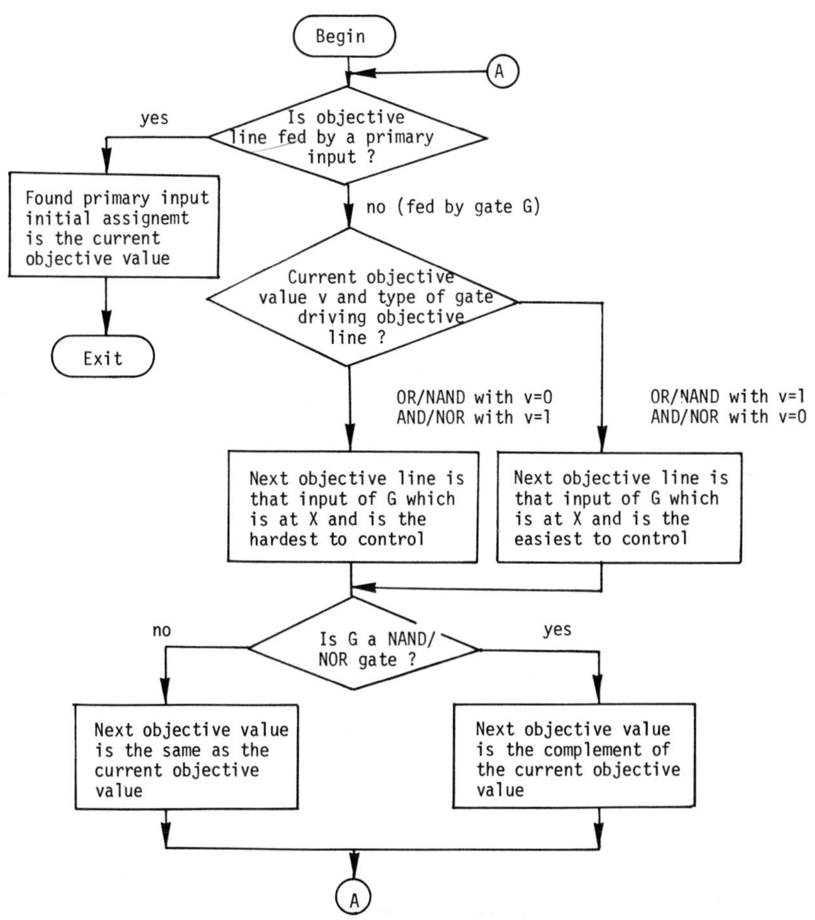

Figure 2.21
Flowchart of backtrace (from Goel 1981a; © 1981 IEEE)

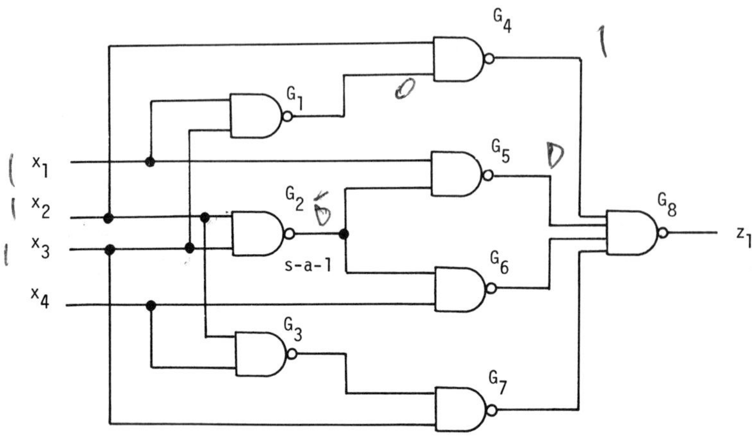

Figure 2.22

sures of controllability for the inputs of the gates could be used. Various types of testability measures that include controllability and observability of internal lines of circuits will be discussed in section 5.1.

Example 2.7 Consider the circuit of figure 2.22 and the fault G_2 output s-a-1. To provide a faulty signal on the output of G_2, the initial objective is determined to be $(0, G_2)$. The backtrace causes the assignment $x_2 = 1$. Again, the initial objective is set to $(0, G_2)$, and the backtrace causes the assignment $x_3 = 1$. By implication, we have $G_2 = \bar{D}$ and the D-frontier $\{G_5, G_6\}$. To propagate the faulty signal through gate G_5, the initial objective is set to $(0, G_5)$ and then the backtrace selects the assignment $x_1 = 1$. By implication, we have $G_1 = 0$, $G_4 = 1$, and $G_5 = \text{D}$, and hence the D-frontier has changed to $\{G_6, G_8\}$. To propagate the faulty signal further through gate G_8, the backtrace begins with the initial objective $(0, G_8)$ and ends in the assignment $x_4 = 0$. However, by implication we obtain $G_3 = 1$, $G_7 = 0$, and $G_8 = 1$, and thus the propagation of the faulty signal through gate G_8 has failed. Since no test exists under the assignment $x_1 = x_2 = x_3 = 1$ and $x_4 = 0$, we backtrack to the last node at which a choice existed. This is illustrated as a decision tree in figure 2.23. The last primary input assignment was $x_4 = 0$, and so the alternative is assigned this time. Performing the implication of $x_1 = x_2 = x_3 = x_4 = 1$ at this stage results in $G_1 = G_3 = 0$, $G_2 = \bar{D}$, $G_4 = G_7 = 1$, $G_5 = G_6 = D$, and $G_8 = \bar{D}$.

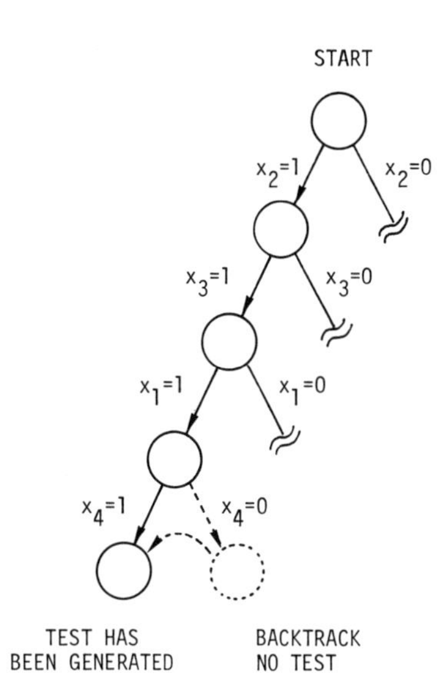

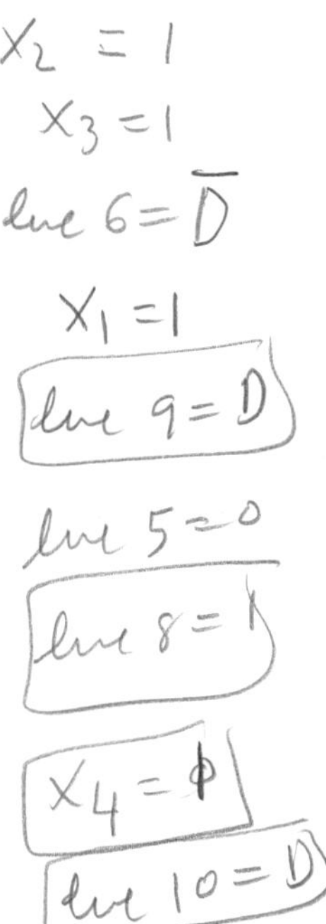

Figure 2.23
Decision tree for example 2.7

2.4 The FAN Algorithm

The PODEM algorithm has indeed succeeded in reducing the occurrences of backtracks in comparison with the D-algorithm. However, there still remain many possibilities of reducing the number of backtracks in the algorithm. This section discusses several techniques to accelerate test-generation algorithms and presents a new test-generation algorithm: the fanout-oriented test-generation algorithm FAN, which was developed by Fujiwara and Shimono (1983a,b).

With respect to the acceleration of test generation, the PODEM algorithm has some defects. Let us consider several effective techniques to eliminate these disadvantages.

In generating a test, the PODEM algorithm creates a decision tree with more than one choice available at each decision node. The initial choice is arbitrary, but it may be necessary during the execution of the algorithm to return and try another possible choice. In order to accelerate the algorithm, it is necessary to reduce the number of these backtracks and to shorten the processing time between backtracks. The reduction of the number of backtracks is particularly important.

In order to reduce the number of backtracks, it is important to find the nonexistence of the solution as soon as possible. In the "branch and bound" algorithm, when we find that there exists no solution below the current node in the decision tree we should backtrack immediately to avoid the subsequent unnecessary search. The PODEM algorithm lacks careful consideration in this regard.

The following strategies are used in the FAN algorithm.

Strategy 1 In each step of the algorithm, determine as many signal values as possible that can be *uniquely* implied.

To do this we take the implication operation that completely traces such signal determination both forward and backward through the circuit. Moreover, we carry out the following process.

Strategy 2 Assign a faulty signal D or $\bar{D}$ that is *uniquely* determined or implied by the fault in question.

Example 2.8 Consider the circuit of figure 2.24. For the fault L s-a-1, we assign the value $\bar{D}$ to the line L and the value 1 to each of the inputs J, K, and E. Then, after the implication, we have a test for the fault without backtracks as shown in figure 2.24(a). On the other hand, in PODEM, the initial objective $(0, L)$ is determined to set up the faulty signal $\bar{D}$ to L, and backtrace starts. As shown in figure 2.24(b), the backtrace causes a path from L backward to a primary input B. The assignment $B = 0$ implies $L = 1$ and fails to provide the faulty signal on L. As seen in this example, by assigning uniquely determined values we can avoid the unnecessary choice.

Consider the circuit of figure 2.25(a). Supposing that the D-frontier consists of a single gate, we often have specific paths such that every path from the site of the D-frontier to a primary output always goes through those paths. In this example, every path from gate G_2 to a primary output passes through the paths F-H and K-M. In order to propagate the value D or $\bar{D}$ to a primary output, we have to propagate the faulty signal along both F-H and K-M. Therefore, if there exists a test at this point, paths F-H and K-M should be sensitized. Then we have the assignment $C = 1$, $G = 1$, $J = 1$, and $L = 1$ to sensitize them. This partial sensitization, which is uniquely determined, is called a *unique sensitization*. In figure 2.25(a), after the implication of this assignment we have $A = 1, B = 0, F = \bar{D}$, and $H = D$ without backtracking. On the other hand, PODEM sets the initial objec-

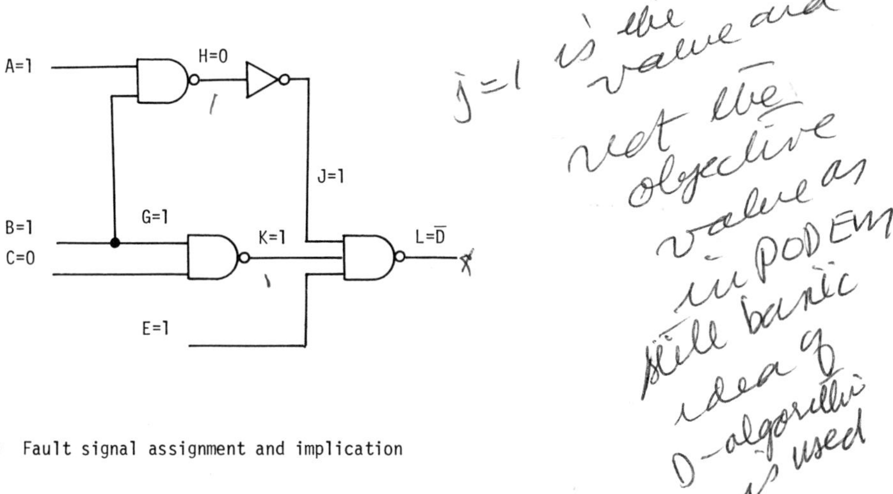

(a) Fault signal assignment and implication

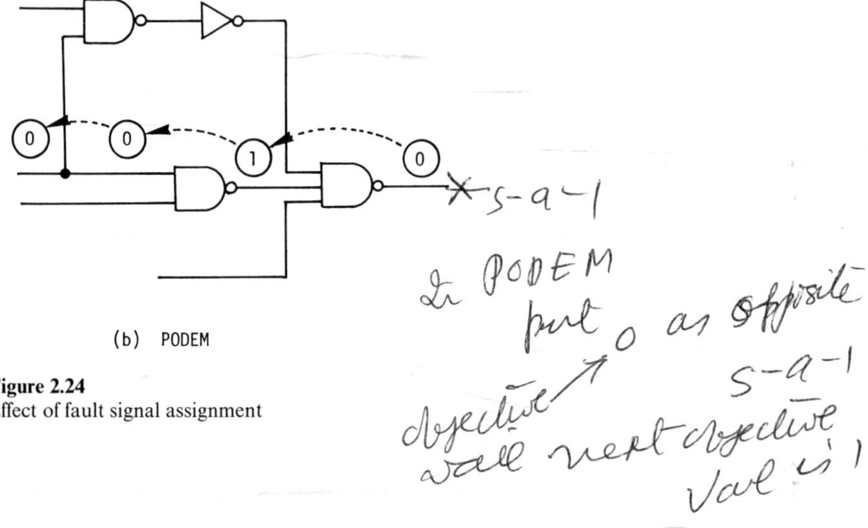

(b) PODEM

Figure 2.24
Effect of fault signal assignment

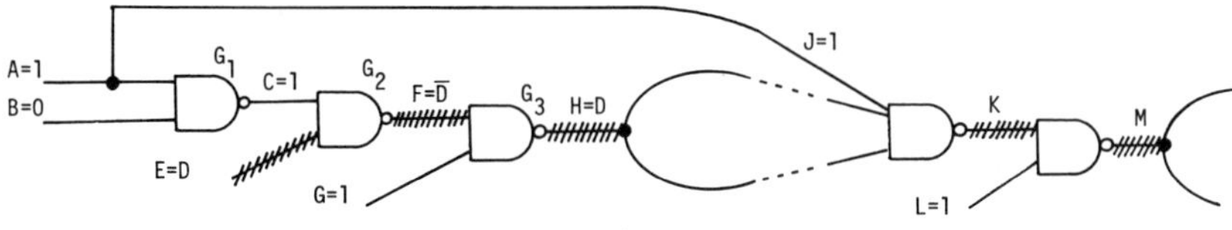

(a) Unique sensitization and implication

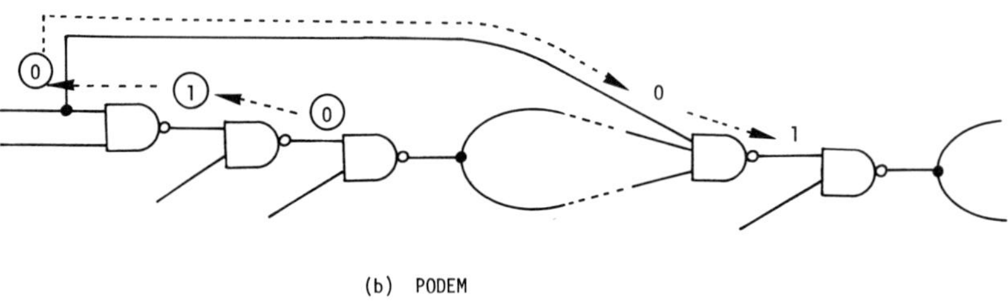

(b) PODEM

Figure 2.25
Effect of unique sensitization

tive $(0, F)$ to propagate the faulty signal to line F and performs the backtrace procedure. If the backtrace performs along the path as shown in figure 2.25(b), we have the assignment $A = 0$, which implies $J = 0$ and $K = 1$. Though no inconsistency appears at this point, an inconsistency or the disappearance of the D-frontier will occur in the future when the faulty signal propagates from H to K. Although the PODEM algorithm can find such an inconsistency by using X-path check, backtracking from $A = 0$ to $A = 1$ is unavoidable.

Strategy 3 When the *D*-frontier consists of a single gate, apply a *unique sensitization.*

As seen in the above example, in order to reduce the number of backtracks it is very effective to find as many uniquely determined values as we can in each step of the algorithm. This is because the assignment of the uniquely determined values could decrease the number of possible choices.

The execution of the techniques mentioned above may specify the output of a gate G but leave the inputs of G unspecified. It is necessary to specify input values so as to produce the specified output values for these unjustified lines. In PODEM, since all the lines are first assigned only to the

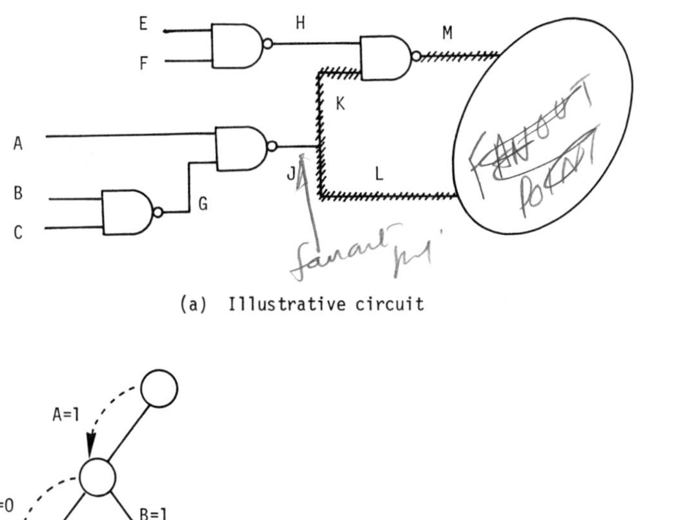

(a) Illustrative circuit

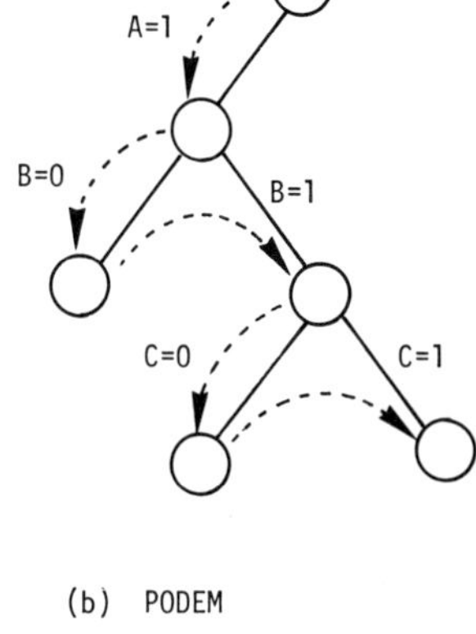

(b) PODEM

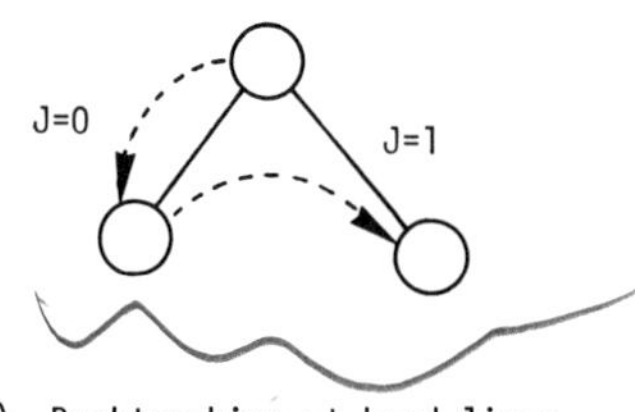

(c) Backtracking at head lines

Figure 2.26
Effect of head lines

primary inputs and only the forward implication is performed, unjustified lines never appear. However, if we employ the techniques mentioned above, the unjustified lines may appear. Thus, in this case some initial objectives will be produced simultaneously so as to justify them. We will manage this by introducing a multiple backtrace procedure that is an extension of the backtrace procedure of PODEM.

When a signal line *L* is reachable from some fanout point (that is, when there exists a path from some fanout point forward to L), we say that *L* is *bound*. A signal line that is not bound is said to be *free*. When a free line *L* is adjacent to some bound line, we say that *L* is a *head line*. As an example, consider the circuit of figure 2.26(a). Lines *A, B, C, E, F, G, H*, and *J* are all free, and lines *K*, *L*, and *M* are bound. Among the free lines, *J* and *H* are head lines of the circuit since J and H are adjacent to the bound lines L and M, respectively.

The backtrace procedure in PODEM traces a single path backward to a primary input. However, it suffices to stop the backtrace at a head line for the following reasons. The subcircuit composed of only free lines and the associated gates is a fanout-free circuit, since it contains no fanout point. For fanout-free circuits, line justification can be performed without backtracking. Hence, we can find the values on the primary inputs that justify all values on the head lines without backtracking. It is sufficient to let the line justification for head lines wait until the last stage of test generation.

Strategy 4 Stop the backtrace at a head line, and postpone the line justification for the head line to later.

As an illustration of strategy 4, consider the circuit of figure 2.26(a). Suppose that we want to set $J = 0$ but do not yet know that there exists no test under the condition $J = 0$. In PODEM, the initial objective is set to $(0, J)$ and the backtrace may result in the assignment $A = 1$. Since the value of J is not determined yet, PODEM starts the backtrace procedure again and gets the assignment $B = 0$. $A = 1$ and $B = 0$ imply $J = 0$. Now, suppose that there exists no test under $J = 0$, and thus an inconsistency occurs for the current assignment and PODEM backtracks to change the assignment on B as shown in figure 2.26(b). In this case, if we stop the backtrace at the head line J we can decrease the number of backtracks, as shown in figure 2.26(c).

In performing a unique sensitization, we need to identify the paths that would be uniquely sensitized. Also, we need to identify all the head lines in the circuit. These must be identified, and this topological information should be stored somehow, before the test generation starts. The computation time of these preprocesses can be, however, as small as negligible compared with the total computation time for test generation.

Strategy 5 Multiple backtracing (concurrent backtracing of more than one path) is more efficient than backtracing along a single path.

Consider the circuit of figure 2.27. For the objective to set $C = 0$, PODEM backtraces three times along the same path C-B-A and also along the same path C-F-E before the value 0 is specified on C by the implication. Backtracing along a single path wastes time. This could be avoided by multiple backtracing along plural paths.

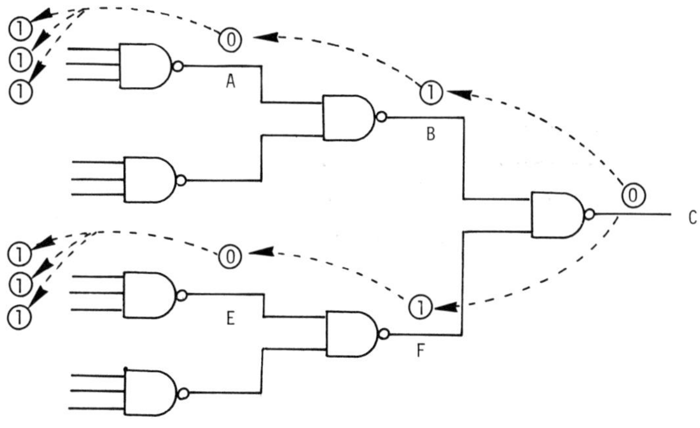

Figure 2.27
Backtrace

In the backtrace of PODEM, an objective is defined by a pair of a objective value and an objective line. An objective that will be used in the multiple backtrace in FAN is defined by the triplet

$$(s, n_0(s), n_1(s))$$

where s is an objective line, $n_0(s)$ is the number of times the object value 0 is required to be set on s, and $n_1(s)$ is the number of times the object value 1 is required to be set on s.

The computation of $n_0(s)$ and $n_1(s)$ will be described later. The multiple backtrace starts with more than one initial objective, that is, a *set of initial objectives*. Beginning with the set of initial objectives, a set of objectives that appear during the procedure is called a set of *current objectives*. A set of objectives that will be obtained at head lines is called a set of *head objectives*. A set of objectives on fanout points is called a set of *fanout-point objectives*.

An initial objective required to set 0 to line s is

$$(s, n_0(s), n_1(s)) = (s, 1, 0),$$

and an initial objective required to set 1 to s is

$$(s, n_0(s), n_1(s)) = (s, 0, 1).$$

Working breadth-first from these initial objectives backward to head lines, we determine the next objectives from the current objectives successively as follows:

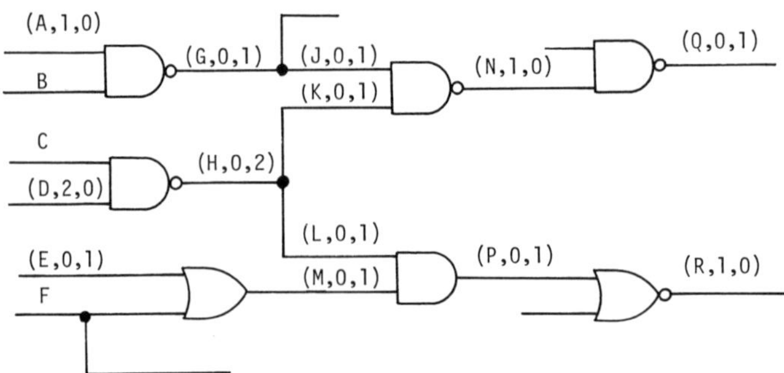

Figure 2.28
Computation of $n_0(s)$ and $n_1(s)$

AND gate: Let X be an input that is the easiest to set to 0. Then

$$n_0(X) = n_0(Y), \qquad n_1(X) = n_1(Y)$$

and for other inputs X_i

$$n_0(X_i) = 0, \qquad n_1(X_i) = n_1(Y)$$

where Y is the output of the AND gate.

OR gate: Let X be an input which is the easiest to set to 1. Then

$$n_0(X) = n_0(Y), \qquad n_1(X) = n_1(Y)$$

and for other inputs X_i

$$n_0(X_i) = n_0(Y), \qquad n_1(X_i) = 0.$$

NOT gate:

$$n_0(X) = n_1(Y), \qquad n_1(X) = n_0(Y).$$

Fanout point:

$$n_0(X) = \sum_{i=1}^{k} n_0(X_i), \qquad n_1(X) = \sum_{i=1}^{k} n_1(X_i)$$

where line X fans out to $X_1, \ldots, X_k$.

Example 2.9 Figure 2.28 shows an example of the computation of $n_0(s)$ and $n_1(s)$. The initial objectives are $(Q, 0, 1)$ and $(R, 1, 0)$; that is, Q and R are first required to be set to 1 and 0, respectively. At the fanout point H, $n_1(H)$ is obtained by summing $n_1(K)$ and $n_1(L)$.

Figure 2.29 is a flowchart of the multiple-backtrace procedure. Each current objective is backtraced until either a fanout point or a head line is reached. At that point, the objective becomes, respectively, a fanout-point objective or a head-line objective. After the set of current objectives becomes empty, the fanout-point objective closest to a primary output is taken out, if one exists. If the fanout-point objective satisfies the following condition, the objective becomes the final objective in the backtrace process and the procedure ends at exit D in figure 2.29. The condition is that the fanout point p is not reachable from the site of the fault and both $n_0(p)$ and $n_1(p)$ are nonzero. In this case, we assign a value [0 if $n_0(p) > n_1(p)$ or 1 if $n_0(p) < n_1(p)$] to the fanout point and perform the implications. The first part of the condition is necessary to guarantee that the value assigned is binary, that is, neither D nor $\bar{D}$.

In PODEM, the assignment of a binary value is allowed only to the primary inputs. In the FAN algorithm, a binary value may be assigned to fanout points as well as to head lines, and thus backtracking occurs only at fanout points and head lines but not at primary input. The reason we assign a value to a fanout point p is that there might exist a great possibility of an inconsistency when the objective in backtracing has an inconsistent requirement such that both $n_0(p)$ and $n_1(p)$ are nonzero. To avoid fruitless computation, we assign a binary value to the fanout point as soon as the objective involves a contradictory requirement. This leads to the early detection of inconsistency, which decreases the number of backtracks.

Strategy 6 In the multiple backtrace, if an objective at a fanout point p has a contradictory requirement, that is, if both $n_0(p)$ and $n_1(p)$ are nonzero, stop the backtrace so as to assign a binary value to the fanout point.

When an objective at a fanout point p has no contradiction, that is, when either $n_0(p)$ or $n_1(p)$ is zero, the backtrace continues from the fanout point. If all the objectives arrive at head lines, that is, if both sets of current objectives and fanout-point objectives are empty, then the multiple-backtrace procedure terminates at exit C in figure 2.29. After this, taking out head lines one by one from the set of head objectives, we assign the relevant value to the head line and perform the implication.

The flowchart of the FAN algorithm is given in figure 2.30. Each box in the flowchart is explained in the list on pages 64–66.

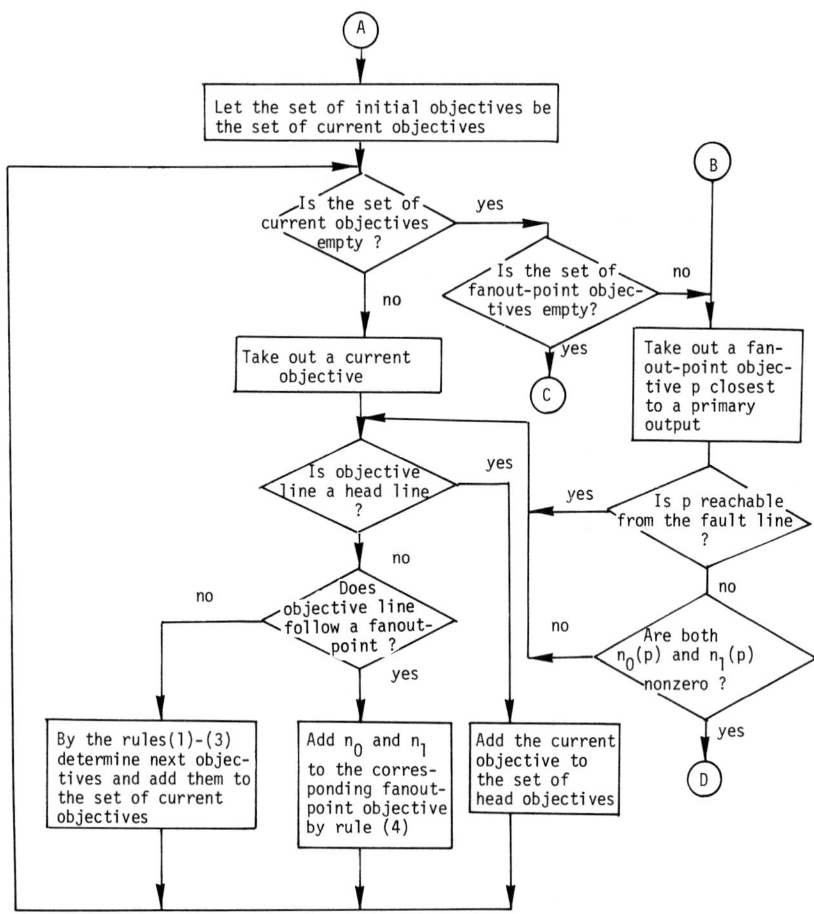

Figure 2.29
Flowchart of multiple backtrace

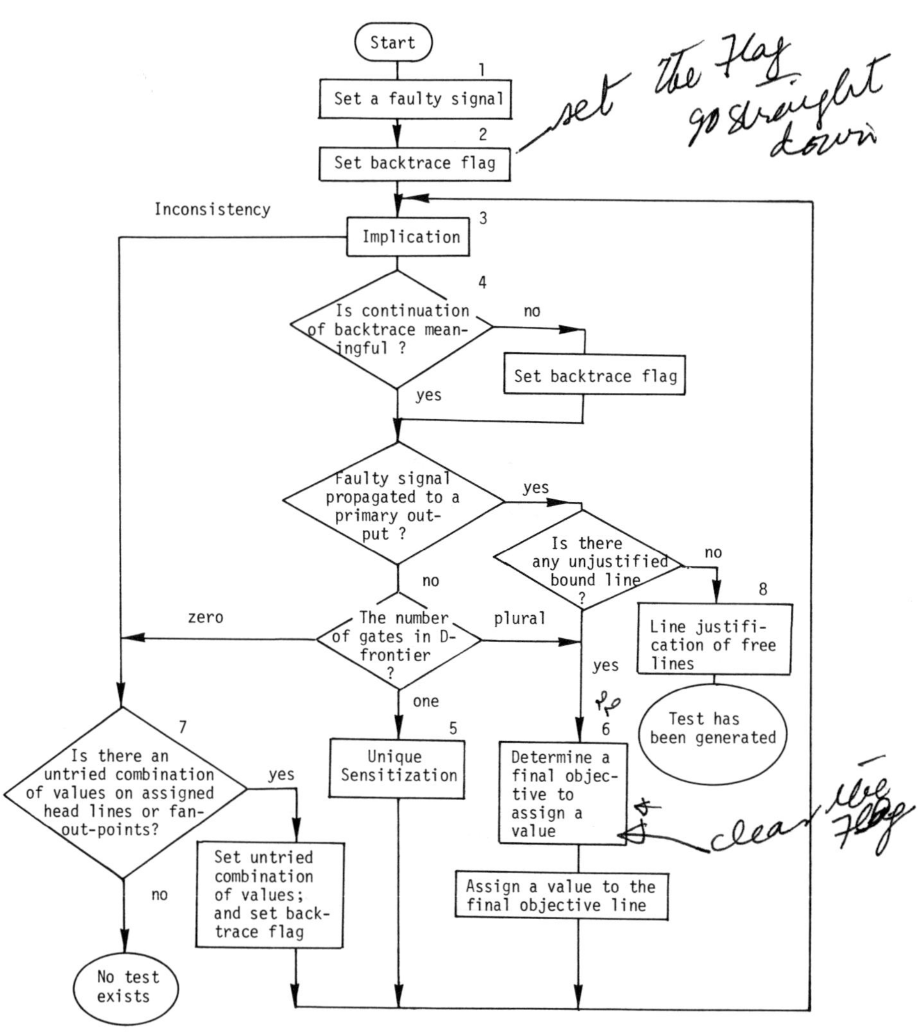

Figure 2.30
Flowchart of FAN algorithm

• Assignment of faulty signal: In box 1, a uniquely determined faulty signal D or $\bar{D}$ is assigned.

• Backtrace flag: The multiple backtrace procedure of figure 2.29 has two entries. One entry is (A), where the multiple backtrace starts from a set of initial objectives, and the other entry is (B), where the multiple backtrace starts with a fanout-point objective to continue the last multiple backtrace that terminated at a fanout point. The backtrace flag is used to distinguish the above two modes.

• Implication: We determine as many values as possible that can be uniquely implied. To do this we take the implication operation that completely traces such signal determination both forward and backward through the circuit. In PODEM, since all the values are assigned only to the primary inputs and only forward implication is performed, unjustified lines never appear. However, in FAN, since both forward and backward implications are performed, unjustified lines might appear. Thus, so as to justify those lines, the multiple backtrace is necessary not only to propagate the faulty signal but also to justify unjustified lines.

• Continuation check for multiple backtrace: In box 4, we check whether it is meaningful to continue the backtrace or not. We consider that it is not meaningful to continue the backtrace if the last objective was to propagate D or $\bar{D}$ and the D-frontier has changed, or if the last objective was to justify unjustified lines and all the unjustified lines have been justified. When it is not meaningful to continue, the backtrace flag is set so as to start the multiple backtrace with new initial objectives again.

• Unique sensitization: The unique sensitization is performed in the manner mentioned above (see figure 2.25). Although the unique sensitization might leave some lines unjustified, those lines will be justified by the multiple backtrace.

• Determination of a final objective: The detailed flowchart of box 6 is described in figure 2.31. By using the multiple backtrace procedure, we determine a final objective; that is, we choose a value and a line such that the chosen value assigned to the chosen line has a good likelihood of helping to meet the initial objectives.

• Backtracking: The decision tree is identical to that of PODEM (that is, an ordered list of nodes with each node identifying a current assignment of either 0 or 1 to one head line or one fanout point), and the ordering reflects the sequence in which the current assignments were made. A node is flagged if the initial assignment has been rejected and the alternative is being tried.

Pp
Box 6

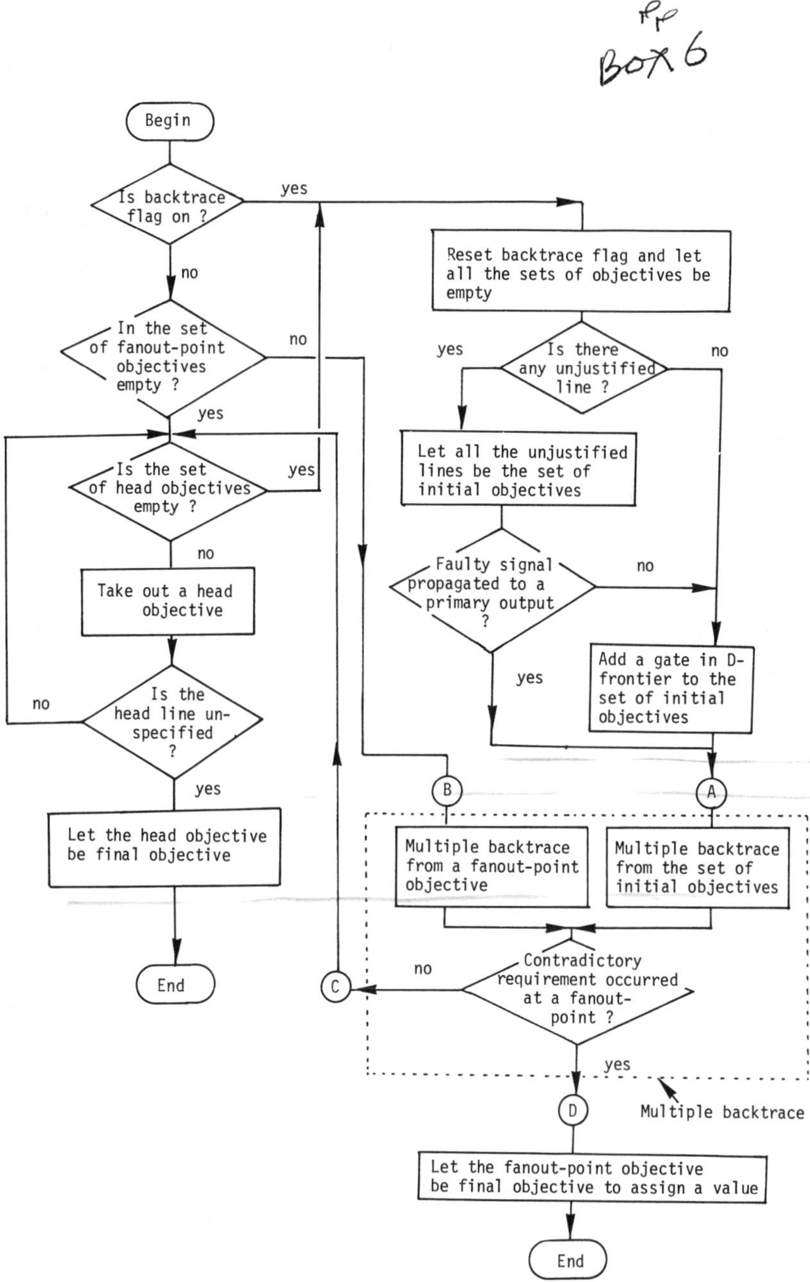

Figure 2.31
Determination of final objective

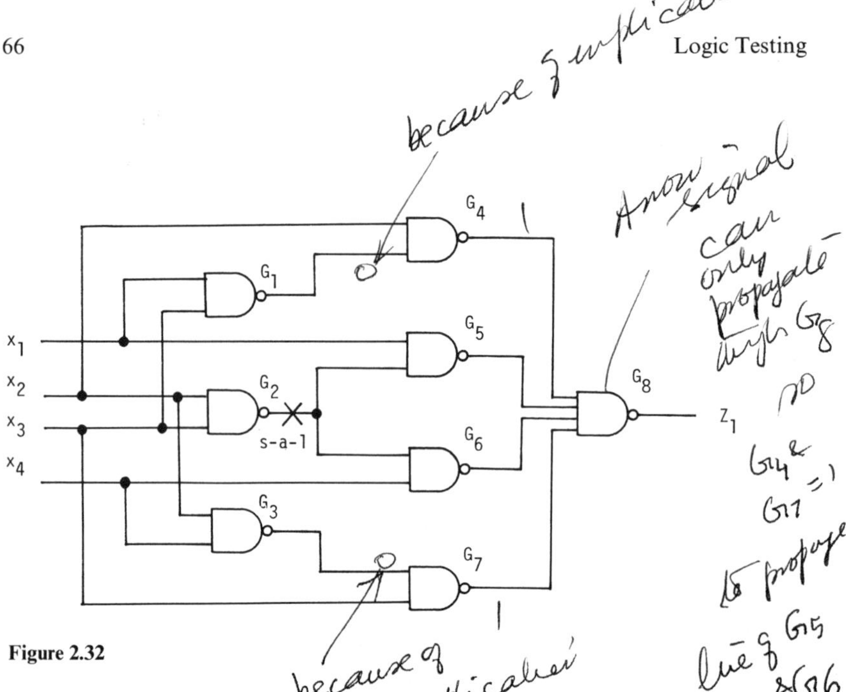

Figure 2.32

When both assignment choices at a node are rejected, then it is removed and the predecessor node's current assignment is rejected. The backtracking done by PODEM does not require saving and restoring of status because at each point the status could be revived only by forward implications of all primary inputs. The same backtracking can be done in FAN, which does not require saving and restoring of status, by implications of all associated head lines and fanout points. However, to avoid the unnecessary repetition of implications, FAN uses saving and restoring of status to some extent.

- Line justification of free lines: We can find the values on the primary inputs that justify all the values on the head lines without backtracking. This can be done by an operation identical to the consistency operation of the D-algorithm.

Example 2.10 To compare the FAN algorithm with the D-algorithm and the PODEM algorithm, consider again the Schneider circuit (figure 2.32). For the fault G_2 output s-a-1. FAN first assigns $x_2 = x_3 = 1$ and $G_2 = \mathrm{D}$ uniquely. At this point, the unique sensitization causes the assignment $G_4 = G_7 = 1$. To justify the unjustified output lines of gates G_4 and G_7, the

are set to $(G_4, 0, 1)$ and $(G_7, 0, 1)$. By the multiple backtrace,

l objectives $(x_1, 0, 1)$ and $(x_4, 0, 1)$. Selecting the first assign-

obtain $G_1 = 0$, $G_4 = 1$, and $G_5 = \mathrm{D}$ by implication. Suc-

cond assignment $x_4 = 1$ implies $G_3 = 0$, $G_6 = \mathrm{D}$, $G_7 = 1$,

onsequently, FAN has generated a test for the fault in

question without backtracking, whereas the D-algorithm and the PODEM backtrack in generating the test.

Three programs—SPS (single-path sensitization), PODEM, and FAN test-generation algorithms—were implemented in FORTRAN on an NEC System ACOS-1000 (15 MIPS) (Fujiwara and Shimono 1983a,b). These programs were applied to a number of combinational circuits, shown in table 2.2. The results are given in tables 2.3, 2.4, and 2.5. To obtain the data, three programs were executed to generate a test for each stuck-at fault. The number of times a backtrack occurs during the generation of each test pattern was calculated by the programs, and the average number of backtracks is shown in table 2.3. Since PODEM and FAN are complete algorithms, given enough time, both will generate tests for each testable fault. However, being limited in computing time, the programs discontinued test generation for those fault for which the number of backtracks exceeded 1,000. (Such faults are called *aborted* faults.) The results shown in tables 2.3 and 2.4 demonstrate that, though PODEM is faster than SPS, FAN is more efficient and faster than PODEM and SPS. The average number of backtracks in FAN is much smaller than the number in PODEM and SPS.

An automatic test-generation system composed of the FAN and the concurrent fault simulation was also reported by Fujiwara and Shimono (1983a, b). In this system, the fault simulator is used after each test pattern is generated to find what other faults are detected by the tests. The results of this system are given in table 2.5.

2.5 Test Generation for Sequential Circuits

For sequential circuits, there are few test-generation algorithms that are of practical significance. Known procedures that are good for use are the extended D-algorithm of Kubo (1968) and Putzolu and Roth (1971) and the nine-valued model of Muth (1976). This section describes these algorithms. We consider synchronous sequential circuits and then asynchronous sequential circuits.

A synchronous sequential circuit M can be modeled as shown in figure 2.33. Cutting the feedback loops where the clocked flip-flops are, we can form the iterative combinational circuit M^p of figure 2.34. The combinational circuits $C(i)$, where $i = 1, \ldots, p$, are all identical to the combinational portion C of the original sequential circuit M. In this transfor-

Table 2.2

Characteristics of circuits

Circuit	Number of gates	Number of lines	Number of inputs	Number of outputs	Number of fanout points	Number of faults
1 Error-correcting circuit	718	1,925	33	25	381	1,871
2 Arithmetic logic unit (ALU)	1,003	2,782	233	140	454	2,748
3 ALU	1,456	3,572	50	22	579	3,428
4 ALU and selector	2,002	5,429	178	123	806	5,350
5 ALU	2,982	7,618	207	108	1,300	7,550

Source: Fujiwara and Shimono 1983a, b. Copyright © 1983 IEEE.

Table 2.3
Normalized computing time and average number of backtracks

	Normalized computing time (sec)			Average number of backtracks		
Circuit	SPS	PODEM	FAN	SPS	PODEM	FAN
1	5.2	1.3	1	31.2	4.9	1.2
2	4.5	3.6	1	51.7	42.3	15.2
3	14.5	5.6	1	189.7	61.9	0.6
4	3.1	1.9	1	1.5	5.0	0.2
5	3.4	4.8	1	38.1	53.0	23.2

Source: Fujiwara and Shimono 1983a, b. Copyright © 1983 IEEE.

mation, the clocked flip-flops of M are modeled as combinational elements $F(i)$, where $i = 1, \ldots, p$. These are referred to as *pseudo flip-flops*. For example, the pseudo flip-flops corresponding to a D flip-flop and an SR flip-flop will be represented as shown in figure 2.35. In this figure the pseudo SR flip-flop has two excitation inputs S and R plus an additional input representing the present state of the flip-flop.

In figure 2.34, $C(i)$ and $F(i)$ correspond to time frame i. Suppose that an input sequence $x(1), x(2), \ldots, x(p)$ is applied to the sequential circuit M of figure 2.33 in initial state $y(1)$ and that M generates the output sequence $z(1), z(2), \ldots, z(p)$ with the state sequence $y(1), y(2), \ldots, y(p+1)$. Then, the iterative combinational circuit M^p obtained from the sequential circuit M will respond as shown in figure 2.34. The time-domain response of the sequential circuit is mapped into a space-domain response of the iterative combinational circuit. In this sense, the iterative combinational circuit M^p is logically equivalent to the sequential circuit M whose input/output response is of length p.

Suppose that we wish to find a test sequence of length p for a single fault in a sequential circuit M. For this purpose we construct the iterative combinational circuit with p identical combinational circuits. A test sequence of length p will be mapped into the test pattern as shown in figure 2.36. In this figure, each cell $M(i)$ consists of the combinational portion C and pseudo flip-flops of the original sequential circuit M. States $y(i)$ and $y(i+1)$ are called *pseudo-inputs* and *pseudo-outputs* of cell $M(i)$, respectively. The iterative circuit M^p is combinational; thus, most of the test-generation algorithms for combinational circuits can be applied to this model. However, we have to note the following points.

Table 2.4

Test coverage

	Percentage of tested faults			Percentage of aborted faults			Percentage of untestable faults		
Circuit	SPS	PODEM	FAN	SPS	PODEM	FAN	SPS	PODEM	FAN
1	99.04	99.20	99.52	0.48	0.48	0.11	—	0.32	0.37
2	91.15	94.25	95.49	4.70	3.49	1.38	—	2.26	3.13
3	66.25	92.53	96.00	16.25	5.05	0	—	2.42	4.00
4	98.77	98.75	98.90	0.07	0.26	0	—	0.99	1.10
5	94.73	94.38	96.81	3.54	4.79	2.17	—	0.82	1.02

Source: Fujiwara and Shimono 1983a, b. Copyright © 1983 IEEE.

Table 2.5

Experimental results from FAN with concurrent simulator

Circuit	Computing time (sec)			Percentage of tested faults	Percentage of aborted faults	Number of test patterns
	FAN	Concurrent simulator	Total			
1	3.8	4.6	8.4	99.52	0.11	151
2	34.6	3.7	38.3	95.74	1.13	159
3	7.4	9.5	16.9	96.00	0	215
4	4.0	10.5	14.5	98.90	0	195
5	76.5	18.9	95.4	98.20	0.78	283

Source: Fujiwara and Shimono 1983a, b. Copyright © 1983 IEEE.

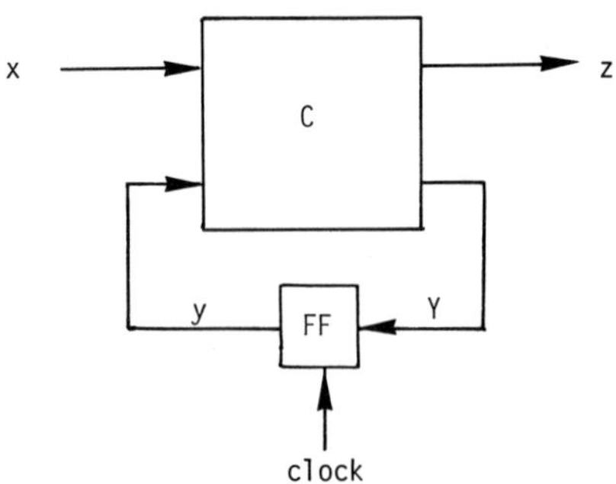

Figure 2.33
Synchronous sequential circuit

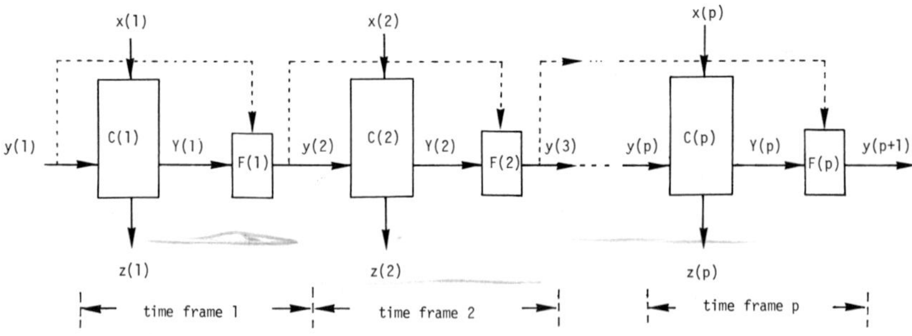

Figure 2.34
Corresponding iterative combinational circuit M^p

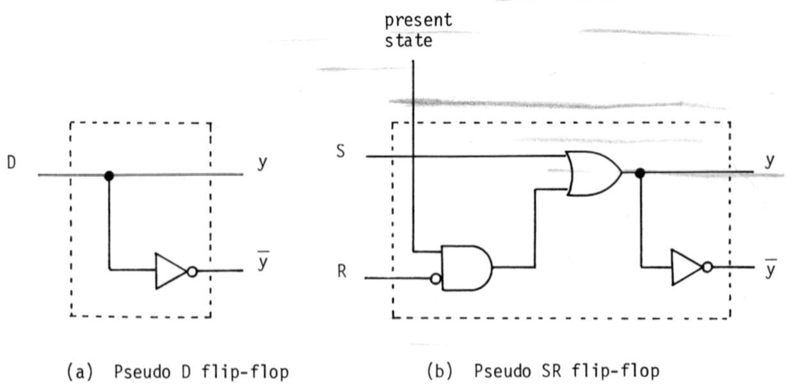

Figure 2.35
Pseudo flip-flops

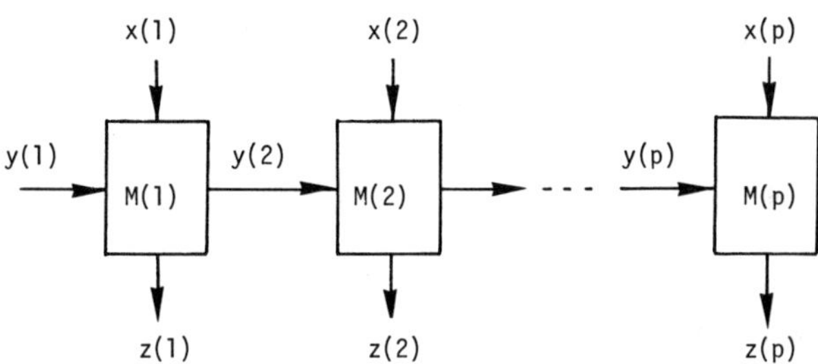

Figure 2.36

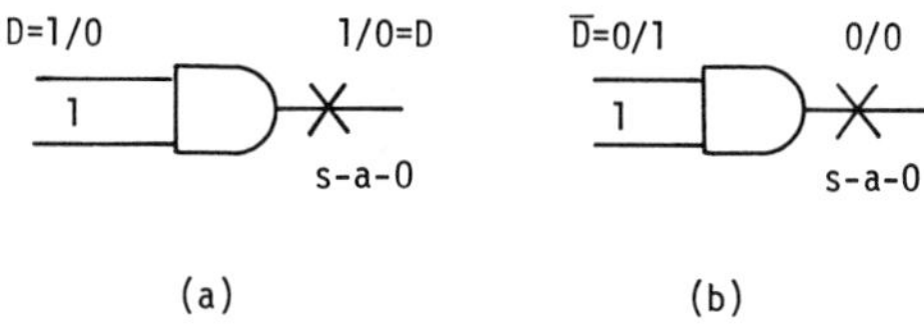

Figure 2.37

- A single fault f in M corresponds to the multiple fault f^p consisting of the same fault f in every cell $M(i)$ of the iterative circuit M^p. In a combinational circuit with a multiple fault, a faulty signal D or D may be propagated onto a line that is itself faulty. Figure 2.37 shows the signal that results when a D or a $\bar{D}$ propagates onto a faulty line. For example, if a D propagates onto a line that is s-a-0, then the line has value 1 in the normal circuit and value 0 in the faulty circuit, and thus the resultant signal on the line is D. This is shown in figure 2.37(a). If a $\bar{D}$ propagates onto a faulty line that is s-a-0, both the normal and the faulty circuit will have value 0 on the line; that is, the effects of the multiple faults cancel each other. This is illustrated in figure 2.37(b).
- In general, the initial state of M is unknown, and hence the pseudo-inputs $y(1)$ of M^p are unknown. Thus, their values must remain at the indeterminate X.
- The distinction between the outputs from the test for normal and faulty circuits must appear on at least one of the primary outputs $z(1), \ldots, z(p)$; that is, at least one of these primary outputs must have the value D or $\bar{D}$. If no test is found, we have to increment p by 1 and repeat generating a test for M^p.

The algorithm for generating a test for the multiple fault f^p in M^p can be obtained by modifying the combinational D-algorithm, with special attention to pseudo-inputs and fault multiplicity, as indicated above. The procedure is as follows.

The Extended D-algorithm for Synchronous Circuits

Step 1 Decide the maximum value P for p, i.e., P is the maximum number of time frames allowed for test generation.

Step 2 Select an initial value for p and construct the iterative combinational circuit M^p of figure 2.36.

Step 3 By choosing the time frame q from which the D-drive must be organized, apply the combinational D-algorithm (section 2.2) to find a test for the multiple fault f^p in M^p, ensuring that the pseudo-inputs of frame 1 retain only X values, i.e., $y(1) = (X, \ldots, X)$. If a test is found, exit; otherwise, continue.

Step 4 If possible, increment p by 1 and return to step 3; otherwise, exit with no test.

Example 2.11 Consider the synchronous sequential circuit of figure 2.38 and the fault a s-a-1 on G_1. We first select $p = 3$ and construct M^3 as shown in figure 2.39(a). Choosing the time frame 2, we begin the D-drive from the site of the fault in $M(2)$. First we set $y_2(2) = 0$ to provide a $\bar{D}$ on line a. Since it is impossible to propagate the faulty signal onto the primary output $z(2)$, we try to propagate it toward $z(3)$. Setting $x(2) = 1$, $y_1(2) = 0$, and $x(3) = 1$ allows the faulty signal $\bar{D}$ to propagate onto $z(3)$, and the D-drive is successfully completed. At this point, since $y_1(2) = 0$ and $y_2(2) = 0$ are unjustified, the line justification begins. However, we cannot set $y_1(2) = y_2(2) = 0$, ensuring $y_1(1) = y_2(1) = X$. Whenever an inconsistency is discovered, the process must backtrack to the last decision point and make an alternative selection. In this case there are no alternatives, and hence we increment the number of frames by 1, i.e., $p = 4$. For the iterative combinational circuit M^4, we can find a test successfully, as shown in figure 2.39(b).

When the logic circuit is combinational, the D-algorithm guarantees to generate a test if one exists. However, for sequential circuits, the extended D-algorithm mentioned above does not guarantee a test sequence for a fault even if one exists. Consider the circuit of figure 2.40. Suppose we wish to find an input combination (x_1, x_2) that forces $f = 1$ by retaining $y = X$.

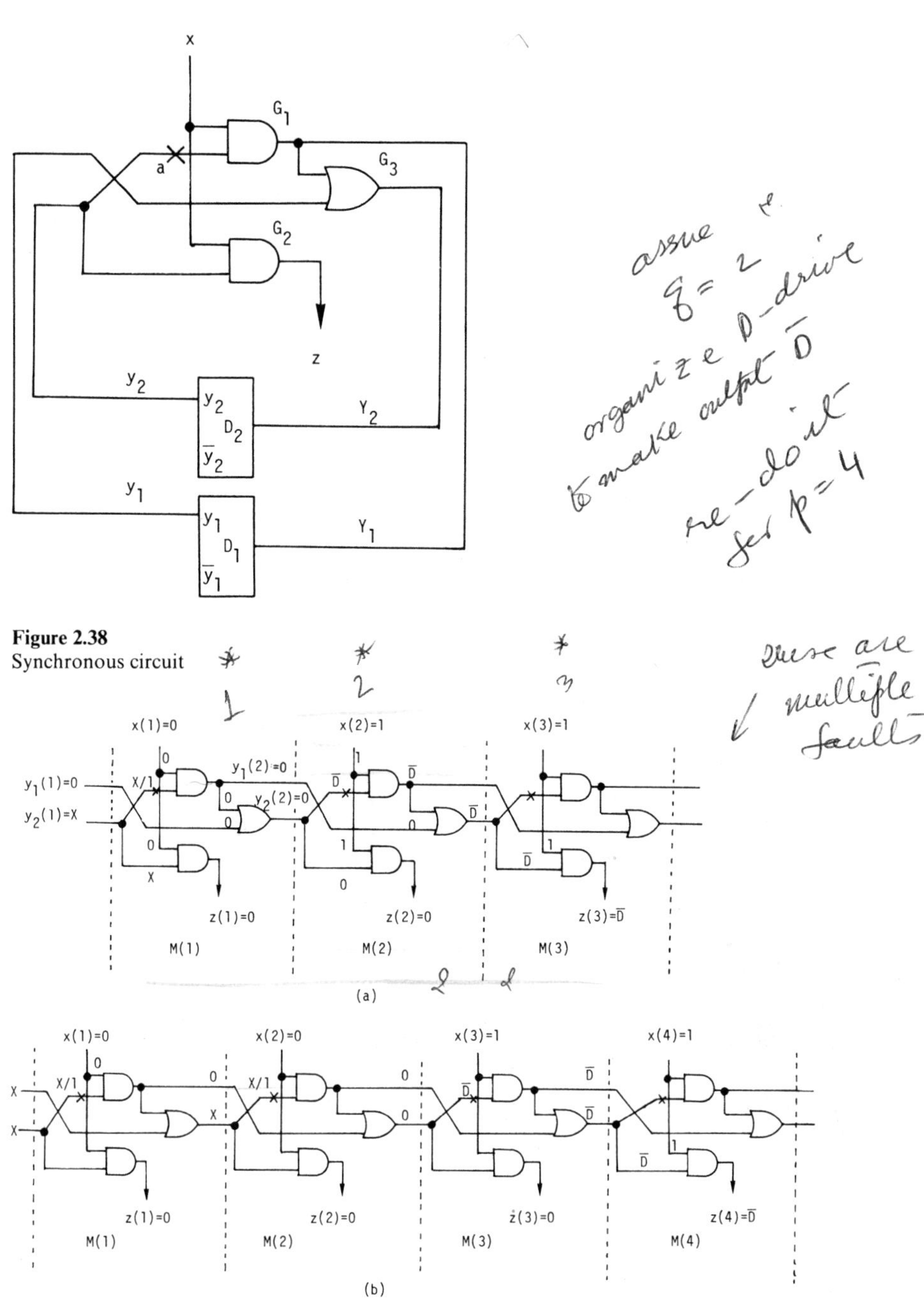

Figure 2.38
Synchronous circuit

Figure 2.39
Iterative combinational circuits

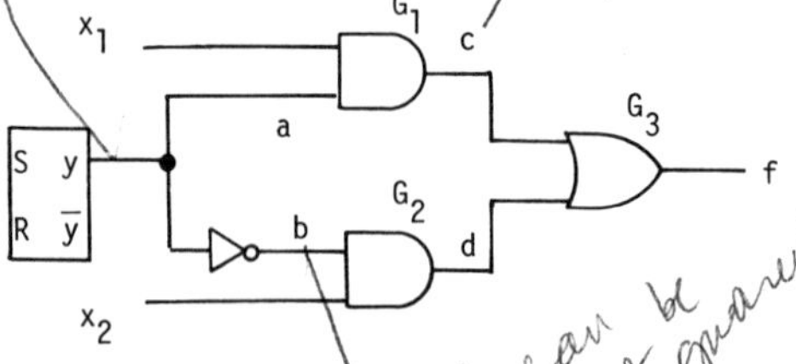

Figure 2.40

First, $f = 1$ requires $c = 1$ or $d = 1$. If $c = 1$ is chosen, then it implies $x_1 = 1$ and $a = 1$, and thus $y = 1$. If $d = 1$ is chosen, then it causes $x_1 = 1$, $b = 1$, and $y = 0$. Both cases contradict $y = X$, and this seems to imply that no input combination forces $f = 1$ by ensuring $y = X$. However, $f(x_1, x_2, y) = x_1 y + x_2 \overline{y}$ and $f(1, 1, y) = y + \overline{y} = 1$. Thus, f has the value 1 independent of the value of y if $x_1 = x_2 = 1$.

If the circuit M has a *synchronizing sequence* (an input sequence that when applied to M results in a unique final state independent of the initial state), then the above problem may be settled. However, the extended D-algorithm still cannot guarantee the generation of a test sequence when one exists. For example, consider the circuit of figure 2.41(a) and the fault d s-a-1. The extended D-algorithm fails to generate a test sequence for the fault, as shown in figure 2.41(b). In this figure, trying line justification ends with the contradiction that $d(1)$ must be 0 while d is stuck-at-1 because of the fault. Further, it can be shown that there is no way to generate a test for the iterative combinational circuit, even if more than two copies of the circuit are considered. However, we can find a test sequence for the fault if we apply a test-generation procedure using a nine-value model.

A *nine-value circuit model* for test generation of sequential circuits was presented by Muth (1976). The nine-value algorithm guarantees the generation of a test sequence, if one exists, for every stuck-at fault in a synchronous sequential circuit having a synchronizing sequence.

The nine values of the model are derived by distinguishing between a normal and a faulty circuit. Each of the nine values n_i, where $i = 1, \ldots, 9$, is defined by an ordered pair of binary values:

$$n_i = a_i/b_i$$

where a_i is a value in the normal circuit, b_i is a value in the faulty circuit, and a_i and b_i are 0, 1, or X (unspecified binary value). Values 0/0, 1/1, 1/0, and 0/1

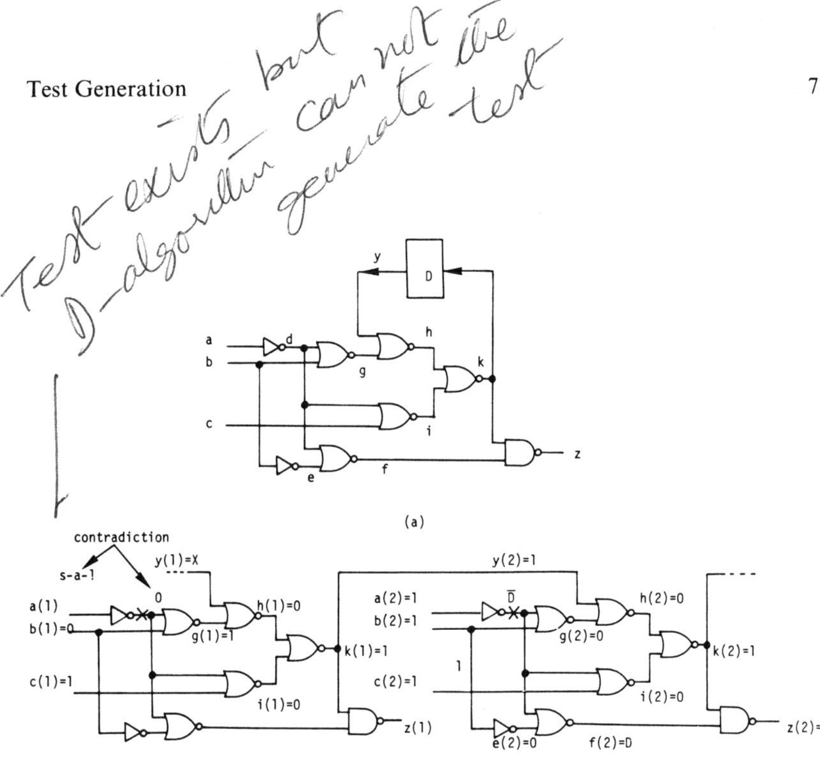

(b)

Figure 2.41
Test generation for fault *d* s-a-1

are fully specified and identical to the values 0, 1, D, and $\bar{D}$, respectively, of the D-algorithm. Value X/X is identical to X, which is an unspecified value in both the normal and the faulty circuit. If a binary value need be specified only in the normal circuit, we have $0/X$ and $1/X$; if it need be specified only in the faulty circuit, we have $X/0$ and $X/1$. The calculus for the nine-value model is as shown in table 2.6. For example, consider a three-input AND gate. If one input has $1/0 = D$ and the other two inputs have $1/X$, then the output of the AND gate will have $1/0 = D$.

The test-generation procedure based on the nine-value model is similar to that of the extended D-algorithm. To derive a test sequence for a fault f in a synchronous sequential circuit M, we construct the corresponding iterative combinational circuit M^p and then try to generate a test for the multiple fault f^p in the iterative combinational circuit M^p.

A primitive D-cube of a fault in the nine-value model is defined as a cube that specifies a minimal input condition to the gate, required to provide a

Table 2.6
Calculus of nine values

AND	0	0/x	$\bar{D}$	x/0	x	x/1	D	1/x	1
0	0	0	0	0	0	0	0	0	0
0/x	0	0/x	0/x	0	0/x	0/x	0	0/x	0/x
$\bar{D}$	0	0/x	$\bar{D}$	0	0/x	$\bar{D}$	0	0/x	$\bar{D}$
x/0	0	0	0	x/0	x/0	x/0	x/0	x/0	x/0
x	0	0/x	0/x	x/0	x	x	x/0	x	x
x/1	0	0/x	$\bar{D}$	x/0	x	x/1	x/0	x	x/1
D	0	0	0	x/0	x/0	x/0	D	D	D
1/x	0	0/x	0/x	x/0	x	x	D	1/x	1/x
1	0	0/x	$\bar{D}$	x/0	x	x/1	D	1/x	1

OR	0	0/x	$\bar{D}$	x/0	x	x/1	D	1/x	1
0	0	0/x	$\bar{D}$	x/0	x	x/1	D	1/x	1
0/x	0/x	0/x	$\bar{D}$	x	x	x/1	1/x	1/x	1
$\bar{D}$	$\bar{D}$	$\bar{D}$	$\bar{D}$	x/1	x/1	x/1	1	1	1
x/0	x/0	x	x/1	x/0	x	x/1	D	1/x	1
x	x	x	x/1	x	x	x/1	1/x	1/x	1
x/1	x/1	x/1	x/1	x/1	x/1	x/1	1	1	1
D	D	1/x	1	D	1/x	1	D	1/x	1
1/x	1/x	1/x	1	1/x	1/x	1	1/x	1/x	1
1	1	1	1	1	1	1	1	1	1

	0	0/x	$\bar{D}$	x/0	x	x/1	D	1/x	1
NOT	1	1/x	D	x/1	x	x/0	$\bar{D}$	0/x	0

faulty signal on its output. For example, consider a three-input AND gate and the s-a-0 fault on the output. To provide the faulty signal D on the output, all the inputs of the gate need to take value 1 only in the normal circuit. Hence, the primitive D-cube of the fault is

1	2	3	4
$1/X$	$1/X$	$1/X$	D

In the D-algorithm, the primitive D-cube of the fault is

1	2	3	4
1	1	1	D

This cube 111D includes the unnecessary condition that all the inputs of the gate take the value 1 even in the faulty circuit. In the nine-value model we can describe the minimal conditions precisely, since behaviors of the normal and the faulty circuit are distinguished by using nine values. For the s-a-1 fault on input 1 of the three-input AND gate, the primitive D-cube is

1	2	3	4
$0/X$	$X/1$	$X/1$	$\bar{D}$

For the s-a-1 fault on the output of the AND gate, the primitive D-cubes are

1	2	3	4
$0/X$	X	X	$\bar{D}$
X	$0/X$	X	$\bar{D}$
X	X	$0/X$	$\bar{D}$

A propagation D-cube of a gate in the nine-value model is similar to that of the D-algorithm. Suppose that a faulty signal D or $\bar{D}$ is on input line 1 of a three-input AND gate. Then the propagation D-cubes for this fault are

1	2	3	4
D	$1/X$	$1/X$	D
$\bar{D}$	$X/1$	$X/1$	$\bar{D}$

In the D-algorithm the corresponding propagation D-cubes are

1	2	3	4
D	1	1	D
$\bar{D}$	1	1	$\bar{D}$

Similarly to the D-algorithm, after the D-drive, line justification or consistency operation is performed. For example, consider a three-input AND gate whose inputs are all unspecified but whose output has value $0/X$. Line justification will choose one of the following cubes to justify the required value $0/X$.

1	2	3	4
$0/X$	X	X	$0/X$
X	$0/X$	X	$0/X$
X	X	$0/X$	$0/X$

When the inputs are all unspecified but the output has value $X/1$, line justification assigns the following cube.

1	2	3	4
$X/1$	$X/1$	$X/1$	$X/1$

In circuits with reconvergent fanout, line justification may result in two or more values being required simultaneously at a branching point. In such cases, the consistency of the required values has to be checked by means of an intersection operation in the nine-value model. Nine-value intersection is defined by the intersection of the set of binary values for the normal and the faulty circuit. If either of these intersections is empty, the required values are inconsistent. For example, suppose that a line L fans out to lines M and N and values $M = 1/X$ and $N = X/0$ are required at the same time. Binary intersection is nonempty in both the normal and the faulty circuit, and we have $L = 1/0$, that is, $L = D$.

Line justification always ends at the primary inputs of the circuit, where values $0/X$ and $X/0$ are replaced by 0, and $1/X$ and $X/1$ by 1. Values D and $\bar{D}$ must not occur at primary inputs unless faults in these inputs are to be tested. Value D is replaced by 1, and $\bar{D}$ by 0. Having thus completed line justification, we have test patterns consisting of values 0, 1, and X.

Example 2.12 Consider the circuit of figure 2.41(a) and the fault d s-a-1. As previously stated, the extended D-algorithm cannot find a test sequence for this fault. We will now try to find a test sequence for the fault by the procedure using the nine-value model. Here, we consider two copies of the circuit, that is, the iterative combinational circuit M^p with $p = 2$. The first step in test generation is to assign the value $X/1$ to the corresponding lines, $d(1)$ and $d(2)$, since in the faulty circuit both lines d will take the value 1. Arbitrarily, we start the D-drive at the second copy $M(2)$ of the circuit. The primitive D-cube of the fault is $a(2) = 1/X$ and $d(2) = 0/1$. Driving the faulty signal from $d(2)$ to the output $z(2)$ through $f(2)$ requires $e(2) = 0/X$ and $k(2) = 1/X$. Line justification of these will yield the values shown in figure 2.42. At this point, the value $1/X$ is assigned to the pseudo-input $y(2)$. Thus the line justification is continued backward into $M(1)$ along the lines $k(1)$, $h(1)$, $g(1)$, and $d(1)$. In this case, as shown in figure 2.42, the intersection of $X/1$ and $0/X$ on line $d(1)$ is performed successfully, and thus a test has been derived.

Most of the advantages of the nine-value model are due to the higher

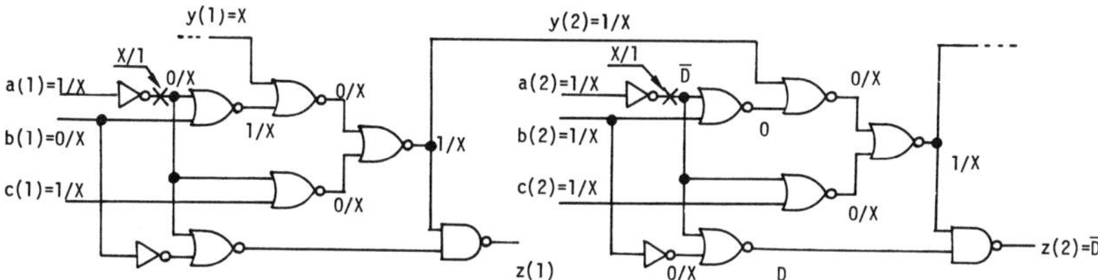

Figure 2.42
Test generation for fault d s-a-1 using nine-value model

degree of freedom afforded by the partly specified values $0/X$, $1/X$, $X/0$, and $X/1$ as compared with the values 0, 1, D, and $\bar{D}$ of the D-algorithm. The D-algorithm does not take into account correctly the repeated effects of faults on the internal state of a circuit; the test-generation procedure using the nine-value model does take them into account precisely. Moreover, the D-drive along any path using the nine-value model simultaneously takes account of all the possibilities of sensitizing this path as part of a multiple-path sensitization. Thus, at a fanout point having a fanout of N, at most N attempts have to be made at sensitizing a path. However, in the D-algorithm it may be necessary to try all $2^N - 1$ possible selections of one or more of the N branches to sensitize all possible single or multiple paths. Although the nine-value model has these advantages, it also has some disadvantages. One is the natural increase of computing time due to the greater complexity of its calculus in comparison with that of the five-value model of the D-algorithm.

Up to now we have considered the generation of tests for synchronous sequential circuits only. Test generation is much more difficult for asynchronous circuits than for synchronous circuits because of races, hazards, or oscillations. We will next briefly consider asynchronous circuits. In an approach that is analogous to that taken for synchronous circuits, an iterative combinational circuit model will be adopted for asynchronous circuits in order to utilize test-generation procedures for combinational circuits. Test generation for asynchronous circuits is performed in two steps. First, a potential test is generated for the multiple fault in the iterative combinational circuit that corresponds to a given fault in the original asynchronous circuit. This potential test is then simulated for both the normal and the faulty circuit to check its validity. In the real asynchronous circuit the potential test might be invalid because of races, hazards, or oscillations.

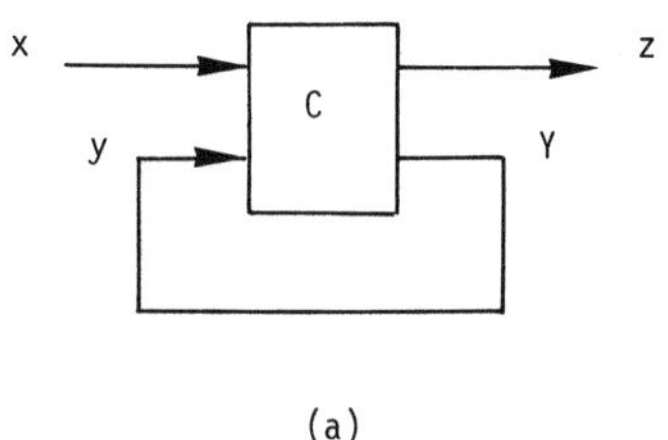

(a)

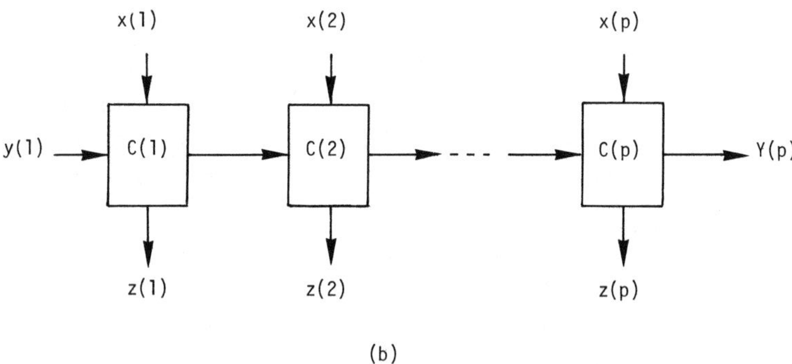

(b)

Figure 2.43
Asynchronous circuit

Figure 2.43(a) shows a model of an asynchronous circuit M, and figure 2.43(b) shows the corresponding iterative combinational circuit M^p. For the circuit M^p and a corresponding multiple fault f^p, the extended D-algorithm or the test-generation algorithm based on the nine-value model might be used to generate a test. Having obtained a potential test, we perform a simulation to check that the test is valid. For the test simulation, a three-value simulator of Eichelberger (1965), or other multivalue simulators for hazard detection, such as the model of Fantauzzi (1974), might be used by simulating the test on both the normal and the faulty circuit and comparing the values on primary outputs. Eichelberger's approach first modifies the sequence of patterns by inserting between each pair of adjacent patterns a new pattern having X values corresponding to changing variables and values as in the adjacent patterns for the nonchanging variables. For example, consider a circuit with three inputs x_1, x_2, and x_3 and the input sequence

x_1	0	1	0	0
x_2	1	1	0	1
x_3	0	0	1	0

Then, the modified input sequence is

x_1	0	X	1	X	0	0	0
x_2	1	1	1	X	0	X	1
x_3	0	0	0	X	1	X	0

This modified input sequence is then simulated using three-value logic. The simulator due to Eichelberger (1965) will detect any possible race, hazard, or oscillation.

3 Fault Simulation

Fault simulation of logic circuits is an important part of the test-generation process. It is used for the purpose of generating fault dictionaries and for verifying the adequacy of tests (test patterns or test sequences) intended to detect and locate logic faults. Moreover, fault simulation is often necessary to determine the fault coverage of a given test, that is, to find all the faults detected by the test.

Fault simulation is also employed for analyzing the operation of a circuit under various fault conditions in order to detect circuit behavior not considered by the designer. For example, faults can create races and hazards that did not exist in the fault-free circuit, or change a combinational circuit into a sequential one. To analyze these faults it is desirable to employ timing analysis of circuits, which requires the simulation of timing (delay) faults.

This chapter introduces three typical methods of fault simulation: *parallel*, *deductive*, and *concurrent* fault simulation. These methods are compared, and concurrent fault simulation is shown to be the most effective. For very large circuits, these fault-simulation methods based on software are all very time-consuming and costly. A new approach to this problem has been reported. The proposed solution involves *hardware simulators*—special-purpose, highly parallel, programmable computers, with a capacity and speed hundreds or thousands of times that of existing software simulators. In section 3.4 we consider these hardware simulators.

3.1 Simulation Methodology

In general, simulators can be separated into two classes: compiler-driven simulators and table-driven event-directed simulators. In *table-driven simulators*, the description of the logic circuit to be simulated is stored in tables in the host computer. The tables are accessed by the simulation program as necessary. The simulation program is circuit-independent, but a new set of tables is required for each distinct circuit to be simulated. In contrast, *compiler-driven simulators* have the circuit implicitly described in the program, as compiled code.

The first step in compiler-driven simulation is *levelizing*. We define the logic level of element i by level(i) recursively as follows:

- level(i) $= 0$ for all primary input lines and feedback lines.
- level(i) $= n + 1$ if level (j) $< n + 1$ for all immediate predecessors j of i; level(k) $= n$ for some immediate predecessor k of i.

If circuit elements (gates or flip-flops) are simulated in the order of ascending value of their logic level, the logic value of each element can be determined properly, since whenever an element at logic level k is evaluated the logic value of each of its inputs has already been evaluated. After levelizing, the compiler-driven simulation translates the description of the circuit into a machine-executable code, such as an assembly-language program. Simulation of a logic circuit is performed by executing the compiled code in the order of ascending value of logic level.

Compiler-driven simulators are usually employed for simulating logic circuits in a zero-delay model, and hence they handle only synchronous logic circuits, where race and hazard conditions are often ignored. A more accurate simulation is obtained with table-driven event-directed simulators.

A table-driven event-directed simulator models the dynamic behavior of the simulated circuit, updating its computations at successive, uniform intervals of simulated time, $1T$, $2T$, $3T$, ..., where the time interval T is chosen equal to the average gate delay. An *event* is a change in value of a signal line. The output of a logic element will change value only when one or more of its inputs have changed in the preceding time interval. Hence, an element need be simulated only when an event occurs at one of its inputs. When an event occurs, every element to which this line fans out has the possibility of a new event. We need only to simulate those potentially active elements that are successors of a signal line where an event occurred. The technique based on this observation is called *event-directed* (*selective trace*) simulation. Deductive and concurrent fault simulators are table-driven event-directed simulators. In contrast, almost all compiler-driven simulators are parallel fault simulators (although parallel fault simulation can also be carried out by table-driven event-directed simulators).

3.2 Parallel Fault Simulation

A computer has several bit-oriented instructions, including logical instructions such as the AND, OR, Exclusive OR, and NOT operations. During execution of instructions from this group the several bits of a single computer word are manipulated identically and independently. The AND, OR, and Exclusive OR instructions each operate on a pair of operands; the ith bits of each operand are combined to give the ith bit of the result. For example, the AND operation of 4-bit words is processed as follows:

[1010] .AND. [1100] = [1000]

Each ith bit of two words is simultaneously ANDed, and the resultant value is stored in the ith bit of the third word. Several advantages accrue from adopting a bit-oriented view of the contents of computer words instead of the one-symbol-per-word view. One advantage is that memory can be used with great efficiency if many items per word, instead of just one, are stored. Another advantage is that parallel computation is possible because there are instructions that operate on all the bits of a word concurrently.

Fault simulation based on this parallel process of bit-oriented operations is called *parallel fault simulation*. Parallel fault simulation is an old method, and it has been widely accepted in automated test-generation systems. Representative of this approach are the Sequential Analyzer (Seshu 1965), the IBM simulator used in the design of the Saturn computer (Hardie and Suhocki 1967), and the TEGAS simulator (Szygenda et al. 1970).

In parallel fault simulation, if a word or a string has n bits, then n different problems can be processed in parallel. If we want to simulate a circuit for m different faults, then $\lceil m/n \rceil$ passes must be made with n faults being simulated during each pass, when $\lceil x \rceil$ is the smallest integer equal to or greater than x.

In the fault simulation, a logical effect of a fault is injected into the computation of the faulted element. This procedure is called *fault injection*. Two masks mask(S) and fvalue(S) associated with each signal line S are used to inject faults. Each fault injected on S corresponds to a unique bit position i in mask(S) and fvalue(S). This bit position must be different from the bit positions in the corresponding masks of any other remaining $n-1$ faults being simulated in parallel with the fault on S. These masks are defined as follows: mask$(S)_i = 1$ if a fault exists on the signal line S when the ith bit of the computer word is simulated, mask$(S)_i = 0$ otherwise; fvalue$(S)_i = 1$ if the fault on S is stuck-at-1, fvalue$(S)_i = 0$ if the fault on S is stuck-at-0, where the subscript i denotes the bit position.

These two masks are used to inject faults into each bit of the word S, and the masked word S' is formed as follows (figure 3.1):

$$S' = S \cdot \overline{\text{mask}(S)} + \text{mask}(S) \cdot \text{fvalue}(S)$$

where $\cdot$, $+$, and $\overline{}$ mean bit-oriented logical operations AND, OR, and NOT, respectively.

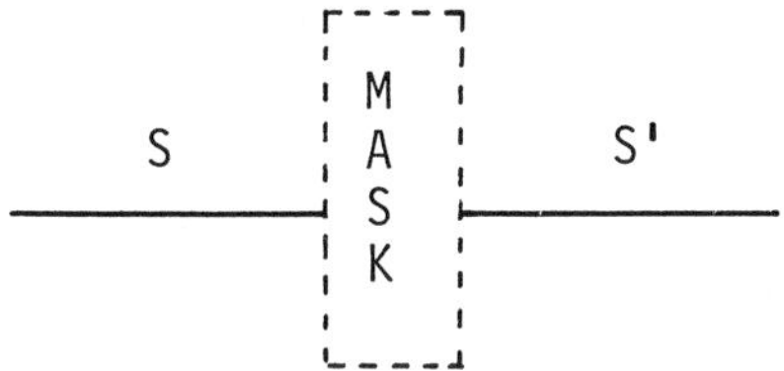

Figure 3.1
Model of fault injection

Bit Position	Fault
1	Fault-Free
2	A s-a-0
3	B s-a-1
4	C s-a-0
5	C s-a-1

(a)

Line	Mask	Fvalue
A	[01000]	[00000]
B	[00100]	[00100]
C	[00011]	[00001]

(b)

A=[11111] A'=[10111]
B=[00000] B'=[00100]
C=[11011] C'=[11001]

(c)

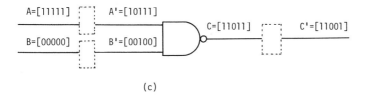

Figure 3.2
Parallel fault simulation

The masks used for fault injection are generated during the preprocessing of the circuit for fault simulation. Except for the overhead required to generate the masks and carry ouut fault injection, n faults can be processed almost as rapidly as one fault.

Consider a two-input NAND gate and the four faults associated with the gate (figure 3.2). The four faults are specified in figure 3.2(a), and the values of the masks associated with signal lines A, B, and C are defined as shown in figure 3.2(b). For example, mask(B) = [00100] since the bit position of the fault associated with line B is bit 3, and fvalue(B) = [00100] because the fault is stuck-at-1 and is processed in bit 3. Similarly, since two faults associated with line C (C s-a-0 and C s-a-1) must be injected into bits 4 and 5 of word C, $\text{mask}(C) = [00011]$ and $\text{fvalue}(C)_4 = 0$ and $\text{fvalue}(C)_5 = 1$.

After the masks for fault injection have been generated, parallel fault simulation is carried out. Suppose we want to simulate an input pattern with $A = 1$ and $B = 0$. First the words A and B are initialized to $A = [11111]$ and $B = [00000]$. The simulation is carried out from primary inputs toward primary outputs. To evaluate properly the logic value of each element, all elements of the circuit should be ordered or levelized. The details of levelization will be described later. In figure 3.2(c), A and B are masked to form A' and B':

$$\begin{aligned} A' &= A \cdot \overline{\text{mask}(A)} + \text{mask}(A) \cdot \text{fvalue}(A) \\ &= [11111] \cdot \overline{[01000]} + [01000] \cdot [00000] \\ &= [11111] \cdot [10111] + [00000] \\ &= [10111], \end{aligned}$$

$$\begin{aligned} B' &= B \cdot \overline{\text{mask}(B)} + \text{mask}(B) \cdot \text{fvalue}(B) \\ &= [00000] \cdot \overline{[00100]} + [00100] \cdot [00100] \\ &= [00000] + [00100] \\ &= [00100]. \end{aligned}$$

Next the NAND gate is simulated:

$$\begin{aligned} C &= \overline{A' \cdot B'} \\ &= \overline{[10111] \cdot [00100]} \\ &= \overline{[00100]} \\ &= [11011]. \end{aligned}$$

Then C is masked:

$$\begin{aligned} C' &= C \cdot \overline{\text{mask}(C)} + \text{mask}(C) \cdot \text{fvalue}(C) \\ &= [11011] \cdot \overline{[00011]} + [00011] \cdot [00001] \\ &= [11000] \cdot [00001] \\ &= [11001]. \end{aligned}$$

On the output C', bits 3 and 4 are different from bit 1 of the fault-free value, and hence the faults corresponding to the bits 3 and 4, that is, *B* s-a-1 and *C* s-a-0, are detectable.

3.3 Deductive Fault Simulation

Deductive fault simulation was developed by Armstrong (1972) and has been used in the LAMP system (Chappell et al. 1974b). This method consists in explicitly simulating the behavior of the fault-free logic circuit only, and simultaneously deducing from the current "good" state of the circuit all faults that are detectable at any internal or output line while in the current state. Using the concept of deductive simulation, we can compute all detectable faults at the same time, and thus we need perform only a one-pass simulation for each applied test pattern. In parallel fault simulation, if m is the total number of faults to be simulated and n faults are simulated during each pass, then $\lceil m/n \rceil$ passes are required. The simulation time per pass for deductive fault simulation is likely to be much longer than the time per pass for parallel fault simulation. However, it is expected to be less than the time for the $\lceil m/n \rceil$ passes required by parallel fault simulation to accomplish equivalent results. Indeed, Chang et al. (1974) have shown experimentally that deductive fault simulation is faster than parallel simulation when a large circuit with a large number of faults is to be simulated. Parallel fault simulation is faster than deductive simulation only for small (e.g., <500 gates), highly sequential circuits. However, comparison indicates that a parallel fault simulator can be designed to require less storage than a deductive fault simulator.

A deductive fault simulator simulates the fault-free circuit and computes lists of faults. A list of faults L_A associated with line A contains the name or index of every fault that produces an error on line A when the circuit is in its current logic state. That is, each fault in a list, if inserted singly in the circuit, would cause complementation of the good state of the associated signal line. These fault lists are propagated from primary inputs toward primary outputs, level by level, through the circuit. In this manner, a fault list is generated for each signal line, and it is updated as necessary with every change in the logic state of the circuit.

A deductive simulator employs the event-directed or selective trace procedure; the output state of a logic element is computed only when an event occurs at one of its inputs. In deductive fault simulation there are two

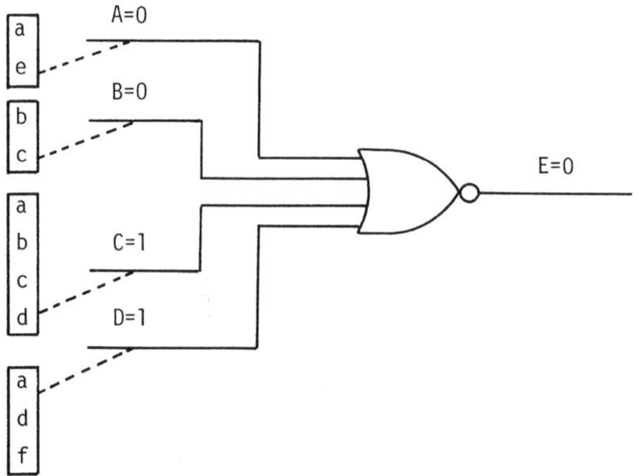

Figure 3.3
Fault lists associated with NOR gate

types of events: *logic events*, which occur when a signal line takes on a new logic value, and *list events*, which occur when a fault list changes. The simulator must recompute a fault list associated with the output of an element when a list event occurs at one of its inputs, even if no logic event occurs at any of its inputs.

Let me first illustrate the procedure for computing fault lists in the case of logic gates. Consider a NOR gate having inputs $A = 0$, $B = 0$, $C = 1$, and $D = 1$. Suppose that inputs A, B, C, and D already have the fault lists shown in figure 3.3. These are the lists currently associated with the logic elements that feed these inputs. Several of the faults appear in more than one input list because of the effects of reconvergent paths in the circuit.

Let a list of faults associated with line X be denoted L_X. In figure 3.3, the fault lists are

$$L_A = \{a, e\},$$

$$L_B = \{b, c\},$$

$$L_C = \{a, b, c, d\},$$

$$L_D = \{a, d, f\}.$$

Consider fault a in figure 3.3. Since fault a appears in L_A, L_C, and L_D, it causes the states of A, C, and D to be complemented (that is, $A = 1$ and $C = D = 0$) and the output E to be 0. This implies that fault a causes no error at E and hence is not contained in L_E. Next, consider fault d. Since fault d

appears in both L_C and L_D, it causes $C = D = 0$ and thus $E = 1$. This implies that fault d causes an error at E and thus is contained in L_E. The faults that propagate to E are the faults that cause the good output of E to be complemented. Therefore, to cause a 1 on E, a fault must cause all ones on E's inputs to change to zeros, and at the same time must not cause any zeros on E's inputs to change to ones. In this example, the fault-free inputs are $A = B = 0$ and $C = D = 1$. Therefore we have

$$L_E = \overline{(L_A \cup L_B)} \cap L_C \cap L_D$$

where $\cup$, $\cap$, and $\overline{}$ denote set union, intersection, and complement, respectively.

For the faults that propagate to the inputs of a logic element, we can compute the list of faults propagating to the output by the above computation using set operations. However, we also have to consider those faults internal to the associated logic element that produce the incorrect output for the current good inputs. In figure 3.3, we have the fault E s-a-1 under the single stuck-at fault assumption. Hence, we have a complete list of faults associated with E in the example of figure 3.3:

$$\begin{aligned} L_E &= (\overline{(L_A \cup L_B)} \cap L_C \cap L_D) \cup \{E/1\} \\ &= \{d, E/1\}. \end{aligned}$$

For the same 4-input NOR gate of figure 3.3, if we consider $A = B = C = D = 0$, and hence $E = 1$, then we have

$$L_E = L_A \cup L_B \cup L_C \cup L_D \cup \{A/1, B/1, C/1, D/1, E/0\}$$

because in this case any fault that causes a 1 on any input line or a 0 on the output will produce the incorrect logical output.

The procedures for computing fault lists for other types of logic gates are straightforward and involve the same considerations as above.

Fault propagation through memory elements is more complicated. Consider the SR latch realized by cross-connected NOR gates shown in figure 3.4. Suppose that the state at time t_1 is $(Q_1, Q_2) = (1, 0)$, and the input is $(S, R) = (0, 1)$. If at time t_2 R changes to 0 (that is, if a nonenabling input is applied at t_2), then the latch will remain in the same state, as shown in figure 3.4. Let $L_{Q_1}^1$ and $L_{Q_2}^1$ be the fault lists present at Q_1 and Q_2 at time t_1, respectively, and let L_S^2, L_R^2, $L_{Q_1}^2$, and $L_{Q_2}^2$ be the fault lists associated with lines S, R, Q_1, and Q_2 at time t_2, respectively.

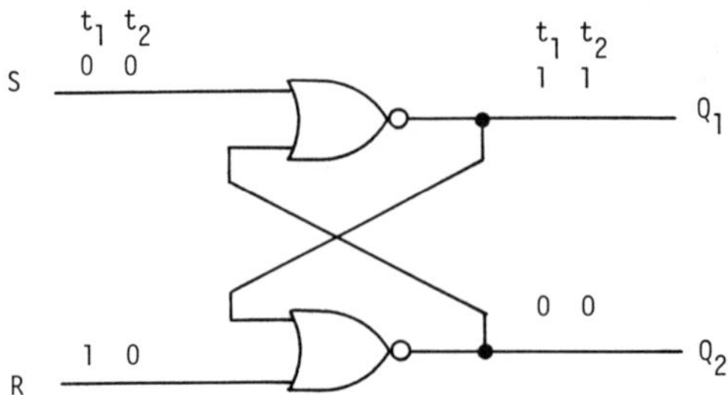

Figure 3.4
Propagation of fault lists through SR latch

The computation of the new lists depends on the previous logic state of the latch at time t_1 and the new logic inputs to the latch at time t_2, as well as on the associated fault lists. That is, $L_{Q_1}^2$ and $L_{Q_2}^2$ can be expressed as a function of $L_{Q_1}^1$, $L_{Q_2}^1$, L_S^2, and L_R^2. In other words, $L_{Q_1}^2$ and $L_{Q_2}^2$ may be expressed as the union of appropriate subsets of the 16 fundamental products:

$L_{Q_1}^1 \cap L_{Q_2}^1 \cap L_S^2 \cap L_R^2$,

$L_{Q_1}^1 \cap L_{Q_2}^1 \cap L_S^2 \cap \overline{L_R^2}$,

…,

$\overline{L_{Q_1}^1} \cap \overline{L_{Q_2}^1} \cap \overline{L_S^2} \cap \overline{L_R^2}$,

In the following, we will compute the lists $L_{Q_1}^2$ and $L_{Q_2}^2$ by examining each of the 16 fundamental products in turn to see if it is included in $L_{Q_1}^2$ or $L_{Q_2}^2$. To keep the discussion simple, we will first consider only faults external to the latch.

Any fault in $L_{Q_1}^1 \cap L_{Q_2}^1 \cap L_S^2 \cap L_R^2$ causes both lines Q_1 and Q_2 to be incorrect at time t_1 and both inputs to be incorrect at time t_2. That is, it would cause $Q_1 = 0$, $Q_2 = 1$ at t_1 and $S = R = 1$ at t_2. This also causes $Q_1 = Q_2 = 0$ at t_2, and an error is detected on Q_1 at t_2. Consequently, the product $L_{Q_1}^1 \cap L_{Q_2}^1 \cap L_S^2 \cap L_R^2$ is included in $L_{Q_1}^2$ but not in $L_{Q_2}^2$.

Next, consider the product $L_{Q_1}^1 \cap L_{Q_2}^1 \cap L_S^2 \cap \overline{L_R^2}$. Any fault in this set causes $Q_1 = 0, Q_2 = 1$ at time t_1 and $S = 1, R = 0$ at time t_2. Therefore we have $Q_1 = 0, Q_2 = 1$ at time t_2, which implies that this fault can be detected on both outputs Q_1 and Q_2 at time t_2. Hence, $L_{Q_1}^1 \cap L_{Q_2}^1 \cap L_S^2 \cap \overline{L_R^2}$ is included in both $L_{Q_1}^2$ and $L_{Q_2}^2$.

We can process the remaining 14 products in a similar manner and determine whether each product should be included in $L^2_{Q_1}$ or $L^2_{Q_2}$. However, we have to pay special attention to the following cases:

• Any fault in $L^1_{Q_1} \cap \overline{L^1_{Q_2}} \cap \overline{L^2_S} \cap \overline{L^2_R}$ causes $Q_1 = Q_2 = 0$ at time t_1. This implies that both inputs S and R must be 1 at time t_1 because of the fault. Since such a fault does not affect either input at time t_2, both will be 0 at this time. Hence, both inputs S and R will change from 1 to 0. However, it is not predictable which input changes first, and so it is not known whether the state of the latch will be $(Q_1, Q_2) = (1, 0)$ or $(0, 1)$. If and only if the latch goes to the state $(Q_1, Q_2) = (0, 1)$ as a result of the race, the fault can be detected on both outputs at t_2. Owing to this race condition, any fault in $L^1_{Q_1} \cap \overline{L^1_{Q_2}} \cap \overline{L^2_S} \cap \overline{L^2_R}$ may or may not be detected by the current test.

• There is no fault external to the latch that can cause both outputs Q_1 and Q_2 to be 1 simultaneously. This condition can appear only in the four products containing $\overline{L^1_{Q_1}} \cap L^1_{Q_2}$. Therefore, we can treat these four products as "don't care" to reduce the expressions for $L^2_{Q_1}$ and $L^2_{Q_2}$.

Having examined whether each of 16 fundamental products is included in $L^2_{Q_1}$ and $L^2_{Q_2}$, we can now specify the expressions for $L^2_{Q_1}$ and $L^2_{Q_2}$

$$\begin{aligned}
L^2_{Q_1} = {} & (L^1_{Q_1} \cap \overline{L^1_{Q_2}} \cap \overline{L^2_S} \cap \overline{L^2_R}) \cup (L^1_{Q_1} \cap L^1_{Q_2} \cap L^2_S \cap L^2_R) \cup \\
& (L^1_{Q_1} \cap L^1_{Q_2} \cap L^2_S \cap \overline{L^2_R}) \cup (L^1_{Q_1} \cap L^1_{Q_2} \cap \overline{L^2_S} \cap \overline{L^2_R}) \cup \\
& (L^1_{Q_1} \cap \overline{L^1_{Q_2}} \cap L^2_S \cap L^2_R) \cup (L^1_{Q_1} \cap \overline{L^1_{Q_2}} \cap L^2_S \cap \overline{L^2_R}) \cup \\
& (\overline{L^1_{Q_1}} \cap \overline{L^1_{Q_2}} \cap L^2_S \cap L^2_R) \cup (\overline{L^1_{Q_1}} \cap \overline{L^1_{Q_2}} \cap L^2_S \cap \overline{L^2_R}) \cup \\
& (\overline{L^1_{Q_1}} \cap L^1_{Q_2} \cap L^2_S \cap L^2_R) \cup (\overline{L^1_{Q_1}} \cap L^1_{Q_2} \cap L^2_S \cap \overline{L^2_R}) \cup \\
& (\overline{L^1_{Q_1}} \cap L^1_{Q_2} \cap \overline{L^2_S} \cap \overline{L^2_R}),
\end{aligned}$$

$$\begin{aligned}
L^2_{Q_2} = {} & (L^1_{Q_1} \cap \overline{L^1_{Q_2}} \cap \overline{L^2_S} \cap \overline{L^2_R}) \cup (L^1_{Q_1} \cap L^1_{Q_2} \cap L^2_S \cap \overline{L^2_R}) \cup \\
& (L^1_{Q_1} \cap L^1_{Q_2} \cap \overline{L^2_S} \cap \overline{L^2_R}) \cup (L^1_{Q_1} \cap \overline{L^1_{Q_2}} \cap L^2_S \cap \overline{L^2_R}) \cup \\
& (\overline{L^1_{Q_1}} \cap \overline{L^1_{Q_2}} \cap L^2_S \cap L^2_R) \cup (\overline{L^1_{Q_1}} \cap L^1_{Q_2} \cap \overline{L^2_S} \cap \overline{L^2_R}) \cup \\
& (\overline{L^1_{Q_1}} \cap L^1_{Q_2} \cap L^2_S \cap \overline{L^2_R}).
\end{aligned}$$

The above expressions can be simplified by using "don't care" products containing $\overline{L^1_{Q_1}} \cap L^1_{Q_2}$. The simplification is performed on all the products

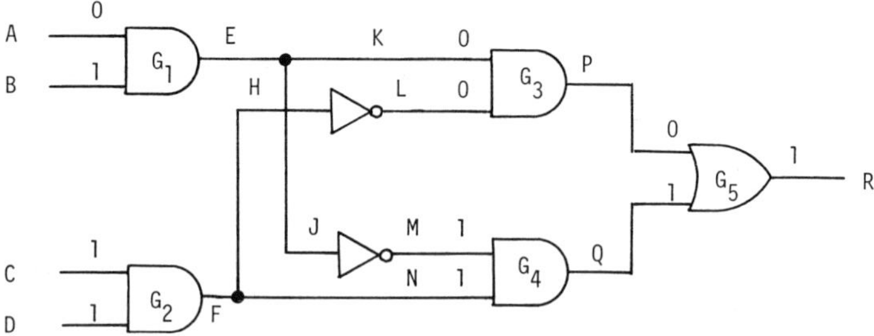

Figure 3.5
Deductive fault simulation

except $L_{Q_1}^1 \cap \overline{L_{Q_2}^1} \cap \overline{L_S^2} \cap \overline{L_R^2}$. Consequently, we have

$$L_{Q_1}^2 = (L_{Q_1}^1 \cap \overline{L_{Q_2}^1} \cap \overline{L_S^2} \cap \overline{L_R^2}) \cup L_S^2 \cup (L_{Q_2}^1 \cap \overline{L_R^2}),$$

$$L_{Q_2}^2 = (L_{Q_1}^1 \cap \overline{L_{Q_2}^1} \cap \overline{L_S^2} \cap \overline{L_R^2}) \cup (L_S^2 \cap \overline{L_R^2}) \cup (L_{Q_2}^1 \cap \overline{L_R^2}).$$

Up to now we have not considered the faults internal to the latch. Any internal fault causes (Q_1, Q_2) to be either $(1, 0)$ or $(0, 1)$. Hence, in the example of figure 3.4, all internal faults causing $(Q_1, Q_2) = (0, 1)$ should be included in the lists $L_{Q_1}^2$ and $L_{Q_2}^2$.

Example 3.1 The propagation of fault lists is illustrated by the circuit of figure 3.5. This example shows how a deductive fault simulator propagates lists of single stuck-at faults on each signal line under the input pattern shown in the figure. The propagation of fault lists is performed from primary inputs toward primary outputs in the order of ascending value of logic level. First, the fault lists associated with inputs A, B, C, and D are obtained as follows:

$$L_A = \{A/1\},$$

$$L_B = \{B/0\},$$

$$L_C = \{C/0\},$$

$$L_D = \{D/0\}.$$

For gate G_1, we have the fault list associated with the output E in

$$L_E = (L_A \cap \overline{L_B}) \cup \{E/1\} = \{A/1, E/1\}.$$

For gate G_2, L_F is obtained from

$$L_F = L_C \cup L_D \cup \{F/0\} = \{C/0, D/0, F/0\}.$$

Similarly, we have

$$L_H = L_F \cup \{H/0\} = \{C/0, D/0, F/0, H/0\},$$

$$L_N = L_F \cup \{N/0\} = \{C/0, D/0, F/0, N/0\},$$

$$L_J = L_E \cup \{J/1\} = \{A/1, E/1, J/1\},$$

$$L_K = L_E \cup \{K/1\} = \{A/1, E/1, K/1\},$$

$$L_L = L_H \cup \{L/1\} = \{C/0, D/0, F/0, H/0, L/1\},$$

$$L_M = L_J \cup \{M/0\} = \{A/1, E/1, J/1, M/0\},$$

$$L_P = (L_K \cap L_L) \cup \{P/1\} = \{P/1\},$$

$$L_Q = L_M \cup L_N \cup \{Q/0\}$$
$$= \{A/1, C/0, D/0, E/1, F/0, J/1, M/0, N/0, Q/0\}$$

$$L_R = (\overline{L_P} \cap L_Q) \cup \{R/0\}$$
$$= \{A/1, C/0, D/0, E/1, F/0, J/1, M/0, N/0, Q/0, R/0\}.$$

Consequently, all faults in L_R can be detected by the current test pattern. Next, suppose that the input B changes to 0. The logic event (B changes from 1 to 0) induces a list event on input B by which $L_B = \{B/0\}$ changes to $\{B/1\}$. Simulating gate G_1 produces no logic event, but now $L_E = \{E/1\}$ and thus a list event has occurred. The simulator must recompute a fault list associated with the output of a gate when a list event occurs at one of its inputs even if no logic event occurs at any of its inputs. Therefore, we have to continue the fault list propagation. The list event on E causes the lists L_K and L_J to change to $\{E/1, K/1\}$ and $\{E/1, J/1\}$, respectively. We still have

$$L_P = \{P/1\},$$

but now

$$L_M = \{E/1, J/1, M/0\}.$$

Thus, a new list event has occurred on M, and so L_Q is reevaluated to

$$L_Q = \{C/0, D/0, E/1, F/0, J/1, M/0, N/0, Q/0\}$$

and L_R to

$L_R = \{C/0, D/0, E/1, F/0, J/1, M/0, N/0, Q/0, R/0\}$.

Up to now we have considered fault simulation at the gate level. However, when the size of the circuit is too large (as in LSI or VLSI circuits), it is often more cost-effective to simulate parts of the circuit, such as memories, registers, and decoders, at a functional level. In functional simulation, only input/output behavior is specified for each functional block for which the actual gate-level realization is unknown. This approach makes the simulation of larger circuits feasible, since large functional blocks will usually make lesser requirements of the host computer's resources than the corresponding gate-level circuits. A method developed by Menon and Chappell (1978) for propagating the effects of faults through functional blocks by a deductive technique was used to implement the functional simulator in the LAMP system.

3.4 Concurrent Fault Simulation

There is another fault-simulation method that like deductive fault simulation, can perform only one pass simulation to compute all detectable faults for each applied test. This method, known as *concurrent fault simulation*, was developed by Ulrich and Baker (1973). Usually, the behavior of a faulty circuit is only slightly dissimilar from the fault-free circuit. Activities in fault-free and faulty circuits are sometimes identical, most of the time almost identical, and only rarely substantially different. Concurrent fault simulation, which is based on this similarity between fault-free and faulty circuits, consists of simulating the fault-free circuit, and concurrently simulating the faulty circuit only if the faulty circuit's activity actually differs from that of the fault-free circuit. There are some similarities between deductive and concurrent simulation. The difference between them will be clarified after the concept and the fundamental operations of concurrent fault simulation have been illustrated.

Figure 3.6 shows an example of a fault list associated with an AND gate. Each entry in the fault list consists of the name or index of every fault that produces an error either at an input or the output of the gate, and of its input and output values. The first entry in the fault list of figure 3.6 is

$A/0$;   010;   0

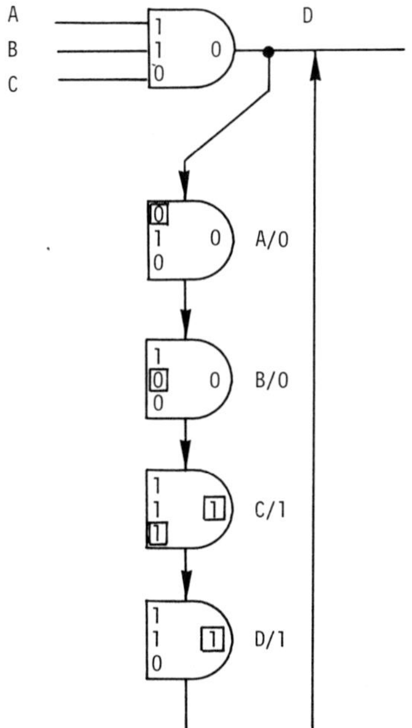

Figure 3.6
Fault list associated with AND gate

which means that fault $A/0$ causes inputs $(0, 1, 0)$ and output 0. (This fault $A/0$ is contained in the list associated with line D although it causes no error on D.) To facilitate fast processing, the entries are sorted by fault index and are stored in the order of their indices in a list structure.

In deductive fault simulation, a fault list L_D associated with line D contains only the names or indices of faults that produce an error on the line D. In the example of figure 3.6, the fault list L_D would be

$$L_D = \{C/1, D/1\}.$$

Hence, the deductive fault list is a subset of the concurrent fault list, and concurrent fault simulation requires more storage than deductive fault simulation.

How fault lists are propagated in concurrent simulation is illustrated in figure 3.7 by a situation wherein input $A = B = C = 0$ is first applied and then input line A changes to a 1. In concurrent simulation, only the gates in the faulty circuit that do not agree, in terms of their input and/or output

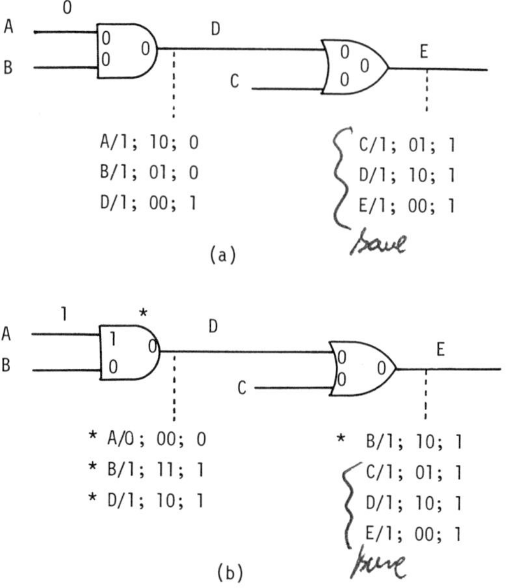

Figure 3.7
Propagation of fault lists

values, with the corresponding gate in the fault-free circuit are explicitly simulated. For gate D, in figure 3.7(a), faults $A/1$, $B/1$, and $D/1$ produce an error at an input and at the output of the gate. Hence, for each of these faults gate D is simulated separately, and the associated fault list is obtained as shown in figure 3.7(a). For example, the first entry ($A/1$; 10; 0) in the list implies that if A is s-a-1, the input to the gate will be $A = 1$, $B = 0$ rather than $A = 0$, $B = 0$, and the output is 0. Here, only fault $D/1$ is propagated to the input of gate E, since the output value of D in the faulty circuit differs from the fault-free value. For gate E, faults $C/1$, $D/1$, and $E/1$ are simulated to evaluate their output values, and the gate's associated fault list is obtained as shown in figure 3.7(a). All the output values for $C/1$, $D/1$, and $E/1$ are ones and differ from the fault-free value, and hence these faults are detectable at E.

Next, suppose that line A changes to 1. Since a logic event has occurred at an input of gate D, the entire fault list associated with D must be processed. For the entry ($A/1$; 10; 0), since $A = 1$, this term is deleted and the term ($A/0$; 00; 0) is added to the list. Similarly, ($B/1$; 01; 0) changes to ($B/1$; 11; 1), and

$(D/1; 00; 1)$ changes to $(D/1; 10; 1)$, as shown in figure 3.7(b). Those gates and entries in fault lists that have been processed are flagged by an asterisk in figure 3.7(b). The fault list associated with D has three entries, all of which have asterisks. Among these, only entry $B/1$ qualifies for further processing, since this fault causes a change in the logic value of line D. Hence, fault $B/1$ is propagated to gate E. The fault list associated with E is then recomputed only for the new fault $B/1$. It is not necessary to reevaluate the other entries, $C/1$, $D/1$, and $E/1$, since their input values do not differ from their previous status.

In this way, concurrent fault simulation simulates only the gates in the faulty circuit that have an error at either an input or the output. If gate G has some activity or event due to faults $f_1, f_2, \ldots, f_n$, then these n faulty circuits are simulated separately and these entries are placed in the fault list associated with gate G. In concurrent fault simulation, the faulty circuits and the fault-free circuit are simulated explicitly. In deductive fault simulation, only the fault-free circuit is simulated explicitly; the faulty circuits are simulated deductively. Another significant difference between deductive and concurrent fault simulation is related to the fact that a concurrent simulator processes only the active circuits. In deductive simulation, if a list event occurs, it is necessary to reevaluate all faults in the list because of the complex process of set operations. In contrast, concurrent simulation need not reevaluate a fault whose status has not changed, but need only resimulate the active faulty circuits. Furthermore, in concurrent simulation, since each fault in a list is processed separately, fast processing is possible throught techniques such as table lookup.

The disadvantages of concurrent fault simulation are that it requires more memory space than does deductive fault simulation. Also, as in deductive simulation, the amount of memory needed by concurrent simulation cannot be predicted accurately before a run. This can become serious for large circuits such as VLSI circuits, and so dynamic memory allocation is desirable.

Example 3.2 The differences between concurrent and deductive fault simulation are clarified by fault simulations for the circuit of figures 3.8 and 3.9 using concurrent and deductive techniques, respectively. Suppose that the input to the circuit is first $A = B = C = 0$, $D = 1$, and then input A changes to 1. We begin with concurrent fault simulation in figure 3.8. For gate E, faults $A/1$, $B/1$, and $E/0$ are simulated to form the fault list

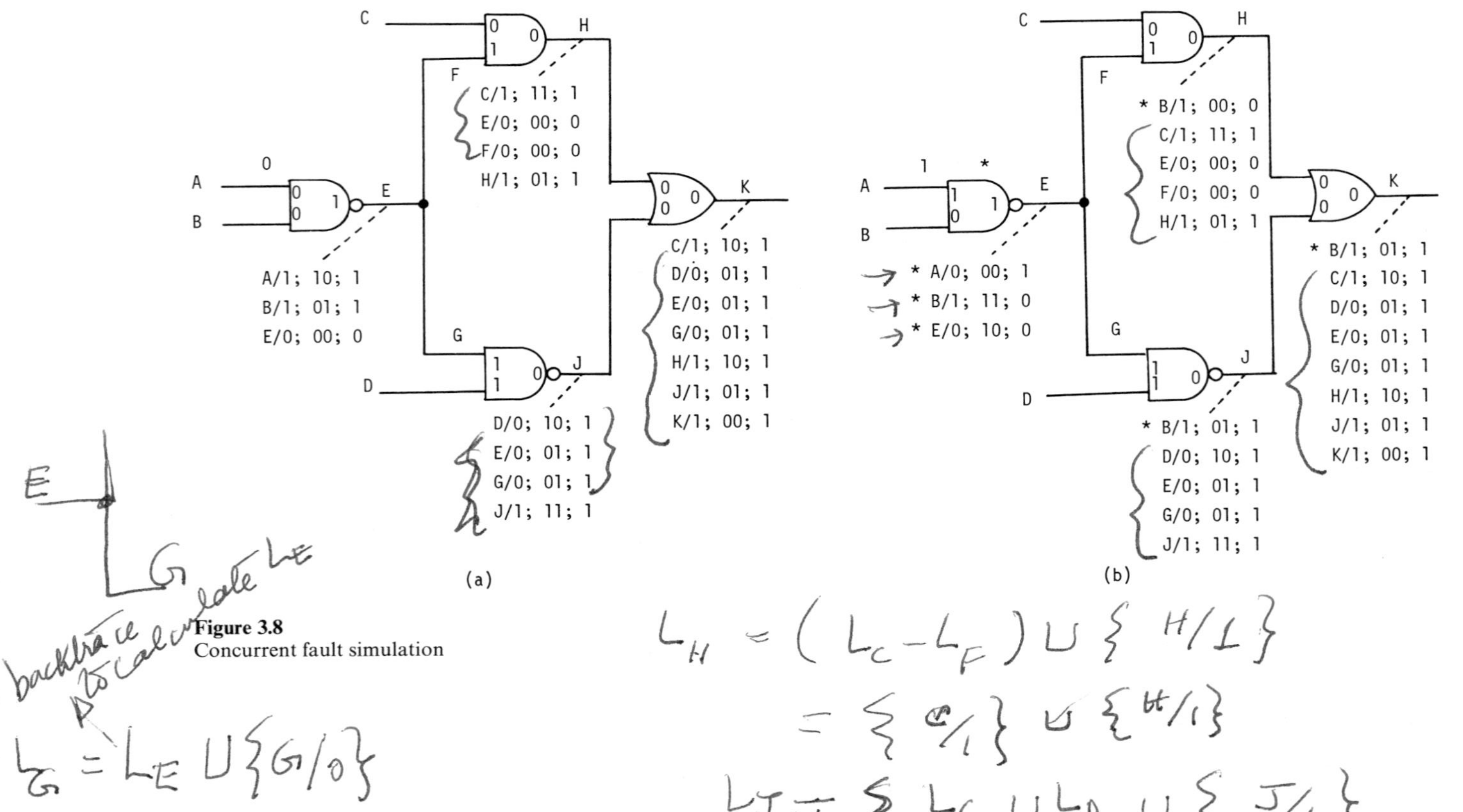

Figure 3.8
Concurrent fault simulation

$A/1$; 10; 1

$B/1$; 01; 1

$E/1$; 00; 0.

Among these faults, only $E/0$ is propagated further since it is the only output value of the gate in the faulty circuit that differs from the fault-free value. For gate H, faults $C/1$, $E/0$, $F/0$, and $H/1$ are simulated; the resulting fault list associated with H is

$C/1$; 11; 1

$E/0$; 00; 0

$F/0$; 00; 0

$H/1$; 01; 1.

Similarly, we have the fault lists associated with J and K as shown in figure 3.8(a). Consequently, faults $C/1$, $D/0$, $E/0$, $G/0$, $H/1$, $J/1$, and $K/1$ are all detectable on the output K.

Next, consider the case where input A changes to 1. Previously the fault list associated with E contained the following faults.

$A/1$; 10; 1

$B/1$; 01; 1

$E/0$; 00; 0

Since A is now 1, the first entry, ($A/1$; 10; 1), is deleted and ($A/0$; 00; 1) is added. Since a logic event has occurred at an input of gate E, the remaining entries, ($B/1$; 01; 1) and ($E/0$; 00; 0), are reevaluated. The resulting fault list is

$A/1$; 00; 1

$B/1$; 11; 0

$E/0$; 10; 0.

Now, since gate E in the fault-free circuit does not alter its output in spite of the change in input A, no logic events occur after this. Only fault $B/1$ causes a change in the logic value of E as compared with the previous status and hence qualifies for further processing. Similarly, only $B/1$ is simulated after this, as shown in figure 3.8(b). In this way, a concurrent fault simulator can simulate each fault separately and thus process only the active circuits. This leads to a significant reduction in computing time.

For the same circuit with the same tests, if we consider deductive fault simulation, we can obtain the results shown in figure 3.9. The result of the simulation with $A = B = C = 0$ and $D = 1$ is shown in figure 3.9(a). Comparing figure 3.9(a) with figure 3.8(a) makes it obvious that concurrent fault simulation requires more memory than deductive simulation. Figure 3.9(b) shows the result of simulation after input A changes to 1. First, since a logic event has occurred at A, the fault list associated with E must be recomputed by set operations, resulting in the fault list $\{B/1, E/0\}$. This new fault list is different from the previous list associated with E, which implies an occurrence of a list event on E. Hence, further computations of fault lists must be continued at the following gates, H and J. For gate K, deductive simulation must resimulate all faults $B/1$, $C/1$, $D/0$, $E/0$, $G/0$, $H/1$, $J/1$, and $K/1$, which are flagged by an asterisk in figure 3.9(b). In concurrent simulation, only the single fault $B/1$ is processed, as shown in figure 3.8(b). The main reason that deductive simulation must process more faults than concurrent simulation is that the deductive technique cannot simulate each of faulty circuits separately.

3.5 Hardware Simulators

The development of increasingly complex logic circuits has created difficult problems in logic design, verification, and testing. The complexity of circuits has led to significantly greater use of CAD (computer-aided design). For example, 1,800 hours of IBM System/370 model 168 CPU time were required to verify the logic design of one-fourth of a medium-range System/370 CPU (Pfister 1982). This fact seems to indicate the limits of current technology supported by general-purpose computers. Recently, attempts to overcome these limits by using special-purpose processors that utilize the parallelism/concurrency in CAD algorithms have received a great deal of attention. The present commercial products are the Logic Evaluator and the Tagas accelerator (Lineback 1982). The other systems, discussed in this section, are a logic-simulation machine proposed by Abramovici et al. (1982), the Yorktown Simulation Engine (Pfister 1982; Denneau 1982; Kronstadt and Pfister 1982), and the Hardware Logic Simulator (Sasaki et al. 1983). These are all special-purpose parallel com-

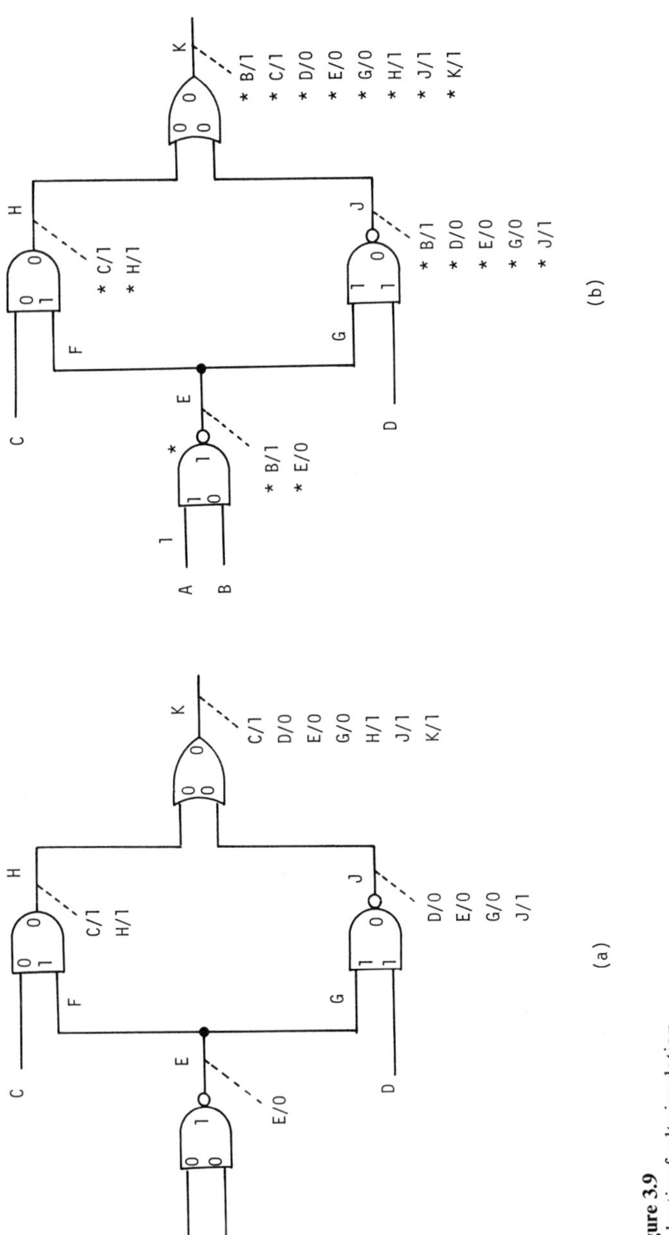

Figure 3.9
Deductive fault simulation

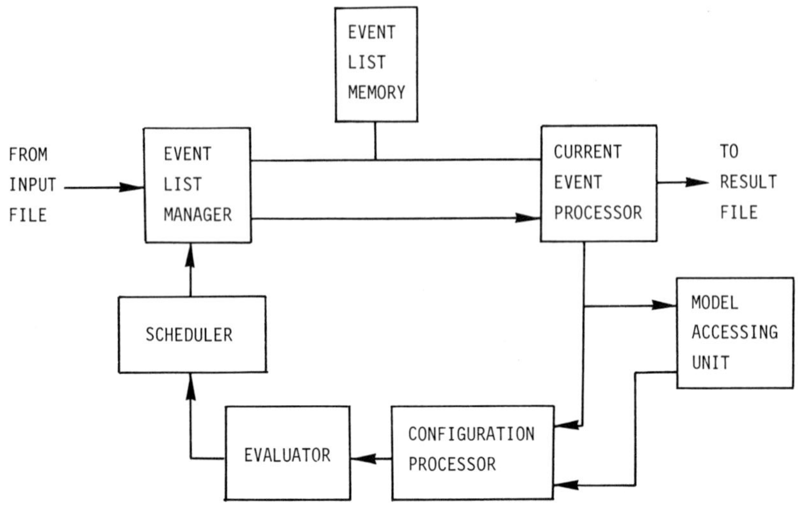

Figure 3.10
Overall architecture of logic-simulation machine (Abramovici et al. 1982; © IEEE 1982)

puters that might be called *hardware simulators* (in contrast with conventional software simulators hosted by general-purpose computers). Although all these hardware simulators are designed primarily for logic simulation, they can be used for fault simulation. By simulating faulty circuits as well as a normal circuit, they can perform fault simulation at high speed.

The basic structure of the logic-simulation machine of Abramovici et al. (1982) is shown in figure 3.10. The machine is organized in a distributed processing architecture in which separate processing units are dedicated to specific tasks of the simulation algorithm. The algorithm adopted here is based on table-driven event-directed simulation. Usually, event-directed simulation performs the following main processes (tasks): The first step is retrieving an event from the event list. The second is updating the configuration of the source element that has generated that event, where the configuration of an element consists of the values of its inputs, outputs, and internal state variables. The fanout elements to which the event propagates are determined to update their configuration. After updating the configuration of all the elements associated with the event, the simulator determines (that is, evaluates) the new values of their outputs and state variables. The evaluation of an element may result in events on its outputs and/or state variables. Delays are usually associated with the operation of elements. Hence, the resulting events are scheduled to occur at some time in the future by computing their times of occurrence. These events are inserted in the event list, and the simulation time is advanced. Each processing unit is dedicated to some task of simulation and works concurrently and cooperatively with the other processing units. The execution of a task is initiated by the arrival of the data required for the task, and the data flow between processing units is organized in a pipeline fashion. The tasks of the different processing units are as follows:

The *Event List Manager* receives the future events and their times of occurrence from the Scheduler and inserts them in the Event List Memory. It also transfers events of the primary inputs from a file containing the applied input sequence into the Event List Memory periodically.

The *Current Event Processor* retrieves the events associated with the current time from the Event List Memory and sends them to both the Model Accessing Unit and the Configuration Processor. It also records in the output file the events occurring at the monitored points.

The *Model Accessing Unit* determines the fanout elements to which the current event propagates and sends them to Configuration Processor.

The *Configuration Processor* updates the configuration (i.e., all the values of inputs, outputs, and internal states of the source element and its fanout elements affected by the current event).

The *Evaluator* receives the configurations of the elements from the Configuration Processor and evaluates them. The evaluation of an element may result in new events or may cancel a previously scheduled event. Depending on the results, it sends the new events or a "cancel event message" to the Scheduler.

The *Scheduler* receives the new events and computes the times of occurrence of the events. The new events and their occurrence times or the "cancel event message" are sent to the Event List Manager.

The simulation machine of Abramovici et al. also contains parallel processors, referred to as *Functional Evaluators*, which concurrently perform functional evaluations as shown in figure 3.11.

Abramovici et al. also proposed to use a microprogrammable processor and to implement all the tasks directly in microcode in order to avoid the substantial software overhead involved in fetching and decoding macroinstructions. They estimated that hardware-based simulation would be between 10 and 60 times as fast as software-based simulation.

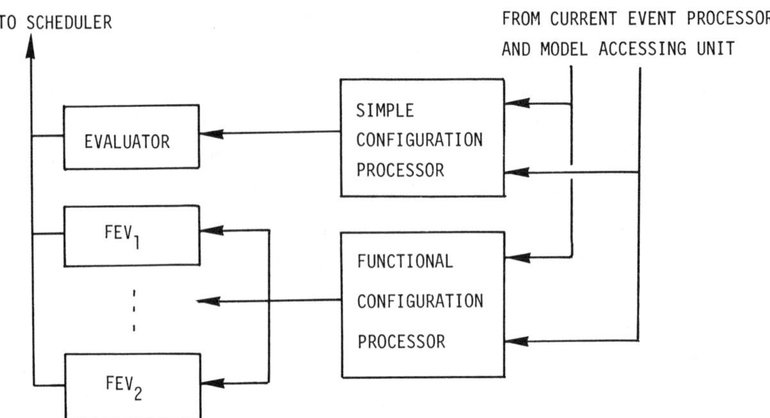

Figure 3.11
Simple and functional evaluations (Abramovici et al. 1982; © IEEE 1982)

In contrast with the low parallelism of the machine of Abramovici et al., the Yorktown Simulation Engine (YSE) (Pfister 1982) exploits the high parallelism of 256 processors. The YSE differs from the machine of Abramovici et al. in that it is designed to execute unit-delay and level-order simulation rather than event-directed simulation. The unit-delay model assumes that every gate has the same delay and that external input changes occur only on integral unit-delay time boundaries. Level-order simulation is a technique used in parallel fault simulation where in all gates are first sorted in ascending order of levels and simulated in the order of ascending value of logic level. The YSE uses these two simulation techniques at the gate level, but not at the functional level. It was built to simulate the logic operation of circuits composed of up to a million gates at a rate exceeding 2 billion gate computations per second.

Figure 3.12 shows the overall architecture of the YSE. It is basically an array of parallel processors. In addition, it has an interprocessor switch and a control processor. A large circuit to be simulated is partitioned into subcircuits, and each subcircuit is assigned to a logic processor prior to simulation by the control processor. Each logic processor contains an instruction memory, which stores the interconnection and function information for the logic circuit; a data memory, which maintains configurations (i.e., logic values for signal lines in the circuit); and a function unit, which evaulates logic function. During simulation, the logic processors concurrently fetch the information from their instruction memories to access and

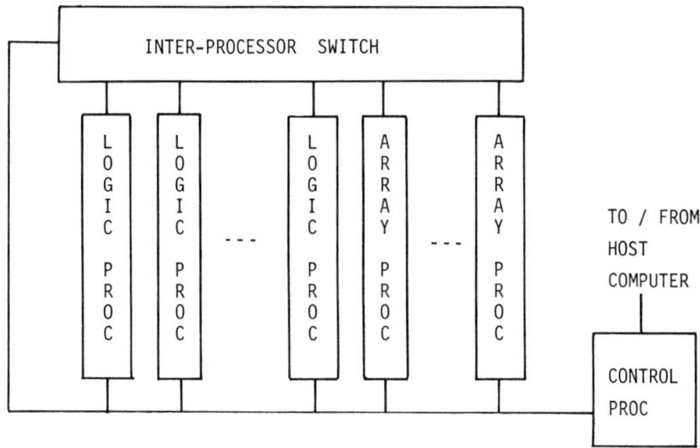

Figure 3.12
Overall architecture of Yorktown Simulation Engine (Pfister 1982; © IEEE 1982)

update values for signal lines stored in their data memories. Each function unit of the logic processors accepts a function code and some operands from the instruction memory and the data memory, respectively; computes the logic function; and finally stores the resultant value back into the data memory. Array processors are used to simulate random-access memories (RAMs) and read-only memories (ROMs).

The interprocessor switch provides communication among up to 256 logic and array processors during simulation. Logic and array processors have to transfer signal values between their data memories. The switch accommodates the required communication introduced by the partitioning.

The control processor takes charge of communication between the host computer and the YSE, including initializing, interrupt handling, and diagnostics of the YSE. The partitioning of the circuit into subcircuits and the sequence of switch routing configurations are all determined and fixed prior to simulation, and affect the initialization of the YSE by the control processor.

The third type of hardware simulator is the Hardware Logic Simulator "HAL" developed by Sasaki et al. (1983). The overall architecture of the HAL, shown in figure 3.13, is similar to that of the YSE. It is also basically an array of parallel processors that contains logic processors, memory processors, a control processor, and an interprocessor network. However,

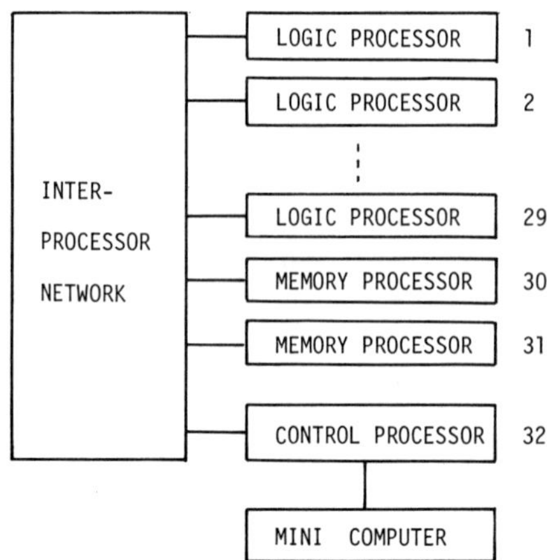

Figure 3.13
Overall architecture of HAL (Sasaki et al. 1983; © IEEE 1983)

the HAL differs in some respects from the YSE. It contains only 32 processors, and thus its parallelism is lower than that of the YSE. It performs table-driven event-directed simulation at the functional level as well as at the gate level. It uses a technique called *block-oriented simulation*, where "block" means a logic collection ranging from several gates to several hundred gates or a memory element in a range from one RAM chip to several hundred RAM chips. The block-level simulator supports LSI-level, functional macro-level, gate-level, and mixed-level simulation.

The hardware of each processor is made up of two parts: an interblock-connection simulator and a block-behavior simulator. The interblock simulator has a block-status memory and a block-interconnection list memory. It reads (in turn) block input values and block type information from the block-status memory, sends them to the block-behavior simulator, receives the resulting output values of the block from the block-behavior simulator, and updates the block-status memory. The block-behavior simulator has a block-function memory. It receives block-input values and block type information from the interblock simulator, evaluates the output values of the block, and sends the result to the interblock simulator.

The HAL has 29 logic processors and two memory processors. Each logic processor can simulate up to 1,024 logic blocks. Each memory processor can also simulate up to 1,024 memory blocks. It was estimated that the HAL can simulate up to 1.5 million gates and 2M byte RAM ICs at a 5-millisecond clock speed.

4 The Complexity of Testing

Testing has two main stages: the generation of tests for a given circuit and the application of these tests to the circuit. Hence, the complexity of testing can be classified into the complexity of test generation and the complexity of test application.

The computational complexity of the algorithms used to generate a test is used to estimate the complexity of test generation. The size of a test set or the length of a test sequence is adopted as a measure of the complexity of test application.

4.1 NP-Completeness

The *time complexity* of an algorithm (that is, the time needed by the algorithm) can be expressed as a function of the size of the problem. If an algorithm processes inputs of size n in time cn^2 for some constant c, then we say that the time complexity of that algorithm is of order n^2. More precisely, a function $f(n)$ is of order $g(n)$ whenever there exists a constant c such that $f(n) \leqslant c \cdot g(n)$ for all values of $n \geqslant 0$. An algorithm whose time complexity is of order $p(n)$ for some polynomial function p is called a *polynomial time algorithm*. Similarly, an algorithm whose time complexity is of order k^n for some constant k is called an *exponential time algorithm*.

In the theory of computation, there is general agreement that a problem should be considered intractable if it cannot be solved in less than exponential time. That is, exponential time algorithms are "too inefficient." To illustrate this, suppose that we have three algorithms whose time complexities are n, n^3, and 2^n. Assuming that time complexity expresses execution time in microseconds, the n, n^3, and 2^n algorithms can solve a problem of size 10 instantly in 0.00001, 0.001, and 0.001 second, respectively. However, the apparent distinction between polynomial time algorithms and exponential time algorithms exists in larger problems. For example, to solve a problem of only size 60, the 2^n algorithm requires 366 centuries whereas the n and n^3 algorithms require only 0.00006 and 0.216 second, respectively.

From this example it is obvious that exponential time algorithms are unsuited for practical use in large problems, and that polynomial time algorithms are much more desirable. Hence, a problem is regarded as intractable if it is so hard that no polynomial time algorithm can possibly solve it. Many intractable problems are known to constitute an equivalent class called the class of *NP-complete problems*. Major fault-detection problems are NP-complete, and thus it appears very unlikely that fault-detection problems can be solved by a polynomial time algorithm in general.

More detailed and precise discussions of NP-completeness may be found in both Aho et al. 1976 and Garey and Johnson 1979. A problem A is said to belong to class P (class NP) if any instance of A is solved in time bounded by a polynomial of the problem size by a deterministic (nondeterministic) computation. (In our problems, the number of gates and lines in a circuit may be regarded as the problem size.)

Problem A is said to be *polynomially transformable* to B if the existence of a deterministic polynomial time algorithm for B implies the existence of a deterministic polynomial time algorithm for A. For decision problems, we say that A is polynomially transformable to B if any instance of A can be transformed in polynomial time of the deterministic computation to an instance of B such that the former has an answer "yes" if and only if the latter has an answer "yes." Now we can define NP-completeness as follows: A problem B is said to be NP-complete if (1) it belongs to NP and if (2) every problem A in NP is polynomially transformable to B. If some problems are already known to be NP-complete, condition 2 is rather easily checked: It is sufficient to show that (2′) at least one problem A, which is known to be NP-complete, is polynomially transformable to B.

"Is P = NP?" is a long-standing open problem in complexity theory. If for at least one NP-complete problem A any instance of A is solved in polynomial time, then P = NP. However, it appears very unlikely that $P = NP$, and hence NP-complete problems are regarded as intractable in the sense mentioned above.

The first NP-complete problem, usually referred to as the satisfiability (SAT) problem, was reported by Cook (1971). A brief description of this problem follows; we need it in our discussion of the NP-completeness of fault-detection problems.

A *literal* is either x or $\bar{x}$ for some variable x, and a *clause* is a sum of literals. A Boolean expression is said to be in *conjunctive normal form* (CNF) if it is a product of clauses. For example, $(x_1 + x_2)\cdot(\bar{x}_1 + x_3 + x_4)$ is in CNF, but $x_1 + x_2\bar{x}_3$ is not. A Boolean expression is *satisfiable* if and only if there exists some assignment of zeros and ones to the variables that gives the expression the value 1. Then the SAT problem is specified as follows.

Satisfiability (SAT) Is a Boolean expression satisfiable?

THEOREM 4.1 (Cook 1971) The satisfiability problem is NP-complete.

It is known that, even with a more stringent condition, the satisfiability problem is NP-complete. An expression is said to be in k-conjunctive normal form (k-CNF) if it is a product of sums of at most k literals. The k-satisfiability problem (k-SAT) is to determine whether an expression in k-CNF is satisfiable. For $k = 1$ or 2 there exist polynomial algorithms to test k-satisfiability. However, 3-SAT is known to be NP-complete.

THEOREM 4.2 (Cook 1971) 3-SAT is NP-complete.

An expression is said to be *clause-monotone* if each clause contains either only negated variables or only unnegated variables. The satisfiability for clause-monotone expressions (CM-SAT, for short) is also known to be NP-complete (Gold 1974). Since this is the key NP-complete problem for the following discussions, a proof is given here.

THEOREM 4.3 CM-SAT is NP-complete.

Proof It is easy to see that CM-SAT is in NP. We transform 3-SAT to CM-SAT. Given a 3-CNF of a Boolean expression $F = C_1 \cdot C_2 \cdot \cdots \cdot C_k$ where each clause C_i $(1 \leqslant i \leqslant k)$ is composed of exactly three literals, we shall construct a clause-monotone expression F' such that F' is satisfiable if and only if F is satisfiable.

To construct F' we merely replace each individual clause C_j $(1 \leqslant j \leqslant k)$ by a clause C_j' or a product of two clauses $C_j' \cdot C_j''$ as follows:

Case 1 $C_j = a + b + c,$ $C_j' = C_j.$

Case 2 $C_j = \bar{a} + \bar{b} + \bar{c},$ $C_j' = C_j.$

Case 3 $C_j = a + b + \bar{c},$ $C_j' \cdot C_j'' = (a + b + v_j) \cdot (\bar{v}_j + \bar{c})$

where v_j is a new variable for C_j.

Case 4 $C_j = \bar{a} + \bar{b} + c,$ $C_j' \cdot C_j'' = (\bar{a} + \bar{b} + \bar{v}_j) \cdot (v_j + c).$

Obviously, this transformation can be performed in polynomial time. To prove that this is indeed a transformation, we must show that F' is satisfiable if and only if F is satisfiable. However, one can easily prove that. ∎

Although SAT, 3-SAT, and CM-SAT are all NP-complete, the satisfiability problem is solvable in polynomial time if a Boolean expression is monotone or unate. An expression is said to be *monotone* if it contains only unnegated variables. An expression is said to be *unate* if each variable is either only negated or only unnegated. A negated (unnegated) variable in a unate expression is called to be *negative* (*positive*) unate.

One can easily see that if an expression is monotone then it is unate and also clause-monotone. However, every unate expression is not always clause-monotone. For example, $(x_1 + x_2)\cdot(x_2 + \bar{x}_3)$ is unate but not clause-monotone. In this expression, x_1 and x_2 are positive unate and x_3 is negative unate. Moreover, $(x_1 + x_2)\cdot(\bar{x}_2 + \bar{x}_3)$ is clause-monotone but not unate.

The satisfiability problem for unate expressions (U-SAT, for short) is shown to be solvable in time $O(L)$, where L is the length of an expression, in the following theorem.

THEOREM 4.4 U-SAT is solvable in time $O(L)$ where L is the length of an expression.

Proof Let $E(x_1, x_2, \ldots, x_p)$ be a unate expression. Let $(a_1, a_2, \ldots, a_p)$ be an assignment such that $a_i = 0$ if x_i is negative unate and $a_i = 1$ if x_i is positive unate. Since the expression E is unate, if $E(a_1, a_2, \ldots, a_p) = 0$ then $E(x_1, x_2, \ldots, x_p) = 0$ for any assignment. This implies that $E(a_1, a_2, \ldots, a_p) = 1$ if E is satisfiable. Hence, E is satisfiable if and only if $E(a_1, a_2, \ldots, a_p) = 1$. We can determine whether $E(a_1, a_2, \ldots, a_p) = 1$ in time $O(L)$ and so that U-SAT is solvable in time $O(L)$. ■

The satisfiability of a monotone expression (M-SAT, for short) is also solvable in time $O(L)$, since a monotone expression is also unate. Thus we have the following corollary.

COROLLARY 4.1 M-SAT is solvable in time $O(L)$ where L is the length of an expression.

Now we shall consider the following fault-detection problem:

Fault detection (FD) Is a given single struck-at fault detectable?

Ibarra and Sahni (1975) reported that the FD problem is NP-complete. However, their proof is rather long and complicated. The much simpler proof given by Fujiwara and Toida (1982a, b) showed that the FD problem is still NP-complete even for k-level ($k \geqslant 3$) monotone/unate circuits though it is solvable in polynomial time for 2-level monotone/unate circuits.

In this section, NP-completeness proof of fault-detection problems given

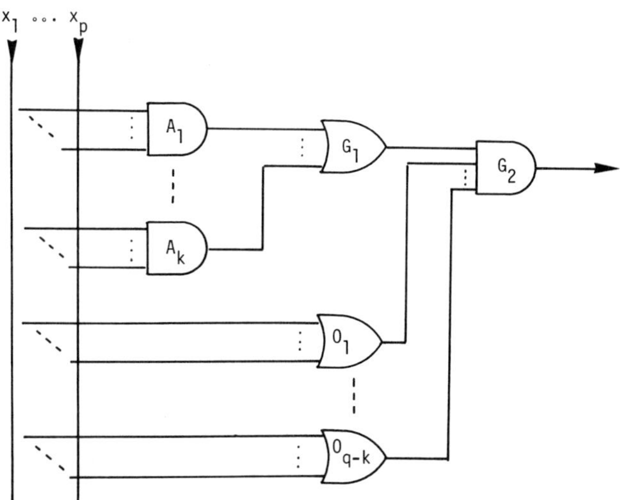

Figure 4.1
A 3-level monotone circuit Q_1

by Fujiwara and Toida (1982a,b) will be described. The following expressions will be used:

kM-FD fault-detection problem for k-level monotone circuits
kU-FD fault-detection problem for k-level unate circuits.

Let us begin with the following theorem.

THEOREM 4.5 3M-FD is NP-complete.

Proof Obviously 3M-FD is in NP. Hence, it suffices to show that some NP-complete problem is polynomially transformable to 3M-FD. We shall transform CM-SAT to 3M-FD.

Given any clause-monotone expression E with variables $x_1, x_2, \ldots, x_p$ and clauses $C_1, C_2, \ldots, C_q$, we construct a 3-level monotone circuit Q_1 as folows (figure 4.1).

Without loss of generality, we assume that $C_1, C_2, \ldots, C_k$ are the clauses with negated variables and $C_{k+1}, C_{k+2}, \ldots, C_q$ are the clauses with unnegated variables.

Step 1: Construct AND gates $A_1, A_2, \ldots, A_k$ from clauses $C_1, C_2, \ldots, C_k$ with negated variables so that each AND gate A_i has the input variables of

C_i. For example, suppose a clause C_i is equal to $\bar{a} + \bar{b} + \bar{c}$; then the output of A_i is $a \cdot b \cdot c$.

Step 2: Construct the above AND gates to OR gate G_1 as shown in figure 4.1.

Step 3: Construct OR gates $O_1, O_2, \ldots, O_{q-k}$ from clauses $C_{k+1}, C_{k+2}, \ldots, C_q$ with unnegated variables. For example, the output of O_i is $a + b + c$ if the clauses C_i is equal to $a + b + c$.

Step 4: Connect all the OR gates $O_1, O_2, \ldots, O_{q-k}$ and G_1 to AND gate G_2 as shown in figure 4.1.

In this circuit Q_1, a stuck-at-1 fault on the output of gate G_1 is detectable if and only if there exists a test such that all the outputs of AND gates A_1, $A_2, \ldots, A_k$ are 0 and all the outputs of OR gates $O_1, O_2, \ldots, O_{q-k}$ are 1. Suppose that AND gate A_i corresponds to a clause $C_i = \bar{a} + \bar{b} + \bar{c}$. Then the output of A_i is 0 if and only if $C_i = 1$, since $a \cdot b \cdot c = 0$ if and only if $\bar{a} + \bar{b} + \bar{c} = 1$. Hence, the fault G_1 s-a-1 is detectable if and only if the given expression E is satisfiable.

The above construction can be carried out in an amount of time linear in p and q. Therefore, CM-SAT is polynomially transformable to 3M-FD. ∎

Since monotone circuits are also unate, we can see from theorem 4.5 that 3U-FD is also NP-complete.

COROLLARY 4.2 3U-FD is NP-complete.

Now we have seen that the fault-detection problem is NP-complete even for 3-level monotone/unate circuits. These results also imply that the fault-detection problem is in general NP-complete. Hence, we have the following corollary from theorem 4.5.

COROLLARY 4.3 FD is NP-complete.

Next we consider the following test-generation problem with a more stringent condition. Suppose we know that a circuit C is not only monotone but also irredundant and we wish to know how long it will take to find a test for a given fault in C. The following theorem shows that this problem is still NP-complete.

THEOREM 4.6 The problem of finding a test to detect a given fault f in an arbitrary monotone and irredundant circuit C is NP-complete.

Proof It suffices to show that a polynomial time algorithm for finding a test for f in C can be used to develop a polynomial time algorithm for solving 3M-FD.

Assume that we have a polynomial time algorithm A that finds a test for a given fault f in an arbitrary monotone and irredundant circuit C. Using this algorithm, we can construct a polynomial time algorithm that solves 3M-FD as follows:

Algorithm A:

Input: an irredundant monotone circuit C and a single stuck-at fault f.

Output: a test to detect f in C.

Let $p(\cdot)$ be the polynomial time bound of A.

Algorithm B:

Input: a 3-level monotone circuit C' and a single stuck-at fault f'.

Output: "yes" if there is a test to detect f'; "no" otherwise.

Method:

Apply algorithm A to f' and C'.

If A does not halt on f' and C' after $p(\cdot)$ steps, then there is no test for f' and the answer is "no."

If A halts on f' and C' in $p(\cdot)$ or fewer steps, then check whether or not the output is a test for f'. If it is a test for f', then the answer is "yes." Otherwise, there is no test for f', and the answer is "no." ∎

4.2 Polynomial Time Class

The choice has been made to show that the fault-detection problem is NP-complete. However, there are many circuits for which the fault-detection problem can be solved in polynomial time—for example, linear circuits, decoder circuits, and parallel adders. This section presents a class of circuits that contains the above circuits and for which the fault-detection problem can be solved in polynomial time (Fujiwara and Toida 1982a, b).

First, we introduce an extended operation of implication, called an *extended implication.*

Consider a combinational circuit C in which the values 0, 1, D, and $\bar{D}$ may be assigned at some lines. Let $V(s_i)$ be a subset of $\{0, 1, D, \bar{D}\}$ with respect to line s_i in C. We construct each set $V(s_i)$ working breadth-first from primary inputs to primary outputs as follows: For each primary input x_i $(1 \leqslant i \leqslant n)$, we let $V(x_i) = \{a\}$ if the value a is already assigned at x_i, where a is 0, 1, D, or $\bar{D}$, and let $V(x_i) = \{0, 1\}$ otherwise.

For an AND gate with inputs $X_1, X_2, \ldots, X_p$ and output Y, we construct $V(Y)$ in the following steps:

If 0 is in $V(X_i)$ for some X_i, then 0 is in $V(Y)$.
If D is in $V(X_i)$ and $\bar{D}$ is in $V(X_j)$ for some X_i and X_j, then 0 is in $V(Y)$.
If 1 is in $V(X_i)$ for all X_i, then 1 is in $V(Y)$.
If D is in $V(X_i)$ for some X_i and D or 1 is in $V(X_j)$ for all other X_j $(j \neq i)$, then D is in $V(Y)$. If $\bar{D}$ is in $V(X_i)$ for some X_i and $\bar{D}$ or 1 is in $V(X_j)$ for all other X_j $(j \neq i)$, then $\bar{D}$ is in $V(Y)$.

We can construct $V(Y)$ similarly for other types of gates (OR, NAND, NOR, NOT).

When we encounter a line s_i on which a value V is already assigned, we check whether or not $V(s_i)$ contains v. If it does not, then an inconsistency occurs. Otherwise, we redefine $V(s_i) = \{v\}$ and continue the computation.

When we encounter a line L with a fault, we check whether or not $V(L)$ contains 1 (0) if the fault is s-a-0 (s-a-1). If it does not, then an inconsistency occurs. Otherwise, we redefine $V(L) = \{D\}$ for a s-a-0 fault and $V(L) = \{\bar{D}\}$ for a s-a-1 fault and continue the computation.

Obviously, the above computation requires at most $O(m)$ time, where m is the number of lines in C.

A set S of points in a circuit C is called a *head-point* set of C if for any reconvergent fanout point p, either p belongs to S or any path from each primary input to p contains at least one point in S.

THEOREM 4.7 Let C be a circuit and let S be a head-point set with k head points. Then there is an algorithm of time complexity $O(4^k \cdot m)$ to find a test for a single stuck-at fault in C, where m is the number of lines in C.

Proof The test generation for a fault on line L can be performed in the following steps:

(1) Fix a value of L to D ($\bar{D}$) if a fault is a stuck-at-0 (s-a-1). Assign a value 0, 1, D, or $\bar{D}$ to each head point in C to do the following steps for each combination of values on the head points. If there is no untried combination remaining and no test has been found, then there exists no test, so stop.
(2) For each assignment, determine the implications, that is, determine all the line values that are implied uniquely by the values assigned on the head

points. If any inconsistency occurs, then go back to step 1. If no inconsistency occurs, the values of all (head and nonhead) reconvergent fanout points are determined uniquely.
(3) Perform extended implications, working breadth-first from primary inputs to primary outputs; that is, compute $V(s_i)$ for all lines s_i. If any inconsistency occurs, then go back to step 1.
(4) Check whether or not every D-path starts at the line L under test, where a D-path is a path such that $V(s_i)$ contains either D or $\bar{D}$ for all lines s_i on the path. If not, then go back to step 1.
(5) Check whether or not there is at least one D-path ending at a primary output. If not, then go back to step 1. Otherwise, you have found a test, so stop.

The above algorithm requires the enumeration of at most 4^k combinations of values on head points. We can see that steps 2, 3, and 5 can be performed in time $O(m)$, where m is the number of lines. Hence, the above algorithm can be carried out in $O(4^k \cdot m)$ time. ■

The algorithm shown in the proof of theorem 4.7 generates all the combinations of values 0, 1, D, or $\bar{D}$ on all head points, i.e., 4^k assignments from the beginning. This can be improved by an implicit enumeration technique. In generating a test, the algorithm creates a decision tree in which at each decision node the value of a line is chosen from among a number of possible values. The initial choice is arbitrary, but it may be necessary during the execution of the algorithm to return to the same node and consider another possible choice. This is called a *backtrack*. In order to guarantee the time complexity $O(4^k \cdot m)$, we have to make sure that backtracks occur only at k head points.

Next, consider a combinational circuit C, which is partitioned into subcircuits called *blocks*: $B_1, B_2, \ldots, B_t$. A fanout point p in a block B_i is called a *reconvergent fanout point with respect to* B_i if there exist two paths, both of which start from p and either reconverge within B_i or arrive at an adjacent block B_j $(j \neq i)$. A nonprimary input of B_i is a signal line coming into B_i from another block.

A *head-point set* S_i *of a block* B_i is a set of points such that all nonprimary inputs of B_i are contained in S_i and such that, for any reconvergent fanout point p with respect to B_i, either p belongs to S_i or any path from each primary input to p contains at least one point in S_i.

For a combinational circuit C partitioned into blocks, we define a

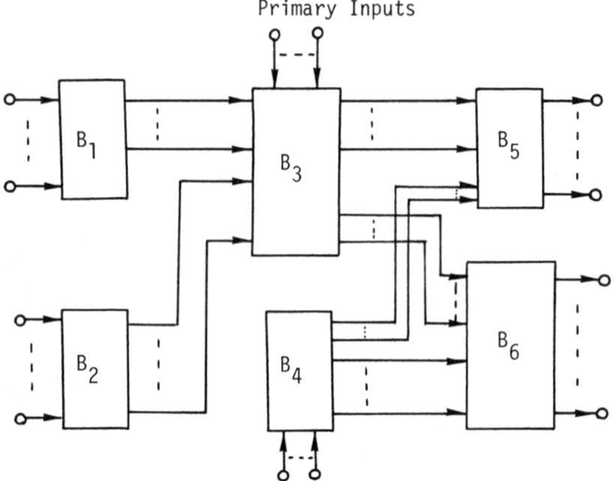

(a) Circuit C partitioned into blocks

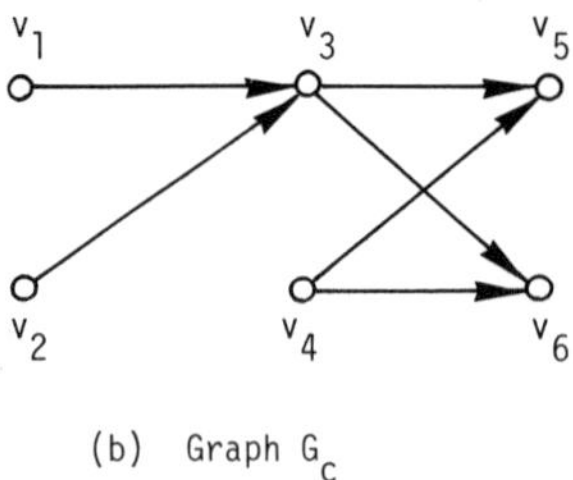

(b) Graph G_C

Figure 4.2
A k-head-bounded circuit

directed graph G_c with respect to the circuit C and its blocks such that each vertex represents a block and each arc represents a connection between blocks (figure 4.2).

A combinational circuit C is said to be *k-head-bounded* if C can be partitioned into blocks B_i $(i = 1, 2, \ldots, t)$ such that the graph G_c with respect to C and B_i is acyclic and has no reconvergent path and such that, for each block B_i $(1 \leqslant i \leqslant t)$, there is a head-point set S_i with at most k head points.

Example 4.1 Consider a parallel binary adder of p bits constructed by cascading p stages of one-bit full adders called ripple-carry adders. Figure 4.3 shows p-stage ripple-carry adder. If we partition this adder so that each

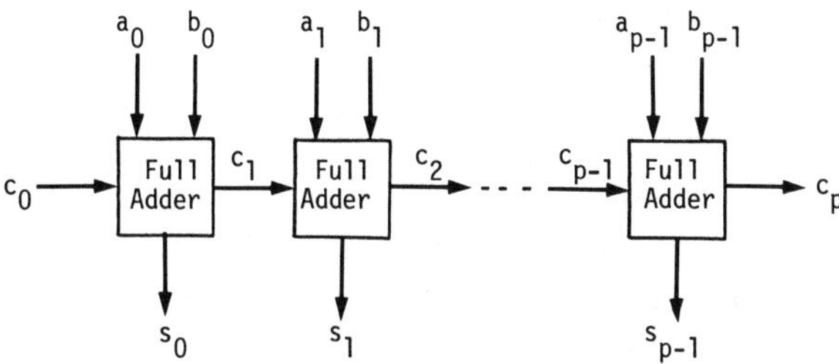

Figure 4.3
Ripple-carry adder

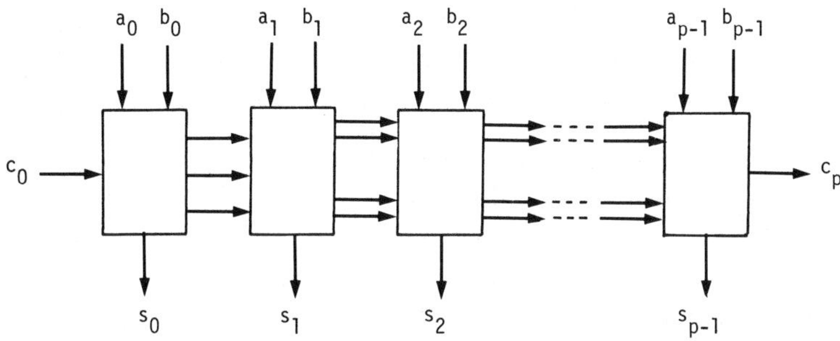

Figure 4.4
Gate-minimum p-bit adder

block corresponds to a full adder, we see that the ripple-carry adder is a 3-head-bounded circuit.

Example 4.2 The gate-minimum p-bit parallel adder (Lai and Muroga 1979) diagrammed in figure 4.4 is 6-head-bounded.

Example 4.3 The exclusive-OR tree realization of a linear function is a 2-head-bounded circuit.

Example 4.4 A p-bit decoder can be realized by a circuit with p nonreconvergent fanout points and 2^p AND gates. Hence, it is a 0-head-bounded circuit.

In theorem 4.7 it was shown that for a circuit with k head points there exists an algorithm of time complexity $O(4^k \cdot m)$ to find a test for a given fault of the circuit. We can easily extend the result to a class of k-head-bounded circuits as in the following theorem.

THEOREM 4.8 Let C be a k-head-bounded circuit. Then there is an algorithm of time complexity $O(16^k \cdot m)$ to find a test for a single stuck-at fault in C, where m is the number of lines in C.

In the proof of theorem 4.8, we consider 4^k possible values for each block and $4^k \times 4^k$ possible tests for each pair of adjacent blocks. Hence, the time complexity becomes $O(16^k \cdot m)$ instead of the $O(4^k \cdot m)$ of theorem 4.7. The proof is omitted. For details, see the proof of theorem 11 in Fujiwara and Toida 1981c. Notice that k-head bounded circuit will have more than k head points.

From Theorem 4.8 we have the following corollary.

COROLLARY 4.4 Let C be a k-head-bounded circuit such that $k = \log_2 p(m)$ for some polynomial $p(m)$, where m is the number of lines in C. Then the fault-detection problem for C is solvable in time complexity $O(p(m)^4 \cdot m)$.

For a k-head-bounded circuit, in order to solve the fault-detection problem in polynomial time it is sufficient that $k = \log p(m)$. As mentioned earlier, parallel adders, linear circuits, and decoder circuits are all k-head-bounded for some constant k. Hence, the fault-detection problem for these circuits is solvable in time complexity $O(m)$.

4.3 Closedness under Faults

Let Ω be the set of all logic function. Let Ω_1 be the set of all single-input logic functions, i.e., $\Omega_1 = \{0, 1, I, N\}$ where 0 and 1 denote the constant functions, I denotes the identity function, and N denotes the NOT function, i.e., $0(x) = 0$, $1(x) = 1$, $I(x) = x$, and $N(x) = \bar{x}$.

Let F be a set of logic functions. Let $[F]$ be the set of all logic functions that can be obtained as finitary compositions of functions from F. (each f may appear any number of times.) $[F]$ is said to be the *closure* of F. F is said to be *closed under composition* if $F = [F]$.

The classical closedness problem in logic and switching theory was completely solved for the binary case, and all the closed classes under composition were classified (Kuntzmann 1968). Figure 4.5 shows all the closed classes that contain constants 0 and 1. The notations in the figure are defined as follows:

L= the class of linear functions. An n-input linear function can be represented in the form $c_0 \oplus c_1 x_1 \oplus \cdots \oplus c_n x_n$ where $c_i = 0$ or 1 for $i = 0, 1, \ldots, n$.

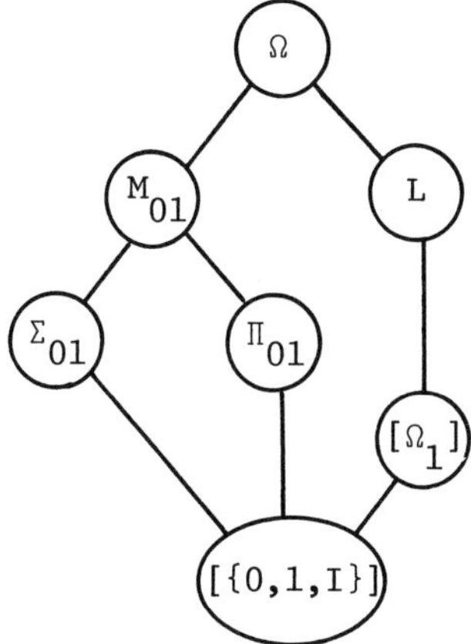

Figure 4.5
Closed sets containing constants 0 and 1

M_{01} = the class of monotone functions including 0 and 1.
Σ_{01} = the class of OR functions including 0 and 1.
Π_{01} = the class of AND functions including 0 and 1.

Let F be a set of logic functions, and let f be a logic function in F. If a logic circuit that realizes the function f is composed of the elements realizing functions in F, then such a realization is called a *closed composition with respect to F*. Henceforth we assume that any realization of a function f in F is a closed composition with respect to F. As an example, consider a function f in F such that f can be expressed in the form

$$f(x_1, x_2, x_3, x_4) = g_1(g_1(x_1, x_2), g_2(x_2, x_3, x_4))$$

where g_1 and g_2 is in F. Then we obtain a closed composition as shown in figure 4.6, where E_1 and E_2 are the elements realizing functions g_1 and g_2, respectively.

We will assume the standard stuck-at fault model, according to which all faults can be modeled by lines stuck at logical 0 or at logical 1.

A set of logic functions F is said to be *closed under stuck-at faults* if any multiple stuck-at fault changes a function in F to a faulty function in F. Let $S(F)$ be the set of all faulty functions that can occur from each function in F when a multiple stuck-at fault is present. Then we can say that F is closed under stuck-at faults if and only if F covers $S(F)$.

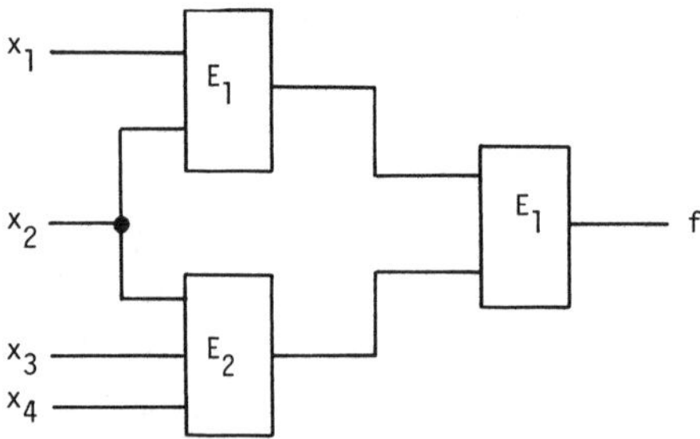

Figure 4.6
Circuit realizing function f

THEOREM 4.9 (Fujiwara 1981) For any subset F of Ω such that $F = [F]$, F covers $S(F)$ if and only if F contains constants 0 and 1.

Proof Suppose that F covers $S(F)$. Obviously $S(F)$ contains constants 0 and 1. Therefore, F also contains 0 and 1. Conversely, suppose that F contains 0 and 1. Let C be a circuit realizing a function f in F. Let α be a multiple stuck-at fault such that lines $s_1, s_2, \ldots, s_k$ are stuck at $\alpha_1, \alpha_2, \ldots, \alpha_k$, respectively. Let C_α be the faulty circuit due to the fault α, and let f_α be the faulty function realized by the circuit C_α. Clearly, the circuit C_α is equivalent to the circuit in which the lines $s_1, s_2, \ldots, s_k$ are cut and connected with constant elements $\alpha_1, \alpha_2, \ldots, \alpha_k$, respectively. By hypothesis, F is closed under composition, and moreover F contains 0 and 1. Therefore, the faulty function f_α is also in F which implies that F covers $S(F)$. ■

From this theorem and figure 4.5 we have the following corollary:

COROLLARY 4.5 If $F = [F]$ and F covers $S(F)$, then F is Ω, M_{01}, L, Σ_{01}, Π_{01}, $[\Omega_1]$, or $[\{0, 1, I\}]$.

Corollary 4.5 shows that all the sets of logic functions that are closed under both composition and stuck-at faults are Ω, M_{01}, L, Σ_{01}, Π_{01}, $[\Omega_1]$, and $[\{0, 1, I\}]$.

So far, we have considered only the sets that are closed under composition. However, there still exist many sets of logic functions that are not closed under composition but are closed under stuck-at faults. Indeed, it can be shown that there exist infinitely many sets of logic functions F such that $F \neq [F]$ and F covers $S(F)$. The classes of fanout-free functions and unate functions are the examples of such sets of logic functions.

A single-output circuit C is *fanout-free* if every line in C is connected to an input of at most one gate, where the gates are assumed to be AND, OR, NAND, NOR, and NOT gates. A logic function is said to be a *fanout-free function* if f can be realized by a fanout-free circuit. The class of fanout-free functions is not closed under composition. As an example, consider three functions f, g_1, and g_2 such that

$$f(x_1, x_2, x_3) = x_1 x_2 + x_2 x_3 + x_3 x_1,$$

$$g_1(x_1, x_2, x_3) = x_1 + x_2 + x_3,$$

$$g_2(x_1, x_2) = x_1 x_2.$$

The function f can be expressed using g_1 and g_2 in the form

$$f(x_1, x_2, x_3) = g_1(g_2(x_1, x_2), g_2(x_2, x_3), g_2(x_3, x_1)).$$

Although g_1 and g_2 are fanout-free functions, f is not fanout-free. Hence, the class of fanout-free functions is not closed under composition.

Now we define a restricted composition as follows. Let F be a set of logic functions. If a logic circuit C that realizes a function f in F is composed of the elements realizing functions in F, and if every line in C is connected to any input of at most one element in C, then such a realization is called a *closed tree composition* or simply a *tree composition.*

The class of fanout-free functions is not closed under composition. However, if we restrict our realization of a given fanout-free function to a tree composition, we can easily show that the class of fanout-free functions is closed under composition and that it it also closed under stuck-at faults. Various properties of fanout-free functions have been studied by Hayes (1975) and Agarwal (1978).

Similarly, although the class of unate functions is not closed under composition, it can be shown to be closed under some restricted composition. One example of such composition is a *unate gate network* introduced by Reddy (1973). We extend the unate gate network to the closed composition as follows. If a circuit C that realizes a unate function is composed of the elements realizing unate functions, and if the number of inversions in any path connecting two points in C has the same parity (odd or even), then such a realization is called a *unate composition.*

As an example, consider two unate functions g_1 and g_2 such that $g_1(x_1, x_2) = x_1 + \bar{x}_2$ and $g_2(x_1, x_2) = x_1 \bar{x}_2$. Figure 4.7 shows a unate composition using the elements realizing g_1 and g_2. In this figure, a plus sign

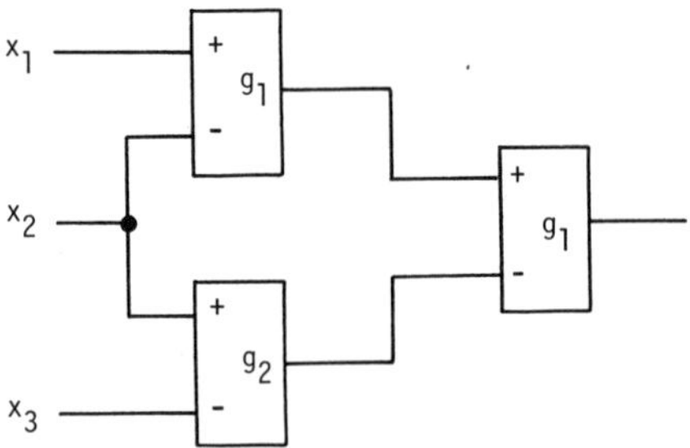

Figure 4.7
Unate composition

denotes a positive unate variable and a minus sign denotes a negative unate variable. The function f realized in figure 4.7 can be expressed as

$$\begin{aligned} f(x_1, x_2, x_3) &= g_1(g_1(x_1, x_2), g_2(x_2, x_3)) \\ &= (x_1 + \bar{x}_2) + (\overline{x_2 \bar{x}_3}) \\ &= x_1 + \bar{x}_2 + x_3. \end{aligned}$$

It can be easily shown that the following theorem holds.

THEOREM 4.10 The class of unate functions is closed under both composition and stuck-at faults provided that the circuit under consideration is realized by a unate composition.

Next we will apply the property of the closedness under stuck-at faults to the fault detection and location problem. For nontrivial sets of logic functions that are closed under stuck-at faults, M_{01} and L, we will consider the test complexity (the minimum number of fault-detection and fault-location tests) and present the universal test sets derived only from the functional description of the circuits.

Given a circuit C, the minimum numbers of tests required to detect all single faults in C and all multiple faults in C are denoted by $\delta_s(C)$ and $\delta_m(C)$, respectively. The minimum numbers of tests required to locate (to within an indistinguishability class) all single faults in C and all multiple faults in C will be denoted by $\lambda_s(C)$ and $\lambda_m(C)$, respectively.

First, we consider the class of monotone and unate functions. An input vector X is said to *cover* the input vector Y if X has ones everywhere Y has ones. A *minimal true vertex* of a logic function is the input vector that does not cover any other true vertex except itself, and a *maximal false vertex* of a function is the input vector that is not covered by any other false vertex except itself.

Betancourt (1973) has shown that the set of all maximal false vertices and minimal true vertices of a unate function f are sufficient to detect any stuck-at-0 or stuck-at-1 fault in any AND/OR realization of f. Betancourt's result has been extended to multiple faults and unate gate networks by Reddy (1973). The number of maximal false vertices plus minimal true vertices of an n-input unate function is at most

$$\binom{n+1}{\left\lfloor \frac{n+1}{2} \right\rfloor}$$

where

$$\binom{x}{y}$$

denotes the number of combinations choosing y things out of x things and $\lfloor z \rfloor$ denotes the integer part of z (Akers 1973). These results can be extended to the unate composition as follows.

THEOREM 4.11 If C is any realization of an n-input unate function under unate composition, then

$$\delta_m(C) \leqslant \binom{n+1}{\left\lfloor \frac{n+1}{2} \right\rfloor}.$$

This theorem can be proved similarly to the proofs in the literature (Akers 1973; Reddy 1973), using the "closedness under stuck-at faults" of theorem 4.10 (i.e., the property that if one or more stuck-at faults are introduced into a unate circuit under a unate composition, the resulting circuit is still unate).

COROLLARY 4.6 If C is any realization of an n-input monotone function under closed composition with respect to M_{01}, then

$$\delta_m(C) \leqslant \binom{n+1}{\left\lfloor \frac{n+1}{2} \right\rfloor}.$$

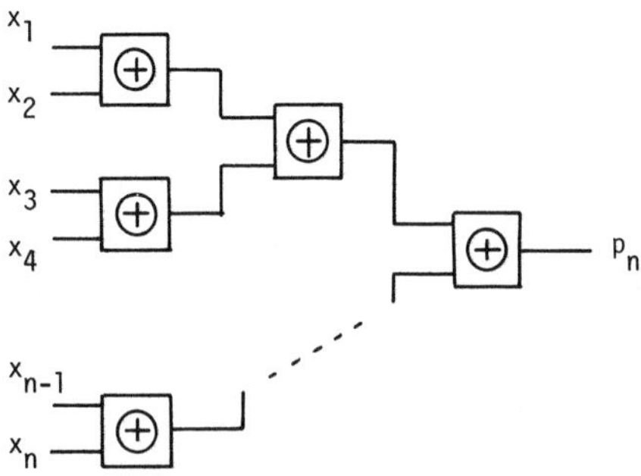

Figure 4.8
EOR tree realization

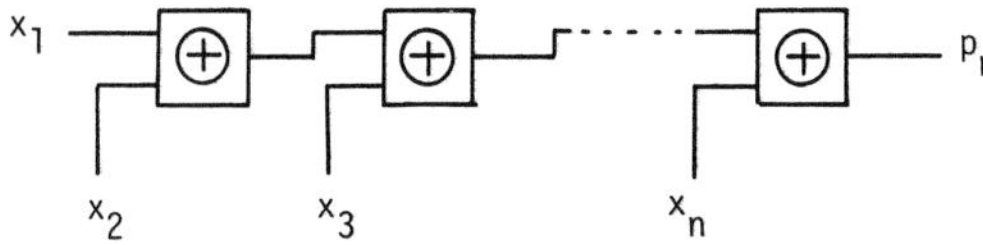

Figure 4.9
EOR cascade realization

Next we shall consider the test complexity for the class of linear functions. A linear function $f(x_1, x_2, \ldots, x_n)$ can be expressed in the form

$$c_0 \oplus c_1 x_1 \oplus \cdots \oplus c_n x_n$$

where $c_i = 0$ or 1 for $i = 0, 1, \ldots, n$. If $c_0 = 0$ ($c_0 = 1$), then the function is called an odd (even) linear function. There are 2^{n+1} linear functions of n variables, of which only two are nondegenerate: $x_1 \oplus x_2 \oplus \cdots \oplus x_n$ and $1 \oplus x_1 \oplus x_2 \oplus \cdots \oplus x_n$. The two nondegenerate functions are complements of each other. Thus, it is sufficient to consider only the odd linear functions in order to clarify the test complexity of linear functions. Henceforth, we restrict ourselves to odd linear functions, which will be denoted by p_n.

Many works on the test complexity of linear functions have been reported. Figures 4.8 and 4.9 show EOR tree and cascade realizations, respectively. For these circuits, under the assumption that any stuck-at fault within EOR gates is considered, we have the following theorems.

THEOREM 4.12 (Hayes 1971b) If C is any EOR tree realization of an n-input linear function, then $\delta_s(C) = 4$.

THEOREM 4.13 (Seth and Kodandapani 1977) If C is any EOR tree realization of an n-input linear function, then

$$\delta_m(C) \leqslant \lfloor 3n/2 \rfloor + 1.$$

THEOREM 4.14 (Hayes 1971b) If C is a cascade realization of an n-input linear function, then $\delta_m(C) \leqslant n + 2$.

Under the more stringent fault assumption that permits only stuck-at faults on the input and output lines of EOR gates, we have the following theorem.

THEOREM 4.15 (Breuer 1972) If C is any EOR tree realization of an n-input linear function, then $\delta_s(C) = 3$.

The linear function is usually realized in either cascade or tree structure of EOR gates. However, these realizations are special cases of closed compositions. There exist some other realizations closed under composition that are neither cascade nor tree. The next theorem shows the test complexity for such closed compositions.

THEOREM 4.16 (Fujiwara 1981) If C is any realization of p_n under closed composition with respect to L, then $n + 1$ tests $t_0, t_1, \ldots, t_n$ are sufficient to locate or distinguish all distinguishable multiple stuck-at faults in C, where

$$t_0 = (0, 0, \ldots\ldots, 0),$$

$$t_1 = (1, 0, \ldots\ldots, 0),$$

$$t_2 = (0, 1, 0, \ldots\ldots, 0),$$

$\ldots,$

$$t_n = (0, \ldots\ldots\ldots, 1).$$

Proof Any linear function of n or fewer variables can be expressed in the form

$$p_A(x_1, x_2, \ldots, x_n) = a_0 \oplus a_1 x_1 \oplus a_2 x_2 \oplus \cdots \oplus a_n x_n$$

where $a_i = 0$ or 1 and $A = (a_0, a_1, \ldots, a_n)$. Since the class of linear functions L is closed under composition, any faulty function of linear circuits under closed composition is also a linear function of k ($k \leqslant n$) variables, and thus it can be expressed in the above form. When $A = (0, 1, \ldots, 1)$, the linear function p_A represents the fault-free linear function p_n. Let $p_B = b_0 \oplus b_1 x_1 \oplus \cdots \oplus b_n x_n$ be a linear function realized by a circuit under test where $b_i = 0$ or 1. Applying the vectors $t_o, t_1, \ldots, t_n$ to

$$p_A(x_1, x_2, \ldots, x_n) = p_B(x_1, x_2, \ldots, x_n),$$

we obtain

$$a_o = b_0,$$

$$a_0 \oplus a_1 = b_0 \oplus b_1,$$

$$\ldots,$$

$$a_0 \oplus a_n = b_0 \oplus b_n,$$

which implies

$$a_i = b_i, \qquad i = 0, 1, \ldots, n.$$

Therefore we can uniquely determine the values of a_i, and thus distinguish all 2^{n+1} linear functions p_A, applying $n + 1$ tests $t_0, t_1, \ldots, t_n$. ■

Since the test set $T = \{t_0, t_1, \ldots, t_n\}$ is independent of the structural description of a given circuit, it is a universal test set under closed composition.

THEOREM 4.17 (Fujiwara 1981) If C is any realization of an n-input linear function under closed composition with respect to L, then $\delta_m(C) = \lambda_m(C) = n + 1$.

Proof By theorem 4.16, $\delta_m(C) \leqslant \lambda_m(C) \leqslant n + 1$. Therefore, it suffices to prove that $\delta_m(C) \geqslant n + 1$.

Let C be any arbitrary realization of an n-input linear function p_n under closed composition. If it can be shown that $n + 1$ tests are necessary to detect all multiple stuck-at faults on the primary inputs of C, then we can say $\delta_m(C) \geqslant n + 1$. This will be proved in the following.

When we consider all the multiple stuck-at faults on the primary inputs $x_1, x_2, \ldots, x_n$ of C, there exist exactly $2^{n+1} - 2$ faulty functions p_A such that

$$A = (0, \ldots\ldots\ldots, 0, 0)$$

$$(0, \ldots\ldots\ldots, 0, 1)$$

$$(0, \ldots\ldots\ldots, 1, 0)$$

$(0, \ldots\ldots\ldots, 1, 1)$

$\ldots$

$(1, \ldots\ldots\ldots, 1, 1)$

except $A = (0, 1, \ldots, 1)$ and $(1, 1, \ldots, 1)$. Therefore p_A is a faulty function if any only if $a_i = 0$ for some i $(1 \leqslant i \leqslant n)$.

Applying all the 2^n input combinations of $(x_1, x_2, \ldots, x_n)$ to the equation $p_A(x_1, x_2, \ldots, x_n) = x_1 \oplus x_2 \oplus \cdots \oplus x_n$, we have 2^n equations as follows:

$$a_0 = 0,$$

$$a_0 \oplus a_1 = 1,$$

$$\ldots,$$

$$a_0 \oplus a_n = 1,$$

$$a_0 \oplus a_1 \oplus a_2 = 0,$$

$$a_0 \oplus a_1 \oplus a_3 = 0,$$

$$\ldots,$$

$$a_0 \oplus a_1 \oplus \cdots \oplus a_n = \begin{cases} 0 & \text{if } n \text{ is even,} \\ 1 & \text{if } n \text{ is odd.} \end{cases}$$

The maximum number of linearly independent equations among the above 2^n equations is $n + 1$. Therefore, $n + 1$ equations are necessary to determine the values $a_1, a_2, \ldots, a_n$ uniquely. In other words, $n + 1$ tests are necessary to detect all multiple stuck-at faults on the primary inputs of C. Hence, we obtain $\delta_m(C) \geqslant n + 1$. ■

II DESIGN FOR TESTABILITY

5 Introduction to Design for Testability

With the development of increasingly complex circuits, boards, and systems, testing has become more difficult and more expensive. As compared with the increasing cost of testing, the cost of manufacturing is steadily decreasing. This suggests that circuits should be designed to be tested easily—that testability should be adopted as a design parameter. It is now generally agreed that designers should consider design for testability to a certain extent.

5.1 Testability

The testability of a logic circuit has a great effect on the cost of generating and applying tests for the circuit. The greater the testability of a circuit is, the easier the testing will be. Testability can be defined as the ease of testing or as the ability to test easily or cost-effectively.

As discussed in chapter 4, the problem of test generation is in general NP-complete and thus very intractable for very large circuits. This demonstrates the necessity of designing easily testable circuits. With the advent of VLSI circuits, the need for methods of design for testability becomes more and more urgent. One approach to reducing the difficulty of test generation is to consider the testability of a circuit as early as possible in the design cycle and then to improve its testability. To accomplish this objective, it is necessary to have a means of knowing how easy or difficult it will be to generate tests for a circuit and of identifying the areas of poor testability. This is called *testability analysis.*

Testability analysis requires a *testability measure* by which the testability of a circuit can be quantified as accurately as possible. The testability measure must indicate the ease or the difficulty of test generation in the circuit in a manner that can be interpreted by logic-circuit designers. The computational complexity of the testability measure should be much less than that of the test generation. Further, since the information produced by a testability measure is used to modify or to redesign circuits, it must be accurate enough to improve their testability. If the testability computation is fast and if it accurately predicts the difficulty of test generation, then the testability measure will be useful in reducing the cost of testing.

Many methods for meauring testability in logic circuits have been proposed (see, e.g., Stephenson and Grason 1976; Keiner and West 1977; Dejka 1977; Dussault 1978; Wood 1979; Goldstein 1979; Kovijanic 1979; Bennetts et al. 1981; Berg and Hess 1981; Brglez 1984). These methods in common introduce two measures, controllability and observability, to estimate testability. *Controllability* is defined as a measure of how easily the internal logic of the circuit can be controlled from its primary inputs. *Observability* is defined as a measure of how easily the internal logic of the circuit can be observed at its primary outputs.

The process of test generation consists of the tasks of controlling and observing internal logic values. Representatives of controlling and observing tasks in test generation are the consistency and D-drive operations of the D-algorithm, respectively. If each of these tasks is easily achievable, then the test-generation process can be easily accomplished. This means that testability has a close relation with both controllability and observability.

The two typical testability measures are those of Stephenson and Grason (1976) and Goldstein (1979). The measures of Stephenson and Grason were developed for register-transfer-level circuits, though they can also be applied at the gate level. These measures are normalized between 0 and 1 to reflect the ease of controlling and observing the internal logic values. On the other hand, Goldstein (1979) considered gate-level logic circuits and intended to provide measures of the difficulty of controlling and observing the logical values of internal signal lines. His measures are represented as cost functions of each signal line in the circuit.

The Testability Measure of Stephenson and Grason (1976)

A register-transfer-level circuit can be assumed to be a network of *components* (e.g., adders, registers, multiplexers, controllers) interconnected by unidirectional *links*. In general, a link may be many conductors carrying more than one bit of information; however, to simplify our discussion we assume here that all links have a single conductor. A link is thus referred to as a signal line carrying logic values 0 and 1.

A controllability value $CY(s)$ and an observability value $OY(s)$ ranging from 0 to 1 are assigned to each signal line s. The values for the CYs and the OYs of all the signal lines in the circuit are derived by solving a system of simultaneous equations with the CYs and the OYs as unknowns. These equations reflect how the CYs and the OYs of input/output lines of each component are related to one another.

Consider the component illustrated in figure 5.1. The expression used to calculate CY for each output z_j is

$$CY(z_j) = \text{CTF} \times \frac{1}{n} \sum_{i=1}^{n} CY(x_i) \tag{5.1}$$

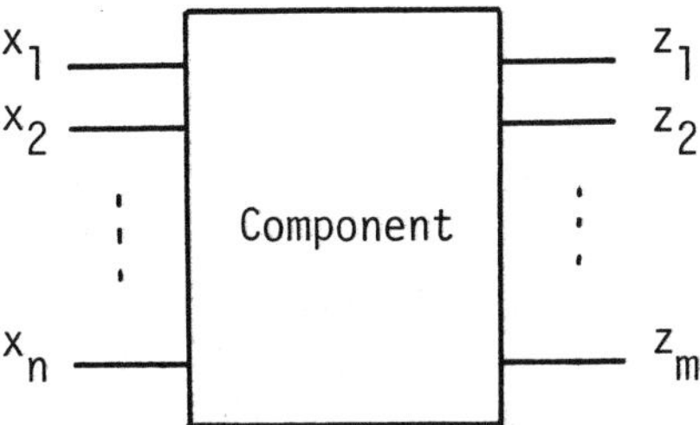

Figure 5.1

where CTF is the *controllability transfer factor* of the component and n is the number of inputs of the component. Note that each output controllability is assigned the same value.

The concept of the CTF is used to account for the potential diminishing of control information as it is propagated through the circuit. The CTF of a component must represent the ability to control outputs of the component by applying input values. It is defined by the following equation, depending only on the input-output relation of the component:

$$\mathrm{CTF} = \frac{1}{m}\sum_{j=1}^{m}\left(1 - \frac{|N_j(0) - N_j(1)|}{2^n}\right) \tag{5.2}$$

where m is the number of outputs of the component and $N_j(0)$ and $N_j(1)$ are the numbers of input values for which output z_j has output value 0 and 1, respectively. The CTF of a component ranges between 0 and 1. It takes the maximum value 1 when the component has a uniform input-output relation, and decreases to 0 as the degree of uniformity decreases. For example, the CTFs for a NOT gate and an EOR gate are 1, since $N(0)$ and $N(1)$ are equal. On the other hand, the CTF of an n-input NAND gate is $1/2^{n-1}$.

Consider again the component diagrammed in figure 5.1. The expression used to calculate OYs for each input x_i is

$$OY(x_i) = \mathrm{OTF} \times \frac{1}{m}\sum_{j=1}^{m} OY(z_j) \tag{5.3}$$

where OTF is the *observability transfer factor* of the component. Note that each input observability is assigned the same value.

The OTF of a component must represent the ease of propagating a fault value through the component. It is expressed as

$$\text{OTF} = \frac{1}{n}\sum_{i=1}^{n}\frac{NS_i}{2^n} \tag{5.4}$$

where NS_i is the number of input values for which outputs resulting from changing the input value of x_i are different. NS_i also means the number of input values that can sensitize a path from x_i to the outputs of the component. The OTF measures the probability that a faulty value at any input of the component will propagate to its outputs. The values of OTFs also vary between 0 and 1.

For example, the OTF of a NOT gate is 1, since $n = 1$ and $NS_1 = 2$. For an EOR gate, $n = 2$ and $NS_1 = NS_2 = 4$, and thus the OTF is 1. For an n-input NAND gate, $NS = 2$ and so the OTF is $1/2^{n-1}$.

The set of equations 5.1 for all signal lines consists of the controllability system. The coefficients for the system are derived from equation 5.2 for each component. The constants $(CY = 1)$ for the system are assigned for all primary inputs, since primary inputs have perfect controllability. Similarly, the observability system consists of the set of equations 5.3 for all signal lines. The coefficients are derived from equation 5.4. The constants $(OY = 1)$ are assigned for all primary outputs, since primary outputs have perfect observability. By solving these two system, we can obtain all the controllability and observability values for signal lines.

For sequential components with storage elements, clock lines, and fanout points, special rules are considered. Sequential components are modeled by adding feedback links around the components that represent internal state. Clock lines that originate as primary inputs to the entire circuit and that only define transition periods for a component are not considered. For the fanout points, the controllability and observability values are calculated as follows: Let s be a fanout line and lef f denote the number of fanout branches from s. Then the CYs of the fanout branches are deduced by dividing $CY(s)$ by $(1 + \log f)$. This is based on the assumption that the CYs of fanout branches are less than the CY of the fanout line. The observability value represents the probability that a fault value there can be detected at the primary outputs, and thus the OY of a fanout line s is defined as

$$OY(s) = 1 - \prod_{i=1}^{f}[1 - OY(s_i)] \tag{5.5}$$

where s_i $(i = 1, 2, \ldots, f)$ are fanout branches of s.

Stephenson and Grason (1976) evaluated the quality of the proposed measure by comparing actual test-generation effort to testability values for two or three circuits. The correlation appeared to be good.

The Testability Measure of Goldstein (1979)

The logic circuits under consideration are composed of combinational and sequential standard logic cells, such as AND gates, OR gates, NOT gates, flip-flops, and more complex logic modules. Goldstein's measures consist of six functions: combinational 0 and 1 controllabilities, sequential 0 and 1 controllabilities, and combinational and sequential observabilities. In contrast with the testability measures of Stephenson and Grason (1976), Goldstein's measures are intended to represent the costs of controlling and observing internal logic values. These are defined as follows.

The combinational 0 and 1 controllabilities of a signal line s, $CC^0(s)$ and $CC^1(s)$, are defined as the minimum number of combinational lines that must be set in order to, respectively, produce a 0 or a 1 on line s. A combinational line is defined as a primary input or an output line of a combinational logic cell. Sequential controllabilities of a signal line s, $SC^0(s)$ and $SC^1(s)$, are defined as the minimum number of sequential lines that must be set in order to, respectively, produce a 0 or a 1 on line s. A sequential line is defined as an output line of a sequential logic cell.

The combinational and sequential observabilities, CO and SO, are defined as the minimum numbers of combinational and sequential nodes, respectively, that must be set in order to propagate the logical value on line s to a primary output of the circuit.

For all primary inputs I, the costs of controllabilities are defined as $CC^0(I) = 1$, $CC^1(I) = 1$, $SC^0(I) = 0$, and $SC^1(I) = 0$. For all primary outputs U, the costs of observabilities are defined as $CO(U) = 0$ and $SO(U) = 0$.

Working breadth-first from primary inputs toward primary outputs of the circuit, we calculate the controllability of the output line of each logic cell as a function of the controllabilities of input lines of the logic cell. As an example, consider a 3-input AND gate with output y and inputs x_1, x_2, and x_3. The output y can be set to 0 if one of three inputs is set to 0. Hence,

$$CC^0(y) = \min\{CC^0(x_1), CC^0(x_2), CC^0(x_3)\} + 1. \tag{5.6}$$

To assign y to 1 we have to set all three inputs to 1. Hence,

$$CC^1(y) = CC^1(x_1) + CC^1(x_2) + CC^1(x_3) + 1. \tag{5.7}$$

Since an AND gate is not sequential, the sequential controllability values are not incremented by 1:

$$SC^0(y) = \min\{SC^0(x_1), SC^0(x_2), SC^0(x_3)\}, \tag{5.8}$$

$$SC^1(y) = SC^1(x_1) + SC^1(x_2) + SC^1(x_3). \tag{5.9}$$

As an example of a sequential-logic cell, consider a D flip-flop with data input D, clock line C, reset line R, and output Q. The output Q of the flip-flop can be set to 1 only if D is set to 1, R is held at 0, and a clock pulse is applied to C. Hence, we have

$$CC^1(Q) = CC^1(D) + CC^0(C) + CC^1(C) + CC^0(R), \tag{5.10}$$

$$SC^1(Q) = SC^1(D) + SC^0(C) + SC^1(C) + SC^0(R) + 1. \tag{5.11}$$

Similarly, we have

$$CC^0(Q) = \min\{CC^1(R) + CC^0(C), CC^0(D) + CC^1(C) + CC^0(C) + CC^0(R)\}, \tag{5.12}$$

$$SC^0(Q) = \min\{SC^1(R) + SC^0(C), SC^0(D) + SC^1(C) + SC^0(C) + SC^0(R)\} + 1. \tag{5.13}$$

Such a calculation process from primary inputs to primary outputs through the circuit is iterated until all the controllability values stabilize when the circuit has feedback loops external to logic cells.

The observabilities are calculated working backward from primary outputs to primary inputs of the circuit. For a 3-input AND gate with inputs x_1, x_2, and x_3 and output y, the observabilities $CO(x_1)$ and $SO(x_1)$ are calculated by

$$CO(x_1) = CO(y) + CC^1(x_2) + CC^1(x_3) + 1, \tag{5.14}$$

$$SO(x_1) = SO(y) + SC^1(x_2) + SC^1(x_3). \tag{5.15}$$

The observability of a fanout line is defined as the minimum value of the observabilities of fanout branches. These calculation processes are iterated until the observability values stabilize.

Two typical testability measures with different features have been described above. Though existing testability measures (including the measures mentioned above) seem to provide some information about circuit testability, it is not necessarily good information to use in the interpretation of whether or not the actual testability of the circuit is sufficient. The existing testability measures have some limitations due to the restricted information source (circuit structure only) on which they rely. The quality of a testability measure depends on how accurately it can decide whether a design is satisfactorily testable and on the areas in the design where a modification can ease the test generation.

The testability measure can also be applied to test generation. As described in chapter 2, test-generation algorithms using heuristics usually apply a kind of testability measure to their heuristic operations. For example, in path sensitization various testability measures are used to estimate the difficulty of sensitizing paths.

5.2 Minimizing the Cost of Testing

One way to reduce the cost of testing is to add extra logic. Formerly, the criteria of logic-design problems were the minimization of hardware cost and the maximization of performance (e.g., circuit speed). However, because of the increasing testing cost and the decreasing hardware cost, design for testability is now becoming a cost-effective approach to LSI and VLSI testing.

Since design for testability requires extra circuitry, there occur some problems such as increased hardware cost and performance degradation. It might be undesirable for many manufacturers to allocate any significant area of a circuit to extra circuitry and to degrade the speed of the circuit. Therefore, both the testing cost and the cost of design and production should be estimated. In practice, an attempt should be made to maximize the testability of the circuit and to minimize the cost of its testing within the limitations of permitted extra hardware cost and tolerated performance degradation.

However, if we ignore these penalties, what is the optimal design that minimizes the cost of testing; i.e., to what extent can the cost of testing be decreased and the testability of circuits can be increased? Though this problem stems from theoretical interest, it is important to solve such a fundamental problem in order to develop design techniques for testability.

The complexity or the cost of testing can be classified into two categories: the ease of test generation and the ease of test application. For the first category, the optimal design to minimize the test-generation cost can be accomplished by a technique called *universal testing* or *function-independent testing*. Universal testing is performed with a test set that is independent of the function realized by the circuit. Usually, such a universal test set depends only on the size of the circuit.

In conventional testing, test patterns are generated laboriously for every circuit under test, since the circuits differ from one another. On the other hand, in universal testing, test patterns can be predetermined independent of the function being realized. Hence, these test patterns can be generated easily at a very small cost. A trivial example of universal testing is *exhaustive testing*, which requires that all 2^n patterns be applied to the input of a circuit. Some design techniques for testability using exhaustive testing have been proposed. Representative are autonomously testable design (McCluskey and Bozorgui-Nesbat 1980) and syndrome-testable design (Savir 1980).

Various other designs for nontrivial universal testability have been reported to be successful for circuits with regular structures, such as Reed-Muller canonic circuits and programmable logic arrays. Reddy (1972) has shown that for an arbitrary logic function there exist realizations, based on Reed-Muller canonic expressions, that have function-independent test sets that detect all single stuck-at faults in the circuits. The size of test sets can be only $n + 4$, for any n-input Reed-Muller canonic circuit, if an extra AND gate whose output is observable is added. Unfortunately, however, the Reed-Muller canonic circuits are composed of a cascade of EOR gates driven by AND gates connected to the circuit inputs, and thus the circuit delay is so large as to make the method of only theoretical interest.

The other regular structure that can be modified to have universal testability is a programmable logic array (PLA). The PLA, which is conceptually a two-level AND-OR, is attractive in LSI and VLSI because of its memorylike array structure and has become a popular and effective tool for implementing logic functions. In the first contributions to the design of universally testable PLAs, Fujiwara et al. (1980) and Hong and Ostapko (1980) independently proposed designs of PLAs that can be tested easily by function-independent test patterns. The output responses of the test patterns are also independent of the function realized by the PLA under test. The number of tests is of order $n + m$ where n and m are the numbers of inputs and product lines of the PLA, respectively. Although the designs of Fujiwara et al. (1980) and Hong and Ostapko (1980) differ in implementation, the essential idea is almost the same. They both have extra circuitry to select each row line of AND array, a shift register to select each product line, and two EOR cascades or trees to check the parity of the row and the column in the array.

Next, we consider the optimal design for ease of test applicaton. Here, we adopt the number of test patterns as a measure of the cost of applying test patterns to the circuit under test. The minimum cost never becomes zero, since at least one test pattern must be applied to the circuit to test it. Therefore, the minimum cost of test application might be some positive constant independent of the size of the circuit. If the cost of test application never increases as the circuit becomes larger, we can say that the circuit design achieves optimal testability in the test application. Such designs have been reported by Hayes (1974), Saluja and Reddy (1974), Inose and Sakauchi (1972), and DasGupta et al. (1980). Hayes has shown that any combinational and sequential circuit can be modified by embedding EOR gates so that five test patterns are sufficient to detect all single and multiple stuck-at faults in the circuit. Saluja and Reddy (1974) extended the result of Hayes to obtain minimally testable designs. They presented a design technique to modify a circuit so that it is fully tested by only three test patterns. Consider a two-input AND gate. It is obvious that three test patterns 01, 10, and 11 are necessary to detect all single and multiple stuck-at faults on the input/output lines of the AND gate. Hence, we can consider that the three tests of Saluja and Reddy constitute a minimum test set.

All the design methods mentioned above involve a lot of extra hardware and very large circuit delays, and thus they are impractical. However, the results show that if sufficient extra circuitry can be added to a circuit, we can design a circuit with optimal testability such that it requires only three test patterns to detect all single and multiple stuck-at faults in the circuit. We can further reduce the number of tests from three to two if we restrict our fault assumption to the more stringent condition that we test only for faults at input/output terminals of components or modules in the circuit. Kuhl and Reddy (1978) have shown that by adding extra circuitry and extra inputs and outputs it is possible to detect all stuck-at faults occurring at module inputs/outputs with three function-independent tests. Inose and Sakauchi (1972) developed a method of designing easily testable circuits that require only two test patterns to detect all terminal stuck-at faults. The same result was obtained by DasGupta et al. (1980), who used almost the same idea as Inose and Sakauchi. These methods are based on the idea of dual-mode logic, in which a circuit is tested in one mode while the normal function of the circuit is performed in another mode, with neither mode interfering with the other.

A different approach, called *compact testing*, can reduce greatly the cost of testing. (As mentioned in section 1.4, compact testing is modeled by the scheme of figure 1.22.) The circuit under test is usually fed pseudorandom input patterns. The output responses of the circuit are compressed and then compared against a reference value. In conventional testing, for each distinct circuit under test a set of tests must be produced by a detailed analysis of the logic circuits, and these tests must be stored before testing. Compact testing, however, does not require prior test generation. The test-pattern generator is independent of the circuit under test and may be implemented in hardware such as a linear feedback shift register. Hence, the cost of test generation is considerably reduced. Further, a much smaller amount of data needs to be compared against the reference value because of data compression. In this way, compact testing can decrease the cost of testing in both stages of test generation and test applicaton. One of the most widely used methods of compact testing is signature analysis.

5.3 Combinational Logic versus Sequential Logic

As described in section 2.4, there are fast test-generation algorithms that can obtain high fault coverage for rather large-scale combinational circuits. These algorithms seem to be reasonably satisfactory for combinational circuits. However, particularly intense difficulties arise in the case of sequential circuits, where there are problems of setting the initial state of a circuit and checking its final state after a test.

In section 2.5 we considered test generation for sequential circuits. The approach taken there was to consider an iterative combinational circuit by cutting the feedback loops as shown in figure 2.34. Test-generation algorithms for combinational circuits can be applied to this iterative model. However, we have to consider the following points:

- A single fault in the original sequential circuit corresponds to a multiple fault consisting of the same fault in every cell of the iterative circuit.
- In general, the initial state is unknown. Hence, we must set its state to the initial state required for the test. Controllability is required to set the initial state of the circuit under test.
- The faulty signal must be propagated to at least one of the primary outputs. If the effect of the fault causes an incorrect final state, we must supply a sequence of input patterns that will observe the final state of the circuit. That is, the observability of the internal state of the circuit is required to check the faulty signal propagated to the flip-flops.

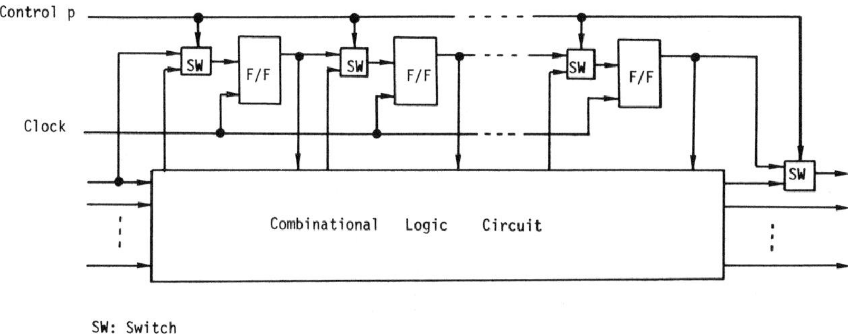

Figure 5.2
Shift-register modification (from Williams and Angell 1973; © 1973 IEEE)

For general sequential circuits, these problems are so difficult that they cannot be solved in reasonable computing time if high fault coverage is desired. However, these problems can be solved completely if a design approach is adopted such that the circuits are designed so that it is easy to set the circuit to any desired internal state and easy to observe any internal state of the circuit. These properties relate to the controllability and observability of the flip-flops or the latches in sequential circuits, respectively.

Several design techniques have been reported to give the ability to control and observe the internal states of a circuit. A representative of these techniques is a scan design approach using a shift register. (Here, the term *scan* refers to the ability to shift into or out of any state of a circuit.) Figure 5.2 shows a scan design technique proposed by Williams and Angell (1973).

In figure 5.2 the circuit is designed so that it has two modes of operation: a normal-function mode and a shift-register mode. A control signal can switch these two modes. In the shift-register mode, all flip-flops of the circuit are connected together in a chain to behave as shift register. Therefore, it is possible to shift an arbitrary test pattern into the flip-flops, and to shift out the contents of the flip-flops. The shift-register mode makes it possible to control and observe the internal state easily. By using this mode, the testing problem for sequential circuits can be completely reduced to one for combinational circuits. The procedure for testing such circuits is roughly as follows:

Switch to the shift-register mode and load the initial state for a test pattern into the flip-flops.

Return to the normal-function mode and apply the test input pattern.
Switch to the shift-register mode and shift out the final state while setting the starting state for the next test.

As this procedure shows, one can design any sequential circuit so that it will be treated as purely combinational by making use of the scan design techniques.

5.4 Ad Hoc Design and Structured Design

The concept of design for testability has a very wide range. One may desire the best testability even if the approach is expensive, or one may wish to enhance testability by a simple and inexpensive method. Hence, there are many different approaches to design for testability, depending on the degree of testability required.

Many of the approaches to design for testability can be classified as either ad hoc or structured (Williams and Parker 1982). The *ad hoc techniques* are directed at solving the testing problem for a given design but are not generally applicable to all designs. These techniques are completely heuristic rather than systematic. They are aimed at making a given design more testable by a simple and inexpensive method. Hence, they usually cost less than the structured approaches. The *structured techniques* are aimed at solving the general problem with a design methodology that uses a set of design rules to achieve good testability. These techniques are applied in the early design state. They are so systematic that when the designer has completed his design in pursuance of design rules, the expected testability will be achieved. Usually the structured approaches are more expensive than the ad hoc methods. However, in return for this added expense, the procedures of test generation and fault simulation are much simpler and more straightforward than those used with the ad hoc approaches. That is, the structured designs generally yield much better testability than the ad hoc designs.

Many products currently under development have boards containing many hundreds of devices, including several VLSI chips. It will be difficult or impossible to achieve the expected fault coverage at a reasonable cost unless structured design techniques are used for these complex circuits. On the other hand, to solve this problem in a simple and inexpensive way, several ad hoc techniques have been investigated.

In ad hoc techniques as well as in structured methods, there are two basic guidelines that lighten the tasks of test generation and test application. The first is to divide the circuit to be tested into small ones. This is based on the "divide and conquer" approach. As mentioned in section 4.1, the problem of test generation is in general NP-complete, and hence it is conjectured that the computing time grows exponentially in the worst case as circuits become larger. Actually, it has been observed that the computer run time to generate tests is approximately proportional to the number of gates to the power of 3 (Goel 1980). Therefore, dividing a circuit in half would reduce the test-generation task to one-eighth for each of the two divided subcircuits. The second guideline is to enhance controllability and observability. As described in section 5.1, the testability of a circuit is closely related to its controllability and observability, and hence enhancing controllability and observability is very effective in reducing the cost of test generation.

Dividing the Circuit

A circuit can be divided mechanically or logically. *Mechanical partitioning* (e.g., dividing a board in half) reduces the number of gates loaded on a board. This goes against the current stream of VLSI technology and defeats the cost advantages of integration.

Logical partitioning can be accomplished by adding extra logic. *Degating* is a simple technique for separating modules in a circuit by inserting extra gates between modules. Figure 5.3 shows two examples of degating logic. For both cases, a degate line and an AND gate are used to block signal propagation from the oscillator and module 1 by forcing their output to noncontrolling values. In figure 5.3(a), when the degate line is at the value 0 the oscillator is blocked and the external clock can propagate through the OR gate. As a result, all the logic in the circuit can easily be controlled by the external clock. Similarly, in figure 5.3(b), the control line can be used to drive directly into module 2 by setting the degate line to 0. In this way, degating can disconnect one portion of a circuit from another portion in order to make testing easier.

Another approach related to partitioning is the use of *bus-structured architecture*. This architecture has been used very successfully in microcomputers. Figure 5.4 shows a typical bus-structured microcomputer. The external tester can access three buses, which go to many different modules (microprocessor, ROMs, RAMs, and I/O interface circuits) on the computer board. Further, it can disconnect any module from the buses by

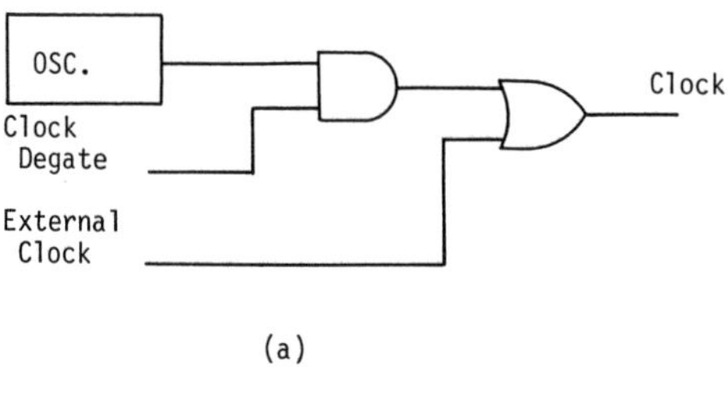

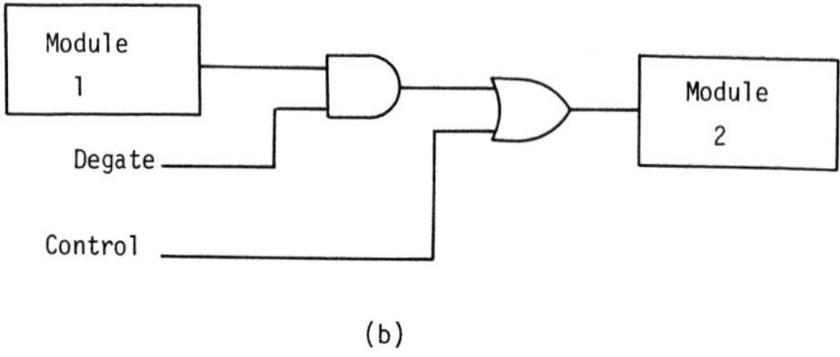

Figure 5.3
Degating logic

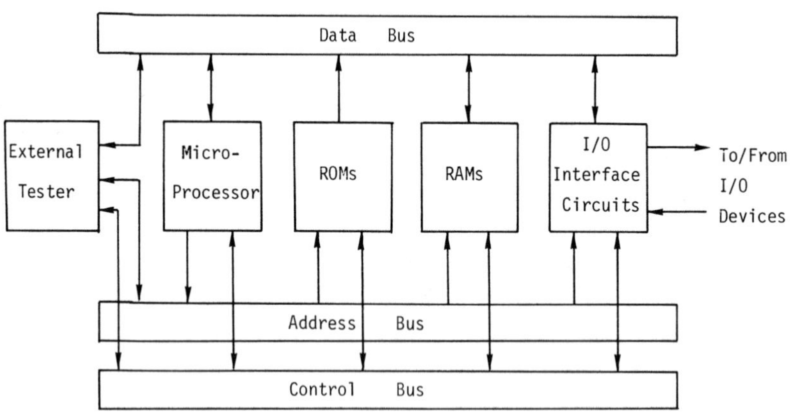

Figure 5.4
Bus-structured microcomputer

putting its output into a high-impedance state. These buses can be used to drive any module, as if they were primary inputs/outputs to that particular module. Since each module can be isolated from the buses, the partitioning is accomplished. The buses make it possible to test the computer boards by applying test patterns to each module separately.

Another technique that partitions the circuit under test is *in-circuit testing*, in which each chip on the board is tested independent of the other chips on the board. Chips not under test are disabled, or their outputs are forced to a desired state by overdriving them with large currents. Such in-circuit testing is usually performed in card testing by a *bed-of-nails* tester (Stewart 1977). The "nails" are spring-loaded pins arranged to contact chip pins on the noncomponent side of the card. That is, the bed-of-nails tester probes the underside of a board to give a larger number of points for controllability and observability. For each chip, the appropriate nails and/or edge pins are driven so as to prevent one chip from being driven by the other chips on the card, and then test patterns are applied to this logically isolated chip. The tests are much simpler and the test generation much easier than in edge-connector testing, since only one chip is tested at a time. On the other hand, this approach has some drawbacks. Since testing of interconnections is incomplete and the interactions among chips are neglected, it is not guaranteed that the board as a whole will work correctly. Also, care must be taken not to damage the circuit when overdriving it. Despite such disadvantages, in-circuit testing is very widely used and will become more necessary because of the increasing complexity of products.

Enhancing Controllability and Observability

A direct approach to enhancing the controllability and observability of a circuit is to use *test points* for the purpose of allowing the internal signals to be controlled and observed. Several techniques to identify how and where to add such test points have been studied theoretically by Hayes (1974), Hayes and Friedman (1974), and Saluja and Reddy (1974). Although these techniques can achieve a high level of testability, they require too many extra gates and pins to be used in practice.

Another technique based on testability analysis is used in practice to identify where to add test points. As mentioned in section 5.1, several testability measures are devised to find the areas of poor testability. A good testability measure indicates the difficulty of test generation in the circuit. This testability analysis can identify the areas of poor controllability and

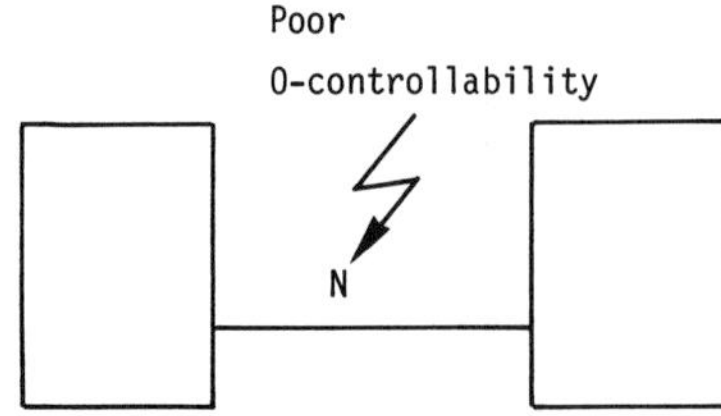

(a) Original circuit

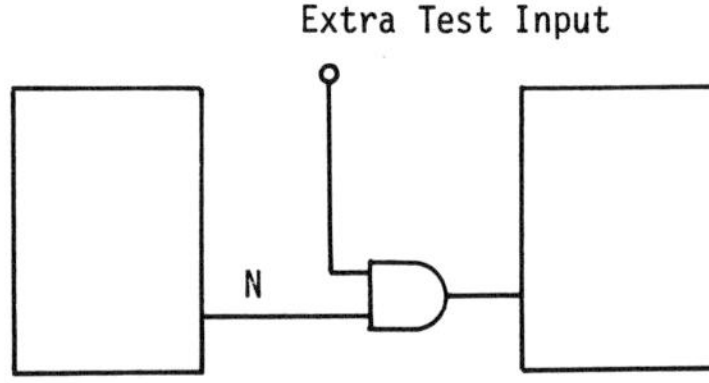

(b) Additional control gate

Figure 5.5
Test point for enhancing controllability

poor observability, and hence one can know where to add control inputs and observable outputs so as to enhance testability.

Using a test point as a primary input can enhance the controllability of a circuit, and using a test point as a primary output can enhance the observability of a circuit. In some cases, a single pin can be used as both an input and an output. For example, suppose that an internal node, say N in figure 5.5(a), is predicted to be too hard to set to value 0 by the testability analysis. Then the 0-controllability of N can be enhanced by a straightforward technique of embedding an AND gate, as shown in figure 5.5(b). Similarly, the 1-controllability can be enhanced by using an OR gate. These extra AND and OR gates may be replaced by wired-AND and wired-OR, respectively, though they depend on the circuit technology. Figure 5.6 shows a technique by which the JK flip-flop can be made directly resettable. This extra facility of resetting (or setting) a bistable flip-flop can significantly enhance the testability of the circuit. Since resetting the flip-flop ensures

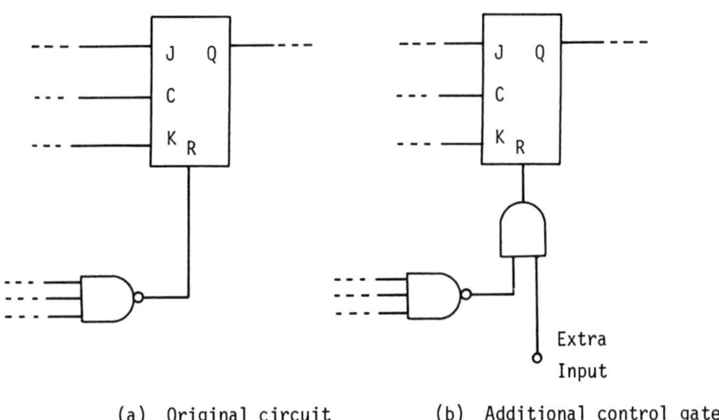

Figure 5.6
Test point for direct resetting

that the initial state is known, this lightens the task of test generation for sequential circuits. The drawback of this general technique for adding test points is that its applicability has a limit of extra pins.

In addition to these techniques, in-circuit testing approaches such as the bed-of-nails tester mentioned above also fall into the category of test points. Each of nails on the bed-of-nails tester can function as a test point. This technique is effective in simplifying test generation, but its applicability is limited since it depends on the physical design of electrical products. Boards that have devices on both sides or that have large numbers of device leads that are inaccessible to external probes cannot be tested by a bed-of-nails strategy. Also, systems might be completely sealed in plastic or be contained in their own cooling units. In such advanced products, in which in-circuit testing is powerless, structured design techniques may be needed to obtain good testability.

6 Design to Minimize the Cost of Test Application

The cost of testing consists mainly of the cost of test generation and the cost of test application. This chapter focuses on design methods that decrease the cost of test application. As a measure of the cost of applying test patterns, we adopt the number of test patterns applied and/or the number of reference comparisons made to test the circuit with the given test patterns. In general, the number of test patterns applied is the same as the number of references. However, in certain compression techniques the two values are independent.

Any circuit can be modified by embedding EOR gates so that the resulting circuit requires only five test patterns. This number of test patterns can be reduced to three by another approach, called a minimally testable design. This number, three, is believed to be minimal under the general fault assumption. However, to test only for faults at input/output terminals of modules or basic elements composing a circuit, two test patterns are sufficient for specially designed circuits using dual-mode logic. In addition to these design techniques, there is a technique in which the response patterns are compressed and compared with the expected value of only two bits.

In this chapter we consider only combinational circuits, since any sequential circuit can be designed so as to be treated as purely combinational by the scan design techniques proposed in chapter 8.

6.1 EOR Embedding

Hayes (1974) accomplished the design of logic circuits requiring very few test patterns for fault detection or location by embedding EOR gates in a given circuit so that the resulting circuit required only five test patterns. The procedure is very simple and can be described as follows. (Here, we assume that a given circuit N is composed only of NAND gates and inverters.)

Modification Procedure

Step 1 Decompose all NAND gates in N into a tree circuit of 2-input NAND gates and inverters.
Step 2 Remove all inverters.
Step 3 Insert an EOR gate with a controllable input and an observable output in the input lines of every gate.

The steps of the procedure can be understood through the example $f = x_1x_2x_3 + \bar{x}_1\bar{x}_2\bar{x}_3$, which is the same function considered by Hayes. A

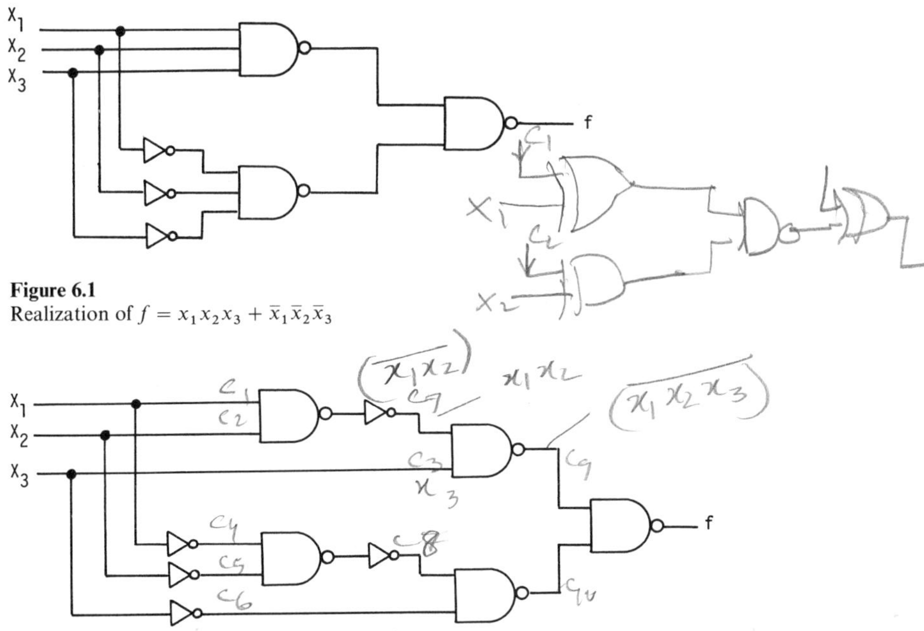

Figure 6.1
Realization of $f = x_1x_2x_3 + \bar{x}_1\bar{x}_2\bar{x}_3$

Figure 6.2
Realization of f after step 1

realization of f using only NAND gates and inverters is given in figure 6.1. Each 3-input NAND gate is replaced by two 2-input NAND gates and an inverter as shown in figure 6.2. After removing the inverters and inserting EOR gates in the input lines of every 2-input NAND gate, we obtain the circuit of figure 6.3. Note that each EOR gate has a primary input for controllability and a primary output for observability. The circuit of figure 6.3 can be made to realize $f = x_1x_2x_3 + \bar{x}_1\bar{x}_2\bar{x}_3$ by assigning $C_1 = C_2 = C_3 = C_9 = C_{10} = 0$ and $C_4 = C_5 = C_6 = C_7 = C_8 = 1$. From this, we can easily see that the circuit modified by the above-mentioned procedure can be made to realize the same function as the original circuit by applying 1 or 0 to the control inputs of the EOR gates.

The modified circuit can be decomposed into basic components like that shown in figure 6.4. Each basic component consists of two EOR gates with controllable inputs and observable outputs followed by a 2-input NAND gate. In order to fully test such a component, four test patterns 00, 01, 10, and 11 are needed to detect all stuck-at faults in each EOR gate, and

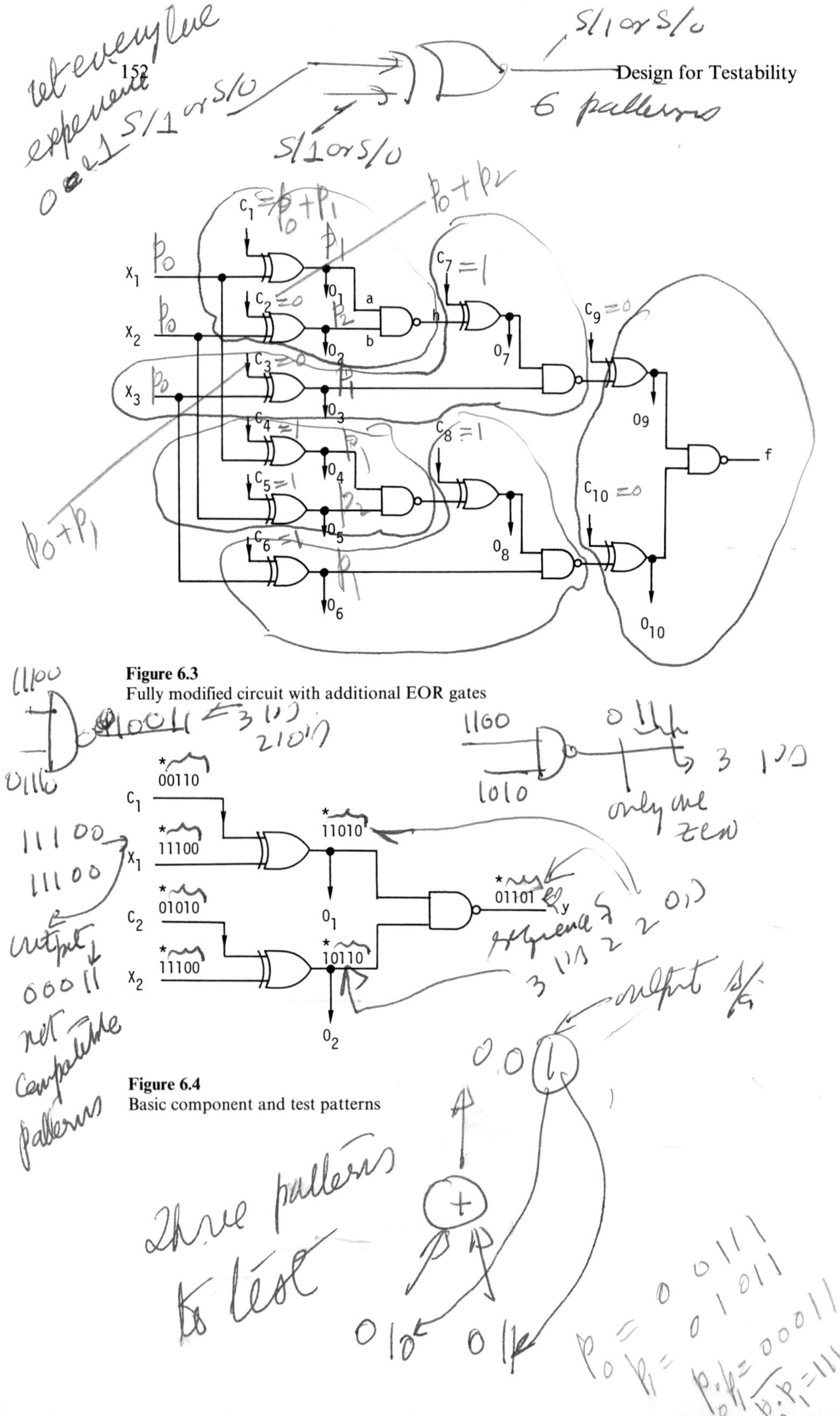

Figure 6.3
Fully modified circuit with additional EOR gates

Figure 6.4
Basic component and test patterns

three test patterns 01, 10, and 11 are needed for the 2-input NAND gate. This is accomplished by the four test patterns not flagged by an asterisk in figure 6.4. In these test patterns, only one 0 appears at the output y of the NAND gate. Hence, if the NAND gate is followed by another EOR gate, an additional 0 must appear at y. This extra test pattern is flagged by an asterisk in figure 6.4.

These five test patterns have the property that each five-bit sequence on the input and output lines except the control lines of EOR gates is a permutation of the sequence 00111. There are ten such permutations, denoted by the set $P = \{p_0, p_1, \ldots, p_9\}$ where

$p_0 = 00111,$

$p_1 = 01011,$

$p_2 = 01101,$

$p_3 = 01110,$

$p_4 = 10011,$

$p_5 = 10101,$

$p_6 = 10110,$

$p_7 = 11001,$

$p_8 = 11010,$

$p_9 = 11100.$

Now we define Boolean operations on n-bit sequences. If $s = a_1 a_2 \ldots a_n$ is an n-bit sequence, then the complement of s, denoted by $\bar{s}$, is the sequence $\bar{a}_1 \bar{a}_2 \ldots \bar{a}_n$. If $s = a_1 a_2 \ldots a_n$ and $t = b_1 b_2 \ldots b_n$ are two n-bit sequences, then their AND is

$$s \cdot t = (a_1 \cdot b_1)(a_2 \cdot b_2) \ldots (a_n \cdot b_n)$$

and their OR is

$$s + t = (a_1 + b_1)(a_2 + b_2) \ldots (a_n + b_n).$$

Two sequences p_i and p_j in P are said to be *compatible* if their NAND product, on a bit-for-bit basis, is in P. For example, $\overline{p_0 \cdot p_1} = 11100 = p_9$,

Table 6.1
$\overline{p_i p_j}$ for all compatible pairs in P

p_i \ p_j	0	1	2	3	4	5	6	7	8	9
0	—	9	8	7	9	8	7	—	—	—
1	9	—	6	5	9	—	—	6	5	—
2	8	6	—	4	—	8	—	6	—	4
3	7	5	4	—	—	—	7	—	5	4
4	9	9	—	—	—	3	2	3	2	—
5	8	—	8	—	3	—	1	3	—	1
6	7	—	—	7	2	1	—	—	2	1
7	—	6	6	—	3	3	—	—	0	0
8	—	5	—	5	2	—	2	0	—	0
9	—	—	4	4	—	1	1	0	0	—

and thus p_0 and p_1 are compatible; however, p_0 and p_9 are not compatible, since $\overline{p_0 \cdot p_9} = 11011$ is not in P. The results of $\overline{p_i \cdot p_j}$ for all compatible pairs in P are shown in table 6.1.

Hayes (1974) presented the following fundamental lemmas for compatible sequences.

LEMMA 6.1 If two compatible sequences are applied to a 2-input NAND gate G, they apply all four possible input patterns to G.

LEMMA 6.2 Let p_i in P be applied to the noncontrolled input of an EOR gate E and let a sequence s_i of length 5 be applied to the control input of E such that the output sequence $p_j\ (= p_i \oplus s_i)$ is in P. All four possible input patterns are applied to E by s_i and p_i if p_i and p_j are compatible.

Lemmas 6.1 and 6.2 guarantee that all stuck-at faults in the modified circuit can be detected by five test patterns if we can assign five-bit sequences to all internal lines in the circuit that satisfy the following conditions:

The two sequences applied to the inputs of each NAND gate are compatible.

The two sequences appearing on the output and on the noncontrolled input of each EOR gate are compatible.

Hayes called this the *compatibility constraint*. The existence of such assignments satisfying the compatibility constraint is guaranteed by the following lemma.

LEMMA 6.3 Given any (not necessary distinct) sequence p_i and p_j in P, there exists p_k in P such that both pairs $\{p_i, p_k\}$ and $\{p_j, p_k\}$ are compatible.

On the basis of the above observation, Hayes (1974) presented a procedure for assigning five-bit sequences to all lines such that the compatibility constraint is satisfied.

Assignment Procedure

Step 1 Apply any p_i in P to each primary input line.
Step 2 Suppose that p_i is applied to the noncontrolled input of an EOR gate E whose output is connected to input A of a NAND gate G. If no sequence has yet been assigned to the other input B of G, select any p_j that is compatible with p_i and apply $p_i \oplus p_j$ to the control input of E. Thus, p_j is assigned to line A. On the other hand, if p_k has already assigned to line B, then select a sequence p_m such that $\{p_i, p_m\}$ and $\{p_k, p_m\}$ are compatible pairs. Assign $p_i \oplus p_m$ to the control input of E.
Step 3 Repeat step 2 until sequences have been assigned to all lines of the circuit.

To understand this procedure, consider the circuit of figure 6.3. First, we assign p_0 to all primary inputs, i.e., $x_1 = x_2 = x_3 = p_0 = 00111$. We select p_1, which is compatible with p_0, and assign it to line a. Hence, $p_0 \oplus p_1 = 00111 \oplus 01011 = 01100$ is assigned to the control input C_1. Line b must be assigned a sequence that is compatible with both p_0 and p_1. From table 6.1 we find that both $\{p_0, p_2\}$ and $\{p_1, p_2\}$ are compatible pairs. Thus, we assign p_2 to line b. This implies that the output h of the gate has p_6. In this way we can assign five-bit sequences satisfying the compatibility constraint to all lines, as shown in table 6.2.

From lemmas 6.1 and 6.2 we can easily see that all four possible input patterns are applied to each EOR gate and the response is observed directly at the output of the EOR gate, and similarly that all four input patterns are applied to each NAND gate and the response is observed at the output of the following EOR gate. Hence, all stuck-at faults in the circuit are completely detected by these five test patterns, and we have the following theorem.

Table 6.2
Assignment satisfying compatibility constraint

Input	Sequence		Output	Sequence	
x_1	p_0	00111	O_1	p_1	01011
x_2	p_0	00111	O_2	p_2	01101
x_3	p_0	00111	O_3	p_1	01011
C_1	$p_0 + p_1$	01100	O_4	p_1	01011
C_2	$p_0 + p_2$	01010	O_5	p_2	01101
C_3	$p_0 + p_1$	01100	O_6	p_1	01011
C_4	$p_0 + p_1$	01100	O_7	p_0	00111
C_5	$p_0 + p_2$	01010	O_8	p_0	00111
C_6	$p_0 + p_1$	01100	O_9	p_2	01101
C_7	$p_6 + p_0$	10001	O_{10}	p_3	01110
C_8	$p_6 + p_0$	10001	f	p_4	10011
C_9	$p_9 + p_2$	10001			
C_{10}	$p_9 + p_3$	10010			

THEOREM 6.1 (Hayes 1974) Every combinational circuit N can be modified by adding control logic to yield a circuit N' that requires five test patterns to detect all single and multiple stuck-at faults.

The procedures and results mentioned above can be extended to sequential circuits. For further discussion see Hayes (1974).

6.2 Minimally Testable Design

Saluja and Reddy (1974) reduced the number of test patterns further. They showed that any circuit can be modified such that three test patterns are sufficient to detect all single and multiple stuck-at faults in a circuit.

In general, any n-input gate of AND, OR, NAND, or NOR requires $n + 1$ test patterns to detect all single and multiple stuck-at faults on its inputs or its outputs. For a primitive 2-input AND gate, at least three test patterns, 01, 10, and 11, are needed to detect all stuck-at faults. Therefore, three might be considered the lower bound on the number of test patterns needed to test all stuck-at faults in a circuit. In this sense, the design of Saluja and Reddy can be said to be the minimally testable design.

First, consider the 3-input AND gate illustrated in figure 6.5(a). Figure

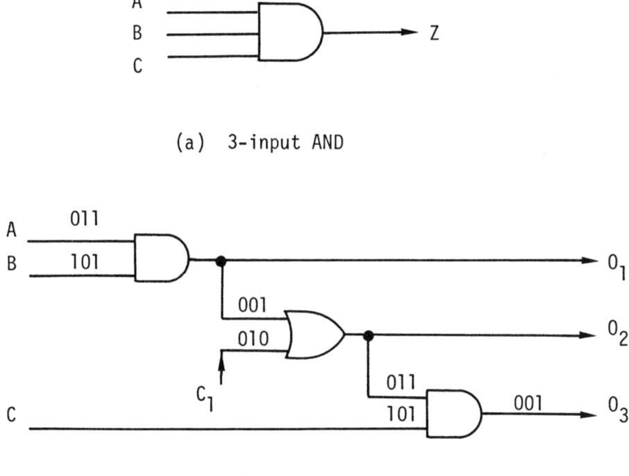

Figure 6.5
Minimally testable 3-input AND

6.5(b) gives a realization in which three input patterns can fully test all single and multiple stuck-at faults on their inputs or outputs in the circuit. In this figure the 3-input AND gate has been replaced by two 2-input AND gates, and a 2-input OR gate has been inserted between them with a controllable input C_1 and observable outputs O_1, O_2, and O_3. By expanding a 3-input gate into 2-input gates, we can apply the three input patterns shown in the figure to each 2-input gate and observe the response at the output of each gate. It is easy to see that those three input patterns can test all single and multiple stuck-at faults in the circuit.

Similarly, we can obtain the minimally testable circuit that realizes an n-input AND gate, as shown in figure 6.6. Three test patterns are given in the figure. For other types of gates, such as OR, NAND, and NOR gates, we can consider similar circuits. Figure 6.7 illustrates the minimally testable realization for a 3-input OR gate and its test patterns.

The test patterns for a 2-input AND gate, 01, 10, and 11, can be obtained by applying any two distinct sequences from the set $S_1 = \{011, 101, 110\}$. Similarly, the test patterns for a 2-input OR gate are 01, 10, and 00, which can be applied by taking any two distinct sequences from the set $S_2 = \{100, 010, 001\}$. Hence, the application of any two distinct sequences from S_1 (S_2) is necessary and sufficient to detect any stuck-at fault in the 2-

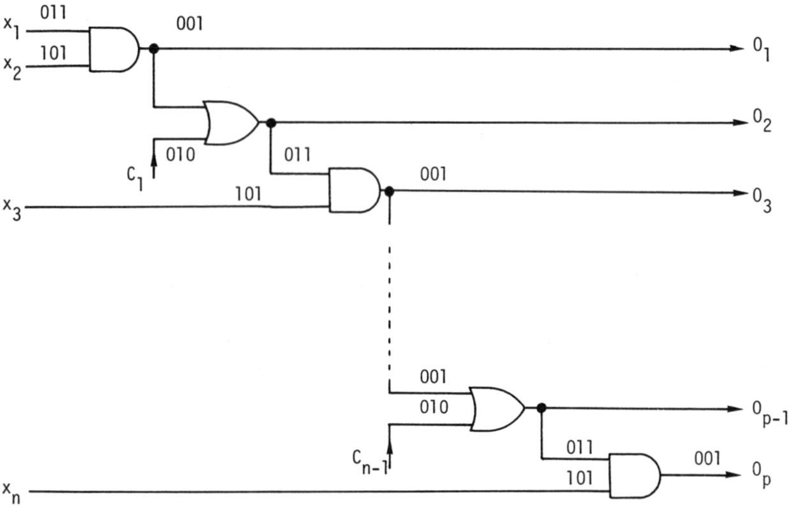

Figure 6.6
Testable realization of n-input gate

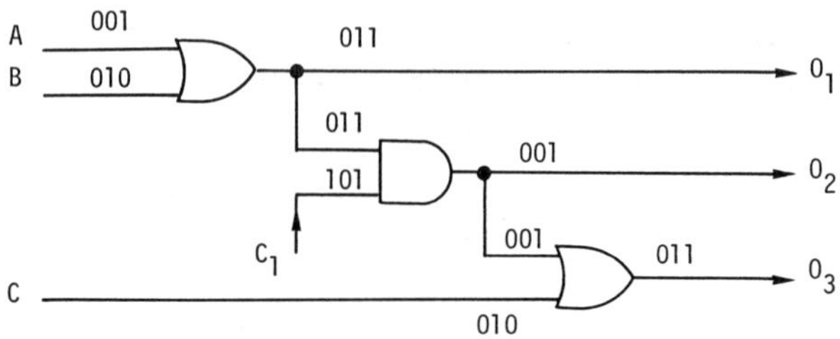

Figure 6.7
Minimally testable 3-input OR

input AND/NAND (OR/NOR) gate. In figure 6.5, 6.6, and 6.7, we can see that all test sequences assigned to the gates are taken from set S_1 or set S_2, depending on whether the gate is of the AND type (AND or NAND) or the OR type (OR or NOR). Furthermore, these sets S_1 and S_2 satisfy the following properties:

If s is in S_1 (S_2), then $\bar{s}$ is in S_2 (S_1).
If both s_1 and s_2 are in S_1, then $s_1 \cdot s_2$ is in S_2, where $s_1 \neq s_2$.
If both s_1 and s_2 are in S_2, then $s_1 + s_2$ is in S_1, where $s_1 \neq s_2$.

Saluja and Reddy also introduced the term *compatible* in the same sense as in section 6.1, though it is defined differently as follows: Two 3-bit sequences appearing at the two inputs of a gate are said to be compatible if they can detect all stuck-at fault on its inputs or its output. Hence, for an AND gate, if s_1 and s_2 are in S_1 and $s_1 \neq s_2$, then s_1 and s_2 are compatible. However, all other pairs are incompatible. For example, {110, 011} is a compatible pair, but {110, 110}, {110, 001}, and {100, 001} are incompatible pairs for a 2-input AND gate.

The procedure for modifying a given circuit so that it can be tested only by three test patterns is as follows. (Here, for the sake of simplicity of argument, the circuit is assumed to be composed only of AND, OR, and NOT gates, though the procedure can be applied to more general circuits including NAND and NOR gates.)

Modification Procedure

Step 1 Change all AND/OR gates in the realization to a tree of 2-input AND/OR gates.
Step 2 Assign arbitrary sequences from $S_1 \cup S_2$ to all the primary inputs.
Step 3 If the two sequences applied to the inputs of a gate are incompatible, then modify the gate by introducing control logic such that only the compatible sequences appear at the inputs of the gate.

There are many cases for this modification. Figure 6.8 illustrates modification for an AND gate with incompatible sequences. Figure 6.8(a) shows an instance where both sequences are from set S_1 and are the same. Figure 6.8(b) gives the modification for an instance where one sequence is from S_1 and the other from S_2. In figure 6.8(c), both sequences are from S_2.

Step 4 Repeat step 3 until all gates in the circuit have been assigned only by compatible sequences.

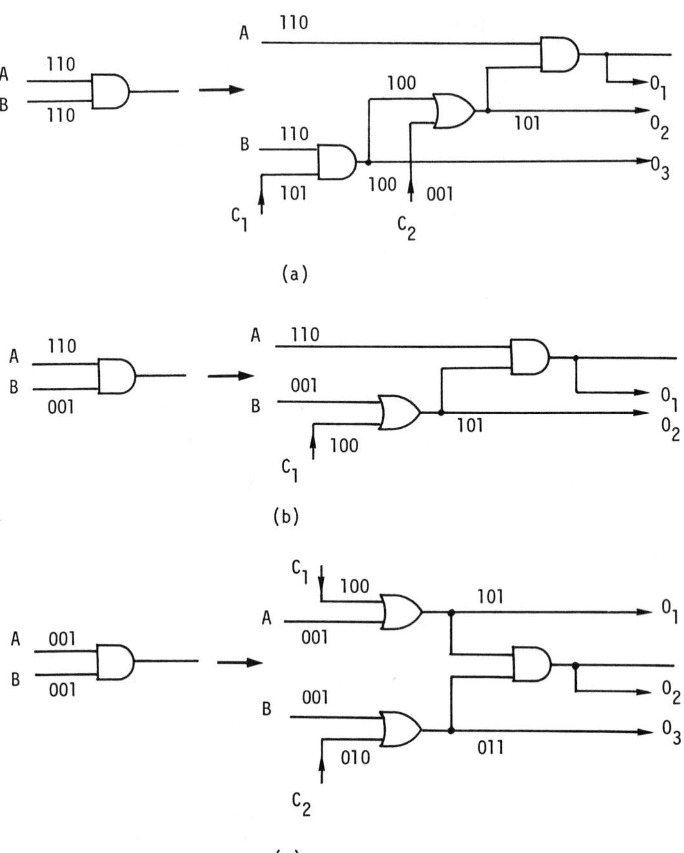

Figure 6.8
Modification for incompatible pairs

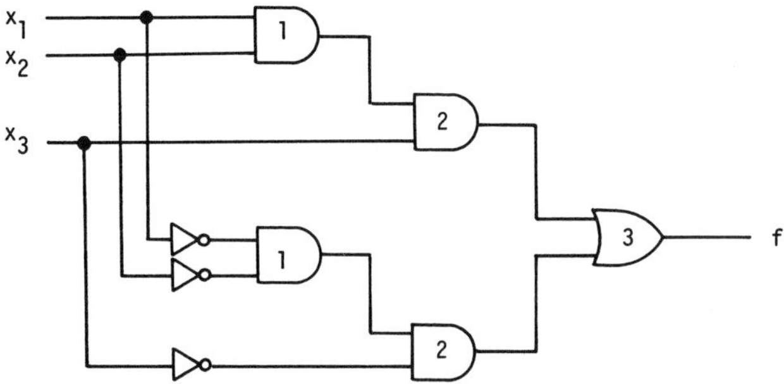

Figure 6.9
Realization of $f = x_1 x_2 x_3 + \bar{x}_1 \bar{x}_2 \bar{x}_3$ after step 1

As an illustration of this procedure, consider the circuit realizing $f = x_1 x_2 x_3 + \bar{x}_1 \bar{x}_2 \bar{x}_3$, which is the same example considered in section 6.1. After step 1, we obtain the circuit of figure 6.9. With the assignments $x_1 = 110$, $x_2 = 101$, and $x_3 = 010$, two incompatible sequences first appear, as shown in figure 6.10. Using the modification technique illustrated in figure 6.8, we can finally obtain the circuit of figure 6.11, in which only compatible sequences appear at the inputs of all the gates. Since all the gates in the modified circuit are applied by compatible sequences, the tests can detect all single and multiple stuck-at faults. Thus, we have the following theorem.

THEOREM 6.2 (Saluja and Reddy 1974) Every combinational circuit can be modified by the addition of control logic to yield a circuit that requires three test patterns to detect all single and multiple stuck-at faults.

6.3 Dual-Mode Logic

As was shown in the preceding section, any circuit can be modified by the addition of extra logic so that all single and multiple stuck-at faults can be tested with only three test patterns. This number, three, is believed to be minimal under the general fault assumption. However, if we assume a more stringent fault condition, we can arrive at a method of designing circuits that require only two test patterns to detect those faults. Inose and Sakauchi (1972) and DasGupta et al. (1980) have shown that logic circuits built with modules they define can be tested with two test patterns. Both of these approaches are based on the idea of *dual-mode logic*, where a circuit is tested in one mode while the normal function of the circuit is performed in another mode.

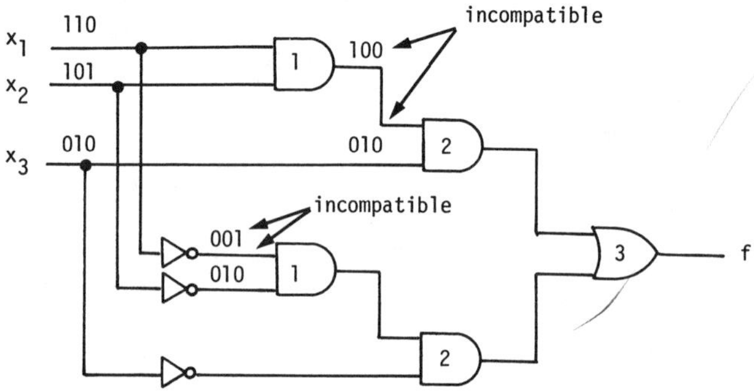

Figure 6.10
Compatible and incompatible pairs

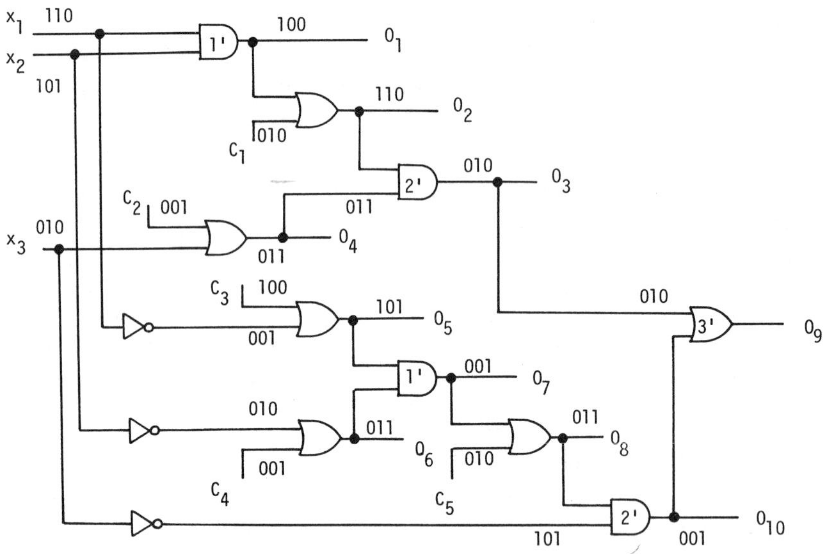

Figure 6.11
Minimally testable realization of $f = x_1 x_2 x_3 + \bar{x}_1 \bar{x}_2 \bar{x}_3$

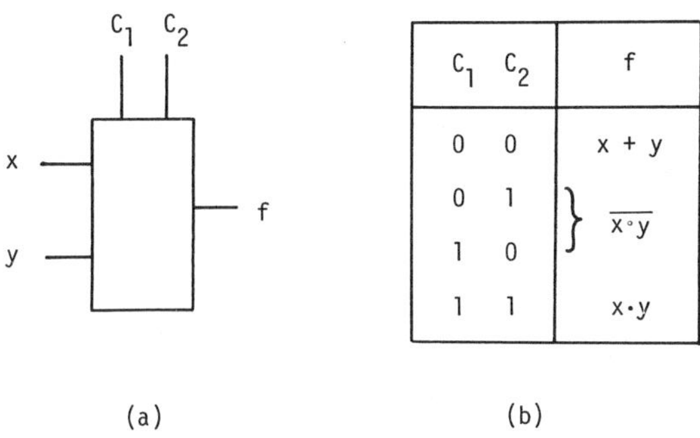

Figure 6.12
Module M_1

First, consider the module M_1, illustrated in figure 6.12(a). The module has two inputs (x and y) and two control inputs (C_1 and C_2). It realizes three functions (OR, NAND, and AND) by changing the control inputs C_1 and C_2 as shown in figure 6.12(b). Such a module is called a *function-conversion unit* by Inose and Sakauchi (1972). The logic circuits of the proposed method are constructed by using such a function-conversion unit as shown in figure 6.13. The normal function of the circuit can be realized by converting all modules into NANDs, since NAND is functionally complete. When the circuit is tested, all the modules in the circuit are converted into ANDs or ORs. After converting all the modules into ANDs (i.e., setting $C_1 = C_2 = 1$), we apply the test pattern $(x_1, x_2, \ldots, x_n) = (1, 1, \ldots, 1)$. This test pattern can detect any multiple stuck-at-0 fault at input/output terminals of modules provided that the control inputs are fault-free, since such a stuck-at-0 fault causes 0 at some output of the circuit. Similarly, after changing all the modules into OR functions (i.e., setting $C_1 = C_2 = 0$), we apply the test pattern $(x_1, x_2, \ldots, x_n) = (0, 0, \ldots, 0)$, which can detect any multiple stuck-at-1 fault at input/output terminals of modules provided that the control inputs are fault-free. Hence, for a circuit built with such modules, as shown in figure 6.12, two test patterns—all zeros and all ones—are sufficient to detect any stuck-at-0 or stuck-at-1 fault at input/output terminals of the modules except control lines.

This is illustrated by the circuit realization of $f = x_1 \oplus x_2$ as shown in figure 6.14. The test patterns are $(C_1, C_2, x_1, x_2) = (0, 0, 0, 0)$ and $(1, 1, 1, 1)$. Suppose there is a stuck-at-1 fault at input A of module 2. When the test pattern $(0, 0, 0, 0)$ is applied, all the modules are converted into ORs and

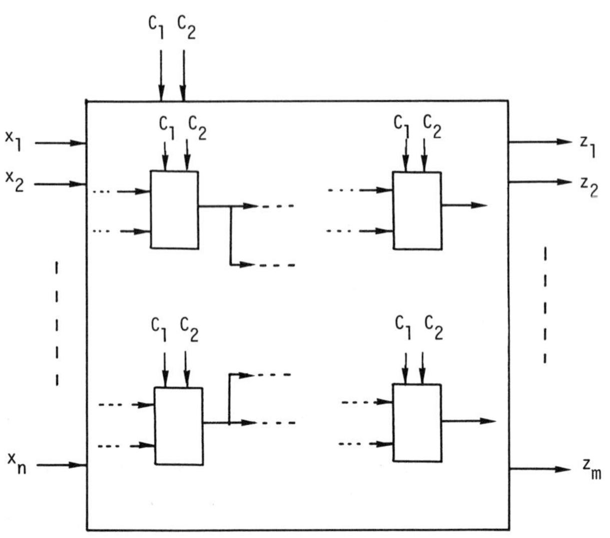

Figure 6.13
Logic circuit built with modules

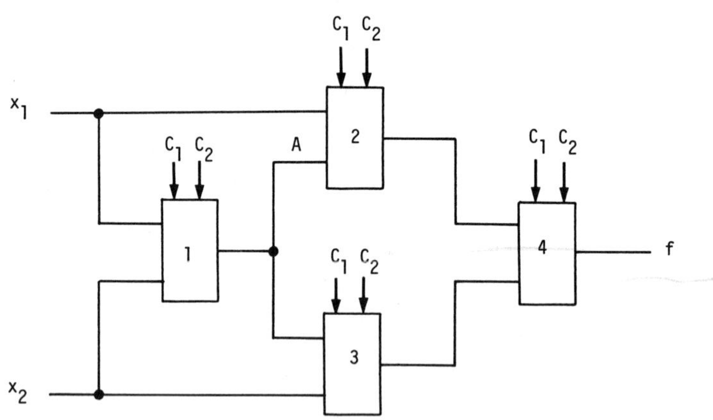

Figure 6.14
Realization of $f = x_1 \oplus x_2$ using module M_1

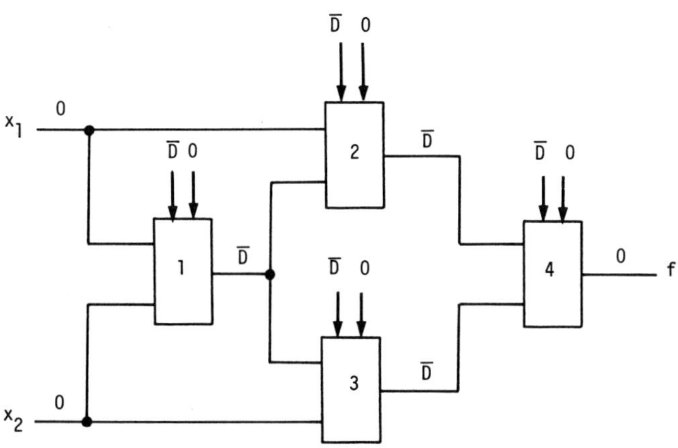

Figure 6.15
Untestable fault at control line

thus the above fault causes value 1 on the output of module 2, which propagates to the output of the circuit. From the principle of duality, we can see that the other test pattern, (1, 1, 1, 1), detects a stuck-at-0 fault at input *A* of module 2. However, it is not guaranteed that the above two test patterns can detect any single stuck-at fault at control lines C_1 and C_2. For example, consider a stuck-at-1 fault at line C_1. Obviously, the test pattern (1, 1, 1, 1) cannot detect the fault. Further, the other test pattern, (0, 0, 0, 0), cannot detect it either, as figure 6.15 shows. It has been proved by DasGupta et al. (1980) that at least four control inputs are necessary to detect all single stuck-at faults, including control input faults, with two function-independent test patterns.

A dual-mode logic circuit proposed by DasGupta et al. (1980) also has the structure shown in figure 6.13. A dual-mode logic circuit is composed of modules, and extra control inputs are common to all these modules. DasGupta et al. showed that four control inputs are necessary and sufficient to derive a dual-mode logic circuit that allows function-independent testing of faults at the terminals with two predefined test patterns. Table 6.3 is the general truth table of dual-mode logic modules with four control inputs: C_1, C_2, C_3, and C_4. If a circuit with input $x_1, x_2, \ldots, x_n$ is built with modules whose truth table is that shown in table 6.3, then we can show that two test patterns, $(C_1, C_2, C_3, C_4, x_1, \ldots, x_n) = (0, \ldots, 0)$ and $(1, \ldots, 1)$, detect all single stuck-at faults at input/output terminals of modules. From table 6.3

Table 6.3
Truth table of dual-mode logic modules

C_1	C_2	C_3	C_4	$d_1 \ldots\ldots d_{m-1}$	d_m	f
0	0	0	0	0 0	0	0 test
0	0	0	0	0 0	1	1
0	0	0	0	0 1	0	1
	⋮			⋮		⋮
0	0	0	0	1 1	1	1
0	0	0	1			
0	0	1	0	x x	x	1
0	1	0	0			
1	0	0	0			
0	0	1	1			
0	1	0	1	At least one		
1	0	0	1	segment for an		
0	1	1	0	arbitary function		
1	0	1	0			
1	1	0	0			
0	1	1	1			
1	0	1	1	x x	x	0
1	1	0	1			
1	1	1	0			
1	1	1	1	0 0	0	0
	⋮			⋮		⋮
1	1	1	1	1 1	0	0
1	1	1	1	1 1	1	1 test

it is easily seen that if the test pattern $(C_1, C_2, C_3, C_4, d_1, \ldots, d_m) = (0, \ldots, 0)$ (or $(1, \ldots, 1)$) is applied, any pattern of m or fewer stuck-at-1 (or s-a-0) faults at $d_1, d_2, \ldots, d_m$ changes the output to the complement of the expected output, where $d_1, d_2, \ldots, d_m$ are inputs of the module. Hence, any stuck-at-1 (or s-a-0) fault at noncontrol input/output terminals of modules is detected by the test pattern $(0, \ldots, 0)$ (or $(1, \ldots, 1)$). Similarly, in table 6.3 all the input patterns Hamming distance 1 from $(0, \ldots, 0)$ and $(1, \ldots, 1)$ have the different output values from that of $(0, \ldots, 0)$ and $(1, \ldots, 1)$, respectively. Hence, any single stuck-at fault at control inputs can be detected by test patterns $(0, \ldots, 0)$ and $(1, \ldots, 1)$. Consequently, the following theorem holds.

THEOREM 6.3 (DasGupta et al. 1980) In any n-input dual-mode logic circuit built with modules whose truth tables are as shown in table 6.3, two

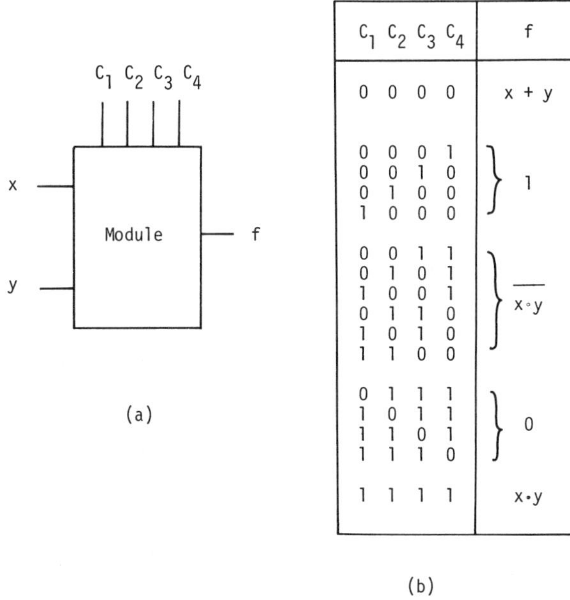

C_1 C_2 C_3 C_4	f
0 0 0 0	x + y
0 0 0 1 0 0 1 0 0 1 0 0 1 0 0 0	1
0 0 1 1 0 1 0 1 1 0 0 1 0 1 1 0 1 0 1 0 1 1 0 0	$\overline{x \circ y}$
0 1 1 1 1 0 1 1 1 1 0 1 1 1 1 0	0
1 1 1 1	x·y

(b)

Figure 6.16
Module M_2

test patterns, $(C_1, C_2, C_3, C_4, x_1, \ldots, x_n) = (0, \ldots, 0)$ and $(1, \ldots, 1)$, can detect any pattern of stuck-at faults at the input/output terminals of the circuit or the modules, provided that faults in the control inputs affect, at most, one control input of each module.

As an example, consider the module M_2 illustrated in figure 6.16, which has two inputs (x and y) and four control inputs, realizes a NAND function in the normal mode, and satisfies the truth table 6.3. For any dual-mode logic circuit constructed by this module, two test patterns, $(0, \ldots, 0)$ and $(1, \ldots, 1)$, detect all single stuck-at faults at input/output terminals of modules in the circuit.

6.4 Testing with Fixed Reference Values

In the preceding sections, we considered several deign approaches to minimizing the number of test patterns. Each technique described there achieves a very low cost of test application. However, all require so much extra

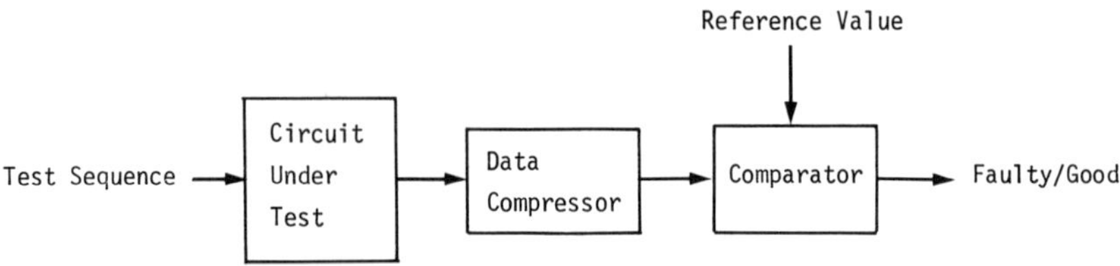

Figure 6.17
Testing scheme for data compression

hardware, including gates and I/0 pins, that they can hardly be put to practical use. This section presents another approach (described in Fujiwara and Kinoshita 1978) to minimizing the cost of test application without changing or modifying the circuit under test. The approach is a test-data-compression technique in which the response patterns are compressed and compared with the expected value of only two bits.

The scheme considered here is illustrated in figure 6.17. A sequence of test patterns are applied to the circuit under test. The response of the circuit is transformed by some data-compression function and then compared against a previously obtained reference value. The circuit under test is certified to be fault-free if and only if the two values are identical.

We first consider single-output combinational circuits. In the data-compression box of figure 6.17, data-compression functions called *count functions* are used. Let $R = r_1 r_2 \ldots r_m$ be any binary sequence. Here we consider the count functions

$$c_1(R) = \sum_{i=2}^{m} r_{i-1} \oplus r_i \qquad \text{(transition count)},$$

$$c_2(R) = \sum_{i=2}^{m} \overline{r_{i-1}} \cdot r_i \qquad \text{(rising edge count)},$$

$$c_3(R) = \sum_{i=2}^{m} r_{i-1} \cdot \overline{r_i} \qquad \text{(falling edge count)}.$$

Let T be any multiple-fault test set for a single-output combinational circuit. Let T^0 (T^1) be all test patterns in T producing output 0 (1), and let $n = |T|$, $n_0 = |T^0|$, and $n_1 = |T^1|$ where $|A|$ is the cardinality of the set A. We define a test sequence denoted by α_T with respect to the test set T as

$$t_1^0 t_2^0 \cdots t_{n_0}^0 t_1^0 t_1^1 t_2^1 \cdots t_{n_1}^1 t_1^1$$

where $T^0 = \{t_1^0, t_2^0, \ldots, t_{n_0}^0\}$ and $T^1 = \{t_1^1, t_2^1, \ldots, t_{n_1}^1\}$.

In the schemes proposed in this section, one or more count functions will be used to implement the data compressor shown in figure 6.17. In general, we assume that an m-tuple $C = (c_{i_1}, c_{i_2}, \ldots, c_{i_m})$, where $m \geqslant 1$, of count functions is being used for testing.

For a given class of faults, a circuit under test is called *testable* by a count function C and a test sequence S if, for every fault in the class, the value of C is different from the reference value.

Before we consider testing schemes that provide considerable compression of test response data such that the response data can be compressed into two bits independent of the number of test patterns, note the following fundamental lemma, which gives an equivalence class of count functions.

LEMMA 6.4 The following conditions are all equivalent:

(1) $R = 0^p 1^q$ for some $p > 0$ and $q > 0$.
(2) $c_2(R) = 1$ and $c_3(R) = 0$.
(3) $c_1(R) = 1$ and $c_2(R) = 1$.
(4) $c_1(R) = 1$ and $c_3(R) = 0$.

Proof It is obvious that condition 1 implies conditions 2–4.

Assume that condition 2 holds, i.e., $c_2(R) = 1$ and $c_3(R) = 0$. Then, $c_3(R) = 0$ implies that R has the form $0^p 1^q$ where $p \geqslant 0$ and $q \geqslant 0$. Moreover, $c_2(R) = 1$ implies that both p and q are positive. Therefore, we have that condition 2 implies condition 1. From the definitions of count functions c_1, c_2, and c_3 we have $c_1(R) = c_2(R) + c_3(R)$. Hence, it is obvious that conditions 2, 3, and 4 are all equivalent. ■

THEOREM 6.4 Let T be any multiple-fault test set for a single-output combinational circuit. Then the circuit is testable by the test sequence α_T and any distinct pair (c_i, c_j) of count functions. The reference values of c_1, c_2, and c_3 are 1, 1, and 0, respectively.

Proof Let $T = \{T^0, T^1\}$, $T^0 = \{t_1^0, t_2^0, \ldots, t_{n_0}^0\}$, and $T^1 = \{t_1^1, t_2^1, \ldots, t_{n_1}^1\}$. The test sequence α_T has the form

$$t_1^0 t_2^0 \cdots t_{n_0}^0 t_1^0 t_1^1 t_2^1 \cdots t_{n_1}^1 t_1^1,$$

and the fault-free response R is $0^{n_0+1} 1^{n_1+1}$.

Let (c_i, c_j) be any distinct pair of count functions, and let e_i and e_j be reference values of c_i and c_j, respectively. Then, from lemma 6.4, $R = 0^{n_0+1} 1^{n_1+1}$ implies $c_i(R) = e_i$ and $c_j(R) = e_j$.

Conversely, assume that another sequence S also has $c_i(S) = e_i$ and $c_j(S) = e_j$. Then, from lemma 6.4, S has the form 0^p1^q where $p > 0$ and $q > 0$ and $p + q = n + 2$. If both sequences S and R are distinct, then either $n_0 + 1 > p$ or $n_0 + 1 < p$. In the case of $n_0 + 1 > p$, the output value of test t_1^0 in S must be 1. Thus, the leftmost value of S is also 1, and this contradicts that S has the form 0^p1^q for $p > 0$ and $q > 0$. In thc case of $n_0 + 1 < p$, the output value of test t_1^1 in S must be 0, and similarly we have the contradiction.

Hence, R and S must be identical. This implies that any response S satisfying $c_i(S) = e_i$ and $c_j(S) = e_j$ is only $0^{n_0+1}1^{n_1+1}$. ■

If we use the test sequence α_T of length $n + 2$, the testing schemes suggested in theorem 6.4 require storing only two bits of responses, since the reference values of count functions are constants 0 and 1. Thus such testing schemes have the following properties: Considerable compression of test response data is achieved; very simple test equipment is required, and it is independent of the circuit under test; and complete fault detection is provided.

When a logic circuit has more than one output, the problem of compressing test data is not straightforward generalization of the single-output case, because all the outputs are assumed to be monitored simultaneously. Thus, it is no longer possible to order test patterns to suit individual outputs. In Fujiwara and Kinoshita 1978 it was shown that, for multiple-output combinational circuits, response data can be compressed through the use of generalized count functions. For more details, see the literature.

7 Design to Minimize the Cost of Test Generation

The optimal design to minimize the cost of test generation is achieved by eliminating the expensive stage of test generation. This can be accomplished by a technique called universal testing or function-independent testing, in which test patterns can be predetermined independent of the function being realized. Some of the techniques mentioned in chapter 6 belong to this approach. However, though these techniques are of great theoretical interest, the enormous hardware requirement is practically prohibitive.

If it is required only to reduce the cost of test generation within the limitations of permitted extra hardware complexity and tolerated performance degradation, an attempt should be made heuristically through ad hoc methods such as inserting test points. Hayes and Friedman (1974) proposed a method for selecting test points to reduce the number of test patterns for fault detection in combinational circuits, but the number of test points required is still large. Coy and Vogel (1981) developed a method of inserting test points to simplify test generation. The approach of Coy and Vogel—breaking up pairs of reconvergent paths by test points—is based on the fact that the existence of reconvergent paths may force faults to become difficult or impossible to detect.

In this chapter, we consider design for universal testability in which no test generation is required. A trivial example of universal testing is exhaustive testing, which requires that all 2^n patterns be applied to the inputs of the circuit under test. One approach based on exhaustive testing is the partitioning of the circuit into small parts by multiplexing; another is syndrome-testable design. Other approaches to universal testing involve designing circuits with regular structures, such as Reed-Muller canonic circuits and programmable logic arrays.

7.1 Partitioning and Exhaustive Testing

Exhaustive testing requires the application of all 2^n input combinations for n-input circuits. It is obvious that difficulty arises immediately when n becomes large. Exhaustive testing might be tolerable for $n \leqslant 20$, which is equivalent to about 1 second of testing with a 1-MHz machine. For $n > 20$, however, the problem is no more solvable in a reasonable amount of time.

A common approach to solving a large problem is to partition the problem into small parts, find solutions for the parts, and then combine the solutions for the parts into a solution for the whole. This "divide and conquer" approach often yields efficient solutions to problems in which the subproblems are smaller versions of the original problem. Testing is no exception to this rule. The problem of exhaustive testing for large circuits can be overcome by partitioning the circuit into subcircuits such that every subcircuit is small enough to be tested exhaustively in a reasonable amount of time.

This was considered by Sakauchi et al. (1975), Bozorgui-Nesbat and McCluskey (1980) (see also McCluskey and Bozorgui-Nesbat 1981), and Oklobdzija and Ercegovac (1982). Their methods enhance the testability of a circuit by partitioning it into subcircuits with the following properties:

Each subcircuit has few enough inputs that all possible combinations of its inputs can be applied to test it.
It must be possible to directly control the inputs to each of the subcircuits and to directly observe the responses of the subcircuits.

The method proposed by Sakauchi et al. (1975) is based on the concept of bypassing subcircuits. Figure 7.1 presents the block diagrams of the implementation of this technique. In the figure, multiplexers are used to propagate the values on the inputs directly to the outputs by bypassing the subcircuit. Figure 7.1(a) shows the case that satisfies

$$n_i \leqslant n_o \leqslant n_p + n_i$$

where n_p, n_i, and n_o are the number of primary inputs, the number of internal linking inputs, and the number of outputs of the subcircuit, respectively. Figure 7.1(b) shows the implementation in the case of $n_i > n_o$.

In order to test one of these subcircuits, multiplexers are controlled so that all subcircuits except the one under test are bypassed. This makes it possible to access directly all the inputs and outputs of the subcircuit under test from outside the circuit, and thus the subcircuit can be tested exhaustively. In this way, exhaustive testing for all subcircuits is performed by controlling multiplexers in the whole circuit. To speed up the testing of the whole circuit, some subcircuits are tested simultaneously if the propagation paths associated with those subcircuits are disjoint or separated from one another.

The approach of Bozorgui-Nesbat and McCluskey (1980) is similar. Let us decompose a circuit G with input X and output Y into two subcircuits, G_1 and G_2, with disjoint sets of inputs and outputs and internal linking buses (figure 7.2). For direct access to linking lines, some multiplexers are added, as shown in figure 7.3(a). In normal circuit operation, the internal

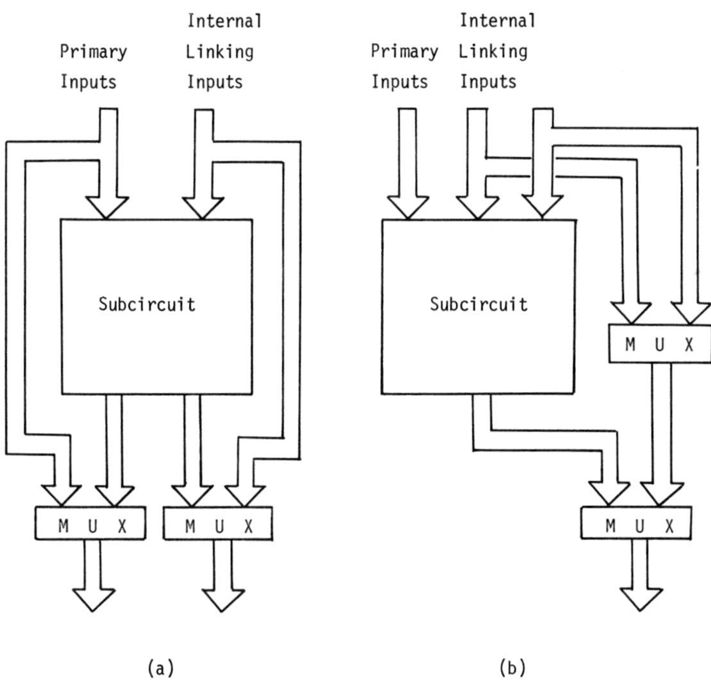

Figure 7.1
Bypassing subcircuits (Sakauchi et al. 1975; © AFIPS 1975)

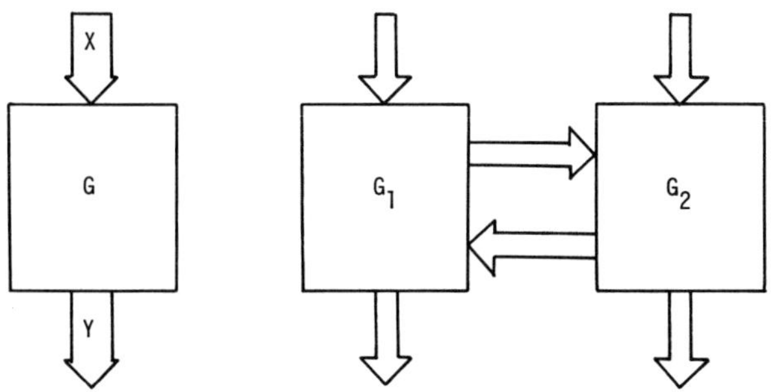

Figure 7.2
Partitioning (Bozorgui-Nesbat and McCluskey 1980; © IEEE 1980)

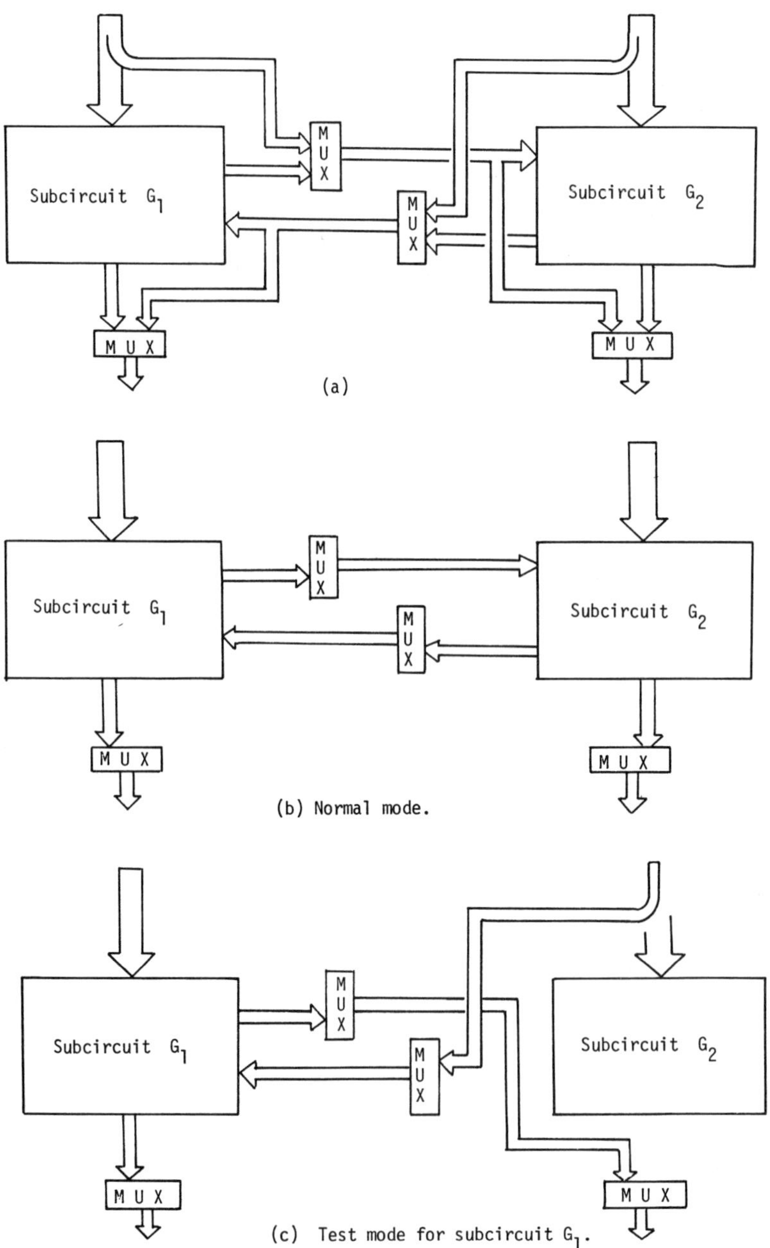

Figure 7.3
Partitioning scheme using multiplexers (Bozorgui-Nesbat and McCluskey 1980; © IEEE 1980)

input of each subcircuit is connected to the internal output of the other subcircuit through the linking multiplexers and the external output of each subcircuit is routed to the output pins via the output multiplexers. This is illustrated in figure 7.3(b). On the other hand, in order to test subcircuit G_1 it is necessary to access the linking lines directly from (to) external inputs (outputs). This is performed by controlling the linking multiplexers as shown in figure 7.3(c). In this mode of testing, test patterns are applied directly to G_1 from external inputs independent of the other subcircuit, G_2. Hence, exhaustive testing for G_1 is possible. Similarly, subcircuit G_2 can be tested exhaustively by controlling multiplexers.

In the implementation shown in figure 7.3, the width of each link must be less than the width of the external input/output of the corresponding subcircuit. Moreover, in order to make such a decomposition meaningful, the width of the input of each subcircuit must be less than the width of the unmodified circuit input.

Bozorgui-Nesbat and McCluskey (1980) also presented a generalized method for including an arbitrary number of partitions instead of two. Figure 7.4 is a block diagram of a circuit partitioned into three subcircuits.

McCluskey and Bozorgui-Nesbat (1981) proposed a technique for designing autonomously testable circuits. The proposed method is based on built-in testing in which test patterns are applied internally by built-in test equipment. A linear-feedback shift register (LFSR) is used as built-in test circuitry. All 2^n input patterns except the $(0, 0, \ldots, 0)$ pattern for an n-input circuit can be generated from an LFSR. Further, an LFSR can compact the output pattern of the circuit under test by generating a "signature," which is compared with the precomputed signature of the fault-free circuit. In this way, LFSRs can be used as both the test-pattern source and the response evaluator.

Figure 7.5 shows an example of a 3-bit reconfigurable LFSR module presented by McCluskey and Bozorgui-Nesbat (1981). The block M realizes three functions, A, B, and $A \oplus B$, depending on the values of the control inputs N and S. Figure 7.6 illustrates these three modes corresponding to the three functions of each block M. In the normal mode with $N = 1$, the module behaves as a register, i.e., a set of D-flip-flops. This is shown in figure 7.6(a). In the test mode with $N = 0$ and $S = 0$, the module realizes a 3-bit LFSR, shown in figure 7.6(b). Here the LFSR transits all the possible seven states, and thus the output of this module provides all the possible input

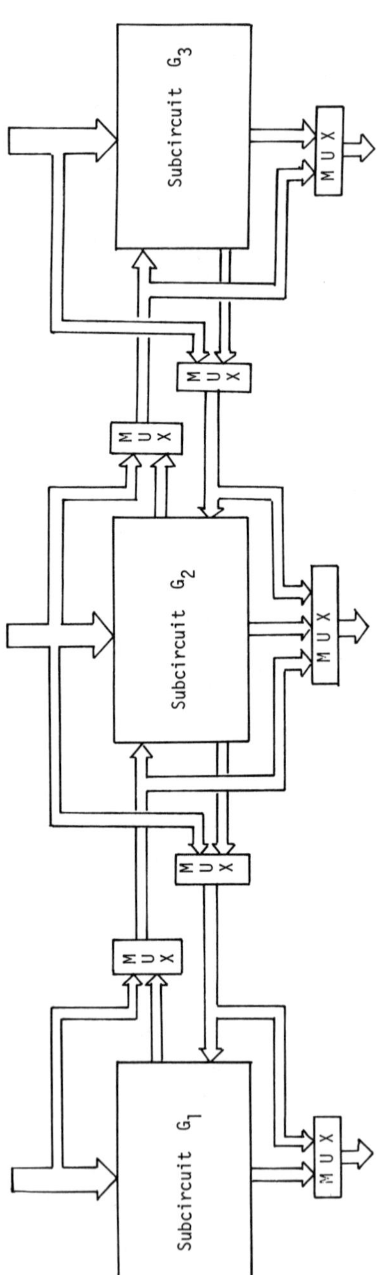

Figure 7.4
Partitioning into three subcircuits

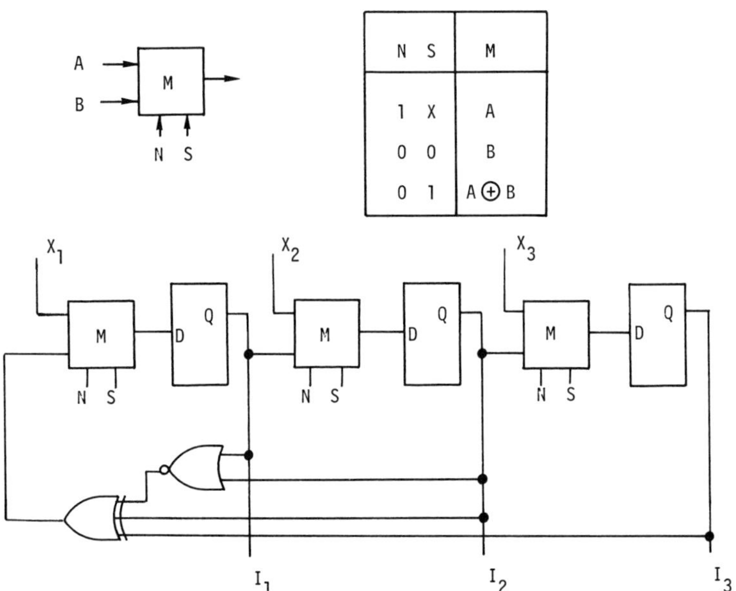

Figure 7.5
Reconfigurable 3-bit LFSR module (McCluskey and Bozorgui-Nesbat 1981; © IEEE 1981)

patterns for the subcircuit being tested. This mode operates as a test-pattern generator. In general, there is a method of designing an LFSR that generates all $2^n - 1$ possible input patterns. The interested reader is referred to Barzilai et al. 1983.

Figure 7.6(c) shows the third mode with $N = 0$ and $S = 1$. In this mode the module functions as a parallel signature analyzer. Generally, an LFSR performs the basic operation of division by a polynomial in GF(2) (Galois fields of two elements) (Peterson and Weldon 1972). Hence, data compression of a sequence of output responses is equivalent to superposition of polynomial division processes. The final signature is composed of the modulo 2 summation of remainders from all the division processes. There are several LFSRs associated with polynomials in GF(2). The LFSR shown in figure 7.6(c) is an example of the LFSRs for parallel data compression.

The techniques mentioned above append multiplexers to the circuit so as to partition it into manageable subcircuits. These subcircuits can be tested exhaustively, so that test-pattern generation and fault modeling can be eliminated. However, these methods have drawbacks; the added multiplex-

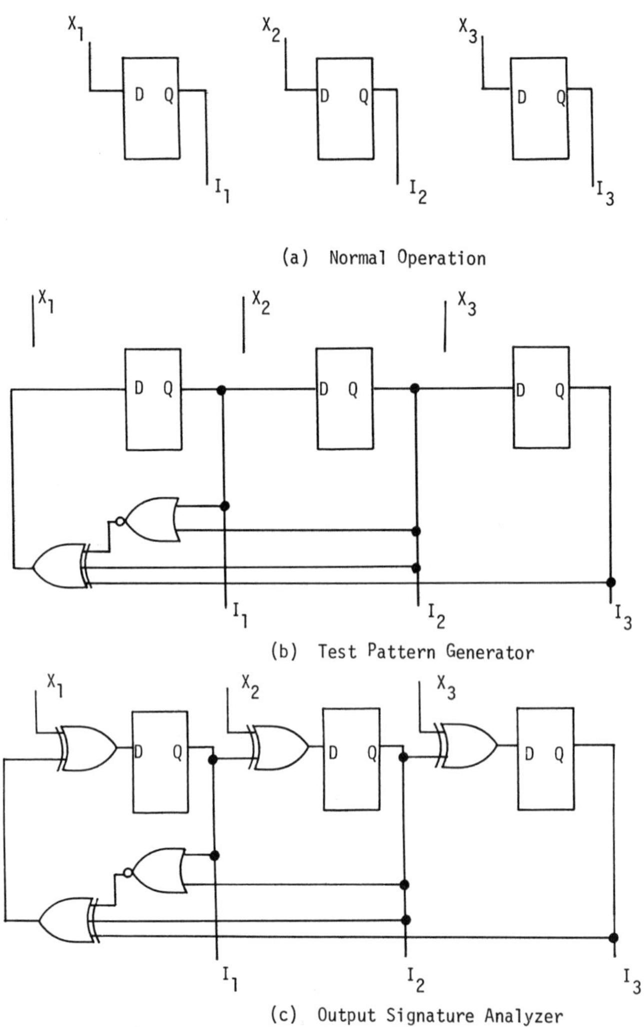

Figure 7.6
Various modes of 3-bit LFSR module (McCluskey and Bozorgui-Nesbat 1981; © IEEE 1981)

ing circuitry introduces an additional delay in the signal-propagation path and a considerable hardware overhead.

Oklobdzija and Ercegovac (1982) presented a circuit-level approach for enhancing the testability of logic circuits. The method proposed there is to change certain gates within a given logic circuit into "controllable gates" so that the controllability and the observability of the circuit are improved. These controllable gates are used in partitioning the circuit into relatively small subcircuits.

A controllable gate is defined as a gate with a control input c whose output y is equal to $f(x_1, x_2, \ldots, x_n)$ if $c = K$ and to $g(x_p)$ if $c = \bar{K}$, where f is the function of the gate in the normal mode, g is a function of the priority input x_p $(1 \leqslant p \leqslant n)$ and K is a constant 0 or 1. Since $g(x_p)$ is either x_p or $\bar{x}_p$, the value on the priority input is transmitted directly or in the complemented form to the output of the controllable gate. This makes it possible to block all paths through the inputs of the gate except x_p and to create the path through x_p. Hence, these controllable gates can be used to create the paths to and from an arbitrary subcircuit in order to control the inputs and observe the outputs. The controllable gate can function as a low-cost multiplexer.

For NAND gates, Oklobdzija and Ercegovac (1982) presented the following three types of controllable gates:

$$f_1 = \begin{cases} \overline{a \cdot b} & \text{if } c = 0 \\ \bar{a} & \text{if } c = 1, \end{cases}$$

$$f_2 = \begin{cases} \overline{a \cdot b} & \text{if } c = 0 \\ x & \text{if } c = 1 \text{ and } a \cdot b = 0, \end{cases}$$

$$f_3 = \begin{cases} \overline{a \cdot b} & \text{if } c = 0 \\ x & \text{if } c = 1. \end{cases}$$

The n-MOS implementations of these controllable NAND gates are shown in figure 7.7. Obviously, the concept of a controllable gate can be applied to other types of gates and to different technologies.

In order to enhance the testability of a circuit, Oklobdzija and Ercegovac (1982) proposed to partition it into small subcircuits by replacing some of the gates with controllable gates capable of blocking or creating propagation paths. In order to test a partitioned subcircuit, the logical values on the control lines of controllable gates are determined in such a way that the

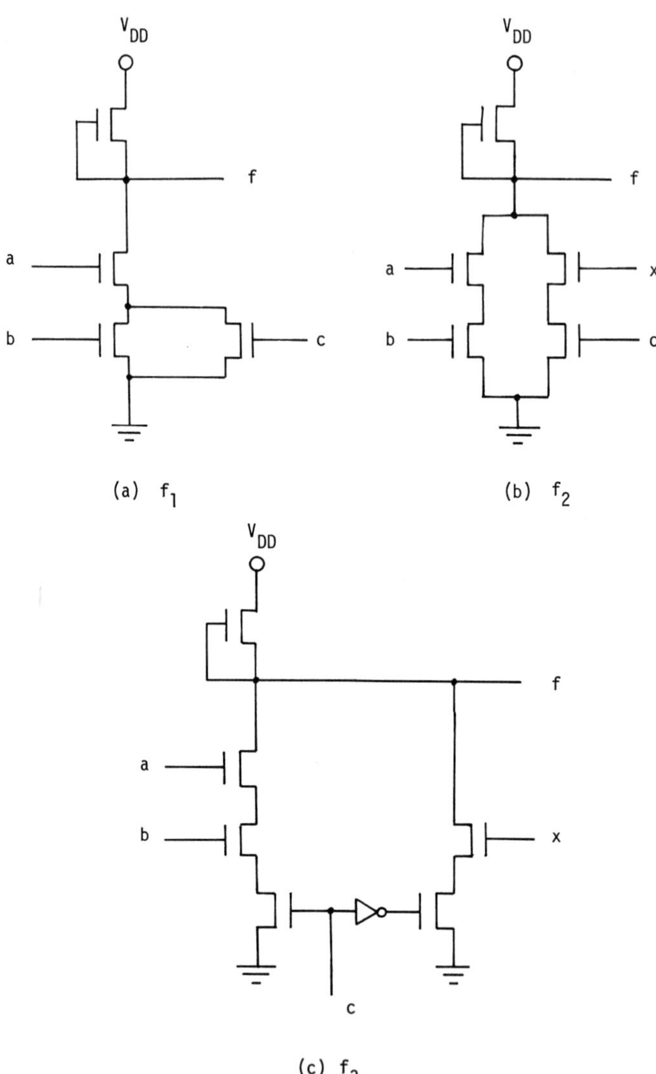

Figure 7.7
The n-MOS implementation of various controllable NAND gates (Oklobdzija and Ercegovac 1982; © IEEE 1982)

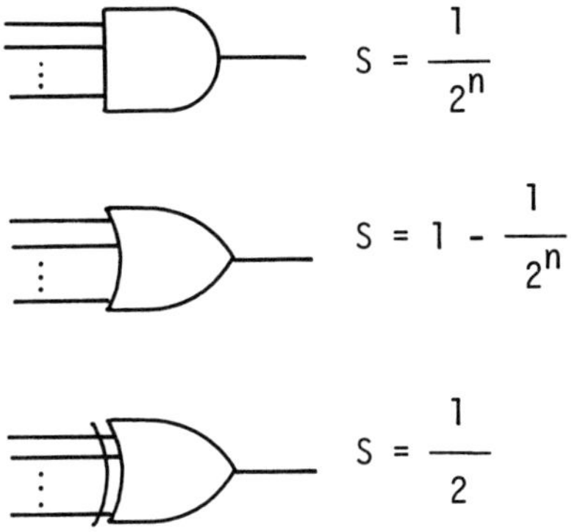

$$S = \frac{1}{2^n}$$

$$S = 1 - \frac{1}{2^n}$$

$$S = \frac{1}{2}$$

Figure 7.8
Syndrome of various n-input gates

subcircuit can be accessed from the outside through the paths created by the controllable gates. The text patterns for this subcircuit are applied from the primary inputs, and the responses are observed on the primary outputs. That is, the subcircuit is tested independent of the other parts of the circuit. This process is repeated for all subcircuits until the whole circuit is tested.

As figure 7.7 shows, each controllable gate has two extra devices. These extra devices cause some speed degradation; however, the delay here is much smaller than that resulting from the addition of an extra gate. The overhead of extra I/O pins for the control lines can be reduced by using a shift register from which the control lines are controlled. The content of the shift register is loaded serially from the outside through an additional pin. Each cell of the shift register has control over one or several controllable gates.

7.2 Syndrome-Testable Design

The *syndrome* $S(f)$ of a logic function f is defined as

$$S(f) = \frac{K(f)}{2^n}$$

where $K(f)$ is the number of minterms realized by the function f and n is the number of inputs of f. Figure 7.8 shows the syndrome of various n-input gates. Obviously $0 \leqslant S(f) \leqslant 1$, and hence the storage requirement for test data is drastically reduced in syndrome testing.

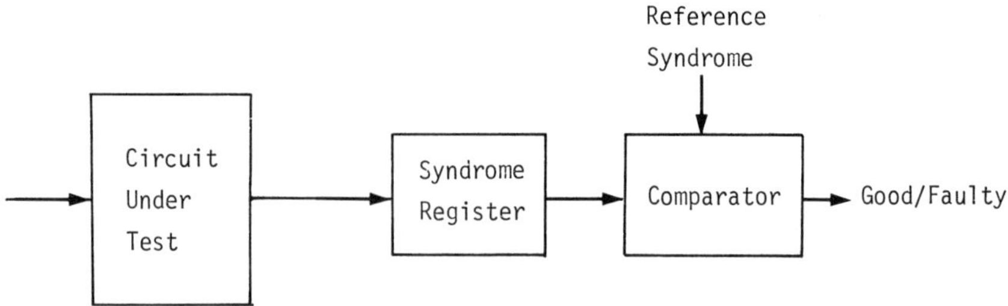

Figure 7.9
Testing scheme for syndrome-testable circuits

A fault in a logic circuit is said to be *syndrome-testable* if the syndrome of the circuit induced by the fault does not equal the syndrome of the fault-free circuit. Further, a logic circuit is said to be syndrome-testable with respect to a class of faults if any fault in the fault class is syndrome-testable. The class of faults considered here is the single stuck-at type. The testing scheme for syndrome-testable circuits is shown in figure 7.9. All 2^n possible input patterns are applied to the circuit under test exactly once, and its syndrome is recorded by counting the number of ones appearing on the output of the circuit. If the actual syndrome equals the expected syndrome, the circuit is fault-free; otherwise the circuit is faulty.

Savir (1980) reported a method of designing syndrome-testable circuits. Here we consider the syndrome-testable design of two-level (AND-OR) circuits. We assume that the circuits are irredundant and that all AND gates realize prime implicants of the functions realized by the circuits.

Consider the function f realized by the circuit diagrammed in figure 7.10:

$$f = x_1 x_2 + x_3 \bar{x}_4 + \bar{x}_3 x_4.$$

The product terms $x_1 x_2$, $x_3 \bar{x}_4$, and $\bar{x}_3 x_4$ are all prime implicants.

Any stuck-at-0 fault at the input to an AND gate causes the prime implicant realized by the AND gate to disappear. For example, the s-a-0 fault at line c causes the function f to be the faulty function

$$f' = x_1 x_2 + \bar{x}_3 x_4.$$

Since $S(f) = \frac{10}{16} \neq \frac{7}{16} = S(f')$, the fault $c/0$ is syndrome-testable. Any stuck-at-1 fault at the input of an AND gate is a growth fault. The fault c/1 changes the term $x_3 \bar{x}_4$ into $\bar{x}_4$, and thus it induces the faulty function

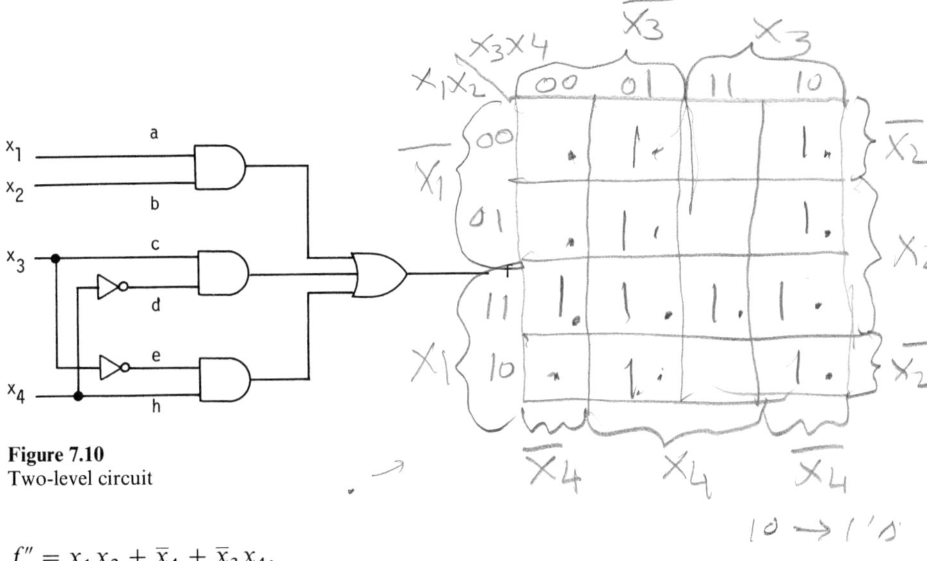

Figure 7.10
Two-level circuit

$$f'' = x_1x_2 + \bar{x}_4 + \bar{x}_3x_4.$$

Since $S(f'') = \frac{13}{16} \neq S(f)$, the fault c/1 is syndrome-testable.

For an irredundant circuit, such a disappearance fault and a growth fault change the number of minterms realized by the function, and thus they are all syndrome-testable. However, there exists a stuck-at fault that does not change the number of minterms, and hence its syndrome. Such a fault exists only at a fanout point of a primary input, say x_i. Suppose that the function is expressed in the form

$$F = A \cdot x_i + B \cdot \bar{x}_i + C$$

where A, B, and C do not depend on variable x_i and where not both of A and B are zero. It can be easily seen that a stuck-at fault (s-a-0 or s-a-1) at the fanout point x_i will cause the faulty syndrome to be identical to the fault-free syndrome if and only if

$$S(A\bar{C}) = S(B\bar{C}).$$

For example, consider the stuck-at-0 fault at the fanout point x_3 shown in figure 7.10. The fault-free function is

$$f = x_1x_2 + x_3\bar{x}_4 + \bar{x}_3x_4,$$

and hence

$$f = Ax_3 + B\bar{x}_3 + C$$

where $A = \bar{x}_4$, $B = x_4$, and $C = x_1x_2$. Computing $S(A\bar{C})$ and $S(B\bar{C})$, we

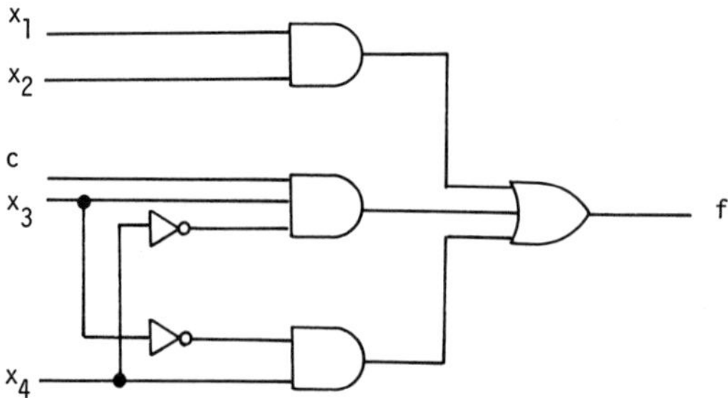

Figure 7.11
Syndrome-testable circuit

have

$$S(A\bar{C}) = S(\bar{x}_4 \cdot \overline{x_1 \cdot x_2})$$
$$= \tfrac{6}{16},$$
$$S(B\bar{C}) = S(x_4 \cdot \overline{x_1 \cdot x_2})$$
$$= \tfrac{6}{16}.$$

The faulty syndrome induced by the fault $x_3/0$ is identical to the fault-free syndrome, and thus such a fault is syndrome-untestable.

Savir (1980) showed that every two-level irredundant combinational circuit can be made syndrome-testable by attaching control (extra) inputs to the AND gates. For example, the circuit of figure 7.10 can be made syndrome-testable by inserting one extra input c to the second AND gate, as shown in figure 7.11. The new function is

$$f = x_1x_2 + cx_3\bar{x}_4 + \bar{x}_3x_4.$$

For this modified circuit, the stuck-at fault at x_3 or x_4 is syndrome-testable, since

$$S(cx_3 \cdot \overline{x_1x_2}) \neq S(\bar{x}_3 \cdot \overline{x_1x_2})$$

and

$$S(c\bar{x}_4 \cdot \overline{x_1x_2}) \neq S(x_4 \cdot \overline{x_1x_2}).$$

Hence, the modified circuit of figure 7.11 is syndrome-testable. The effect of adding extra inputs is to change the "size" of the prime implicants, and thus to create the desired syndrome. In our example, the second product term has shrunk as a result of the addition of input c. In this way the circuit can be made syndrome-testable.

Savir (1980) presented a method of modifying the irredundant function given in a sum of products form by adding a nearly minimal number of control inputs so that the resulting function is syndrome-testable. Roughly speaking, the procedure is to repeat the following process until the function becomes syndrome-testable. That is, the process is to create a new function F' from the present function F by adding a new control input or an already added control input to an appropriate prime implicant of F so that

$$|T(F')| < |T(F)|$$

where

$$T(F) = \{x_i | F \text{ is syndrome-untestable in } x_i\}.$$

As an illustration of the procedure, consider the following function f borrowed from Savir (1980):

$$f = x_1\bar{x}_2 + \bar{x}_1 x_3 + x_2\bar{x}_3 + x_4 x_5 + \bar{x}_4\bar{x}_5.$$

Let $f^{(j)}$ denote the jth modified function, and let $f^{(0)} = f$. The first step is to find all the variables x_i in which $f^{(0)}$ is syndrome-untestable. Then we have

$$T(f^{(0)}) = \{x_1, x_2, x_3, x_4, x_5\}.$$

The next step is to add a new input c_1 to an appropriate prime implicant of $f^{(0)}$ so that $|T(f^{(1)})|$ is minimized, where $f^{(1)}$ is the new modified function. In our example, c_1 is added to the first prime implicant, and we have

$$f^{(1)} = c_1 x_1\bar{x}_2 + \bar{x}x_3 + x_2\bar{x}_3 + x_4 x_5 + \bar{x}_4\bar{x}_5,$$

$$T(f^{(1)}) = \{x_3, x_4, x_5\}.$$

Next, we try to add c_1 to one of prime implicants so as to reduce the size of $T(f^{(1)})$. Adding c_1 to the fourth prime implicant, we have

$$f^{(2)} = c_1 x_1\bar{x}_2 + \bar{x}_1 x_3 + x_2\bar{x}_3 + c_1 x_4 x_5 + \bar{x}_4\bar{x}_5,$$

$$T(f^{(2)}) = \{x_3\}.$$

To make x_3 syndrome-testable, we need a new input c_2. Appending c_2 to the second prime implicant, we have

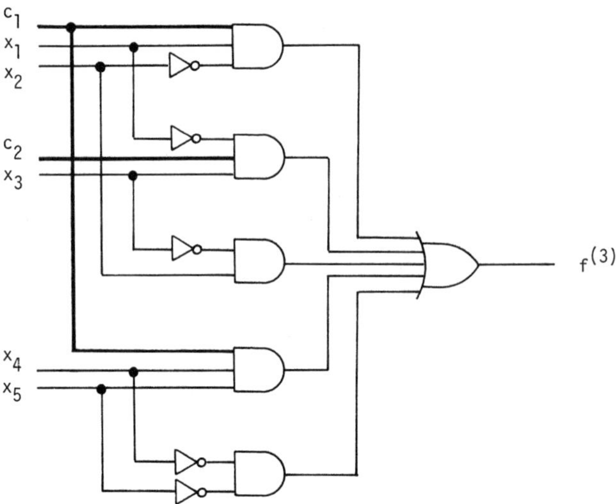

Figure 7.12
Syndrome-testable design

$$f^{(3)} = c_1 x_1 \bar{x}_2 + c_2 \bar{x}_1 x_3 + x_2 \bar{x}_3 + c_1 x_4 x_5 + \bar{x}_4 \bar{x}_5,$$

$$T(f^{(3)}) = \emptyset \text{ (empty)}.$$

Hence, we have the syndrome-testable design shown in figure 7.12.

Savir (1980) also presented a method for modifying the design of a general combinational circuit so that it will be syndrome-testable. However, there was no proof that every multilevel combinational circuit can be modified to be syndrome-testable by extra input insertions. Markowsky (1981) showed that a combinational circuit can always be modified to be syndrome-testable for single stuck-at faults. Savir (1981) presented a method for partitioning a given logic circuit into a minimal number of subcircuits consisting of maximal unate components that are syndrome-testable by themselves. Barzilai et al. (1981) considered syndrome testing for multi-output circuits and proposed the "weighted syndrome sums approach," which is based on multiplying syndromes of different outputs by suitable factors and then summing those to form a composite syndrome. Bhattacharya and Gupta (1983) proposed a method of designing syndrome-testable circuits so that all single stuck-at faults and all short-circuit faults involving any two lines can be detected by checking only the syndrome. Yamada (1983) applied the syndrome-testing approach to PLAs for single stuck-at faults, single bridging faults, and single crosspoint faults.

Syndrome-testing has been extended further to an approach using the Rademacher-Walsh spectral coefficients by Susskind (1981, 1983) and Hsiao and Seth (1982). A Rademacher-Walsh spectral coefficient C_I of an n-variable function $f(x_1, x_2, \ldots, x_n)$, of $f(\mathbf{X})$ for short, can be calculated as follows:

$$C_I = 2^n - 2\sum_x \left[f(X) \oplus \sum X_I \right]$$

where $I = \{i_1, i_2, \ldots, i_k\}$, $\sum X_I = x_{i_1} \oplus x_{i_2} \oplus \cdots \oplus x_{i_k}$, $\sum_x$ is the arithmetic summation for all input combinations, and $C_0 = C_{I=\emptyset}$.

It is obvious that each coefficient has a value that lies in the range from -2^n to $+2^n$. Further, 2^n coefficients characterize the function completely. For a two-variable function we have the following four Rademacher-Walsh coefficients:

$$C_0 = 2^2 - 2\sum_x f(X),$$

$$C_1 = 2^2 - 2\sum_x [f(X) \oplus x_1],$$

$$C_2 = 2^2 - 2\sum_x [f(X) \oplus x_2],$$

$$C_{12} = 2^2 - 2\sum_x [f(X) \oplus x_1 \oplus x_2].$$

The testing scheme using the Rademacher-Walsh spectrum is also based on exhaustive testing; that is, the test patterns are all the possible input combinations. The responses of the test patterns are compressed into the corresponding Rademacher-Walsh spectrum of the circuit. Since each function has a unique Rademacher-Walsh spectrum, we can detect all faults by determining whether or not the circuit under test has the Rademacher-Walsh spectrum intended. However, from a practical standpoint, the number of spectral coefficients is limited to either one or two. It was proved by Susskind (1981, 1983) that, under the assumption of pin faults (i.e., terminal faults), the computation of the single Rademacher-Walsh coefficient C_{ALL} suffices for fault detection, where C_{ALL} is based on all variables, i.e., $I = \{1, 2, \ldots, n\}$. Susskind (1981, 1983) also showed that in a circuit form so restricted that after every initial fanout point every line has unique inversion parity, any combination of stuck-at faults on all the lines up to the initial fanouts can be detected by verifying C_{ALL} and single stuck-at faults on any lines following fanout can be detected by calculating C_0. This result gives us sufficient conditions for designing circuits that can be fully tested for stuck-at faults by verifying only C_0 and C_{ALL}. As an example, every two-level circuit, such as a PLA, satisfies the above conditions.

7.3 Reed-Muller Canonical Forms

Reddy (1972) described a design technique for realizing any arbitrary n-input function using AND and EOR gates. This technique is based on Reed-Muller canonical expansion, in which all single stuck-at faults are detected by only $(n + 4)$ test patterns, independent of the function being realized.

An arbitrary function $f(x_1, x_2, \ldots, x_n)$ can be expressed in the Reed-Muller canonical form as

$$f(x_1, x_2, \ldots, x_n) = c_0 \oplus c_1 \dot{x}_1 \oplus c_2 \dot{x}_2 \oplus \cdots \oplus c_n \dot{x}_n$$
$$\oplus\, c_{n+1} \dot{x}_1 \dot{x}_2 \oplus c_{n+2} \dot{x}_1 \dot{x}_3 \oplus \cdots \oplus c_{2^n-1} \dot{x}_1 \dot{x}_2 \cdots \dot{x}_n$$

where $\dot{x}_i$ is either x_i or $\overline{x}_i$ and c_j is a binary constant 0 or 1. For the sake of simplicity we assume that only uncomplemented variables are used in the expression. To obtain such a Reed-Muller expansion of a given function, we first express the function with a sum of disjoint products, and replace all OR operators in the sum of mutually exclusive products by EOR operators. Then we convert the expression to a complement-free Reed-Muller form using the identity

$$\overline{x}_i = x_i \oplus 1.$$

As candidates for easily testable circuits with function-independent testing, Reddy (1972) considered Reed-Muller canonical circuits, which are direct realizations of Reed-Muller canonical expansions using AND and EOR gates only. For example, consider

$$f_1(x_1, x_2, x_3, x_4) = 1 \oplus x_1 x_2 \oplus x_1 x_3 \oplus x_1 x_3 x_4 \oplus x_2 x_3 x_4.$$

The Reed-Muller canonical circuit realizing f_1 is diagrammed in figure 7.13. Each AND gate forms a product term in the expression. An extra input x_0 is used to supply $c_0 = 1$.

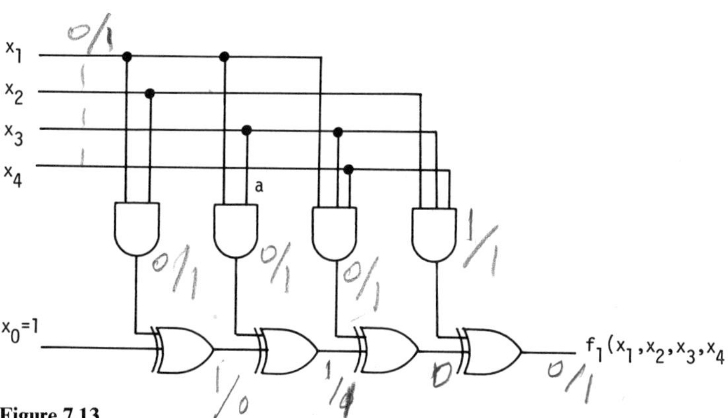

Figure 7.13
Reed-Muller canonical circuit realizing $f_1(x_1, x_2, x_3, x_4)$

Now let us consider the fault detection of these Reed-Muller canonical circuits. We assume that only a single s-a-0 or s-a-1 fault occurs on the inputs and outputs of AND gates or only a single EOR gate is faulty, where any of the 15 other two-variable functions is allowed as the output of the faulty EOR gate.

To detect a single faulty gate in a cascade of EOR gates, it is sufficient to apply a set of test patterns that will apply all possible input combinations to each EOR gate (Kautz 1971). This is performed by applying the following four test patterns, independent of the number of input variables n:

$$T_1 = \begin{array}{c} \begin{array}{cccccc} x_0 & x_1 & x_2 & \cdots & x_n \end{array} \\ \left[\begin{array}{cccccc} 0 & 0 & 0 & \cdots & 0 \\ 0 & 1 & 1 & \cdots & 1 \\ 1 & 0 & 0 & \cdots & 0 \\ 1 & 1 & 1 & \cdots & 1 \end{array}\right] \end{array}$$

It is easy to see that the application of these four test patterns supplies all four input patterns to each EOR gate. Furthermore, as Reddy (1972) mentions, we can see that a s-a-0 fault at any AND gate input or output is detected by applying either of the test patterns $011\ldots1$ and $11\ldots1$. A s-a-1 fault at the output of any AND gate is detected by applying either of the test patterns $00\ldots0$ and $100\ldots0$. Hence, the faults remaining untested are s-a-1 faults at the inputs of the AND gates and s-a-0 or s-a-1 faults at the primary inputs.

To detect a s-a-1 fault at any one of the inputs to the AND gates, one of the n test patterns in the set T_2 is sufficient:

$$T_2 = \begin{bmatrix} x_0 & x_1 & x_2 & x_3 & \cdots & x_n \\ \mathrm{x} & 0 & 1 & 1 & \cdots & 1 \\ \mathrm{x} & 1 & 0 & 1 & \cdots & 1 \\ \mathrm{x} & 1 & 1 & 0 & \cdots & 1 \\ \cdot & & & \cdot & & \cdot \\ \cdot & & & & \cdot & \cdot \\ \cdot & & & & \cdot & \cdot \\ \mathrm{x} & 1 & 1 & 1 & \cdots & 0 \end{bmatrix}$$

where x is "don't care." The ith test pattern in T_2 places a zero on all AND-gate inputs to which x_i is connected, and all the other inputs are 1. Hence, if the input connected to x_i on the jth AND gate is s-a-1, then the output of this gate changes from 0 to 1 and this fault effect is further propagated through the EOR gates to the primary output. For example, to detect a s-a-1 fault at line a in figure 7.13 we need only to set $x_1 = 1$ and $x_3 = 0$. Hence, the fault is detected by either of the test patterns 01101 and 11101 in T_2.

Finally we consider the detection of single stuck-at faults at primary inputs. Suppose that a primary input x_i is connected to an odd number of AND gates; that is, x_i appears an odd number of times in the Reed-Muller canonical expansion. A s-a-0 fault at x_i induces an odd number of changes at the outputs of AND gates if one of the test patterns 011 . . . 1 and 11 . . . 1 is applied. This implies an odd number of changes at the input to the EOR cascade, and hence the fault effect is propagated to the primary output. Similarly, a s-a-1 fault at x_i can be detected by one of the test patterns in T_2. In this way, any single stuck-at faults at a primary input that is connected to an odd number of AND gates can be detected by one of the $(n + 4)$ test patterns in $T = T_1 \cup T_2$. In figure 7.13, x_1 and x_3 are connected to an odd number of AND gates. Hence, a s-a-0 fault at x_1 or x_3 is detected by either of the tests 01111 and 11111. Further, a s-a-1 fault at x_1 (x_3) is detected by either of the tests 00111 and 10111 (01101 and 11101).

However, the $(n + 4)$ test patterns detect no single stuck-at faults at those primary inputs that are connected to an even number of AND gates, since such faults induce an even number of changes at the input to the EOR cascade and thus no change in the output of the cascade. For example, in figure 7.13, x_2 and x_4 are connected to an even number of AND gates. Even if the test patterns 01111 and 11111 are applied to detect a s-a-0 fault at x_2 or x_4, the fault effect propagates to an even number of AND gates; that is,

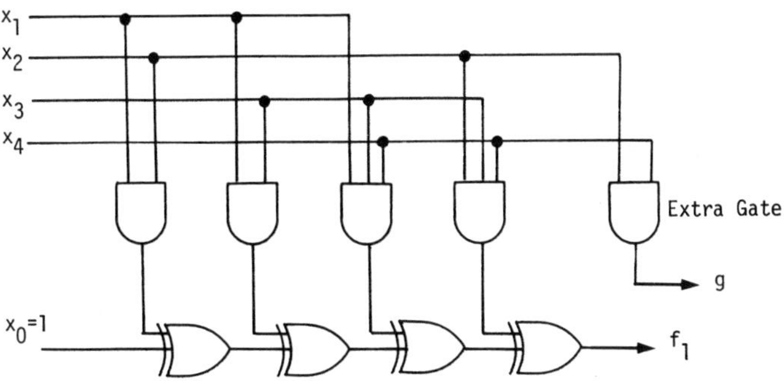

Figure 7.14
Modified circuit for f_1

an even number of changes at the input to the EOR cascade occur and no change at the output of the cascade is induced.

Reddy (1972) proposed an approach to adding an extra AND gate so that any fault at those primary inputs connected to an even number of AND gates can be detected. The inputs to this AND gate are those appearing an even number of times in the Reed-Muller canonical product terms. For the functions f_1 given above, x_2 and x_4 appear in an even number of product terms. Hence, the modified circuit for f_1 is given in figure 7.14 by adding an AND gate whose inputs are x_2 and x_4 and whose output g is allowed to be observed directly. For the modified Reed-Muller canonical circuit, we see that the test patterns in $T = T_1 \cup T_2$ are sufficient to detect single stuck-at faults in the primary inputs and also in this extra AND gate. In the circuit illustrated in figure 7.14, in order to detect single stuck-at faults on primary inputs x_2 and x_4 and inputs/outputs of the extra AND gate, it is sufficient to apply three test patterns supplying $(x_2, x_4) = (1, 1)$, $(0, 1)$, and $(1, 0)$. Obviously these input patterns are included in T.

Summing up Reddy's results, we can state that for an arbitrary function f, by adding one extra AND gate to the Reed-Muller canonical realization of f, with inputs from all those primary input that are connected to an even number of AND gates, we can detect all single stuck-at faults by applying only $(n + 4)$ test patterns, independent of the function f.

The work of Reddy has been extended by Kodandapani (1974), Saluja and Reddy (1975), Pradhan (1978), Page (1980), and others. Kodandapani showed that one of the test patterns in T_1 can be removed by assigning the "don't care" in the test set T_2 in a specific manner. The test patterns in T_2, hence, depend on the function being realized. Saluja and Reddy (1975) extended Reddy's results to the multiple-fault assumption. It has been shown that to detect t stuck-at faults in Reed-Muller canonical circuits, one need only apply a predetermined test set, independent of the function being realized, whose cardinality is

$$4 + \sum_{i=1}^{\lfloor \log_2 2t \rfloor} \binom{n}{i}$$

where $\lfloor x \rfloor$ denotes the integer part of x. The Reed-Muller canonical circuits proposed by Saluja and Reddy (1975) also have an extra AND gate whose output is observable.

7.4 Programmable Logic Arrays

The programmable logic array (PLA) has many attractive features, among them regularity of structure, simplicity of connection, and flexibility of alteration. Because of its regular structure like memory, the PLA is very suitable to LSI and VLSI and has become a popular and effective tool for implementing logic functions.

Much work has been done in recent years on the design of easily testable PLAs (Fujiwara et al. 1980; Fujiwara and Kinoshita 1981; Hong and Ostapko 1980; Pradhan and Son 1980; Son and Pradhan 1980; Saluja et al. 1981, 1983; Yajima and Aramaki 1981; Ramanatha and Biswas 1982, 1983; Khakbaz and McCluskey 1982; Khakbaz 1983; Fujiwara 1984). Most of this work has been concerned with the design of PLAs that can be tested by function-independent test patterns. The first designs of such PLAs with universal testability were proposed independently by Fujiwara et al. (1980), Fujiwara and Kinoshita (1981), and Hong and Ostapko (1980). Although the two designs differ in implementation, the essential idea is almost the same. This section describes the design of Fujiwara and co-workers, since it is much simpler than that of Hong and Ostapko.

A PLA consists of three main sections as shown in figure 7.15. These are the decoder, the AND array, and the OR array. The decoder section usually consists of a collection of one-input or two-input decoders. Both the AND array and the OR array are used to implement multi-output combinational logic with sum-of-product forms. An example of a PLA is shown in figure 7.16. A PLA can be implemented in either bipolar or MOS technology. In

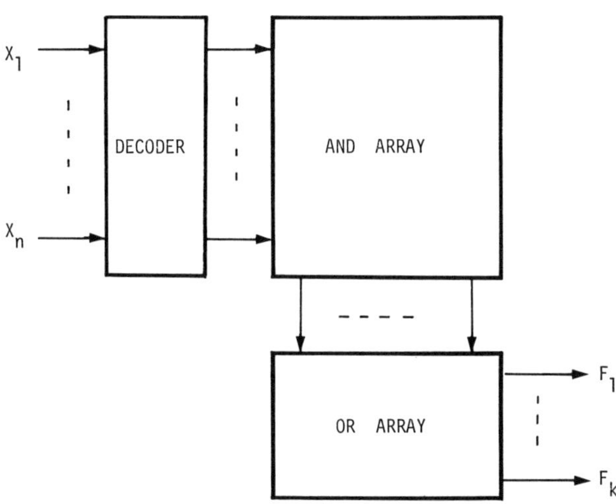

Figure 7.15
General structure of PLA

n-MOS technology, the PLA is typically implemented as a NOR-NOR array. Figure 7.17 is a diagram of the circuit that implements the PLA of figure 7.16 in n-MOS technology. In this section the PLA is assumed to be NOR-NOR implemented and to consist of one-input decorders. These assumptions do not affect our argument. The results given here can easily be modified to be applicable to PLAs implemented in another technology, or with two or more input decoders. A PLA consists of n inputs, $2n$ rows in the AND array, m columns (product terms), and k rows (outputs) in the OR array.

In order to design an easily testable PLA, we augment a given PLA by adding extra logic: a shift register, two cascades of EOR gates, two columns between the decoder and the AND array, and one column and one row to AND and OR arrays, respectively, as shown in figure 7.18. The extra connections shown in figure 7.19 are for an implementation in n-MOS technology.

A shift register is added to select a column (product line) in the AND array. Each column P_i is ANDed by the complement of each variable S_i of the shift register as follows:

$$P_i = p_i \cdot \bar{S}_i \qquad \text{for } i = 1, 2, \ldots, m$$

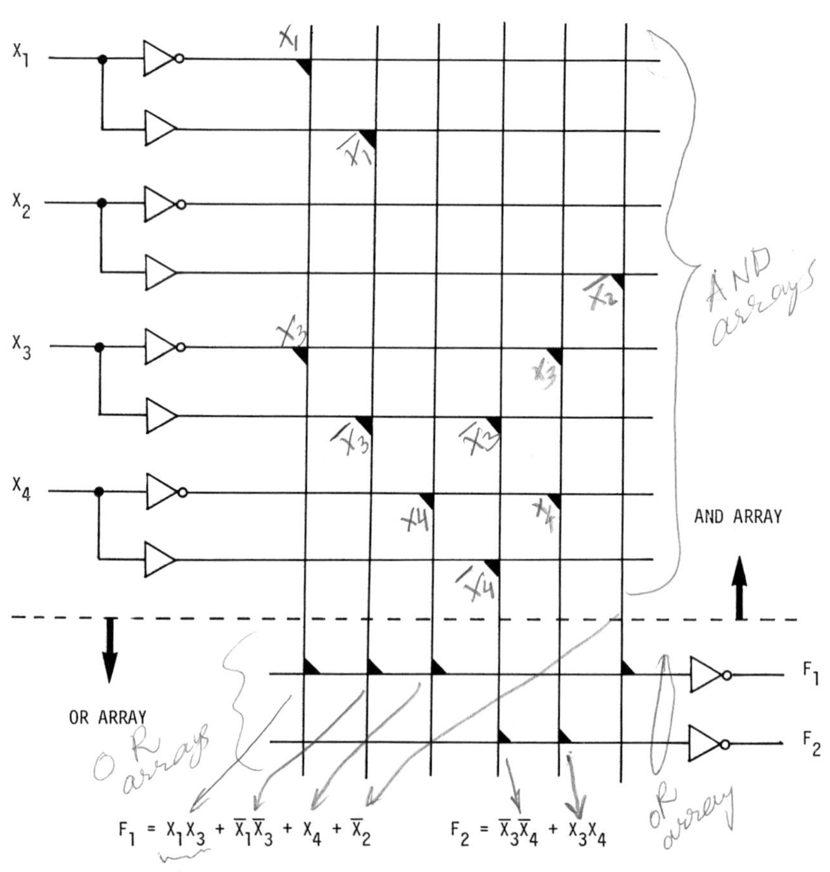

Figure 7.16
Example of PLA

where p_i is a product term generated by the ith column of the original AND array. An extra product line P_{m+1} is arranged so that each row of the AND array has an odd number of connections (devices). Similarly, an extra row of the OR array is arranged so that each column within the OR array has an odd number of connections. Two extra control lines C_1 and C_2 are added to disable all X_is and X_is, respectively, as follows:

$$Q_{2i-1} = \bar{X}_i \cdot C_1,$$

$$Q_{2i} = X_i \cdot \bar{C}_2$$

for

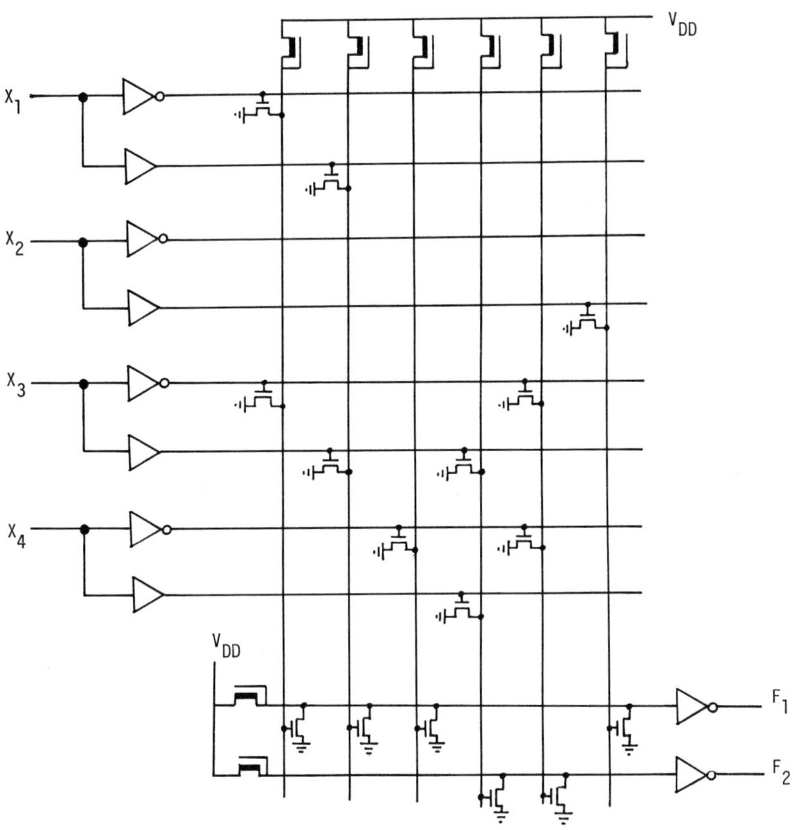

Figure 7.17
Example of PLA in n-MOS technology

$i = 1, 2, \ldots, n$

where X_i is the ith input line and Q_j is the jth row of the AND array. The section, composed of $2 \times 2n$ crosspoints on two control lines, is called the *control array* of the augmented PLA.

The augmented PLA has the following properties:

- The shift register can be used to select an arbitrary column of the AND array by setting 0 to the selected column and 1 to all other columns. Since NOR logic is assumed, to select a column or product line P_i we want S_i to be 0 and all other S_js to be 1.

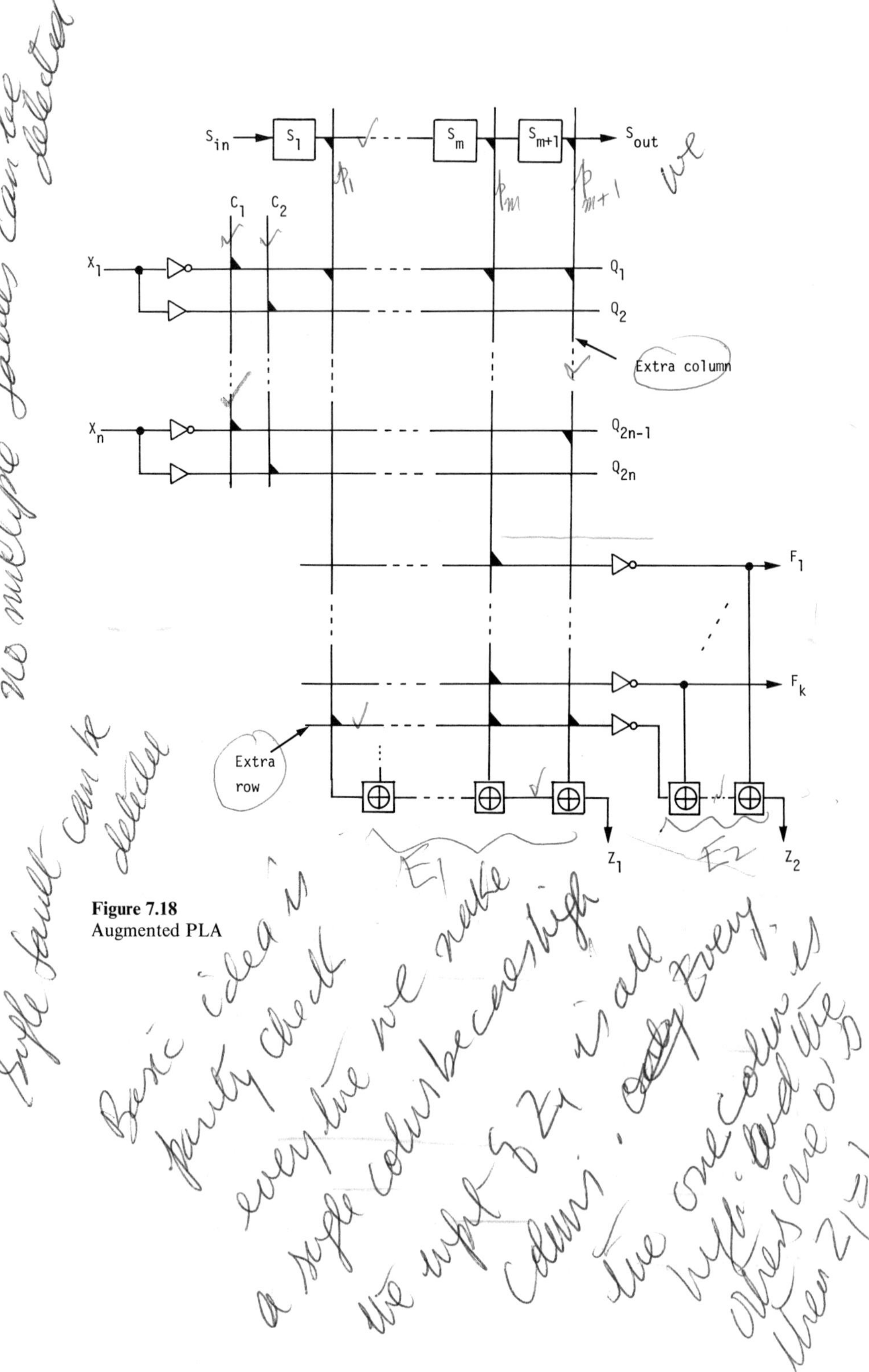

Figure 7.18
Augmented PLA

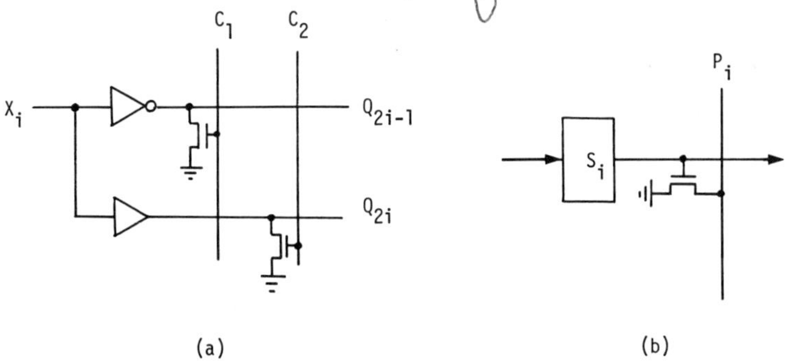

(a) (b)

Figure 7.19
Extra device in n-MOS technology

- The control array can be used to select any row of the AND array, i.e., to sensitize any output line of the decoder. To select Q_{2i-1}, set X_i to 0, all other X_js to 1, C_1 to 0, and C_2 to 1. To select Q_{2i}, set X_i to 1, all other X_js to 0, C_1 to 1, and C_2 to 0. Note that in NOR logic selecting a row is equivalent to setting the row to 1 and all other rows to 0.
- The cascade of EOR gates below the OR array can be used as a parity checker to detect odd errors that propagate to it.
- The cascade of EOR gates on the left of the OR array can be used as a parity checker to detect odd errors that propagate to it.

Utilizing the above properties of the augmented PLA, we can present a universal test set to detect all stuck-at faults in the shift register; single stuck-at faults on the lines of the control array, the AND array, and the OR array; single crosspoint faults in the AND and OR arrays, where a crosspoint fault is an extra-device fault or a missing-device fault at the corresponding crosspoint; and multiple stuck-at faults on the external input/output lines of EOR gates.

Table 7.1 shows the test set $A_{n,m+1}$ used to detect the above types of faults, where n is the number of inputs, m is the number of columns in the original PLA, $\varepsilon_m = 0$ if m is even, $\varepsilon_m = 1$ if m is odd, and x represents "don't care."

For this test set $A_{n,m+1}$ we have the following theorem.

THEOREM 7.1 Let $M_{n,m+1}$ be an augmented PLA as shown in figure 7.18. For any $M_{n,m+1}$, the test set $A_{n,m+1}$ can detect all stuck-at faults in the shift register and all single stuck-at and crosspoint faults in the control array, the AND array, and the OR array.

Table 7.1
Universal test set $A_{n,m+1}$

	$X_1 \dots X_i \dots X_n$	C_1	C_2	$S_1 \dots S_j \dots S_{m+1}$	Z_1	Z_2
I^1	0 0	1	0	1 1	0	0
I_j^2 $(j = 1, \dots, m+1)$	0 0	1	0	1 ...0...1	1	1
I_j^3 $(j = 1, \dots, m+1)$	1 1	0	1	1 ...0...1	1	1
I_i^4 $(i = 1, \dots, n)$	1 ...0 ...1	0	1	0 0	ε_m	x
I_i^5	0 ...1 ...0	1	0	0 0	ε_m	x

Proof By applying the test sequence $I^1 I_1^2 I_2^2 \cdots I_{m+1}^2$ and observing the response from S_{out}, we check whether all the cells can shift in and out both 0 and 1.

When we apply test patterns I_j^2 and I_j^3, the jth column is set to 1 and all the other columns are set to 0. Therefore, both I_j^2 and I_j^3 can detect any crosspoint fault on the jth column of the OR array by observing the output Z_2 and can detect a stuck-at-0 fault on the jth column, stuck-at-1 faults on the other columns, and stuck-at-1 faults on the rows of the AND array by observing the output Z_1. Any stuck-at fault on the row of the OR array can be detected by some of the test patterns I_j^2 and I_j^3 $(j = 1, 2, \dots, m+1)$.

By applying test I_i^4 (I_i^5), we set the $(2i-1)$th $(2i\text{th})$ row of the AND array to 1 and the other rows to 0. Therefore, test I_i^4 (I_i^5) can detect all crosspoint faults and a stuck-at-0 fault on the $(2i-1)$th $(2i\text{th})$ row in the AND array by observing the output Z_1.

The extra-device fault at the crosspoint of C_1 (C_2) with Q_{2i} (Q_{2i-1}) is detected by I_i^5 (I_i^4). The missing-device fault at the crosspoint of C_1 (C_2) and Q_{2i-1} (Q_{2i}) is detected by some of the test patterns I_j^2 (I_j^3) $(j = 1, 2, \dots, m+1)$. The stuck-at-0 fault on C_1 and the stuck-at-1 fault on C_2 are detected by some of the test patterns I_j^2 $(j = 1, 2, \dots, m+1)$. Similarly, the stuck-at-1 fault on C_1 and the stuck-at-0 fault on C_2 are detected by some of the test patterns I_j^3 $(j = 1, 2, \dots, m+1)$. ■

Next, we will see that the test set $A_{n,m+1}$ can also detect any multiple stuck-at fault in the EOR cascades under the fault assumption that permits only stuck-at faults on the external input and output lines of EOR gates. (That is, no fault within EOR gates is considered.)

LEMMA 7.1 If N input vectors are linearly independent, then these N

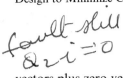

vectors plus zero vector are sufficient to detect any multiple stuck-at fault on the external lines of EOR gates in an N-input EOR cascade.

Let E_1 and E_2 be the EOR cascades having the outputs Z_1 and Z_2, respectively, in the augmented PLA $M_{n,m+1}$ shown in figure 7.18. Let $M_{OR} = [a_{ij}]$ be a matrix of k rows and $m + 1$ columns where $a_{ij} = 1$ if there exists a device at the (i,j)th position of the OR array, and $a_{ij} = 0$ otherwise.

By lemma 7.1 we have the following theorem for the multiple faults in two cascades of EOR gates, E_1 and E_2.

THEOREM 7.2 The test patterns I^1 and I_j^2 $(j = 1, 2, \ldots, m + 1)$ in $A_{n,m+1}$ are sufficient to detect all multiple stuck-at faults in E_1. If the column rank of matrix M_{OR} is equal to the number of inputs of the EOR cascade E_2, then all the multiple stuck-at faults in E_2 can be detected by test patterns I^1, and I_j^2 $(j = 1, 2, \ldots, m + 1)$ in $A_{n,m+1}$.

If the column rank of matrix M_{OR} is not equal to the number of inputs of the cascade E_2, although it hardly occurs, then it is not guaranteed that all multiple stuck-at faults in the cascade E_2 can be detected by the test patterns mentioned above. To overcome this problem, it might be necessary to add an extra OR array so that the rank of M_{OR} is equal to the number of inputs of the EOR cascade E_2. We permit only stuck-at faults on the external input and output lines of EOR gates. However, by adding an extra array it is possible to generate all test patterns for the cascades E_1 and E_2. This technique was reported by Hong and Ostapko (1980).

In the argument mentioned above, fault coverage is not complete since only single faults for stuck-at and crosspoint faults are considered and the bridging faults, which are important in PLAs, are not considered. Fujiwara (1984) proposed a new design of universally testable PLAs having the following properties:

- It can be tested with function-independent test patterns. For the design of PLAs under the single-fault assumption, both the input test patterns and the output responses are function-independent. However, under the multiple-fault assumption the output responses are not function-independent.
- The amount of extra hardware is significantly less than with the previous designs of universally testable PLAs. The ratio of additional hardware to original hardware can be reasonably small for LSI and VLSI chips.
- Very high fault coverage is achieved; that is, any combination of stuck-at

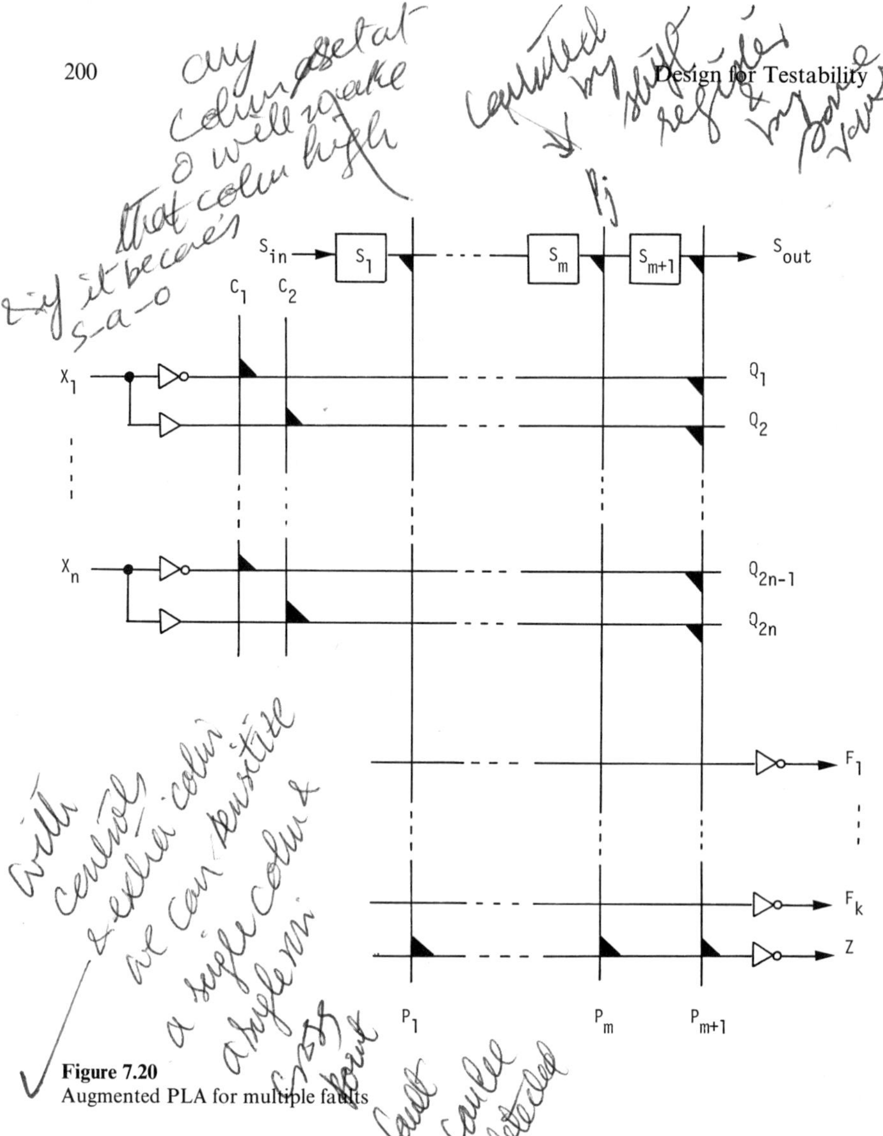

Figure 7.20
Augmented PLA for multiple faults

faults, crosspoint faults, and adjacent-line bridging faults in the PLA is detected.

- It is appropriate for built-in testing approaches, since input test patterns and output responses are both function-independent under the single-fault assumption.
- The design can be applied to the high-density PLAs using array folding techniques.

The augmented PLA is diagrammed in figure 7.20. It can be obtained by excluding two EOR cascades from the PLA of figure 7.18, though the connections of the added column and row in the AND and OR array are different. Obviously, the amount of extra hardware is significantly lower than with the previous designs of universally testable PLAs.

An extra product line P_{m+1} is added. This line has devices on all crosspoints in the AND array, i.e.,

$$P_{m+1} = \bar{Q}_1 \cdot \bar{Q}_2 \cdot \cdots \cdot \bar{Q}_{2n} \cdot \bar{S}_{m+1}$$

where Q_i is the ith row of the AND array. An extra output line Z is added. This line has devices on all product lines, i.e,

$$Z = P_1 + P_2 + \cdots + P_m + P_{m+1}.$$

The extra column P_{m+1} in the AND array can be used to test stuck-at, crosspoint, and bridging faults in the decoder and the control array, and also to test stuck-at and bridging faults on the rows of the AND array. The extra row and output line Z of the OR array can be used to test stuck-at and bridging faults on the columns (product lines) and crosspoint faults in the AND array in cooperation with other extra hardware.

The types of faults considered here are multiple faults such that any combination of the following types of faults occurs simultaneously:

- Stuck faults in the augmented PLA, i.e., stuck-at-0 and stuck-at-1 faults on lines, X_is, C_is, Q_is, P_is, F_is, Z, and S_is.
- Crosspoint faults in the control array, the AND array, and the OR array.
- Adjacent line bridging faults in the control array, the AND array, and the OR array, i.e., bridging faults between C_1 and C_2, Q_i and Q_{i+1}, P_i and P_{i+1}, F_i and F_{i+1}, and F_k and Z.

The technology used will determine what effect the bridging will have. In n-MOS circuits, low voltage will dominate, and hence a bridging fault between two lines will produce an AND function between the lines. However, the results given here can easily be modified to OR-type bridging faults.

Table 7.2 shows the test set $B_{n,m+1}$, which detects all multiple faults mentioned above (where n and m are the numbers of inputs and product terms, respectively) in the original PLA before augmentation. It will be proved that $B_{n,m+1}$ is the multiple-fault test set for the PLAs of figure 7.20 in the following lemmas and theorem.

LEMMA 7.2 I^1 and I_j^2 $(j = 1, 2, \ldots, m + 1)$ can detect all stuck-at faults in the shift register, all stuck-at faults on the product lines and rows of the OR array, all bridging faults between adjacent product lines and between adjacent rows of the OR array, and all devices missing from between the

Table 7.2
Universal test set $B_{n,m+1}$

	$X_1 \ldots X_i \ldots X_n$	C_1	C_2	$S_1 \ldots S_j \ldots S_m$	S_{m+1}
I^1	$0 \ldots\ldots\ldots 0$	1	0	$1 \ldots\ldots\ldots\ldots$	1
I_j^2 $(j = 1, \ldots, m+1)$	$0 \ldots\ldots\ldots 0$	1	0	$1 \ldots 0 \ldots\ldots$	1
I_{m+1}^3	$1 \ldots\ldots\ldots 1$	0	1	$1 \ldots\ldots\ldots 1$	0
I_{ij}^6 $(i = 1, \ldots, n; j = 1, \ldots, m+1)$	$1 \ldots 0 \ldots 1$	0	1	$1 \ldots 0 \ldots\ldots$	1
I_{ij}^7 $(i = 1, \ldots, n; j = 1, \ldots, m+1)$	$0 \ldots 1 \ldots 0$	1	0	$1 \ldots 0 \ldots\ldots$	1

cells of the shift register and from the bottom row (output line Z) of the OR array, independent of the presence of any other faults.

Proof By applying the test sequence $I^1 I_1^2 I_2^2 \cdots I_{m+1}^2$ and observing the response from S_{out}, it is checked whether all the cells can shift in and out both 0 and 1, independent of the rest of the PLA. Therefore, all the faults in the shift register can be detected by the test sequence.

Next, consider each output line (row of the OR array) F_i $(i = 1, 2, \ldots, k)$ and Z. The test sequence $I^1 I_1^2 I_2^2 \cdots I_{m+1}^2$ changes each output line from 0 to 1 at least once if it has at least one device on it. An output line F_i is called redundant if there exists no device on the line in the OR array (i.e., $F_i = 0$) or if there exists another output line F_j realizing the same function (i.e., $F_j = F_i$). We assume here that there are no such redundant output lines in the OR array. If such output lines exist, they should be removed from it since they take unnecessary space. Hence, all the stuck-at faults on the rows of the OR array can be detected by the test sequence. A bridging fault between the adjacent rows of the OR array implies that the corresponding two output functions become the same. This is detected by I^1 and I_j^2 $(j = 1, 2, \ldots, m + 1)$, since no output line is redundant. Hence, all bridging faults between the adjacent rows of the OR array are detected.

Henceforth, we can assume that both the shift register and Z are fault-free. Consider the device D_i^1 at the crosspoint of the cell S_i with the product line P_i, and the device D_i^2 at the crosspoint of the product line P_i with output line Z. Application of the test patterns I^1 and I_i^2 should change Z from 0 to 1. In these test patterns the only change occurs in S_i, which affects only D_i^1, P_i, D_i^2, and Z. If D_i^1 is missing, or P_i is stuck-at-0/1, or D_i^2 is missing, or bridging between P_i and its adjacent column exists, or if any combination of these faults exists, then Z will not change its value. Hence, all devices missing from between the cells of the shift register, all stuck-at faults on product lines, all bridging faults between adjacent product lines, and all devices missing from output line Z are detected by I^1 and I_j^2 ($j = 1, 2, \ldots, m + 1$). ■

By lemma 7.2, we can henceforth assume that the shift register, the product lines, the rows of the OR array, the crosspoints between the cells of the shift register, and the crosspoints on line Z are all fault-free, and that no bridging faults between the adjacent columns or between the adjacent rows of the OR array exist.

LEMMA 7.3 I_j^2 ($j = 1, 2, \ldots, m + 1$) detects any crosspoint faults in the OR array, independent of the presence of any other faults.

Proof By applying I_j^2, we set S_j to 0 and all other cells to 1. By hypothesis, the shift register, the product lines, the rows of the OR array, the crosspoints between the cells of the shift register, and the crosspoints on line Z are all fault-free, and no bridging faults between the adjacent columns or between the adjacent rows of the OR array exist. This guarantees that applying I_j^2 sets P_j to 1 and all other product lines to 0, independent of any other faults, and that all crosspoints in the jth column of the OR array are identified (whether a device exists or not) by the observation of the output lines of the OR array. ■

LEMMA 7.4 I_{m+1}^2, I_{m+1}^3, $I_{i,m+1}^6$, and $I_{i,m+1}^7$ ($i = 1, 2, \ldots, n$) can detect all devices missing from the column P_{m+1} of the AND array, independent of the existence of any other faults.

Proof By hypothesis, the shift register including the crosspoints between the cells, the product lines, and output line Z (including the crosspoints on Z) are fault-free, and no bridging faults between the adjacent product lines or between the adjacent rows of the OR array exist. Consider the device at the crosspoint of the row Q_{2i-1} with the column P_{m+1}. Application of the test patterns I_{m+1}^3 and $I_{i,m+1}^6$ should change Z from 1 to 0. The only change in the two patterns occurs in X_i, which changes Q_{2i-1} from 0 to 1 normally and may change Q_{2i} from 1 to 0 if any faults exist. Suppose that there is a missing-device fault at the crosspoint of Q_{2i-1} with P_{m+1}. If Z does not change from 1 to 0, a fault is indicated. Otherwise, Z changes from 1 to 0 (i.e., P_{m+1} changes from 1 to 0) in spite of the missing-device fault. This is possible only when Q_{2i} changes from 0 to 1. However, Q_{2i} never changes from 0 to 1 in the test patterns I_{m+1}^3 and $I_{i,m+1}^6$. Hence, the missing-device fault at the crosspoint of Q_{2i-1} with P_{m+1} can be detected by I_{m+1}^3 and I_{m+1}^6.

Similarly, one can prove that the missing-device fault at the crosspoint of the row Q_{2i} with the column P_{m+1} can be detected by the two test patterns I_{m+1}^2 and $I_{i,m+1}^7$. ■

By lemmas 7.2 and 7.4, we can henceforth assume that the shift register, the product lines, the rows of the OR array, the crosspoints between the cells of the shift register, and the crosspoints on lines Z and P_{m+1} are all fault-free, and that no bridging faults between the adjacent columns or between the adjacent rows of the OR array exist.

LEMMA 7.5 I_{m+1}^2, I_{m+1}^3, $I_{i,m+1}^6$, and $I_{i,m+1}^7$ $(i = 1, 2, \ldots, n)$ can detect all stuck-at faults on the rows of the AND array and all bridging faults between adjacent rows of the AND array, independent of the existence of any other faults.

Proof Application of the test patterns I_{m+1}^3 and $I_{i,m+1}^6$ changes X_i from 1 to 0 and Q_{2i-1} from 0 to 1. However, if there exists a stuck-at fault on Q_{2i-1} and/or a bridging fault between Q_{2i-1} and its adjacent row, then P_{m+1} never changes from 1 to 0. Hence, such a stuck-at fault and a bridging fault can be detected by observing Z. Similarly, we can show that I_{m+1}^2 and $I_{i,m+1}^7$ can detect a stuck-at fault on Q_{2i} and a bridging fault between Q_{2i} and its adjacent row, independent of the existence of any other faults. ■

By lemmas 7.2–7.5, it has been proved that all faults in the PLA except faults in the control array and crosspoint faults in the AND array are detected by the test set $B_{n,m+1}$. Hence, lemmas 7.6 and 7.7 below assume that the only faults present are the faults in the control array and/or crosspoint faults in the AND array except P_{m+1}.

LEMMA 7.6 I_{m+1}^2, I_{m+1}^3, $I_{i,m+1}^6$, and $I_{i,m+1}^7$ $(i = 1, 2, \ldots, n)$ can detect all stuck-at faults on C_1 and C_2, bridging faults between C_1 and C_2, and crosspoint faults on C_1 and C_2, independent of the existence of any other faults.

Proof The extra-device fault at the crosspoint of C_1 with Q_{2i} is detected by I_{m+1}^2 and $I_{i,m+1}^7$, independent of any other faults. Similarly, the extra-device fault at the crosspoint of C_2 with Q_{2i-1} is detected by I_{m+1}^3 and $I_{i,m+1}^6$. Further, we can see that the missing-device fault at the crosspoint of C_1 and Q_{2i-1} is detected by I_{m+1}^2, independent of any other faults. Similarly, the missing-device fault at the crosspoint of C_2 with Q_{2i} is detected by I_{m+1}^3.

Henceforth, we can assume that all crosspoints in the control array are fault-free. The stuck-at-0 faults on C_1 and C_2 are easily shown to be detected by I^2_{m+1} and I^3_{m+1}, respectively, under the assumption. Similarly, the stuck-at-1 faults on C_1 and C_2 are detected by $I^6_{i,m+1}$ and $I^7_{i,m+1}$, respectively, for any i. ■

LEMMA 7.7 I^6_{ij} and I^7_{ij} $(i = 1, 2, \ldots, n; j = 1, 2, \ldots, m + 1)$ can detect all crosspoint faults in the AND array except the column P_{m+1}, independent of the existence of any other faults.

Proof Now we can assume that the only faults present are the crosspoint faults in the AND array except P_{m+1}, because all other faults are detected by $B_{n,m+1}$ as shown in lemmas 7.2–7.6. By applying I^6_{ij}, we can detect the presence or absence of a device at the crosspoint of Q_{2i-1} with P_j. If the value of Z is 0 (1), then there exists a device (no device) at the crosspoint. Similarly, by the application of I^7_{ij}, it can be checked whether there exists a device at the crosspoint of Q_{2i} with P_j. Hence, all the crosspoint faults in the AND array are detected by I^6_{ij} and I^7_{ij} $(i = 1, 2, \ldots, n; j = 1, 2, \ldots, m + 1)$. ■

Now we can complete the following theorem by collecting lemmas 7.2–7.7.

THEOREM 7.3 The augmented PLA of figure 7.20 can be tested for all multiple faults (that is, any combination of stuck-at faults, crosspoint faults, and bridging faults in the PLA) by the test set $B_{n,m+1}$ given in table 7.2.

By theorem 7.3, the test set $B_{n,m+1}$ is shown to be the multiple-fault test set for the augmented PLAs of figure 7.20. Further the test patterns are function-independent, but their responses are not. However, the responses of test patterns can easily be derived from the personality matrix of the PLA. Another design for PLAs, in which both the input test patterns and their responses are independent of the function under the single-fault assumption, is presented in Fujiwara 1984.

8 Scan Design for Sequential Logic Circuits

In chapters 6 and 7 we considered the problem of enhancing testability in combinational circuits and several methods of designing combinational circuits that are easy to test. This chapter treats the subject of sequential circuits. When we generate a test sequence for a sequential circuit, we are confronted with two added difficulties that do not arise in the case of a combinational circuit:

- In general, the initial state of the circuit is unknown. Hence, we must set its state to the initial state required for the test. That is, the controllability is required to set the initial state of the circuit under test.
- The faulty signal must be propagated to at least one of the primary outputs. If the effect of the fault causes an incorrect final state, we must supply a sequence of input patterns that will observe the final state of the circuit. That is, the observability of the final state of the circuit is required to check the faulty state.

Such controllability and observability requirements are not easily met in general sequential circuits. To overcome this problem, several approaches have been proposed in which a sequential circuit is designed in such a way that the circuit can easily be set to any desired internal state and the internal states of the circuit can easily be observed.

This chapter presents several techniques of designing sequential circuits having such properties. Most of the approaches are based on *scan design*, in which all flip-flops in a circuit are interconnected into one or more shift registers and the contents of the shift registers are shifted in and out.

8.1 State-Shiftable Machines

A sequential machine M is defined by a quintuple $M = (S, I, O, N, Z)$ where $S = \{S_1, S_2, \ldots, S_n\}$ is a set of states, $I = \{I_1, I_2, \ldots, I_m\}$ is a set of input symbols, $O = \{O_1, O_2, \ldots, O_k\}$ is a set of output symbols, $N: S \times I \rightarrow S$ is the next-state function, and $Z: S \times I \rightarrow O$ is the output function. This quintuple can be represented by a state table.

We assume that each fault transforms the normal machine M_0 into some other state table M_i with n or fewer states. That is, any fault that occurs is assumed not to increase the number of states. A test sequence is thus a sequence of inputs that distinguishes M_0 from each of M_i defined by a fault. Such a test sequence is referred to as a *checking sequence*.

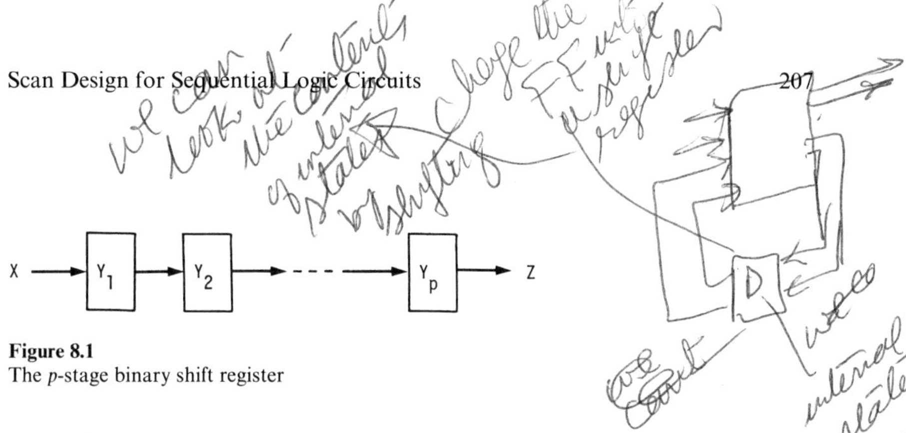

Figure 8.1
The p-stage binary shift register

A *synchronizing sequence* for a sequential machine M is an input sequence whose application is guaranteed to leave M in a certain final state, regardless of the particular initial state of M. A *homing sequence* for M is an input sequence whose application makes it possible to determine the final state of M by observing the corresponding output sequence that M produces. A *distinguishing sequence* is an input sequence whose application makes it possible to determine the initial state of M by observing the corresponding output sequence M produces.

We define an easily testable machine referred to as a *state-shiftable machine* as a reduced and strongly connected machine possessing a distinguishing sequence X_d of length $\lceil \log_2 n \rceil$ that forces the machine into a specific final state S_1 (i.e., X_d is also a synchronizing sequence) and also possesses transfer sequences $T(i)$ with a length that is at most $\lceil \log_2 n \rceil$ to move the machine from state S_1 to state S_i for all i, where n is the number of states of the machine.

Example 8.1 Consider the p-stage binary shift register shown in figure 8.1, a serial connection of p flip-flops interconnected so that at the occurrence of a shift signal the contents of the ith flip-flop are shifted into the $(i + 1)$st flip-flops. Let $Y_1, Y_2, \ldots, Y_p$ be the state variables, let X be the input variable, and let Z be the output variable. For the p-stage shift register, a p-tuple state assignment $Y_1 Y_2 \cdots Y_p$ can be found for each state such that $Y_i(t + 1) = Y_{i-1}(t)$ for $i = 2, 3, \ldots, p$, $Y_1(t + 1) = X(t)$, and $Z(t) = Y_p(t)$, where $Y_1(t)$, $Y_2(t), \ldots, Y_p(t)$, and $Z(t)$ are the values of $Y_1, Y_2, \ldots, Y_p, X$, and Z at time t, respectively. Then it is easily seen that any input sequence of length p will be both a distinguishing and a synchronizing sequence, and that $Y_p Y_{p-1} \cdots Y_1$ is a transfer sequence of length p that carries the p-stage shift register to state S_i with state assignment $Y_1 Y_2 \cdots Y_p$. Therefore, the p-stage shift register shown in figure 8.1 is a state-shiftable machine.

Fujiwara et al. (1975) presented the following procedure to augment a given machine by adding two extra input symbols so that the augmented machine is a state-shiftable machine. Let $M = (S, I, O, N, Z)$ be a given machine, where $S = \{S_1, S_2, \ldots, S_n\}$, $I = \{I_1, I_2, \ldots, I_m\}$, and $O = \{O_1, O_2, \ldots, O_k\}$.

Augmentation Procedure

Add new states $S_{n+1}, S_{n+2}, \ldots, S_{n*}$ to M if n is not an integral power of 2, where $n^* = 2^p$ and $p = \lceil \log_2 n \rceil$.

Assign a p-bit binary code to all states such that each state has only one assignment.

Add new input symbols $\varepsilon_0, \varepsilon_1$ to M. The next function N and the output function Z for the new input symbols $\varepsilon_0, \varepsilon_1$ are defined as follows: For each state S_i, with state assignment $Y_1 Y_2 \cdots Y_p$, $N(S_i, \varepsilon_0) = S_u$, and $N(S_i, \varepsilon_1) = S_v$,

$$
\begin{aligned}
Z(S_i, \varepsilon_0) = Z(S_i, \varepsilon_1) &= O_1 \qquad \text{if } Y_p = 0 \\
&= O_2 \qquad \text{if } Y_p = 1
\end{aligned}
$$

where S_u and S_v have state assignments $O Y_1 Y_2 \cdots Y_{p-1}$ and $1 Y_1 Y_2 \cdots Y_{p-1}$, respectively.

The effect of this state transition is to shift the state assignment one digit to the right and introduce a 0 or a 1 as new leftmost digit according to input ε_0 or ε_1, respectively. Thus, this two-column submachine restricted to inputs ε_0 and ε_1 is isomorphic to the p-stage binary shift register. Since the p-stage shift register is a state-shiftable machine, this two-column submachine is also state-shiftable, and hence the augmented machine M^* is too. Indeed, in the augmented machine M^* obtained above, any input sequence of length $p = \lceil \log_2 n \rceil$ consisting of ε_0 and ε_1 is both a distinguishing sequence and a synchronizing sequence, and $\varepsilon_{Y_p}\varepsilon_{Y_{p-1}} \cdots \varepsilon_{Y_2}\varepsilon_{Y_1}$ is a transfer sequence of length p that transfers M^* from an arbitrary state to state S_i with state assignment $Y_1 Y_2 \cdots Y_p$. The augmented machine M^* has n^* states and $(m + 2)$ input symbols, where $\log_2 n^* = \lceil \log_2 n \rceil$.

Example 8.2 Consider machine A, defined in table 8.1. Machine A is not strongly connected and does not have a distinguishing sequence. By applying the above procedure, we obtain the augmented machine A* (table 8.2). Machine A* has a distinguishing sequence $\varepsilon_0 \varepsilon_0$, which is also a synchronizing sequence whose final state is S_1. The transfer sequences for machine A* are as given in table 8.3. Hence, the augmented machine A* is a state-shiftable machine.

Table 8.1
Machine A

State	Input 0	1
S_1	S_2, 1	S_1, 1
S_2	—	S_3, 0
S_3	S_2, 0	—, 1

Dash means "don't care."

Table 8.2
Augmented machine A*

State		Input 0	1	ε_0	ε_1
00	S_1	S_2, 1	S_1, 1	S_1, 0	S_3, 0
01	S_2	—	S_3, 0	S_1, 1	S_3, 1
10	S_3	S_2, 0	—, 1	S_2, 0	S_4, 0
11	S_4	—	—	S_2, 1	S_4, 1

Table 8.3
Transfer sequences $T(i)$ for machine A*

$T(1)$	$T(2)$	$T(3)$	$T(4)$
Λ	$\varepsilon_1\varepsilon_0$	ε_1	$\varepsilon_1\varepsilon_1$

Λ means the null sequence.

Now let us derive checking sequences for state-shiftable machine. Let $M = (S, I, O, N, Z)$ be an n-state, m-input state-shiftable machine. Let X_d be an input sequence of length $\lceil \log_2 n \rceil$ that is both a distinguishing sequence and a synchronizing sequence. Let S_1 be the final state resulting from the application of X_d. The transfer sequence with a length that is at most $\lceil \log_2 n \rceil$ to move M from state S_1 to state S_i is denoted by $T(i)$.

The checking sequence consists of five parts. The first part of the checking sequence, the initializing part, brings the machine under test to the starting state S_1. This can be done by a synchronizing sequence X_d. Hence, the first part has the form

$$\begin{array}{llll} \text{Input:} & & X_d & \\ \text{State:} & - & & S_1 \\ \text{Output:} & & - & \end{array} \tag{8.1}$$

where the dash means "don't care."

The second part of the checking sequence carries the correctly operating machine through all its states, displays all the different responses to X_d, and thus verifies that X_d is a distinguishing sequence. Thus, the second part has the form

$$\begin{array}{llll} \text{Input:} & & X_d & \\ \text{State:} & S_i & & S_1 \\ \text{Output:} & & Z_i & \end{array} \tag{8.2}$$

for all states S_i of M, where $Z_i = Z(S_i, X_d)$.

The third part of the checking sequence verifies, by the use of a distinguishing sequence, X_d validated by 8.2, that X_d is a synchronizing sequence used to force the correctly operating machine into state S_1. Thus, this part has the form

$$\begin{array}{llllll} \text{Input:} & & X_d & & X_d & \\ \text{State:} & S_i & & S_1 & & S_1 \\ \text{Output:} & & Z_i & & Z_1 & \end{array} \tag{8.3}$$

for all states S_i of M.

The fourth part of the checking sequence verifies that $T(i)$ transfers the rectly operating machine from state S_1 to state S_i. This can be done by istinguishing sequence X_d as follows:

$$\begin{array}{llllllll}
\text{Input:} & & X_{\mathrm{d}} & & T(i) & & X_{\mathrm{d}} & \\
\text{State:} & — & & S_1 & & S_i & & S_1 \\
\text{Output:} & & — & & Z_{1i} & & Z_i &
\end{array} \tag{8.4}$$

for all states S_i, where $Z_{1i} = Z(S_i, T(i))$.

The fifth part of the checking sequence is to be designed to check all the transitions and has the form

$$\begin{array}{llllllllll}
\text{Input:} & & X_{\mathrm{d}} & & T(i) & & I_j & & X_{\mathrm{d}} & \\
\text{State:} & — & & S_1 & & S_i & & S_{ij} = N(S_i, I_j) & & S_1 \\
\text{Output:} & & — & & Z_{1i} & & O_{ij} = Z(S_i, I_j) & & &
\end{array} \tag{8.5}$$

for all states S_i and input symbols I_j.

Because the distinguishing sequence X_{d} and the transfer sequence $T(i)$ have been validated by the previous parts of the checking sequence, S_i is uniquely determined by $T(i)$ and S_{ij} is recognized by X_{d}. If both $N(S_i, I_j)$ and $Z(S_i, I_j)$ are unspecified, then such a transition from S_i under input I_j need not be checked.

Although the checking sequence is functionally subdivided into five parts, these parts need not be physically separated from each other. Parts 1–4 can be completely contained in the sequences

$$\begin{array}{llllllllll}
\text{Input:} & & X_{\mathrm{d}} & & T(i) & & X_{\mathrm{d}} & & X_{\mathrm{d}} & \\
\text{State:} & — & & S_1 & & S_i & & S_1 & & S_1 \\
\text{Output:} & & — & & Z_{1i} & & Z_i & & Z_1 &
\end{array} \tag{8.6}$$

for all states S_i.

Thus, the total checking sequence is to be organized from the subsequences 8.5 and 8.6, and we have the following checking sequence.

$$\begin{array}{llllllllllllll}
\text{Input:} & & X_{\mathrm{d}} & T(1) & & X_{\mathrm{d}}X_{\mathrm{d}} & & T(2) & & X_{\mathrm{d}}X_{\mathrm{d}}\cdots & & & & \\
\text{State:} & — & S_1 & & S_1 & & S_1 & & S_2 & & & S_1 & & \\
 & X_{\mathrm{d}} & & T(n) & & X_{\mathrm{d}}X_{\mathrm{d}} & & T(1) & & I_1X_{\mathrm{d}} & & T(1) & & I_2X_{\mathrm{d}}\cdots \\
 & & S_1 & & S_n & & S_1 & & S_1 & & S_1 & & S_1 & \\
 & X_{\mathrm{d}} & & T(i) & & I_jX_{\mathrm{d}}\cdots & & X_{\mathrm{d}} & & T(n) & & I_mX_{\mathrm{d}} & & \\
 & & S_1 & & S_i & & & & S_1 & & S_n & & &
\end{array}$$

Let us derive the bound on the length of the checking sequence. Since the machine M is a state-shiftable machine, $|X_{\mathrm{d}}| = \lceil \log_2 n \rceil$ and $|T(i)| < \lceil \log_2 n \rceil$ for $i = 1, 2, \ldots, n$, where $|X|$ is the length of X. From the organization of the checking sequence, it can be seen that the total length of the sequence is at most

$$|X_{\mathrm{d}}| + \sum_{i=1}^{n} (|T(i)| + 2|X_{\mathrm{d}}|) + \sum_{j=1}^{m} \sum_{i=1}^{n} (|T(i)| + |I_j| + |X_{\mathrm{d}}|)$$

$$= (2n + 1)|X_{\mathrm{d}}| + \sum_{i=1}^{n} |T(i) + mn(|X_{\mathrm{d}}| + 1) + m \sum_{i=1}^{n} |T(i)|$$

$$\leqslant (2n + 1)\lceil \log_2 n \rceil + n\lceil \log_2 n \rceil + mn(\lceil \log_2 n \rceil + 1) + mn\lceil \log_2 n \rceil$$

$$= (3n + 1)\lceil \log_2 n \rceil + mn(2\lceil \log_2 n \rceil + 1).$$

Thus, the upper bound on the length of the checking sequence is

$$(3n + 1)\lceil \log_2 n \rceil + mn(2\lceil \log_2 n \rceil + 1),$$

which is $O(mn\lceil \log n \rceil)$.

Example 8.3 Let us construct a checking sequence for the machine A* defined by table 8.2. $X_{\mathrm{d}} = \varepsilon_0\varepsilon_0$ is a distinguishing and synchronizing sequence whose final state is S_1. The transfer sequences $T(i)$ from state S_1 to each state S_i are given in table 8.3.

The total checking sequence is

Input:	X_{d}	$T(1)$	X_{d}	X_{d}	$T(2)$	X_{d}	X_{d}	$T(3)$	X_{d}	X_{d}	$T(4)$	X_{d}	X_{d}
Output:	—	Λ	00	00	00	10	00	0	01	00	00	11	00

$T(1)$	0	X_{d}	$T(1)$	1	X_{d}	$T(1)$	ε_0	X_{d}	$T(1)$	ε_1	X_{d}
Λ	1	10	Λ	1	00	Λ	0	00	Λ	0	01

$T(2)$	1	X_{d}	$T(2)$	ε_0	X_{d}	$T(2)$	ε_1	X_{d}	$T(3)$	0	X_{d}
00	0	01	00	1	00	00	1	01	0	0	10

$T(3)$	1	X_{d}	$T(3)$	ε_0	X_{d}	$T(3)$	ε_1	X_{d}	$T(4)$	ε_0	X_{d}
0	1	—	0	0	10	0	0	11	00	1	10

$T(4)$	ε_1	X_{d}
00	1	11

In the above checking sequence, some subsequences are equivalent and thus can be deleted. Then we obtain the reduced checking sequence

Input:	ε_0	ε_0	$T(1)$	ε_0	ε_0	ε_0	ε_0	$T(2)$	ε_0	ε_0	ε_0	ε_0	$T(3)$
Output:	—	—	Λ	0	0	0	0	00	1	0	0	0	0

ε_0	ε_0	ε_0	ε_0	$T(4)$	ε_0	ε_0	ε_0	ε_0	$T(1)$	0	ε_0	ε_0	$T(1)$
0	1	0	0	00	1	1	0	0	Λ	1	1	0	Λ

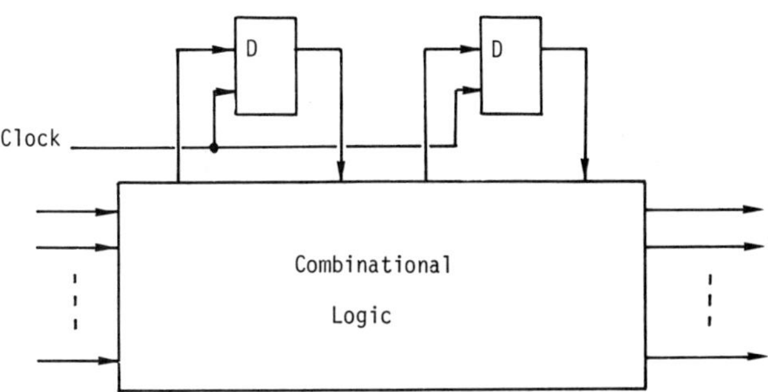

Figure 8.2
Sequential circuit with clocked D flip-flops

$$
\begin{array}{ccccccccccccccc}
1 & \varepsilon_0 & \varepsilon_0 & T(2) & 1 & \varepsilon_0 & \varepsilon_0 & T(2) & \varepsilon_1 & \varepsilon_0 & \varepsilon_0 & T(3) & 0 & \varepsilon_0 & \varepsilon_0 \\
1 & 0 & 0 & 00 & 0 & 0 & 1 & 00 & 1 & 0 & 1 & 0 & 0 & 1 & 0 \\
1 & \varepsilon_0 & \varepsilon_0 & T(4) & \varepsilon_1 & \varepsilon_0 & \varepsilon_0 \\
1 & - & - & 00 & 1 & 1 & 1
\end{array}
$$

8.2 Scan Design Approaches

The term *scan* refers to the ability to shift into or out of any state of sequential circuits. In *scan design approaches*, all flip-flops in the circuit are interconnected into one or more shift registers and the contents of the shift registers are shifted in and out. All the states of the circuit are completely controlled and observed from primary inputs and outputs, and thus all flip-flops can behave as primary inputs/outputs. Therefore, it turns out that the sequential circuit can be thought of as purely combinational and the complexity of test generation for the circuit can be substantially reduced. This section presents three typical scan design approaches: the shift-register-modification approach of Williams and Angell (1973), the Scan Path approach of Kobayashi et al. (1968) and Funatsu et al. (1975), and the Level-Sensitive Scan Design (LSSD) approach of Eichelberger and Williams (1977, 1978).

Shift-Register Modification

Let us consider a sequential circuit in which clocked D flip-flops are used as the storage elements, as shown in figure 8.2. The structure of the shift-register-modification approach proposed by Williams and Angell (1973) is

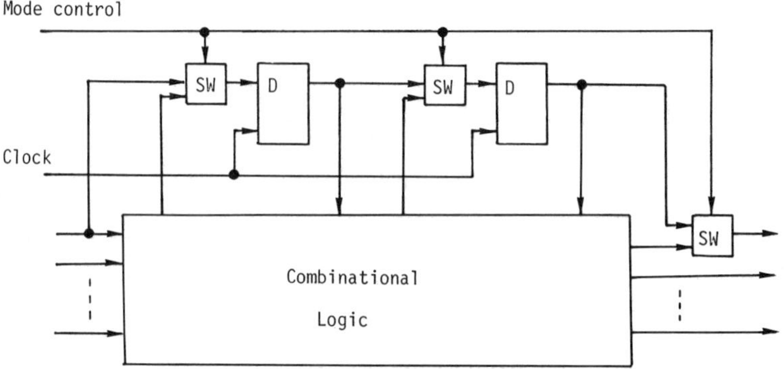

Figure 8.3
Modified sequential circuit (Williams and Angell 1973; © IEEE 1973)

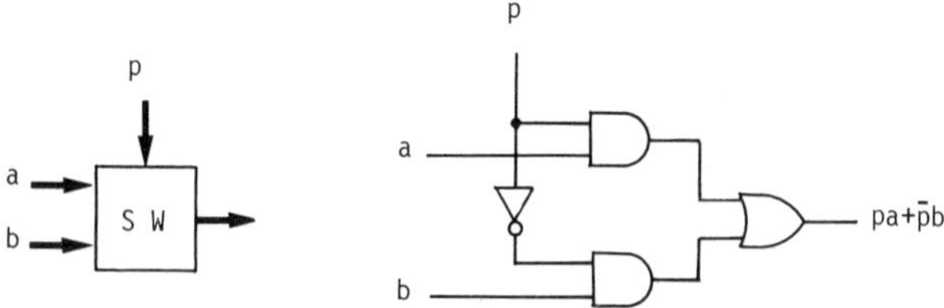

Figure 8.4
Double-throw switch

illustrated in figure 8.3. The modification is done by inserting a double-throw switch at each input lead of every flip-flop and in the lead that drives one of the primary outputs of the circuit. Each of the double-throw switches may be implemented as shown in figure 8.4. The modified sequential circuit shown in figure 8.3 can operate either in its normal mode or in the shift-register mode. When the mode control is supplied with a 0, the circuit operates in the normal mode; that is, it behaves exactly as it did before the modifications were carried out. On the other hand, when the mode-control signal is a 1, all flip-flops in the circuit are connected in a chain and the circuit behaves as a shift register. In this shift-register mode, the first flip-flop can be set directly from a primary input and the output of the last flip-flop can be directly monitored at a primary output. Hence, we can easily set the modified circuit to any desired internal state by supplying the corresponding values to the shift register, and we can easily observe the internal state of the circuit by shifting out the contents of the shift register. Thus the test-generation problem for sequential circuits can be reduced to that of combinational circuits, since all flip-flops can behave as primary inputs/outputs. The procedure for testing the modified circuit is as follows:

(1) Switch to the shift-register mode and check the shift-register operation by shifting in and out an alternating sequence of ones and zeros.
(2) Set the initial state into the shift register.
(3) Return to the normal mode and apply the test input pattern.
(4) Switch to the shift-register mode and shift out the final state while setting the starting state for the next test. Return to step 3.

Here, for the sake of simplicity, we have considered a sequential circuit with D flip-flops. However, shift-register modification can be performed in the same fashion for *JK* and other flip-flops. Since a switch is inserted in each input lead of every flip-flop, the number of switches used is doubled for two-input flip-flops.

Scan Path

Before Williams and Angell presented the shift-register-modification approach mentioned above, an approach to scan design called the Scan Path had already been developed (Kobayashi et al. 1968; Funatsu et al. 1975). Kobayashi et al. reported that the Scan Path approach had been to practical use for a system with 100,000 gates or more (the NEC system 2200/700). The Scan Path approach was the first practical implementation of shift registers for testing to be incorporated in a complete system.

The Scan Path approach uses as a memory element the raceless D-type flip-flop, illustrated in figure 8.5. These raceless D-type flip-flops are connected in a serial scan path as shown in figure 8.6. The flip-flop is composed of two latches operating in master-slave fashion, and has two clocks to select either scan input (called test input) or data input. These clocks operate exclusively so that the value of the data input can be inhibited while the value of the test input is being loaded into the flip-flop and vice versa.

In the normal mode, clock 2 retains logic value 1 to block the test input (scan input) from affecting the values in latch 1, and also not to disturb the values in latch 2. Clock 1 is used to load the value of the data input into the flip-flop. When clock 1 is at value 0, the value of the data input can be loaded into latch 1. After sufficient time has passed to load the data, clock 1

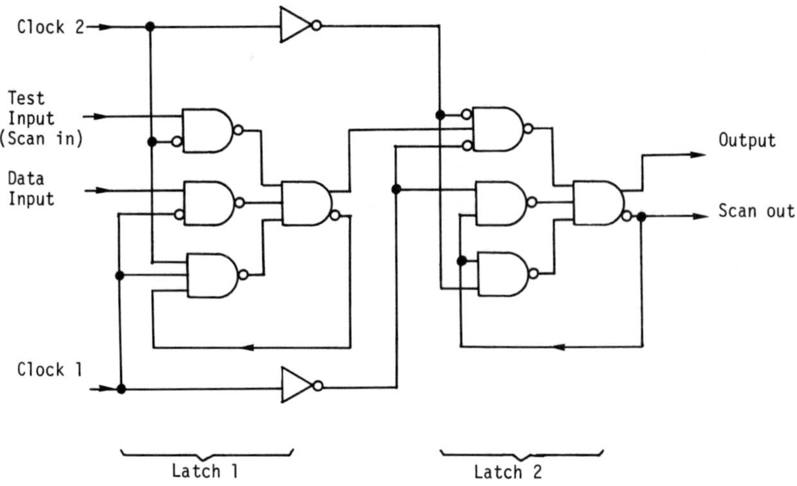

Figure 8.5
Raceless D-type flip-flop with Scan Path (Kobayashi et al. 1968; Funatsu et al. 1975; © IEEE 1975)

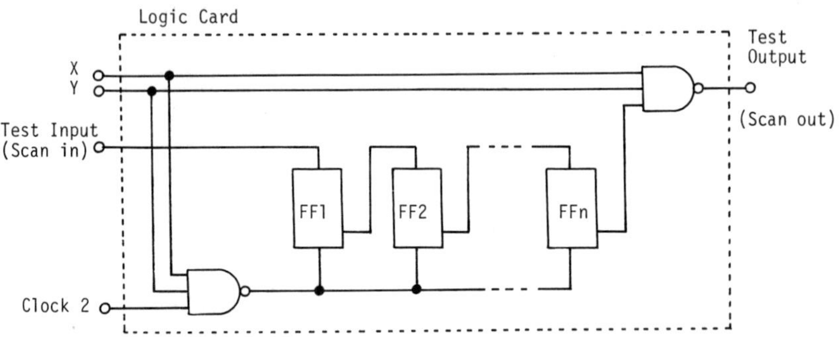

Figure 8.6
Configuration of Scan Path

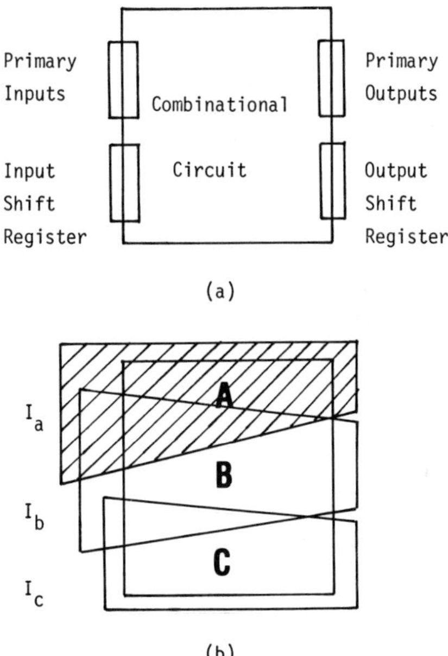

Figure 8.7
Transformed combinational model and partitioning

changes from 0 to 1. It then makes latch 2 sensitive to the data output of latch 1. While clock 1 retains value 1, the data from latch 1 are loaded into latch 2.

In the shift-register mode, clock 1 is set to 1 to prevent the data input from affecting the values in latch 1. The value of the test input is loaded into latch 1 by clock 2 when clock 2 is 0, and the results of latch 1 are loaded into latch 2 when clock 2 is 1. Since all flip-flops are interconnected to form a serial scan path as shown in figure 8.6, test input data applied to the first flip-flop can be shifted through the chain of flip-flops.

Many advantages are brought about by this Scan Path approach. The most prominent one is that a sequential circuit is converted into a combinational circuit, thus reducing the cost of test generation significantly. The circuit can be modeled as shown in figure 8.7(a), where each flip-flop belongs either to the input shift register or to the output shift register. Another advantage of the Scan Path approach is logical circuit partitioning. In the model of figure 8.7(a), it is possible to partition the circuit into small subcircuits. Figure 8.7(b) shows the subcircuits A, B, and C that make up the original circuit. A partition can be generated automatically by backtracing from the flip-flops through the combinational logic until a flip-flop or a primary input is encountered in the backtrace. In figure 8.7(b), outputs of subcircuit A are determined solely by the inputs I_a and do not depend on any other inputs. Subcircuit C and a section of subcircuit B do not have any effect on the test generation of subcircuit A. Hence, test generation for each subcircuit can be performed independent of other parts. When the partition is too large, it can be further partitioned by the insertion of extra flip-flops.

Level-Sensitive Scan Design (LSSD)

Using an approach similar to the Scan Path approach, Eichelberger and Williams (1977, 1978) introduced a concept of level-sensitive design coupled with the scan operation mentioned above. This method, called *Level-Sensitive Scan Design* (LSSD), ensures race-free system operation as well as race-free testing. LSSD is IBM's discipline for structural design for testability and has been used in many IBM systems.

To provide reliable operation in timing, the designer must consider the testing of several AC design parameters, such as rise time, fall time, and delay. However, with LSI and VLSI it will become impossible or impractical to test each circuit for all the AC design parameters. The LSSD approach aims at obtaining logic circuits that are insensitive to those ac characteristics. The term *level-sensitive* is defined by Eichelberger and Williams (1977, 1978) as follows: A logic circuit is level-sensitive if and only if the steady-state response to any allowed input state change is independent of the delays within the circuit. Also, if an input signal, then the response must be independent of the order in which they change. Steady-state response is the final value of all logic gate outputs after all change activity has terminated.

To obtain such level-sensitive logic circuits, we need a level-sensitive memory element that does not contain a hazard or a race condition. Figure 8.8 shows the polarity-hold latch, which is level-sensitive. When $C = 0$, the latch cannot change state. When $C = 1$, the internal state of the latch is set to the value of the data input D. This polarity-hold latch is further augmented to include shift capability. Figure 8.9 shows the *shift register latch* (SRL) used in LSSD as the basic memory element. The polarity-hold SRL consists of two latches, L_1 and L_2, which have the scan input I, the data input

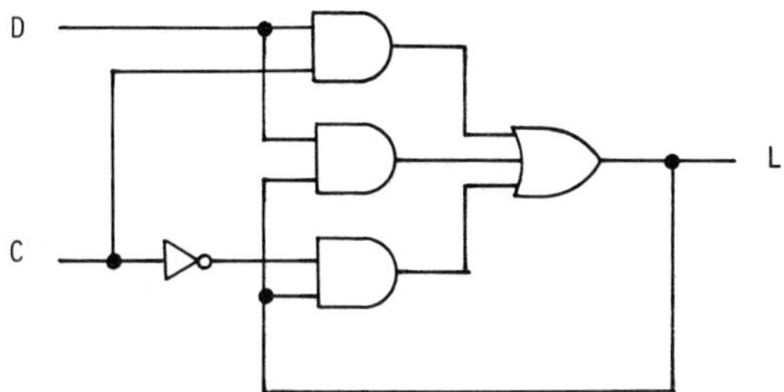

Figure 8.8
Hazard-free polarity-hold latch

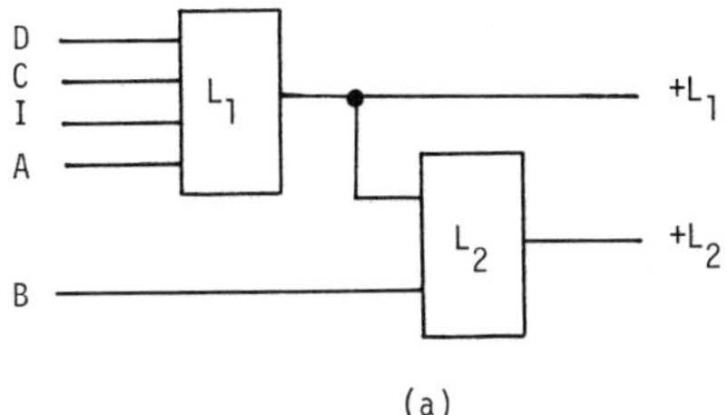

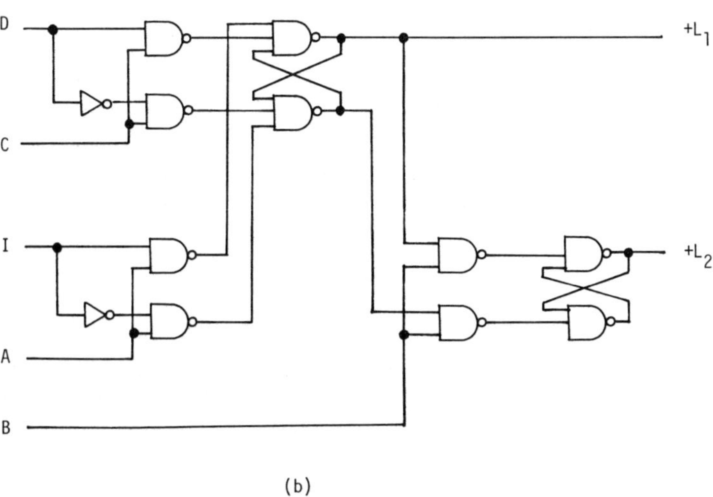

Figure 8.9
Polarity-hold SRL (Eichelberger and Williams 1977, 1978; © IEEE 1977)

D, the system clock C, and two shift-control inputs, A and B. In the normal operation mode, the shift signals A and B are both set to 0 and the L_1 latch operates exactly like a polarity-hold latch. The clock signal C is 0 during the time when the data input D may be changed. After the data input has become stable at either 1 or 0, the clock C will change to 1, which causes the L_1 latch to be set to the value of the data input D. In the shift-register mode, the clock C is set to 0 and both shift signals A and B are alternately changed to shift data through latches L_1 and L_2. First, by changing A to 1, data from the preceding stage can be loaded into latch L_1 through the scan input I. Then, after A has changed back to 0, the B shift signal changes to 1 to load the data from latch L_1 into latch L_2. The $+L_2$ output of latch L_2 is connected to the scan input I of the next-state SRL. All SRLs are interconnected into a shift register, as shown in figure 8.10.

Eichelberger and Williams (1977, 1978) presented the following set of design rules or constraints, which will result in level-sensitive and scannable design to aid testing.

(1) All internal storage is implemented in hazard-free polarity-hold latches.
(2) The latches are controlled by two or more non-overlapping clocks such that
(i) A latch, X, may feed the data port of another latch, Y, if and only if the clock that sets the data into latch Y does not clock latch X.
(ii) A latch, X, may gate a clock C_i to produce a gated clock C_{ig} which drives another latch, Y, if and only if clock C_{ig} does not clock latch X, where C_{ig} is any clock derived from C_i.
(3) It must be possible to identify a set of clock primary inputs from which the clock inputs to SRLs are controlled either through simple powering trees or through logic that is gated by SRLs and/or non-clock primary inputs. Given this structure, the following rules must hold:
(i) All clock inputs to all SRLs must be at their "off" states when all clock primary inputs are held to their "off" state.
(ii) The clock signal that appears at any clock input of an SRL must be contollable from one or more clock PIs such that it is possible to set the clock input of the SRL to an "on" state by turning any one of the corresponding clock PIs to its "on" state and also setting the required gating conditions from SRLs and/or non-clock PIs.
(iii) No clock can be ANDed with either the true or complement value of another clock.

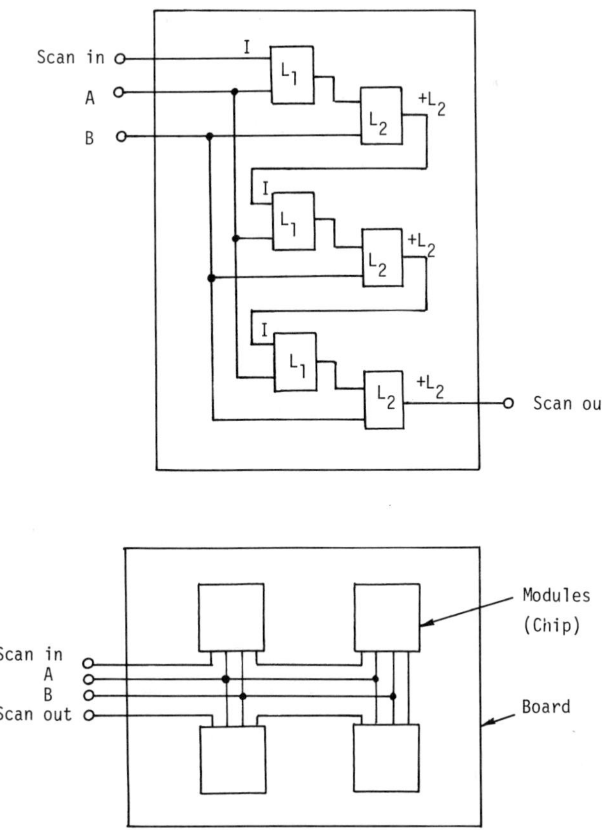

Figure 8.10
Interconnection of SRLs

(4) Clock primary inputs may not feed the data inputs to latches either directly or through combinational logic, but may only feed the clock input to the latches or primary outputs.
(5) All SRLs must be interconnected into one or more shift registers, each of which has an input, an output, and shift clocks available at the terminals of the package.
(6) There must exist some primary-input sensitizing condition (referred to as the scan state) such that
(i) Each SRL or scan-out PO is a function of only the single preceding SRL or scan-in PI in its shift register during the shifting operation.

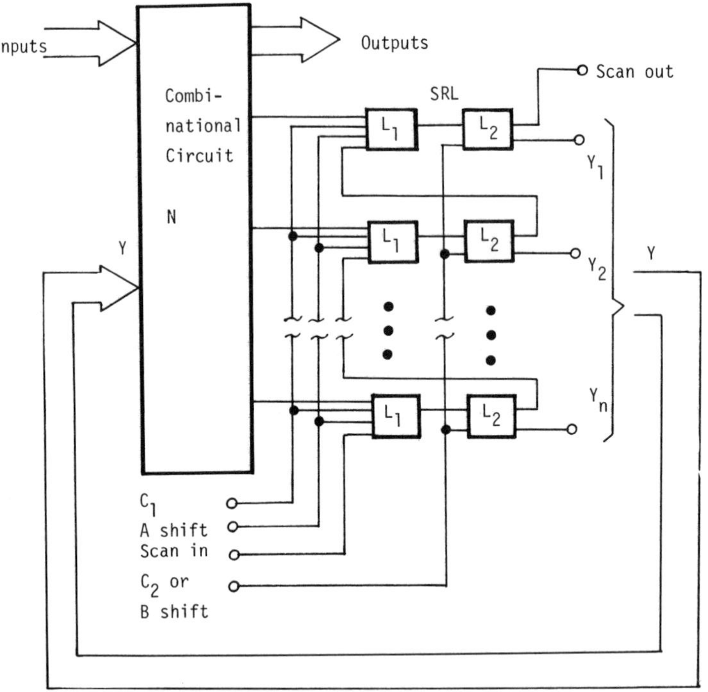

Figure 8.11
General structure for double-latch LSSD (Eichelberger and Williams 1977, 1978; © IEEE 1977)

(ii) All clocks except the shift clocks are held "off" at the SRL inputs.
(iii) Any shift clock to an SRL may be turned "on" and "off" by changing the corresponding clock primary input for each clock.

Whether a logic circuit is designed in compliance with these rules can be checked by a method developed by Godoy et al. (1977). Figure 8.11 shows a general structure for a logic circuit that follows the above LSSD rules. The circuit in figure 8.11 is called a double-latch design, since all the feedback inputs into the combinational circuit N are taken from the L_2 latch.

All storage elements are implemented as a set of master-slave latches L_1 and L_2. Each of the master-slave latches is connected in series and clocked by two nonoverlapping clocks C_1 and C_2, where C_2 is equivalent to B. When C_1 is active, C_2 is 0 and the inputs and outputs of N are stable. Some of the L_1 latches change their states while C_1 is 1. As soon as C_1 is changed back to 0, the next clock C_2 occurs; that is, C_2 changes to 1. The values of the L_1 latches are loaded into the L_2 latches while C_2 is 1.

In the shift-register mode, the SRLs are chained to form a shift register under the control of clocks A and B. Test patterns are applied to the combinational circuit by scanning them into the shift register and applying them at the primary inputs. Then the clock C_1 is set to 1 and the response of the combinational circuit is captured in the L_1 latches and at the primary outputs. The result of the test captured in the register is then scanned out.

Since the LSSD has the scan capability, it also has the same advantages as the shift-register modification of Williams and Angell and the Scan Path. The scan capability reduces the sequential test-generation problem to a combinational one and makes logical partitioning of the circuit possible, thus significantly simplifying the testing problem. Another advantage of the LSSD is that ac testing, test generation, and fault simulation are greatly simplified, because the correct operation of the logic circuit is nearly independent of the ac characteristics and also because hazards and races are eliminated.

However, the LSSD has also some negative aspects. The SRLs are logically 2–3 times as complex as simple latches, requiring up to four additional primary inputs/outputs for control of the shift registers. Eichelberger and Williams (1977, 1978) comment that the actual logic gate overhead for implementing the LSSD has been in the range of 4–20 percent. The difference is due to the extent to which the designer made use of the L_2 latches for the system function. As mentioned earlier, LSSD circuits can be designed in double-latch or single-latch mode. In the former case, as in figure 8.11, system-design considerations require both L_1 and L_2 latches to be in the system path, and both are therefore considered as system latches. In the latter case, however, only the L_1 latch is in the system data path and the L_2 latch is used only for shifting in test mode. Hence, the L_2 latch is an overhead for testability.

DasGupta et al. (1982) have reported a variation of the SRL that can reduce the gate overhead for LSSD (figure 8.12). The difference between the L_2 of figure 8.9 and the L_2^* of figure 8.12 is that the L_2^* latch has two independent data ports. The first port is fed by the related L_1 latch and clocked by shift clock B. This allows the L_2^* latch to behave as the slave latch in the shift-register path. The second data port serves as an independent system data port clocked by system clock C* to permit different system data to be stored in the L_2^* latch during system operation. In this way, the two latches in the new SRL proposed by DasGupta et al. are fully used even in

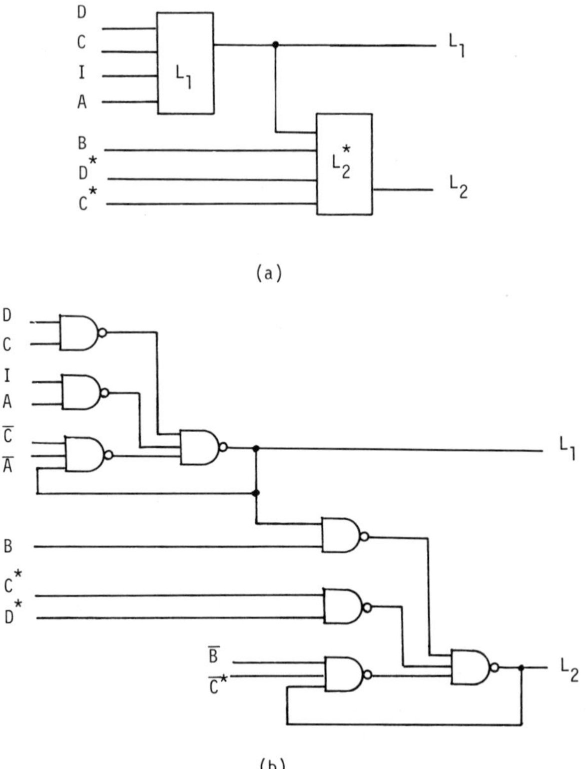

Figure 8.12
SRL with L_2^* latch (DasGupta et al. 1982; © IEEE 1982)

the normal operation. Therefore, the gate overhead for the LSSD is significantly reduced as compared with the single-latch LSSD using the SRLs of figure 8.9.

Another variation of the SRL has been reported by Saluja (1982). Figure 8.13 illustrates this latch, which is called a polarity-hold parallel and shift-register latch (PSRL). The PSRL has two modes of operation, as shown in figure 8.14. The difference between the PSRL and the SRL of Eichelberger and Williams (1977) is that, in the normal mode, Q and $\bar{Q}$ outputs of the PSRL are obtained from two different latches. This allows an increase in the number of controllable inputs to combinational logic, and hence it can be expected that the test-generation process will be easier and will provide better test coverage.

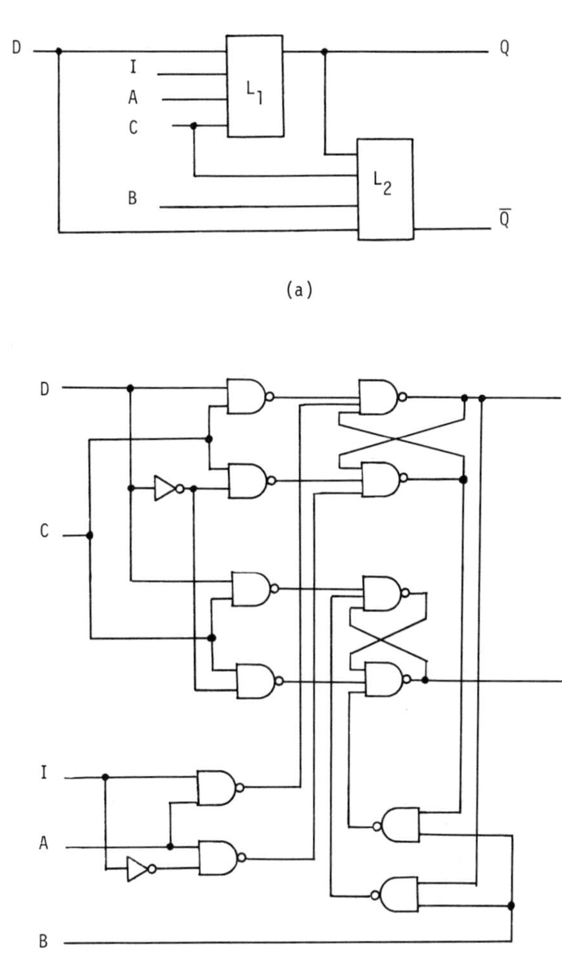

Figure 8.13
Polarity-hold PSRL (Saluja 1982; © IEEE 1982)

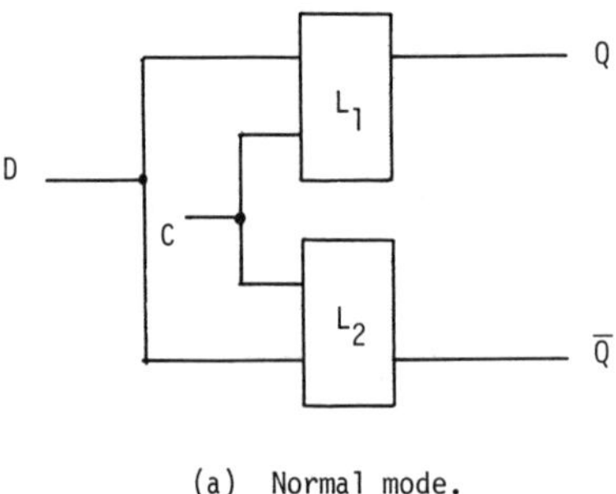

(a) Normal mode.

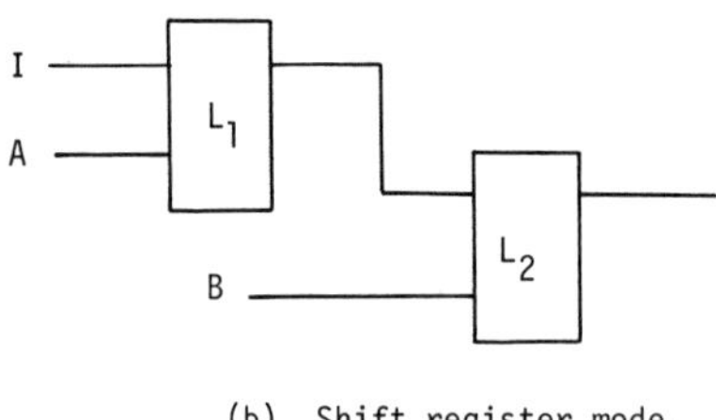

(b) Shift register mode.

Figure 8.14
Two modes of operation for PSRL

8.3 Variations of Scan Design

Some variations of the scan design approach have been proposed by Toth and Holt (1974), Stewart (1977), Mercer et al. (1981), and Ando (1980). The first three are very similar to the scan design techniques mentioned in the preceding section, since shift registers are used to load and unload data. Ando's approach differs from others in that an addressing scheme similar to a random-access memory is used instead of shift registers.

Shift-Register Modification

The approaches of Toth and Holt (1974) and Mercer et al. (1981) are very similar to the shift-register-modification method of Williams and Angell (1973). Toth and Holt presented an implementation using MSI shift registers available on the market. The proposed shift register has the capability of shifting data right and left as well as parallel loading and unloading. Additional control logic is added to the circuit to allow mode control (load/shift) over the shift path.

Whereas most of the scan design techniques have been developed for designing completely synchronous circuits, the approach of Mercer et al. (1981) allows some asynchronous designs. The method is to modify flip-flops in a given sequential circuit to form scan (shift) registers. Figure 8.15 shows a flip-flop modified to allow scan and normal operating modes as specified by the control value of SW. These modified flip-flops are interconnected into one or more scan registers.

As shown in figure 8.15, multiplexers are placed on the clock inputs as well as the data input. Also, preset and clear inputs are gated by control input SW to disable them in scan mode. A realization of a multiplexer using transmission gates is illustrated in figure 8.16. If the normal circuit is already synchronous, the multiplexing of clocks will not be required. Hence, the multiplexers and the disabling gates are used as and where needed. Flip-flops can have asynchronous preset and clear inputs, and clocking by an asynchronous signal is also allowed. In this way, the design rules of Mercer et al. (1981) permit some asynchronous designs and hence are more flexible than those of the Scan Path and the LSSD. However, the price one pays for this design flexibility is that races and hazards may occur in scan-testable circuits, thus complicating test generation.

Scan/Set Logic

A scan design technique called Scan/Set Logic has been used to enhance the controllability and the observability of sequential circuits (Stewart 1977). Scan/Set Logic is separate from the functional logic and provides a data path to observe and/or control some nodes in the circuit. Because of this separation, the performance of the functional logic suffers little degradation. This differs from the Scan Path and LSSD approaches, in which all flip-flops are used to operate in both shift-register and normal modes.

Figure 8.17 shows an example of bit-serial Scan/Set Logic, in which the values of up to 64 nodes in the circuit can be loaded into the 64-bit shift register with a single clock and then serially scanned out through the scan-out pin. This shifting occurs after each test input pattern has been applied, and the scanned data are monitored by the tester as the response data together with the usual primary output response of the circuit under test. The shift register is also used to provide a set capability from the tester. Test patterns are serially shifted into the shift register and then gated into the flip-flops of the functional logic. In this way, any internal node can be scanned and/or set by connecting it to one of the flip-flops in the Scan/Set

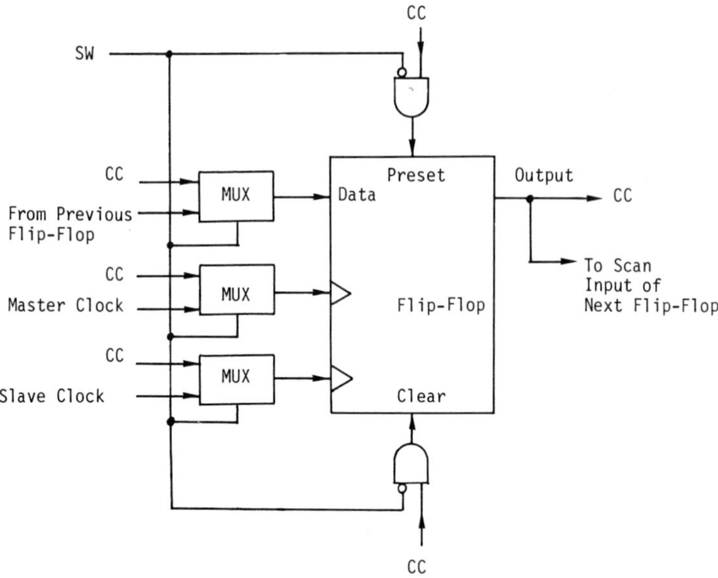

Figure 8.15
Modification of flip-flop to form scan register (Mercer et al. 1981; © IEEE 1981)

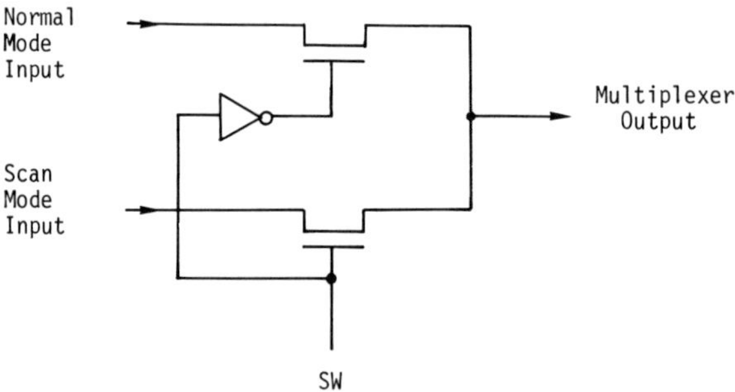

Figure 8.16
Implementation of multiplexer

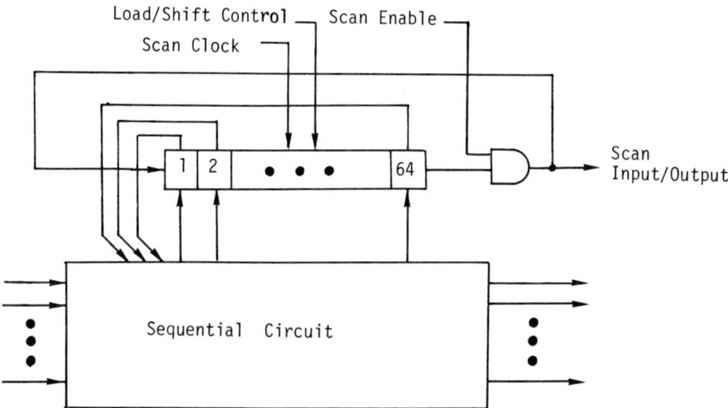

Figure 8.17
Bit-serial Scan/Set logic (Stewart 1977; © IEEE 1977)

shift register. However, not all internal nodes need to be scanned and/or set. To reduce the test-generation problem of sequential logic to a combinational one, it suffices to give scan/set capability to all flip-flops in the functional logic. Of course, not all flip-flops need to be scanned and/or set by the shift register, since some of them are already readily controllable and observable. This design flexibility is one of the advantages of the Scan/Set Logic technique. Another advantage is that the separation of the scan/set logic and the functional logic allow the scan/set operation to be performed during the normal function operation. This enables us to get a "snapshot" of the sequential circuit without degradating its performance.

Random-Access Scan

Random-Access Scan (Ando 1980) is a technique of providing a direct access path to each internal storage element and thereby enhancing its controllability and observability. To create such a direct access path, an addressing scheme very similar to that of a random-access memory is employed in which each latch is selected uniquely to be scanned in/out by specifying its address.

As a basic storage element in the Random-Access Scan approach, an addressable latch or flip-flop is used. Such a latch is one whose state can be controlled and observed through scan in/out lines only when it is selected by addressing. Figure 8.18 illustrates such an addressable latch. The latch has

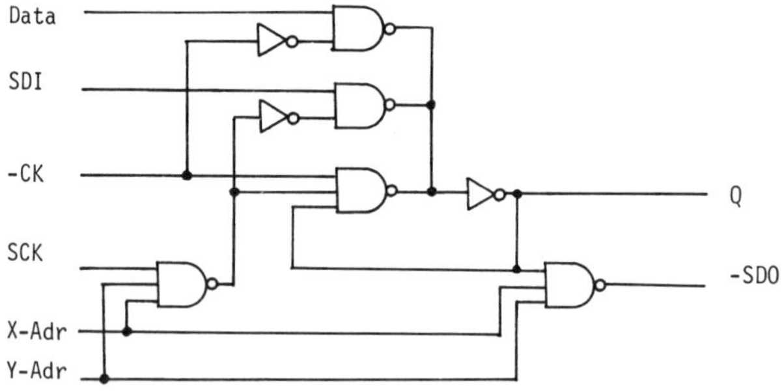

Figure 8.18
Polarity-hold type addressable latch (Ando 1980; © IEEE 1980)

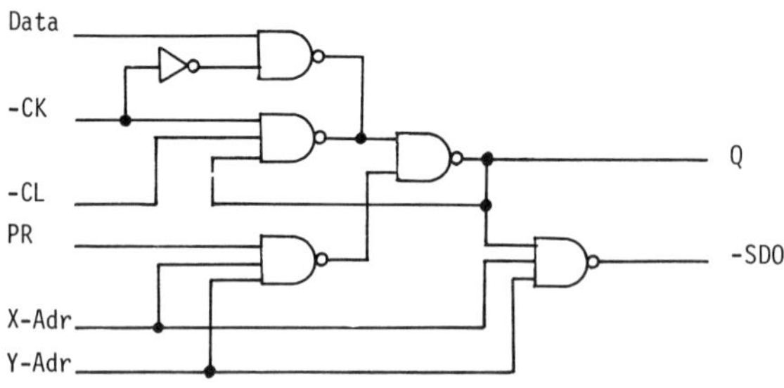

Figure 8.19
Set/reset-type addressable latch (Ando 1980; © IEEE 1980)

two data inputs [one for normal data (DATA) and the other for scan data (SDI)] and two clocks (−CK and SCK). The normal data on DATA are clocked into the latch by the −CK clock independent of the two addressing lines. The scan-in data on the SDI are clocked into the latch by the clock SCK only when both the X and Y addresses are one. The state of the latch can be observed in the complemented form at the Scan Data Output (SDO) when both the X and Y addresses are 1. Latch-state −SDO signals from all latches are ANDed together to produce a scan-out signal of the circuit. Ando (1980) also presented another type of addressable latch, called a set/reset-type addressable latch (figure 8.19).

The configuration of sequential circuits designed by the Random-Access Scan aproach is illustrated in figure 8.20. A pair of address decoders, an AND gate tree to combine all latch-state signals, and several clear inputs are required, as well as the addressable storage elements. An addressable

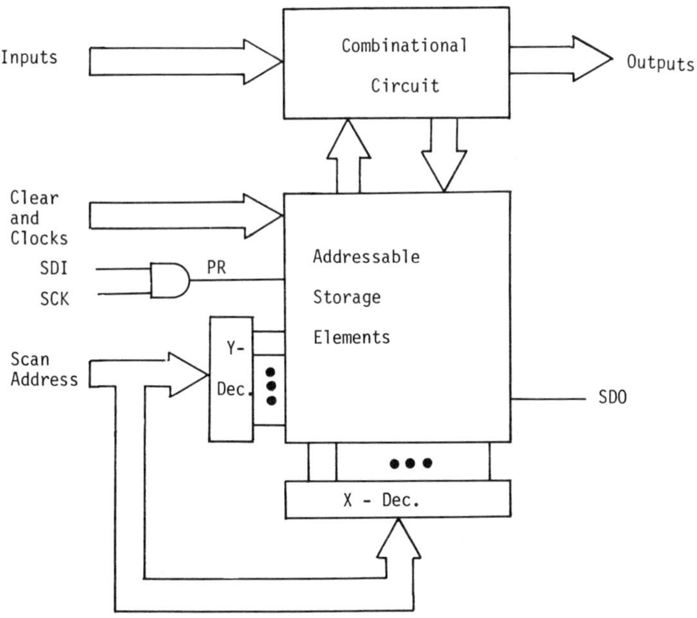

Figure 8.20
Configuration of Random-Access Scan (Ando 1980; © IEEE 1980)

latch located at the intersection of selected X and Y address lines is accessed like a memory cell in an array. The clear inputs of all latches are tied together to form one or several groups depending on the initialization requirement. The preset signal PR gated by the scan clock SCK is propagated to all latches, but only one accessed latch is affected.

The Random-Access Scan technique has the following advantages: By the control and observation of all storage elements, the sequential test-generation problem can be reduced to a combinational one. Since the array of addressable latches is similar to a memory array, both addressable latches and memory arrays can be tested in a unified way. Further, each scanout operation can be performed without disturbing the states of all latches. The drawbacks of the Random-Access Scan approach are as follows: The extra gates are two address gates for each storage element, two address decoders, and an output AND tree. This overhead is about 3–4 gates per storage element. The extra pins are scan control, data, and address pins. This pin overhead is between 10 and 20, which can be reduced to around 6 pins by the use of a serially loadable address counter.

8.4 Incomplete Scan Design and Enhanced Scan Design

Most of the scan design approaches mentioned earlier, such as the Scan Path and the LSSD, require the decomposition of a circuit into a purely combinational part and a scan path. However, in some cases this decomposition is not possible, because of some asynchronous flip-flops or the prohibitive cost of extra hardware. Hence, one needs to consider an incomplete scan design such that only some of the flip-flops can be chained together into the scan path.

A scan design is said to be either *complete* or *incomplete*, depending on whether all or only some of the flip-flops are chained together. Obviously, in the complete scan design the remaining circuit after the scan path has been removed from the original sequential circuit is a purely combinational circuit. On the other hand, in the incomplete scan design the remaining circuit after the scan path has been removed is still a sequential circuit. However, if the sequential depth of the remaining circuit is not so deep (e.g., less than 3), then the cost of test generation will be greatly reduced. To this end, Trischler (1980) proposed the incomplete-scan-path (ISP) approach to enhance circuit testability at a low overhead cost, and presented the design rules and the test-generation methods for the ISP circuits. The rules or recommendations for the implementation of the ISP are the following.

(1) The scan connection in the scan-path (SP) chain must be used as a source of information and not as a point to receive information.

In figure 8.21, connection a is allowed, but connection b is not allowed because the combinational logic acts as a source of information to the scan-in port of the flip-flop.

The sequential part of the circuit that is not included in the SP should not exceed a sequential depth of 3. Also, asynchronous loops through many gates should not be used.

(2) Whether or not a flip-flop should be linked into an SP must be determined by the following rules:
(i) All flip-flops that are easily controllable from primary inputs (directly or through combinational logic) need not be linked into the SP.
(ii) All flip-flops that are easily controllable and observable from primary inputs and outputs (short logical depth) need not be linked into the SP.
(iii) Flip-flops that are not easily accessible must be linked into the SP.

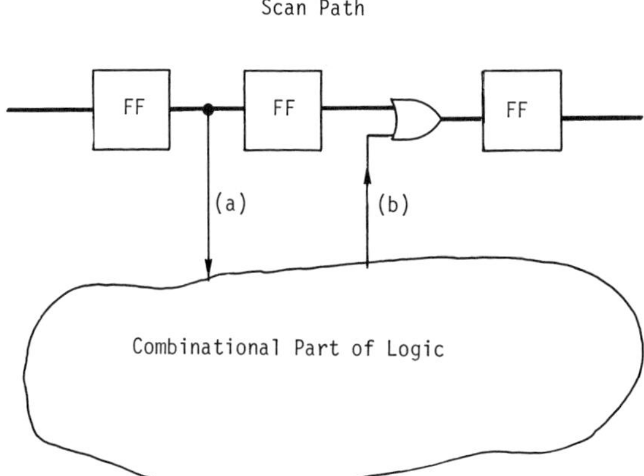

Figure 8.21
Connection of scan path to combinational logic

(iv) When easily controllable asynchronous flip-flops cannot be linked into the SP, they must be at least isolated from influence of the SP.

If the remaining sequential part outside the SP is easily controllable from primary inputs and easily observable either at primary outputs or through the SP, as shown in figure 8.22, then the sequential part outside the SP can be easily tested. Therefore, for such circuits it may be possible to make approximately the same amount of cost reduction in test generation as in the case of the complete scan path. This ISP will be referred to as an optimal ISP (OISP).

In contrast, if the sequential part outside the SP is controlled by the scan path, as shown in figure 8.23, the total circuit with the SP must be simulated. For example, as shown in figure 8.24, the state of the asynchronous flip-flops can be influenced during the shifting operation of the scan path. Hence, the generated test patterns have to be verified for the total sequential circuit. This type of ISP will be referred to as a nonoptimal ISP (NISP). For a circuit with NISP, test patterns are generated for the remaining circuit except the scan path and then the generated test patterns are simulated for the total circuit including the scan path.

A problem for nonoptimal ISP such as that illustrated in figure 8.24 can be solved by enhancing the capability of flip-flops. DasGupta et al. (1981) presented an enhanced LSSD approach that allows interfacing of LSSD logic circuits with non-LSSD circuits. Figure 8.25 shows a modified SRL,

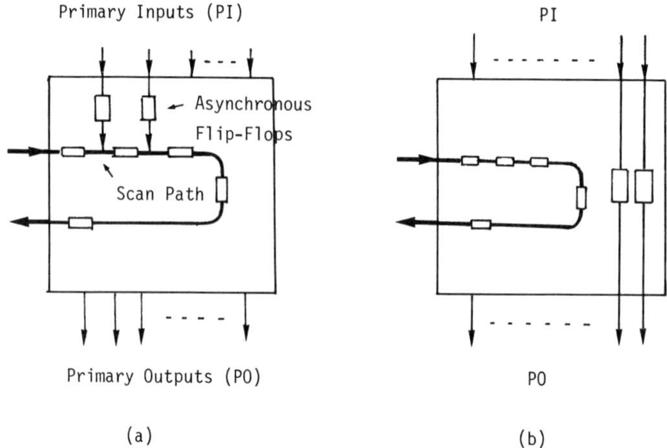

Figure 8.22
Optimal configurations of ISP

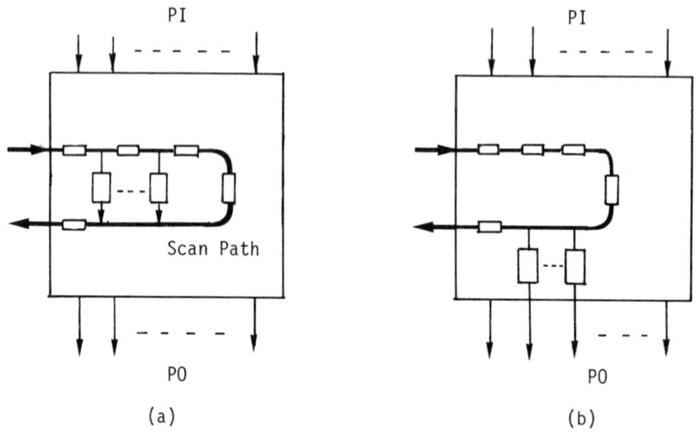

Figure 8.23
Nonoptimal configurations of ISP

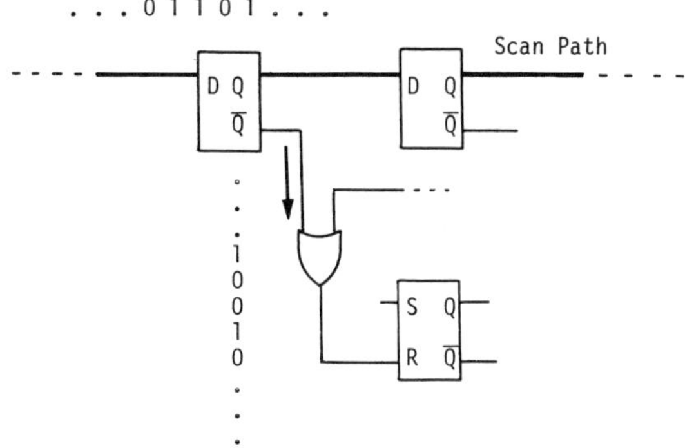

Figure 8.24
Effect of scan-in pattern on flip-flops in scan path

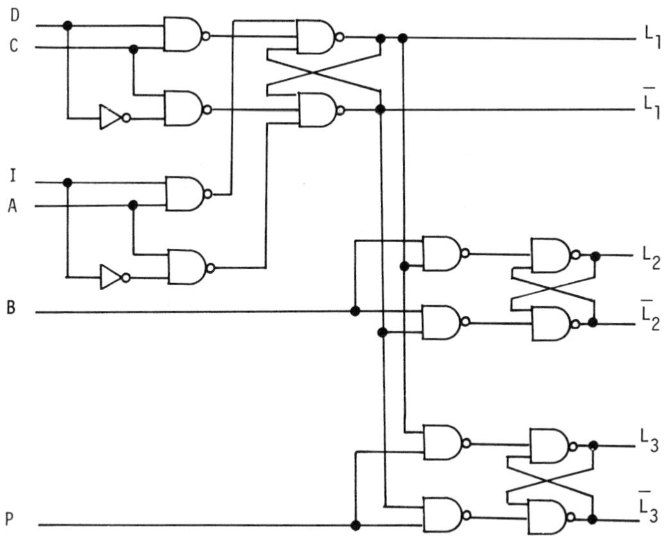

Figure 8.25
Stable shift-register latch (DasGupta et al. 1981; © IEEE 1981)

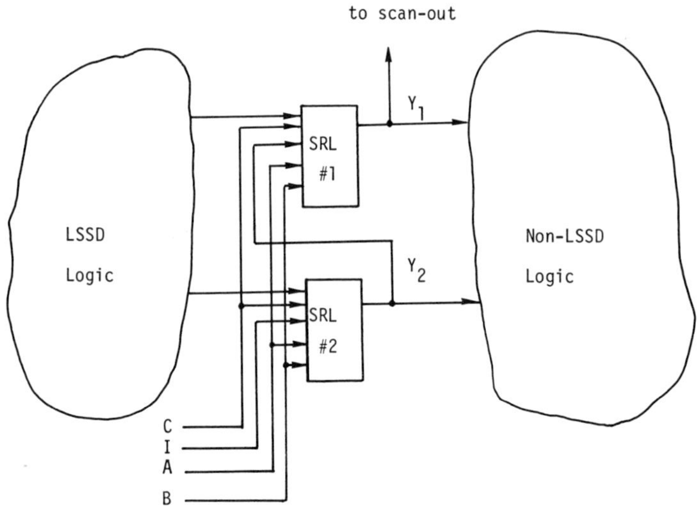

Figure 8.26
Boundary between LSSD and non-LSSD logic

called a stable SRL (SSRL), that is used as the basic storage element together with the SRL proposed by Eichelberger and Williams (1977). The SSRL is composed of an SRL and a third latch, L_3, which is clocked by shift clock P.

Consider the boundary between LSSD and non-LSSD logic shown in figure 8.26. In this circuit, it is impossible to apply a sequence $Y_1 Y_2 = 11$ followed by $Y_1 Y_2 = 01$ only by shifting, since the intermediate pattern $Y_1 Y_2 = 10$ appears between 11 and 01.

The L_3 latch in an SSRL can be used to break a path from an LSSD to non-LSSD circuits so that they do not interfere with each other. For this example, SSRLs are replaced by SRLs as shown in figure 8.27. First, $Y_1 Y_2 = 11$ can be applied from the L_3 latches, and then the pattern 01 is shifted into the SRLs without affecting the states of the L_3 latches. The pattern 01 loaded into the SRLs is then transferred to the L_3 latches by applying the clock P. In this way, with the aid of the L_3 latches in SSRLs, the intermediate pattern 10 is not fed to the non-LSSD circuit.

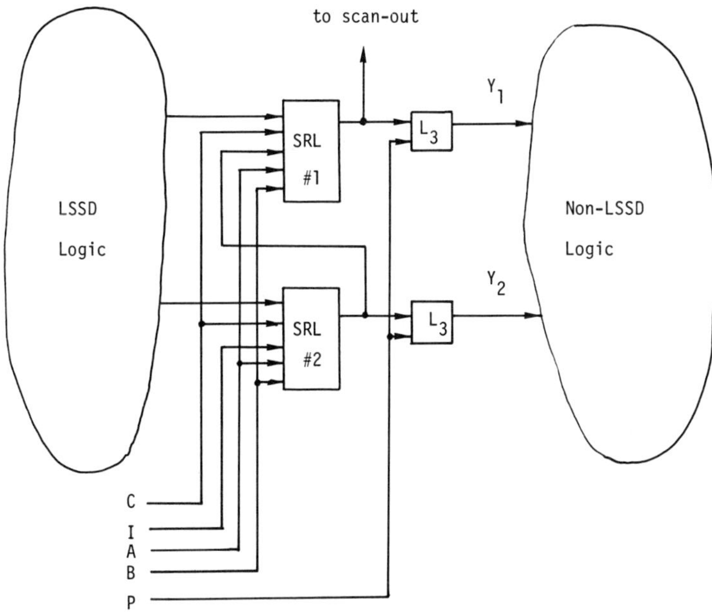

Figure 8.27
LSSD to non-LSSD boundary with SSRL (DasGupta et al. 1981; © IEEE 1981)

To make the most of the SSRL, DasGupta et al. (1981) comment, the following design rules must be followed.

- When an LSSD circuit feeds a non-LSSD circuit, the boundary is defined by SSRLs, whose L_3 outputs feed the non-LSSD circuit. Also, in order for the single-input change format for race-free testing of the non-LSSD circuit to be preserved, the L_1 and L_2 latches of these SSRLs cannot feed the non-LSSD circuit.
- When a non-LSSD circuit feeds an LSSD circuit, the boundary is defined by SRLs.
- A clock that controls the L_3 latch of an SSRL that feeds a non-LSSD circuit cannot clock the system data input of an SRL fed by the same non-LSSD circuit.
- Clocks controlling SRLs and SSRLs on the periphery of a non-LSSD circuit cannot feed the same circuit.

9 Design for Built-In Self-Testing

So far, we have been concerned with external testing—that is, testing approaches in which explicit tests are applied by test equipment external to the unit under test. A primary weakness of a conventional testing philosophy based on externally applied test patterns is that a technique is extremely constrained by limited access to internal points in the unit under test. As digital systems grow more complex and more difficult to test, it becomes increasingly attractive to build self-testing aids into the unit under test. *Self-testing* as used here does not refer to the total self-checking capability defined in section 1.4. In this chapter the term is used in a broad sense to refer to various testing approaches in which test patterns are applied internally to the unit under test without the use of external test equipment. The term *built-in testing* is also used in distinction from external testing approaches. This chapter is concerned mainly with off-line built-in self-testing approaches.

In the preceding chapter we considered various scan design approaches, such as Scan Path and LSSD, to off-line external testing. Although those scan design techniques have indeed succeeded in reducing the difficulty of testing sequential logic, this type of testing still has some drawbacks: Storage of a huge amount of test patterns and responses is required, test-pattern generation is still bothersome since special test-generation software for scan design is required, and testing is slow because of the shifting of patterns through the scan path.

Moreover, two special characteristics of VLSI and VHSI (very-high-speed intergrated) circuits—their very high speed of operation and their very poor accessibility to external probing —will further aggravate the burden of test generation and application. As circuit technologies advance to higher speeds and larger scales of integration, new approaches will be required for the testing, at high logic speeds, of large complex circuits that may contain both multiple stuck-type and non-stuck-type faults. Hence, it might be necessary to consider testing approaches in a new light. Built-in self-test approaches, which will be described in this chapter, seem to be preferred over external testing and hold a good prospect for testing in the future.

9.1 Signature Analysis

In a conventional testing scheme, test responses are all compared with the correct reference values, which usually contain a high volume of data. An

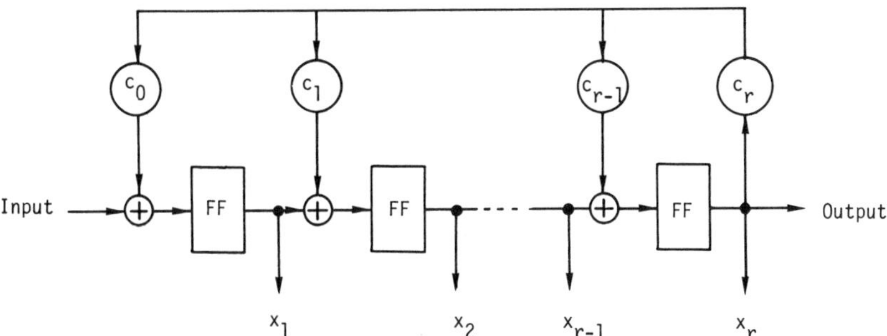

Figure 9.1
LFSR for dividing polynomials

approach called *compact testing* can avoid this difficulty of analysis and storage of huge amounts of test response data. In compact testing, instead of the entire responses, compressed response data are used for comparison. *Signature analysis* falls under the category of compact testing.

Linear feedback shift registers (LFSRs) can be used to compress test response data. Figure 9.1 shows an LFSR that performs polynomial division. As shown in the figure, an LFSR consists of three types of devices; memory elements (D flip-flops), modulo-2 adders (EOR gates), and binary constant multipliers. The constant multiplier for the constant 1 is simply a connection in the LFSR, and that for the constant 0 is simply no connection in the LFSR. Such a data-compression technique using LFSRs is based on the *cyclic redundancy check* (*CRC*) *codes*, which are widely used in systems where data are transmitted or received. The fundamental results of CRC codes can be found in algebraic coding theory (Peterson and Weldon 1972).

A serial input stream into an LFSR corresponds to a polynomial; the coefficients of the polynomial appear on the input line high-order coefficient first. That is, the polynomial

$$p(X) = p_n X^n + p_{n-1} X^{n-1} + \cdots + p_1 X + p_0$$

would be entered on an input line, with p_n coming first, then p_{n-1} one unit of time later, p_{n-2} after another unit of time, and so on. The LFSR shown in figure 9.1 has its *characteristic polynomial* defined by the constants c_0, c_1, ..., c_r as follows:

$$c(X) = c_r X^r + c_{r-1} X^{r-1} + \cdots + c_1 X + c_0.$$

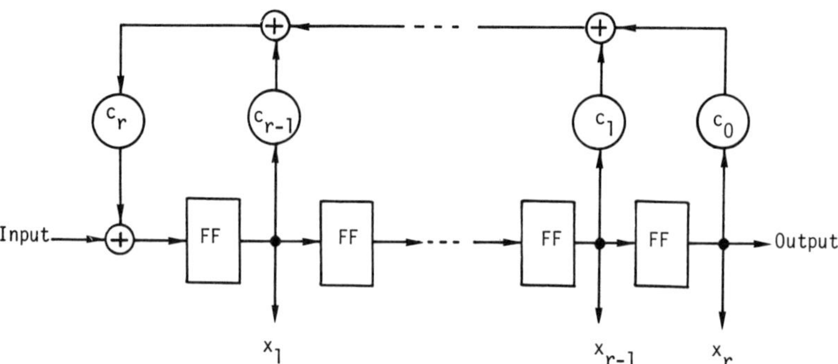

Figure 9.2
Alternative LFSR for dividing polynomials

The LFSR divides any input polynomial $p(X)$ by the characteristic polynomial $c(X)$. All the storage elements are set to 0 initially. The dividend $p(X)$ is shifted in serially via the input of the LFSR, and the quotient appears serially at the output of the LFSR. After a total of n shifts, the entire quotient has appeared at the output, and the remainder is in the shift register.

The LFSR shown in figure 9.1 is called the *internal EOR type*, since EOR gates are located only between shift-register stages. There is an alternative LFSR form that also performs the same division. Figure 9.2 shows the LFSR dividing the input polynomial $p(X)$ by the characteristic polynomial $c(X)$, where selected flip-flop output signals are fed back to the least significant bit position via EOR gates. This type of LFSR is called the *external EOR* type. Note that the order of constant multipliers in figure 9.2 is the reverse of that in figure 9.1. The external EOR type LFSR is more suitable for LSI and VLSI than the internal EOR type, since the former does not require irregularly placed EOR gates between shift-register stages. In the LFSR of figure 9.2, the quotient can be obtained from the output serially, but the final content of the shift register is not the remainder. This differs from the internal EOR type LFSR.

LFSRs of both the internal and the external EOR type compress the serial input stream to the length of the LFSR and form a *signature*. That is, the final contents or the remainder of the LFSR is the signature. By analyzing the signature, one can determine whether the circuit under test is faulty or not. However, some faults are not detected when the erroneous sequences caused by the faults are compressed to the same signature as the correct one.

Let $c(X)$ be the degree r polynomial forming the divisor, that is, the characteristic polynomial of the LFSR. Let $i(X)$ be a polynomial representing an input stream of length k, let $q(X)$ be the quotient, and let $s(X)$ be the signature. Obviously, the degree of $i(X)$ is $k - 1$ and the degree of $s(X)$ is less then r. For an internal EOR type LFSR, the signature is the remainder after division, and thus we have

$$i(X) = c(X) \cdot q(X) + s(X).$$

Errors in the input stream can be expressed by an error pattern such that each nonzero bit represents an error in the corresponding bit position. Each error pattern can be further represented as a polynomial $e(X)$. For example, if the correct input stream is 11001 (i.e., the correct input polynomial is $(X) = X^4 + X^3 + 1$) and if an erroneous input stream is 01011 [i.e., $i'(X) = X^3 + X + 1$], then the error pattern is $11001 \oplus 01011 = 10010$ and is represented by $e(X) = X^4 + X$. In general, an erroneous input polynomial $i'(X)$ can be represented by

$$i'(X) = i(X) + e(X)$$

where $e(X)$ is the corresponding error polynomial.

An error is not detected when $i(X)$ and $i'(X)$ have the same signature. Hence, for an internal EOR type LFSR,

$$i'(X) = c(X) \cdot q'(X) + s(X).$$

Further,

$$i'(X) = i(X) + e(X)$$

and

$$i(X) = c(X) \cdot q(X) + s(X),$$

so

$$e(X) = c(X) \cdot (q'(X) - q(X)).$$

Therefore, it follows that, for an error polynomial $e(X)$, $i(X)$ and $i(X) + e(X)$ have the same signature $s(X)$ if and only if $e(X)$ is a multiple of $c(X)$. The same result also holds true for an external EOR type LFSR (Smith 1980).

Measures of the effectiveness of LFSRs at detecting faults have been proposed by Frohwerk (1977) and Smith (1980). Since faults cannot be observed directly (that is, since only errors can be detected), measures are formulated in terms of errors detected. Frohwerk evaluated the error-detection capability of LFSRs by presenting the following two theorems. Here the proofs are borrowed from Smith (1980) since they are simpler than those of Frohwerk (1977).

THEOREM 9.1 For either the LFSR shown in figures 9.1 or that shown in figure 9.2, if its characteristic polynomial has two or more nonzero coefficients, then it can detect all single-bit errors.

Proof Let $c(X)$ be the characteristic polynomial with two or more nonzero coefficients. Then all nonzero multiples of $c(X)$ must have at least two nonzero coefficients. Hence, any error with only one nonzero coefficient cannot be a multiple of $c(X)$ and must be detectable. ■

THEOREM 9.2 For a k-bit response sequence, if all possible error patterns are equally likely, then the probability of failing to detect an error by either LFSR of length r (figures 9.1 or figure 9.2) is

$$\frac{2^{k-r}-1}{2^k-1}.$$

Proof A k-bit response can be represented by a polynomial of degree $k-1$, and hence an error can be represented by an error polynomial of degree $k-1$ or less. Since there are k coefficients in a polynomial of degree $k-1$, the number of possible error polynomials is $2^k - 1$.

As mentioned earlier, all undetectable errors are represented by one of the multiples of the characteristic polynomial $c(X)$; for example, an error polynomial $e(X)$ is represented by $e(X) = c(X) \cdot p(X)$ for some polynomial $p(X)$. Since the degree of $e(X)$ is less than k and the degree of $c(X)$ is r, the number of nonzero polynomials $p(X)$ satisfying $e(X) = c(X) \cdot p(X)$ is $2^{k-r} - 1$. Hence, the probability of failing to detect an error is

$$\frac{\text{Undetectable errors}}{\text{Total errors}} = \frac{2^{k-r}-1}{2^k-1}. \quad ■$$

For long sequences, the probability of not detecting an error approaches $1/2^r$, and hence the error coverage approaches $1 - 1/2^r$. For a 16-bit LFSR, this gives rise to the certainty of 99.998 percent that an error, if present, can be detected. However, Smith (1980) pointed out that these measures are of questionable validity because of unrealistic fault or error assumptions. For example, theorem 9.2 holds regardless of the polynomial chosen. This indicates that LFSRs based on very simple polynomials such as X^r without feedback are as effective as those based on more complex polynomials such as $X^{16} + X^9 + X^7 + X^4 + 1$ (Frohwerk 1977). That is, the choice of a characteristic polynomial has no effect on error coverage. Therefore, the error coverage proposed in theorem 9.2 cannot be taken as a direct measure of the effectiveness of the LFSR, since errors due to faults are not equally likely and not independent. To provide a more accurate measure, Smith (1980) considered two classes of dependent errors that are likely to occur: burst errors and errors with incorrect bits spaced at intervals equal to some power of 2. However, the best available measure might be the fault coverage as determined by fault simulation.

So far we have considered serial input LFSRs monitoring only one output line of the circuit under test. To monitor multiple outputs of the circuit under test, data compression would require a parallel-to-serial converter to use the serial LFSR described above. However, this is not an effective approach. To implement effective compression of parallel data, parallel input LFSRs are used. Figures 9.3(a) and 9.3(b) show internal and external EOR type parallel LFSRs, respectively. Such a multiple-input LFSR monitoring several lines in parallel is called a *parallel signature analyzer*. On the other hand, the serial-input LFSR mentioned earier is called a *serial signature analyzer*. Analytical results on the effectiveness of parallel signature analyzers in detecting errors in response data from multiple outputs have been reported by Bhavsar and Heckelman (1981), Sridhar et al. (1982), and J. L. Carter (1982).

THEOREM 9.3 (Bhavsar and Heckelman 1981) Let the response sequence consist of L vectors of m bits each. If all possible error sequences are equally likely, then the probability of failing to detect an error in the response sequence by an r-bit parallel signature analyzer is

$$\frac{2^{mL-r} - 1}{2^{mL} - 1}.$$

Proof For L response vectors of m bits each, there are $2^{mL} - 1$ possible error sequences. It can be shown that an r-bit parallel signature analyzer maps 2^{mL} possible sequences into 2^r signatures uniformly. Hence, the num-

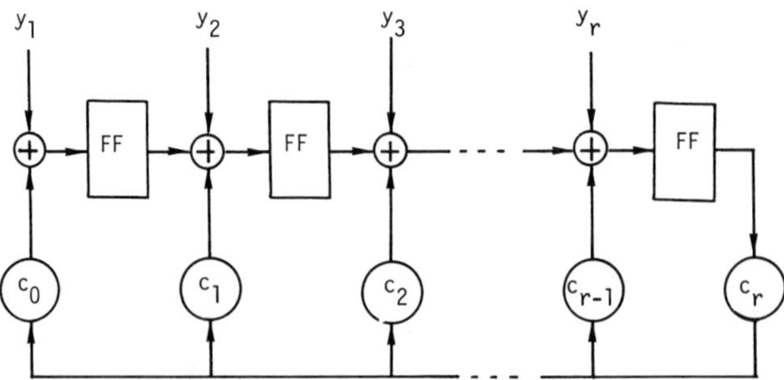

(a) Internal EOR type

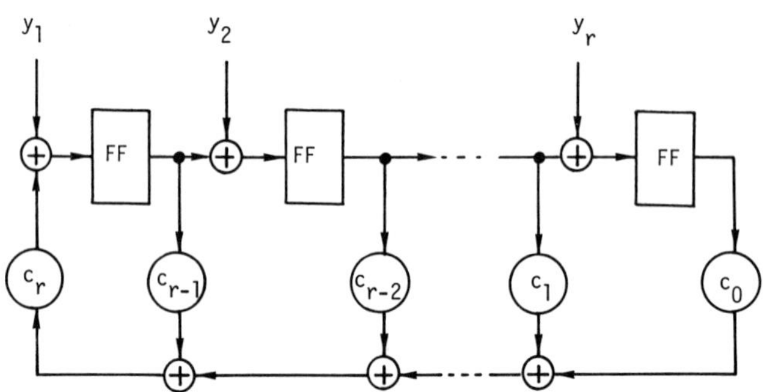

(b) External EOR type

Figure 9.3
Parallel LFSRs

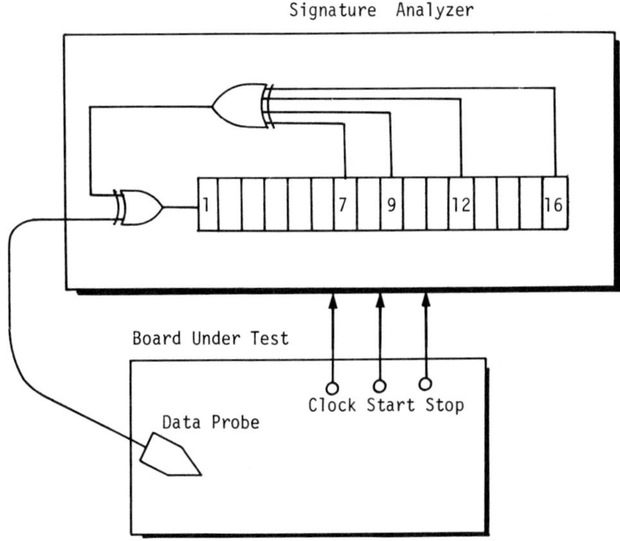

Figure 9.4
Hewlett-Packard signature analyzer

ber of error sequences that results in the same signature as the correct signature is $2^{mL}/2^r - 1$. The probability of failing to detect an error is thus

$$\frac{2^{mL-r} - 1}{2^{mL} - 1}. \blacksquare$$

In theorem 9.3, it is assumed that all possible error sequences are equally likely, i.e., that the erroneous bits produced by a faulty circuit are distributed randomly. However, this assumption is not realistic. J. L. Carter (1982) showed a bound of the probability of masking errors by requiring almost no assumptions about the behavior of faulty circuits. It has been proved that if the order of the L test patterns is chosen randomly, then the probability of failing to detect an error in the response sequence by an r-bit parallel signature analyzer is less than $4/L$, where $r > \log_2(L-1)$. This result holds for a set of randomly generated or carefully chosen test patterns.

Serial signature analyzers are used commercially for field testing of microprocessor-based systems. Figure 9.4 shows the configuration of the Hewlett-Packard signature analyzer (Frohwerk 1977). The signature analyzer uses a 16-bit LFSR. Data streams at designated circuit nodes can be obtained by probing. A serial data stream at a circuit node is compressed to a unique four-digit hexadecimal signature by the signature analyzer. Each signature of suspect circuit nodes is compared with the precomputed correct signature. Three gating signals are supplied to the signature analyzer through an active pad by the unit under test. A clock signal generated by the unit under test ensures synchronous acceptance of data and gating signals by the signature analyzer. A start signal initiates the measurement window during which data are clocked into a 16-bit LFSR in the signature analyzer. A stop signal closes the measurement window.

A microprocessor-based system under test is divided into the kernel and the outlying circuitry. The *kernel* is the minimum configuration of microprocessor and ROM necessary to run the simplest test program, including the clock and the power supply. In order to test the kernel first, a free-running test makes the microprocessor run through its entire address fields. The start/stop signals for the free running are derived from the lines of its address bus. After the free running of the microprocessor, software-driven tests start by running a test program stored in ROM, which generates start/stop signals and sends data streams onto the data bus in order to test the outlying circuitry. The ROM contains a special program for stimulating the various nodes in the circuit under test. Guided by a troubleshooting procedure, the field engineer can discover the cause of an incorrect signature by probing designated nodes, observing signatures, and tracing the faults back to their source. To make the backtracing possible, it is necessary to prevent a fault fom being fed back around and perturbing all data nodes. Hence, feedback paths within the circuit must be broken, either by the use of hardware switches, jumpers, or connectors, or by the disabling of gates with software.

A serial signature analyzer is also used in a built-in test mechanism proposed by Benowitz et al. (1975). The proposed system (figure 9.5) is called the Advanced Avionics Fault Isolation System (AAFIS). In the AAFIS, each sybsystem consisting of several boards contains a test-pattern source, while the evaluation of the test data is performed by a serial signature analyzer on each board.

As mentioned earlier, parallel signature analyzers are more effective than serial signature analyzers. Hence, many methods of incorporating parallel signature analyzers in VLSI circuits for on-chip testing have been explored recently. These methods are described in sections 9.2 and 9.3.

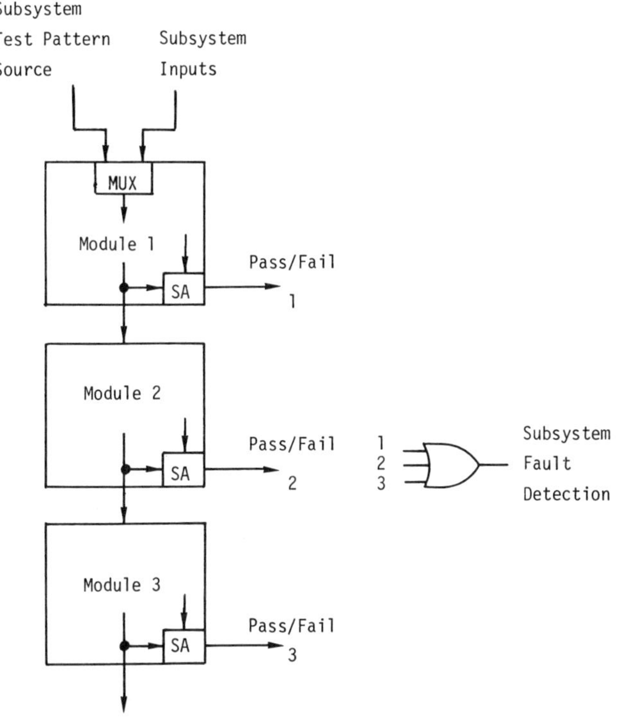

Figure 9.5
AAFIS built-in test mechanism

9.2 Built-In Logic Block Observer

One of the most popular (off-line) built-in self-test approaches is the *built-in logic block observer* (BILBO) of Koenemann et al. (1979), which aims at realizing a built-in self-test mechanism for highly integrated modular and bus-oriented systems, such as microprocessor-based systems. BILBO integrates scan design with signature analysis by making use of an LFSR as an on-chip test generator and analyzer. An LFSR can work as a signature analyzer, as mentioned in section 9.1, and further can generate a pseudorandom data pattern that can be used as a test pattern for a circuit under test.

Figure 9.6(a) is the logic diagram of an 8-bit BILBO composed of eight flip-flops and some gates for shift and feedback operations. S_{in} and S_{out} are the scan-in input and scan-out output for the 8-bit register, respectively. The control inputs B_1 and B_2 can select four functional modes of BILBO:

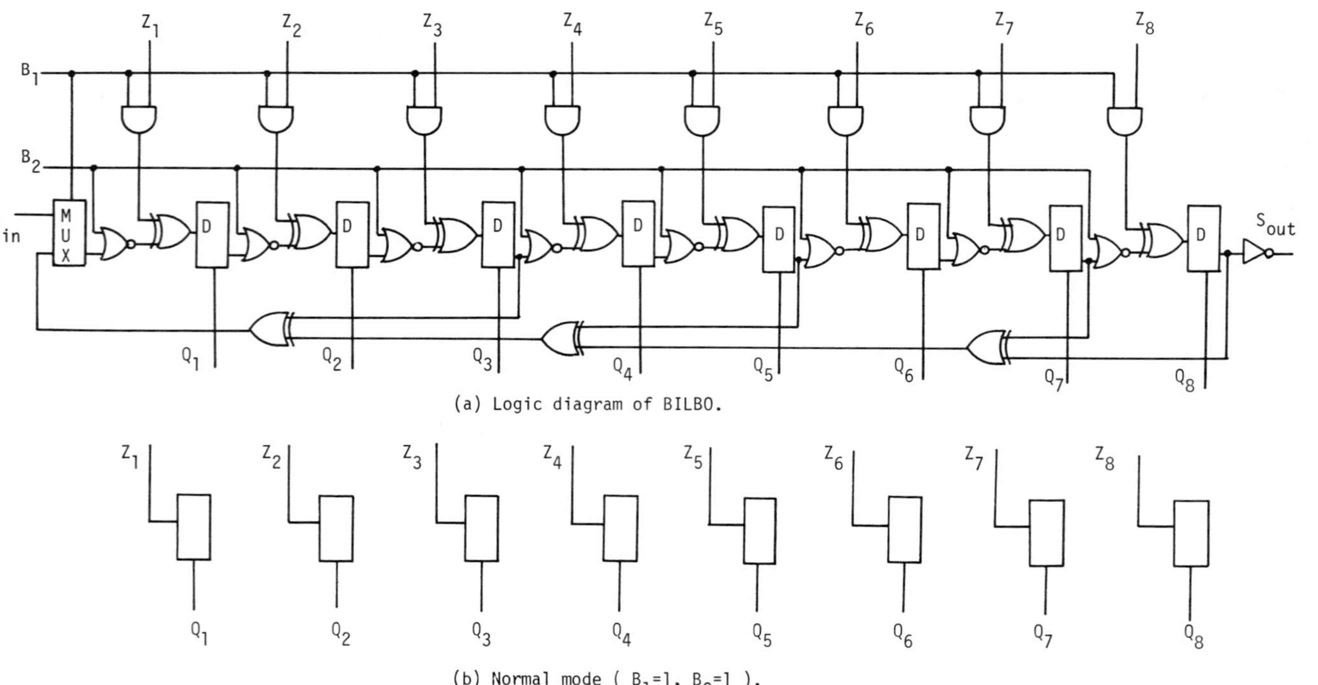

(a) Logic diagram of BILBO.

(b) Normal mode ($B_1=1$, $B_2=1$).

Figure 9.6

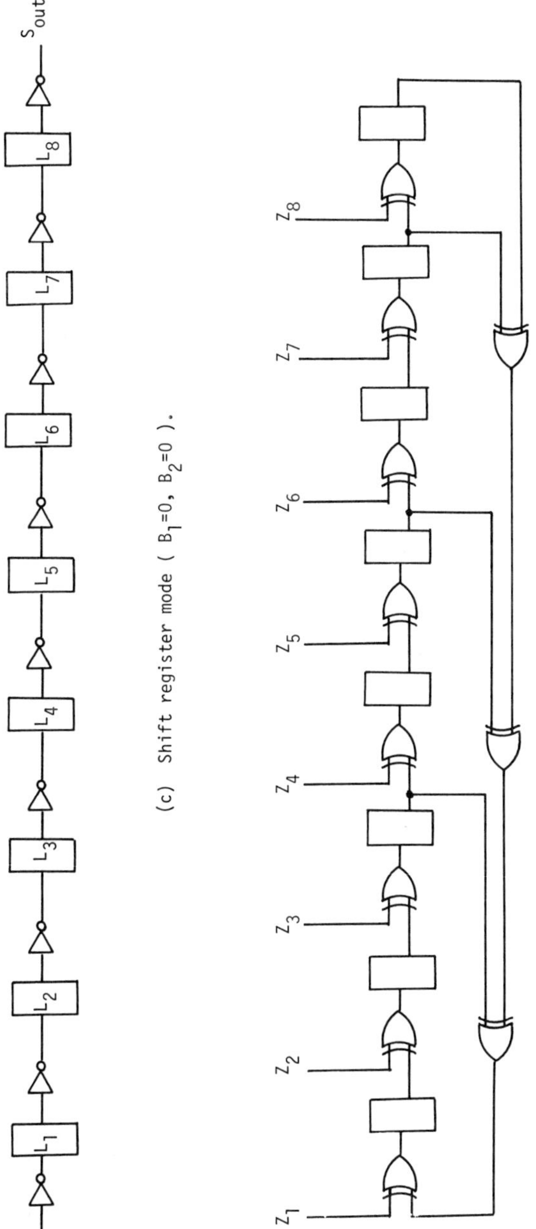

(c) Shift register mode (B_1=0, B_2=0).

(d) Parallel input LFSR mode (B_1=1, B_2=0).

Figure 9.6
Configuration of 8-bit BILBO (Koenemann et al. 1979; © IEEE 1979)

• $B_1 = 1, B_2 = 1$ In this mode BILBO acts as a set of latches, as shown in figure 9.6(b). This is the normal system-operation mode, in which the data $Z_1, Z_2, \ldots, Z_8$ are loaded into the flip-flops and the contents of the flip-flops are read from the outputs Q_i for system operation.

• $B_1 = 0, B_2 = 0$ As shown in figure 9.6(c), this second mode forms a linear shift register. Data are serially loaded into the register through S_{in}, shifted through some inverters, and unloaded from the register through S_{out}. The shift register is used in the test mode in the same fashion as the Scan Path and the LSSD.

• $B_1 = 1, B_2 = 0$ In the third mode, BILBO is functionally converted into a parallel input LFSR as shown in figure 9.6(d). The parallel input LFSR can be utilized as a parallel signature analyzer as discussed in section 9.1. If all inputs $Z_1, Z_2, \ldots, Z_8$ are kept on fixed logical values (say, all zeros), the register becomes an autonomous linear feedback shift register, and hence the contents of the register run through a pseudorandom sequence with maximum period length $2^8 - 1$. In general, the period length of a pseudorandom sequence depends on the number of stages of the LFSR and its characteristic polynomial. Furthermore, the period of a non-maximal-length sequence depends on the initial contents of the LFSR, called the *seed*. In this way, the parallel LFSR can work as a pseudorandom-pattern generator.

• $B_1 = 0, B_2 = 1$ The fourth mode is used for resetting the contents of the register.

The BILBO approach is aimed at applying to highly integrated modular and bus-oriented systems in which functional modules, such as ROMs, RAMs, ALUs (arithmetic logic units), and I/Os, are connected by bus routing. Since clocked latches are usually used to interface the modules and the buses, BILBOs can take the place of the latches, as shown in figure 9.7. Each module has two BILBOs; one is used as a built-in test-pattern generator to stimulate the module, and the other as a parallel signature analyzer to compress the corresponding test responses into a signature.

First, the system is set to a shift-register mode in order to initialize the BILBOs. Each BILBO is initialized to generate pseudorandom patterns or to compress the test responses. The system is then switched to a self-test mode; that is, BILBOs are converted into LFSRs. In this self-test mode, each circuit under test will have pseudorandom patterns applied to its inputs and will have its outputs stored in the parallel signature analyzer. After a fixed number of patterns have been applied, the system is switched

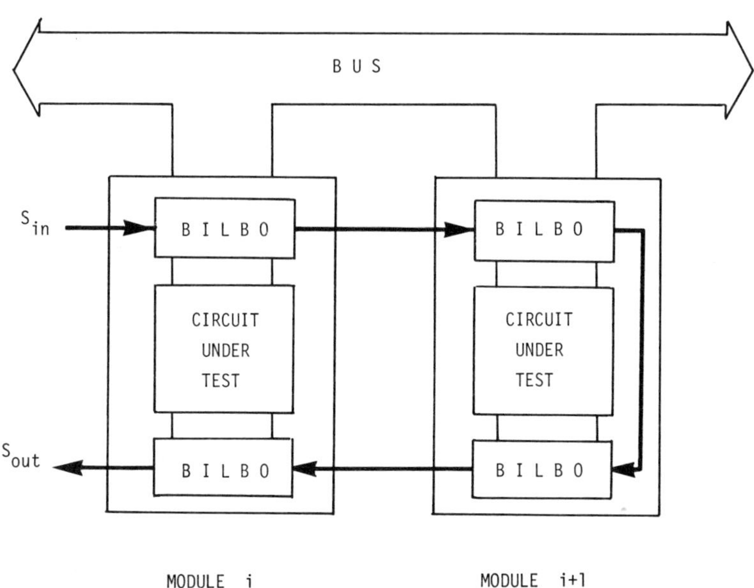

Figure 9.7
Modular bus-oriented design with BILBOs

back to the shift-register mode, and the resulting signatures in BILBOs are scanned out and compared with the expected signatures. In this way, each module can be tested automatically apart from the rest of the system.

Since the LFSR creates pseudorandom patterns, the testing approach mentioned above is suited to those circuits that are susceptible to pseudorandom patterns. However, circuits with large fan-in, such as programmable logic arrays (PLAs), are not tested efficiently by pseudorandom patterns. For example, consider an n-input AND gate. The stuck-at-0 fault on the first input line can be detected only by a test pattern $111\ldots1$. Hence, each pseudorandom pattern would have probability $1/2^n$ of detecting the fault. The random logic circuits with low fan-in of the gates may be tested quite well with pseudorandom patterns. However, most PLAs have large fan-in, and thus the probability of generating an appropriate test pattern becomes quite low if pseudorandom patterns are utilized. To test PLAs efficiently, a set of deterministic test patterns might be required. Daehn and Mucha (1981a) presented a method for designing nonrandom test pattern generators by means of nonlinear feedback shift registers, and applied it with BILBO to the PLA problem.

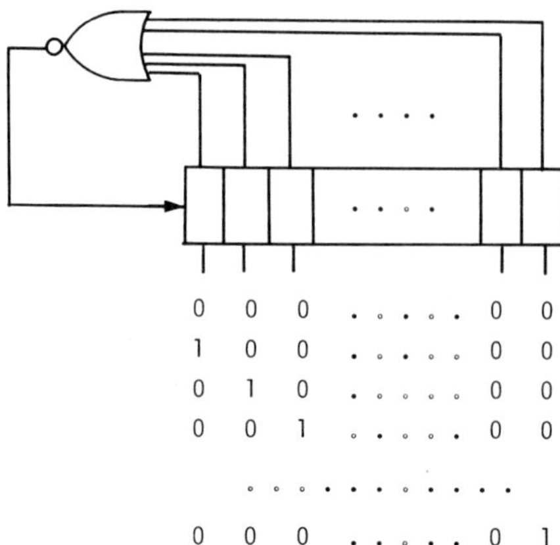

Figure 9.8
Test-pattern generator for NOR arrays

Consider NOR-NOR type PLAs in n-MOS technology. It is easily seen that all the stuck-at faults, crosspoint faults, and bridging faults between adjacent lines in a naked n-input NOR array can be detected by applying the following $n + 1$ patterns:

0 0 0 ··· 0 0
1 0 0 ··· 0 0
0 1 0 ··· 0 0
...
0 0 0 ··· 0 1.

These test patterns are readily generated by means of a nonlinear feedback shift register as shown in figure 9.8. This type of nonlinear feedback shift register can be used for testing NOR arrays. By modifying the BILBO so that it has a mode of a nonlinear feedback shift register, one can use the resulting BILBO for both nonrandom pattern generation and parallel signature analysis of PLAs. Figure 9.9 shows a general structure of built-in self-testable PLAs proposed by Daehn and Mucha (1981b).

Each of the NOR arrays is tested separately. The test patterns for the first NOR array are generated by BILBO 1, and the test responses are monitored by BILBO 2. After $n + 1$ clock cycles, the signature in BILBO 2 is shifted out for inspection. The second NOR array is similarly tested by

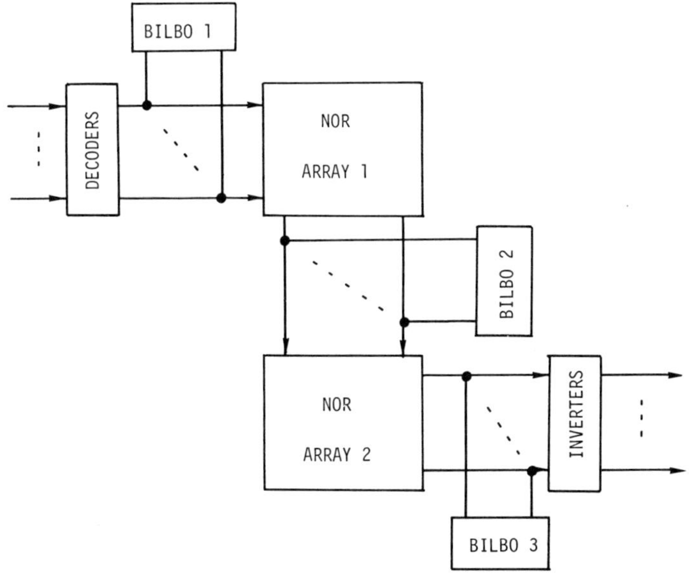

Figure 9.9
Self-testable PLA with BILBOs (Daehn and Mucha 1981; © IEEE 1981)

converting BILBO 2 into a pattern generator and BILBO 3 into a signature analyzer.

Testing of the decoders and the output inverters can be performed by connecting the outputs of the inverters with the inputs of the decoders and by using BILBO 3 as a pattern generator and BILBO 1 as a parallel signature analyzer. When the decoders are all one-bit decoders, the test patterns for NOR arrays are sufficient to detect all the stuck-at and bridging faults in the decoders. However, these test patterns are not sufficient to test two-bit decoders. The test patterns for two-bit decoders are

$$
\begin{array}{cccccc}
0 & 0 & 0 & \cdots & 0 & 0 \\
1 & 0 & 0 & \cdots & 0 & 0 \\
1 & 1 & 0 & \cdots & 0 & 0 \\
0 & 1 & 1 & \cdots & 0 & 0 \\
\ldots \\
0 & 0 & 0 & \cdots & 0 & 1.
\end{array}
$$

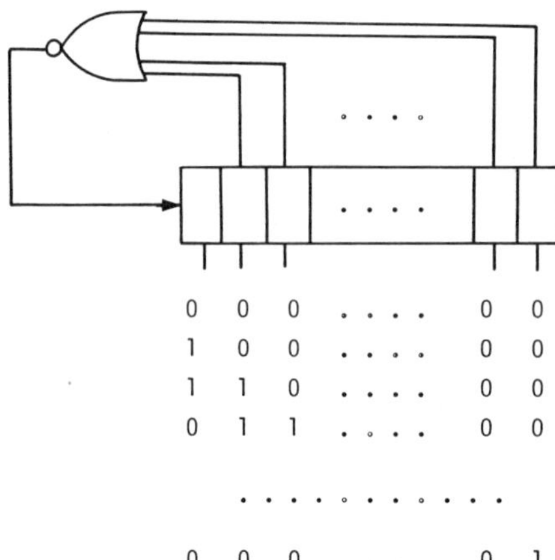

Figure 9.10
Test-pattern generator for two-bit decoders

These patterns can be generated by means of a nonlinear feedback shift register shown in figure 9.10.

As shown in figure 9.11(a), each line of the NOR array passes through the array and hence can be controlled from and observed at either side of the array. Considering this feature, we can place BILBOs properly as shown in figure 9.11(b). Furthermore, if the PLA has input/output registers, the overhead for BILBOs will be reduced by replacing these registers with BILBOs as shown in figure 9.11(c).

The BILBO approach mentioned above has the following advantages.

Since a built-in test-pattern generator is used, the time-consuming process of test generation is eliminated.
Since a built-in data-compression technique is used, the amount of test data is greatly reduced.
External operations are reduced to initializing the registers and checking the signatures.
The circuits are tested at their normal speed.
Simultaneous testing of several modules becomes possible.
The built-in test is also applicable in the field.

In spite of these advantages, the technique has some disadvantages. The overhead is higher than for scan design approaches such as LSSD and Scan

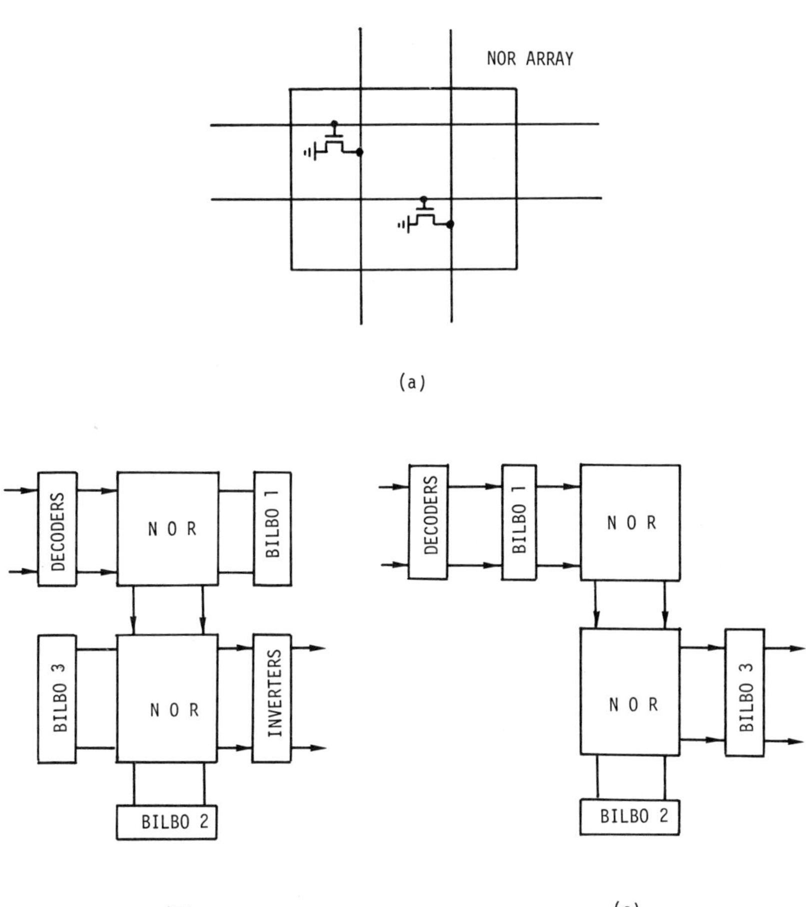

Figure 9.11
Placement of BILBOs

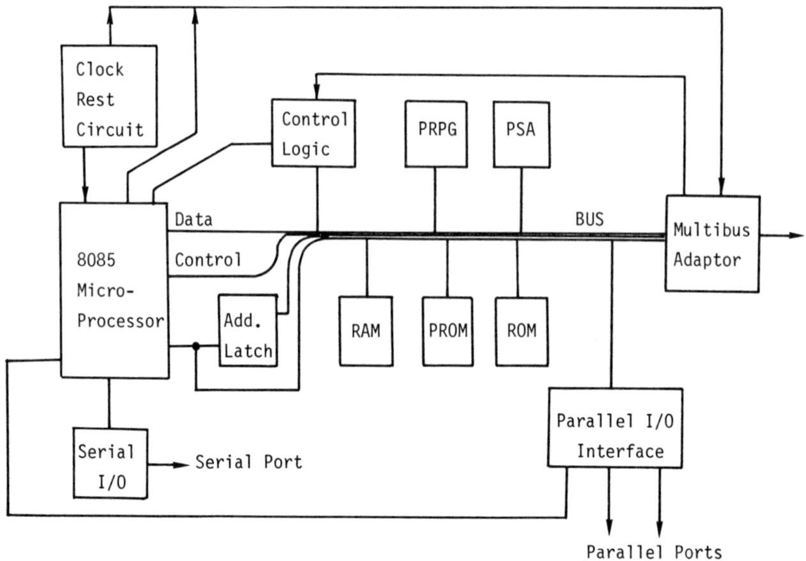

Figure 9.12
Block diagram of MICROBIT 1 (Fasang 1982; © IEEE 1982)

Path because there are extra EOR gates in LFSRs. Furthermore, these extra EOR gates and some gates used for mode switching cause more delay in the system data path than the scan design techniques. However, if we consider the growing cost and complexity of testing VLSI circuits, the built-in self-test approach seems to be an effective and attractive method.

Built-in self-testable architectures for microcomputers have been reported in which parallel signature analysis (BILBO) and serial signature analysis techniques were implemented as on-chip testing aids. Fasang (1982) has reported a microprocessor-based system in which a built-in self-test technique called MICROBIT was implemented. Figure 9.12 is the block diagram of MICROBIT I. The system is typically bus-oriented and composed of the following major blocks: a microprocessor (the 8085), clock and reset circuits, ROM, RAM, parallel input/output ports, a serial I/O port, and an external system bus access arbitrator. The 8085 is an n-MOS 8-bit general-purpose microcomputer chip. In addition to these standard blocks, the MICROBIT has two BILBOs: a pseudorandom-pattern generator (PRPG) and a parallel signature analyzer (PSA). The PRPG generates a repetitive sequence of 255 pseudorandom patterns, which are used for testing RAM and the multibus adaptor. In the MICROBIT system, the functional or operational testing is basically performed. The 8085 microprocessor is tested by running a test program. First, the most fundamental test, called the kernel test, checks the 8085 with respect to only a few instructions, as well as the address, data, and control buses. Then the remaining instructions of the 8085 are executed and compared with the expected results. In the testing of the 8085, BILBOs (PRPG and PSA) are not used. BILBOs are used for testing RAM, ROM, the multibus adaptor, and themselves. In the ROM test, the contents of the ROM are read out, one byte at a time, and compressed by the PSA. The final contents of the PSA are compared with the expected signature by the 8085. In the RAM test, the first 256 bytes of RAM are filled with the 256 patterns from PRPG, the next 256 bytes with the 256 patterns from PRPG + 1, and so on. After all bytes of RAM are filled, the contents are transferred to the PSA, one byte at a time, and compressed into a signature. Then the signature is transferred to the 8085 and compared with the expected signature stored in PROM. In this way, the MICROBIT system implements a microprocessor-based system with built-in self-test function.

Thatte et al. (1982) proposed an architecture for on-chip built-in testable VLSI processors. The proposed methodology is based on bit-sliced, bus-oriented architecture, which is amenable to on-chip built-in implementation using BILBOs. Figure 9.13 shows the general configuration of the processor. In general, a typical single-chip VLSI processor is composed of three main sections; a data-path section, a control section, and an on-chip memory section. The data-path section stores, manipulates, and transfers data. It is usually composed of registers, ALUs, and data buses. The control section, which decodes machine instructions and generates control signals for the data-path section and other logic, is composed of a control ROM, PLA, and decoders. Other on-chip memory, such as program ROM for storing machine-level programs and data RAM for storing data, is contained in the on-chip memory section.

As shown in figure 9.13, the proposed testable processor has two monitors: a control monitor and a data monitor. Both are the same and have four modes of operation: the normal mode, the signature-analysis mode, the scan (shift) mode, and the rotate mode. Except for the rotate mode, the monitor works in the same way as the BILBO. The control monitor can be configured as a parallel signature analyzer to monitor the control signals of the data-path section. The control ROM is tested by reading out the entire

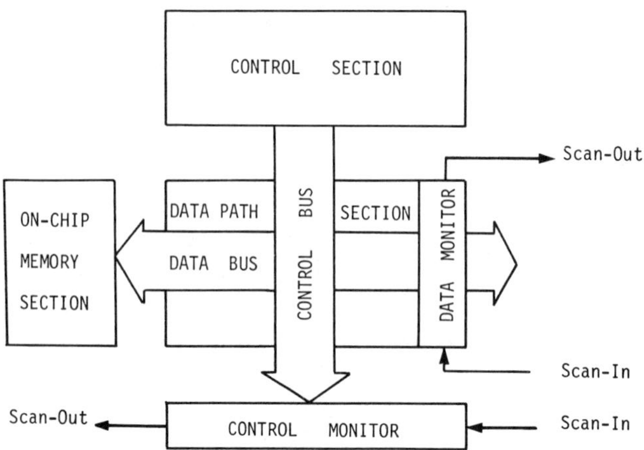

Figure 9.13
A configuration of built-in testable VLSI processors (Thatte et al. 1982; © IEEE 1982)

ROM and compressing the control signals into a signature. In a similar fashion, the data monitor is configured as a parallel signature analyzer to monitor and compress the output data produced by the data-path section. Each functional test pattern for the data-path section consists of control signals and data operands. Data operands can be generated by the use of simple hardware such as counters and sifters. Control signals can be generated by a microprogram stored in an additional ROM or by a machine-instruction program.

The on-chip program ROM is tested by reading out the entire ROM and compressing the ROM outputs into a signature by means of the data monitor. For data RAM testing, test patterns stored in on-chip program ROM are applied to RAM and the outputs are compared with the expected values by means of a comparator.

Thatte et al. (1982) implemented on a CMOS gate array a test vehicle consisting of a four-bit wide, bit-sliced data path equipped with the data and control monitors. According to their study, the additional silicon area required for the data and control monitors is expected to be 4 percent of the total chip area for a 16-bit processor and 2.2 percent for a 32-bit processor.

In the above-mentioned architectures, the BILBO technique based on parallel signature analysis is utilized. Another built-in self-test scheme using an on-chip serial signature-analysis technique has been implemented on a

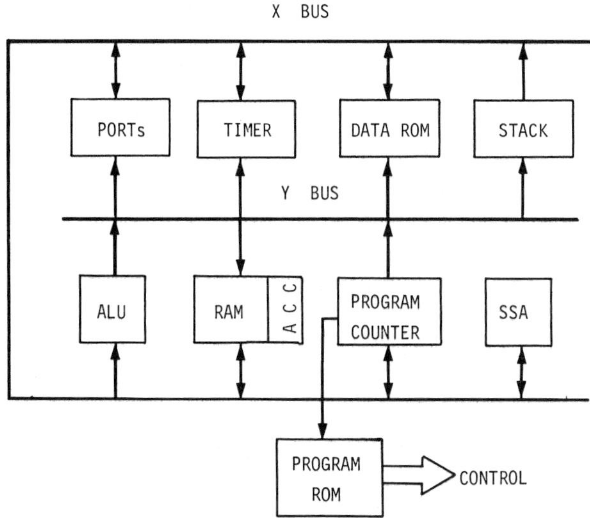

Figure 9.14
Block diagram of MC6804P2 (Kuban and Bruce 1983; © IEEE 1983)

commercial MOS microcomputer, the MC6804P2 (Kuban and Bruce 1983). A block diagram of the MC6804P2 is given as figure 9.14. Since this computer is designed for 4-bit and low-end 8-bit applications, all data transactions are performed serially and parallel conversions are performed locally where necessary. The ALU and the buses are all one bit wide. Because of its serial architecture, the MC6804P2 makes use of a serial signature analyzer (SSA) for the compression of test response data. Each circuit in the MC6804P2 is tested by means of a self-test program stored in program ROM and data ROM. The self-test program occupies 288 bytes of the program ROM and 16 bytes of the data ROM. Test results are compressed into a single 16-bit signature, which is shifted out for off-chip verification. According to Kuban and Bruce, the overhead for the built-in self-test scheme is less than 5 percent of the total chip area.

9.3 Self-Test with Scan Design

As was described in chapter 8, scan design approaches such as the Scan Path and the LSSD can simplify testing of complex sequential logic circuits. Such techniques were developed by mainframe manufacturers and so are

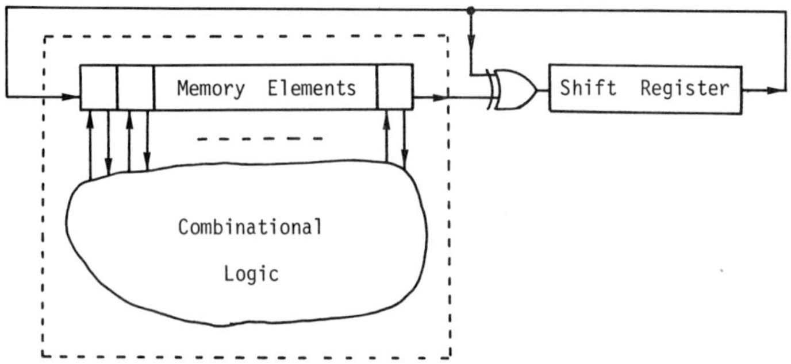

Figure 9.15
External self-test using shift register (Segers 1981; © IEEE 1981)

mainly used in large computers. Even with the scan design approach, test generation is still a heavy burden. Moreover, test application is time consuming, because the test patterns have to be serially shifted in and the responses have to be shifted out through a string of latches. To overcome these shortcomings, a number of self-test approaches combining the scan design concept and linear feedback shift registers (LFSRs) have been proposed. Those techniques that make use of LFSRs as both pseudorandom-pattern generators (PRPGs) and signature analyzers (SAs) have been classified by El-ziq and Butt (1983).

First, the self-test techniques can be classified as either external or internal, depending on the position of the LFSRs. In the *external* technique, all the self-test aids or LFSRs are external to the circuit under test. Hence, the external technique has the advantages that the self-test aids will be just an overlay on an existing scan design, so no changes are needed inside the circuit. ("External" self-testing does not mean the conventional testing using external equipment, nor does it preclude on-chip implementation of external self-test schemes.) The *internal* technique puts the self-test aids into the circuit under test; that is, LFSRs are included in the circuit under test as a part of the scan path. The internal technique seems to be a more attractive solution because it is flexible in realizing various self-test schemes, from low levels to higher levels.

There are four major techniques of the external type. The first is a self-test method proposed by Segers (1981). Figure 9.15 shows the general configuration of the proposed method. The pseudorandom-pattern generator and the signature analyzer are combined into one m-bit feedback (via an EOR

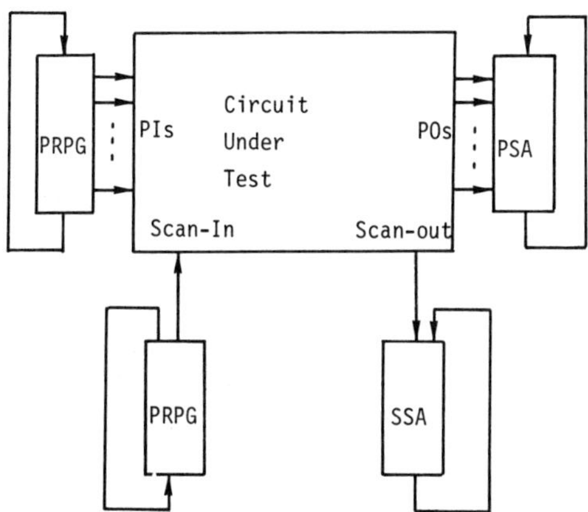

Figure 9.16
External self-test using LFSRs (Bardell and McAnney 1982; © IEEE 1982)

gate) shift register, which is placed outside the module under test. The memory elements or latches of the circuit under test are designed to form a shift register for the scan path technique. Briefly, the self-testing is performed as follows: By shifting a fixed first pattern into the feedback shift register and, as a consequence, into the latches of the scan path, the circuit under test is initialized. After shiftng a test pattern into the latches, the circuit is switched to normal mode and the system clocks are cycled to capture the test responses into the latches. Then the contents of the latches are shifted out and compressed into the feedback shift register. At the same time, the next pseudorandom pattern is shifted into the scan path. After the above operations have been executed a fixed number of times, the final signature of the feedback shift register is compared with the expected signature. This results in a go/no-go signal.

The second external self-test scheme, proposed by Bardell and McAnney (1982), is illustrated in figure 9.16. The primary inputs (PIs) of the circuit under test are driven by an LFSR, which generates pseudorandom patterns. The scan input to the scan path shift register is driven serially by another pseudorandom-pattern generator, an LFSR. The responses at the primary outputs are compressed in parallel into a signature by a parallel signature analyzer, and the response at the scan output is compressed serially by a serial signature analyzer. Both parallel and serial signature analyzers can be implemented using LFSRs, as mentioned in section 9.1.

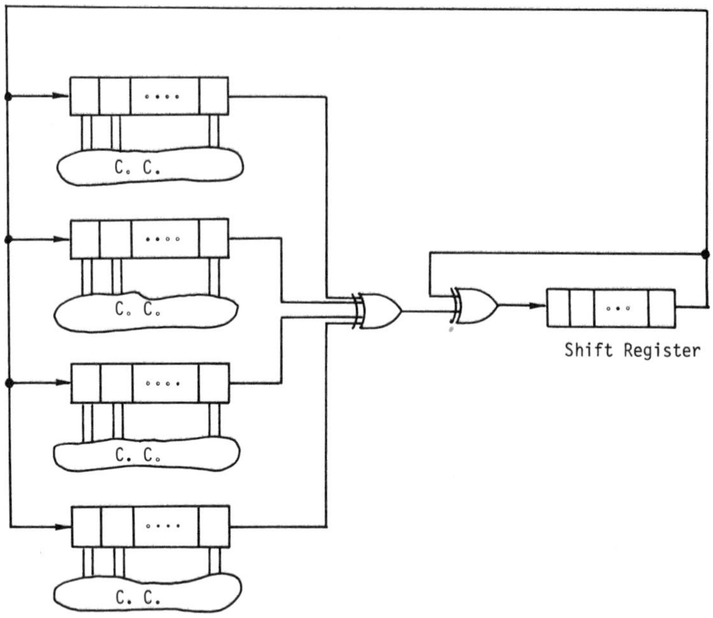

Figure 9.17
Self-test with multiple scan paths (Segers 1981; © IEEE 1981)

The third technique for external self-test is a variation of the above-mentioned scheme of Segers (1981). In order to make the random patterns more effective and to reduce the test time, the scan path is split up into several parallel paths. The configuration of the multiple scan paths is illustrated in figure 9.17.

The fourth technique is also based on multiple scan paths. Figure 9.18 shows the configuration of the self-test scheme, which was presented by Bardell and McAnney (1982). A parallel pseudorandom-pattern generator and a parallel signature analyzer are connected to multiple scan paths, each of which forms a string of latches for each partitioned circuit.

Internal self-test techniques based on LFSRs can be further classified into two types: *centralized* and *distributed*. Figure 9.19 illustrates the centralized technique proposed by Komonytsky (1982). This technique is based on the LSSD and has the following features.

All primary inputs and primary outputs are buffered by additional shift-register latches (SRLs), which are called input latches and output latches,

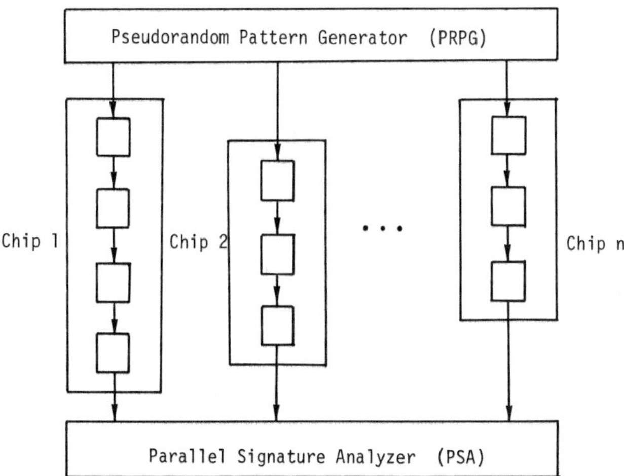

Figure 9.18
Self-test using parallel input LFSRs (Bardell and McAnney 1982; © IEEE 1982)

respectively. Those SRLs that are not input or output latches are called interior latches.
All the SRLs form a shift-register string for parallel and serial pattern loading and unloading.
The first group of SRLs form a pseudorandom-pattern generator.
The last group of SRLs form a signature analyzer.

For the circuit of figure 9.19, the self-testing proceeds as follows.

(1) Initialize all SRLs to 0 but initialize the PRPG latches to 1 in order to provide a deterministic point for the self-test. The PRPG latches must not be cleared to zeros or they will stay locked in a zero state forever. After all latches have been initialized, apply the first test pattern to the combinational logic.
(2) Clock all system clocks, capturing responses from the combinational logic in the interior latches and output latches.
(3) Shift out all interior and output latches to compress the responses into a signature by means of the signature analyzer (the last group of the SRLs). While the contents of latches are shifted, pseudorandom patterns are shifted from the PRPG (the first group of the SRLs) into the interior latches.
(4) Repeat steps 2 and 3 until the test is complete.

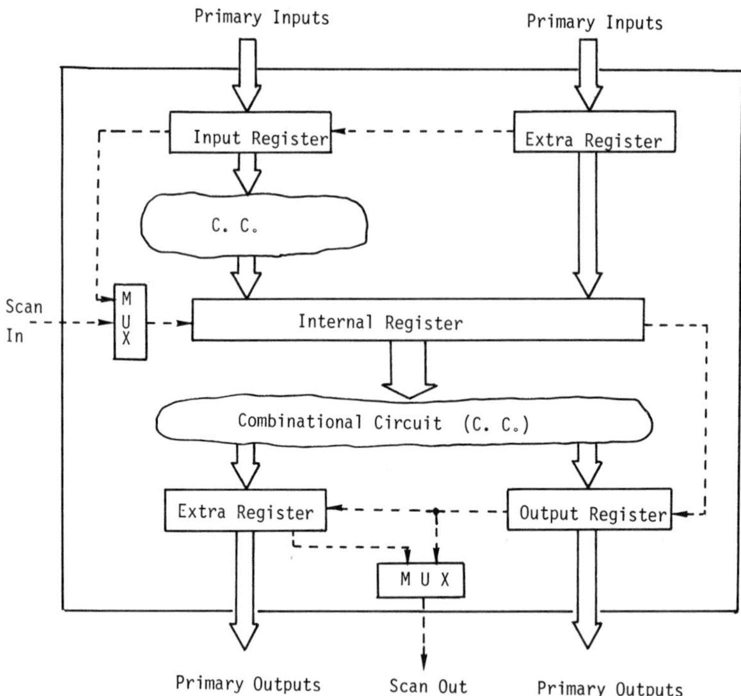

Figure 9.19
Centralized internal self-test approach (Komonytsky 1982; © IEEE 1982)

(5) Compare the final signature compressed in the signature analyzer with the expected signature.

In the self-test technique proposed by Komonytsky (1982), either the test responses are gathered by an external signature analyzer or the signature is computed internally. In both cases, serial signature analysis is used, and hence the testing is relatively slow. If a signature analyzer can compress data from parallel and serial directions, less test time will be required than when only a serial signature analyzer is used. El-ziq and Butt (1983) presented a technique called a mixed-mode built-in self-test (figure 9.20), which is similar to the technique of Komonytsky but differs in signature analysis. Much as in the scheme of figure 9.19, the first group of latches form a pseudorandom-pattern generator, which can feed the output data in both parallel and serial directions. (This is denoted in figure 9.20 as the mixed

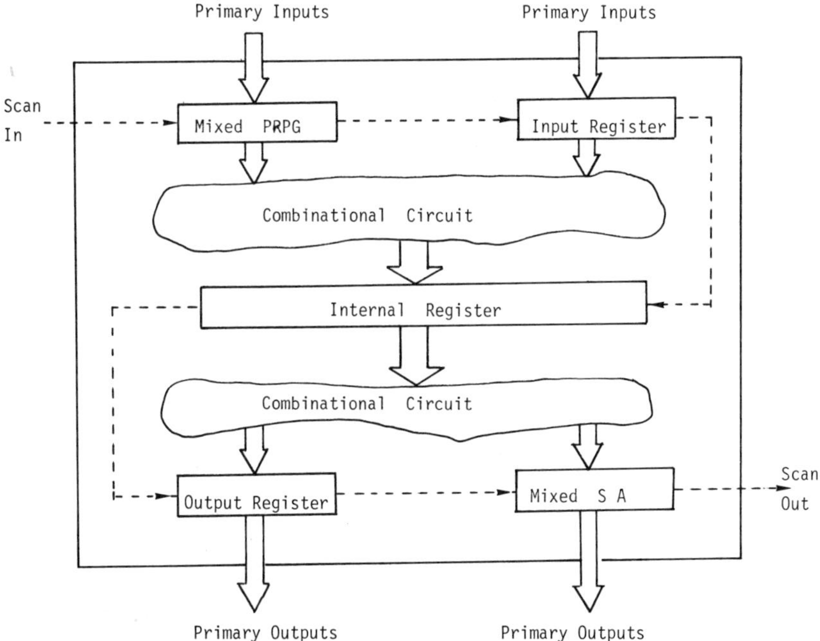

Figure 9.20
Mixed-mode self-test approach (El-ziq and Butt 1983; © IEEE 1983)

PRPG.) The last group of latches form a signature analyzer (called the mixed SA), which collects the output data from the combinational logic feeding into it (in the parallel direction) and mixes it with the output data stored in the output registers (in the serial direction). Note that in the self-test procedure of Komonytsky (1982) all the response data captured in the interior latches are also serially shifted into the signature analyzer.

Another type of internal self-test techniques is the distributed technique, in which every register element has some extra logic that enables it to perform as part of a test-pattern generator or a signature analyzer. The BILBO approach of Koenemann et al. (1979) belongs to this class. Bardell and McAnney (1982) proposed a self-test approach called *simultaneous self-test*, which is also of the distributed type. In this approach, every SRL is required to be replaced by a self-test SRL, as shown in figure 9.21. With +Test Mode at a logical 0, the self-test SRL behaves as an SRL, i.e., a normal system latch or a shift-register element. With +Test Mode at a logical 1 and

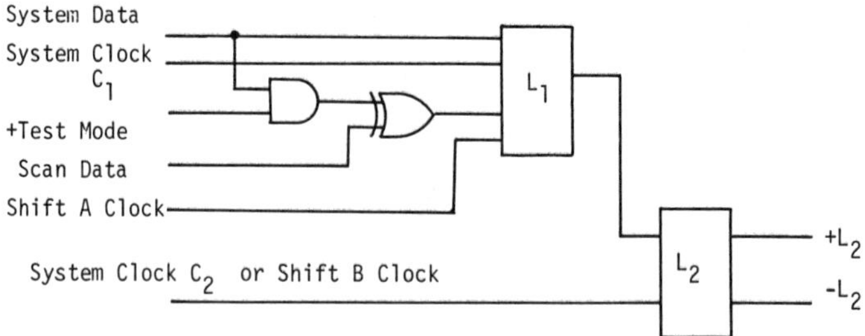

Figure 9.21
Self-test SRL (Bardell and McAnney 1982; © IEEE 1982)

the system clock at a logical 0, the self-test SRL can be used as an element of LFSRs. The configuration of this self-test mode is illustrated in figure 9.22.

The distributed technique is well suited to system-level testing, since the testing can be performed much more rapidly than with all other techniques that need to shift the data through the scan path. However, it requires extra hardware, which may also affect the system performance. Furthermore, it does not test for the I/O logic lying between the PIs and the self-test SRLs and between the self-test SRLs and the POs. Hence, for manufacturing testing of individual modules, the test procedure must be augmented to allow testing of the I/O logic. One approach is to connect the POs and PIs by making use of socket wiring. Another approach is to use external PRPGs and SAs for testing the I/O logic.

9.4 Self-Verification

In general, testing approaches are classified as on-line or off-line. On-line testing is performed during system run time, concurrent with normal system operation. Data patterns from normal computation serve as test patterns, and a failure occurrence caused by some intermittent or solid fault can be detected by means of built-in fault-detection circuits (FDCs). During normal system operation, the FDCs continuously monitor the intermediate as well as the final outputs of the circuit under test and immediately detect any intermittent or solid failures. These FDCs for on-line testing can also be useful for off-line self-testing. Although the object of off-line testing seems different from that of on-line testing, they have a common goal: the detection and isolation of faults and the verification of fault-free operation of

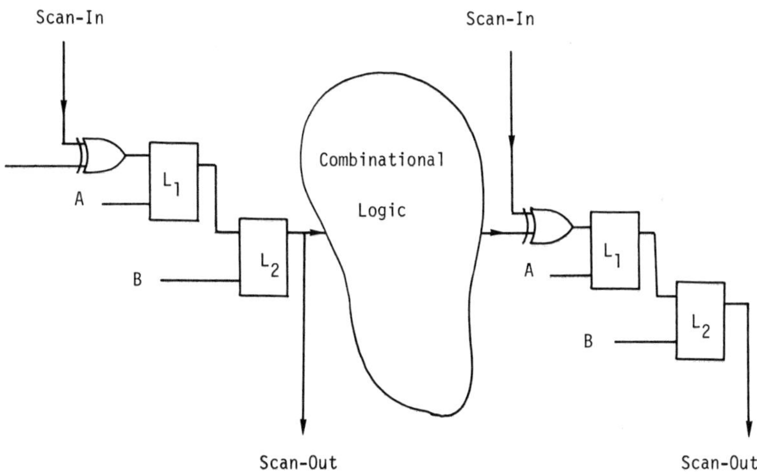

Figure 9.22
Distributed internal self-test approach (Bardell and McAnney 1982; © IEEE 1982)

circuits. This goal may become more achievable if both on-line and off-line techniques are used together harmoniously.

A self-test approach called *self-verification*, proposed by Sedmak (1979), reflects an attempt to merge off-line and on-line testing techniques. Self-verification is defined by Sedmak as the ability of logic to verify a failure-free status automatically, without the need for externally applied test stimuli (other than power and the clock) and without the need for the logic to be part of a running system.

The general configuration of the self-verification approach is illustrated in figure 9.23. As shown in the figure, the self-verification scheme requires automatic fault-detection circuits and test-pattern generators (TPGs). FDCs are used to detect any intermittent or solid failures by monitoring the outputs of the circuit under test. The error-status generator assembles and encodes information about the presence and location of detected faults. Examples of FDCs are checking circuits for error-detecting codes (parity codes, m-out-of-n codes, residue codes, and the like) and comparators for checking duplicated logic. To guarantee the correctness of test results, these FDCs are usually designed so as to be "self-checking."

Test-pattern generators provide the test patterns necessary to stimulate the circuit under test and expose any faults to the FDCs. The TPGs can be implemented in various ways (random-pattern generator, m-out-of-n code

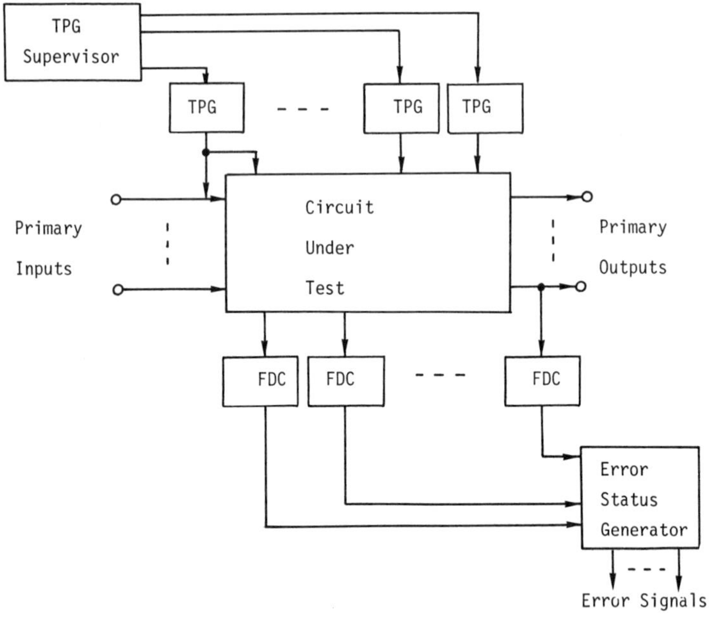

Figure 9.23
General configuration of self-verification approach (Sedmak 1979; © IEEE 1979)

generator, and so on), depending on the nature of the circuit under test. In the proposed self-verification approach, the TPG illustrated in figure 9.24 is utilized. This TPG consists of a binary counter and a parallel-in/serial-out shift register. It generates all 2^n possible input combinations to test exhaustively a combinational circuit having n inputs. Although such exhaustive testing has the advantage that all stuck-at faults as well as non-stuck-at faults can be detected, the test application appears to consume far too much time. However, the test time can be reduced by partitioning the logic to be tested so that partitioned subcircuits have few enough inputs to allow exhaustive testing and so that many of the subcircuits can be tested in parallel.

The TPGs are coordinated by the TPG supervisor shown in figure 9.23. The TPG supervisor is normally used for controlling the starting and the stopping of TPGs only during self-verification and not during normal operation of the system. Hence, in normal system operation, FDCs can also be used for on-line automatic fault detection.

Figure 9.25 shows an example of the application of self-verification using

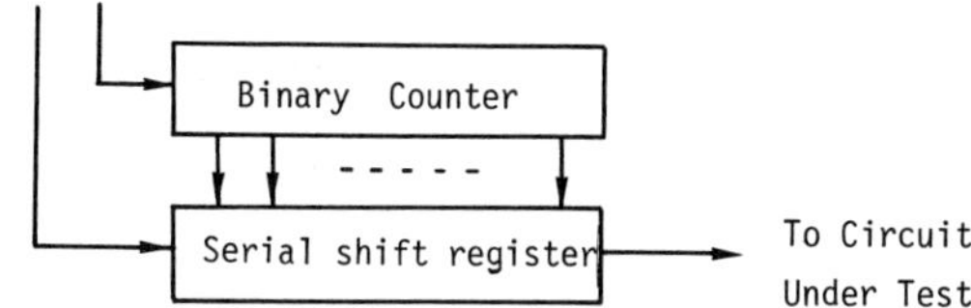

Figure 9.24
Exhaustive test-pattern generator

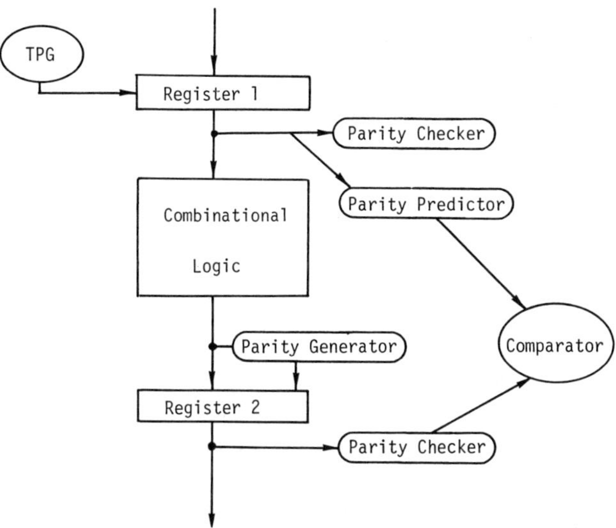

Figure 9.25
Self-verification using parity codes

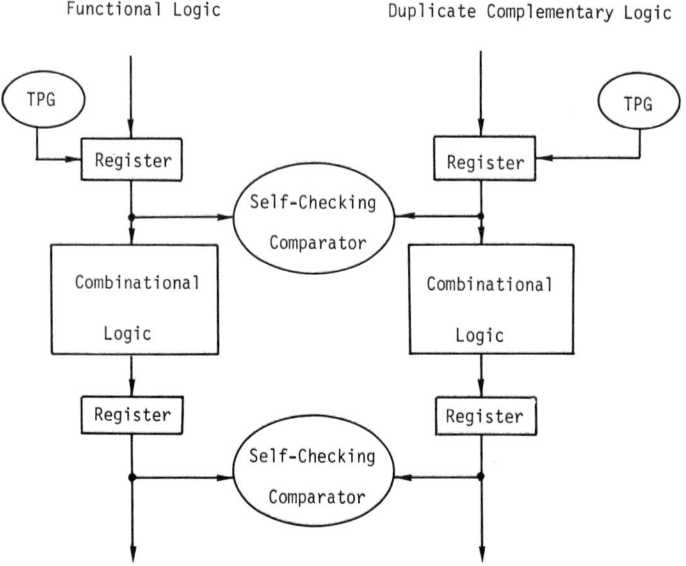

Figure 9.26
Self-verification using duplication

parity codes. Two registers have the added parity bits, and a parity checker is placed at the output of each register. In this example it is supposed that the combinational logic may not preserve parity, and hence the parity bits are regenerated at the outputs by a parity generator. On the other hand, faults in the parity generator can be detected by means of the parity check at register 2 and the parity prediction/comparison check spanning the combinational logic and register 2.

Figure 9.26 shows another example of the self-verification approach. The technique is based on duplication of logic in complementary form. The left side of the figure shows the functional circuit; the right side is the duplicate complementary logic. Comparators compare the functional-logic signals with the duplicate complementary-logic signals at the outputs of registers. Both comparators are designed so as to be self-checking.

As described above, the self-verification approach falls under the category of self-testing. Hence, similar to a number of other self-test approaches, the self-verification approach has the following advantages:

The time-consuming process of test generation is eliminated.
Storage of a huge amount of test data is eliminated.

Circuits are tested at their full machine speed.
Testing is possible at all packaging levels, such as the chip, card, and system levels.

In addition to these advantages, the self-verification approach has a unique attribute: A major portion of the logic required for self-verification is also used for automatic fault detection and recovery during normal operation of the assembled system.

Bibliography

Abramovici, M., Y. H. Levendel, and P. R. Menon. 1982. A logic simulation machine. *Proc. 19th Design Automation Conf.*, pp. 65–73.

Agarwal, V. K. 1978. Fanout-free Boolean functions and L-expressions. *Proc. Conf. Information Sciences and Systems*, Johns Hopkins University, pp. 227–233.

Agarwal, V. K., and A. S. F. Fung. 1981. Multiple fault testing of large circuits by single fault test sets. *IEEE Trans. Comput.* C-30 (11): 855–865.

Aho, A., J. Hopcroft, and J. Ullman. 1976. *The Design and Analysis of Computer Algorithms.* Reading, Mass.: Addison-Wesley.

Akers, S. B. 1973. Universal test sets for logic networks. *IEEE Trans. Comput.* C-22 (9): 835–839.

Akers, S. B. 1976. A logic system for fault test generation. *IEEE Trans. Comput.* C-25 (6): 620–629.

Ando, H. 1980. Testing VLSI with random access scan. *Proc. COMPCON 1980*, pp. 50–52.

Armstrong, D. B. 1966. On finding a nearly minimal set of fault detection tests for combinatorial nets. *IEEE Trans. Electron. Comput.* EC-15 (2): 63–73.

Armstrong, D. B. 1972. A deductive method for simulating faults in logic circuits. *IEEE Trans. Comput.* C-21 (5): 464–471.

Bardell, P. H., and W. H. McAnney. 1982. Self-testing of multichip logic modules. *Proc. 1982 IEEE Test Conf.*, pp. 200–204.

Barzilai, Z., J. Savir, G. Markowsky, and M. G. Smith. 1981. The weighted syndrome sums approach to VLSI testing. *IEEE Trans. Comput.* C-30 (12): 996–1000.

Barzilai, Z., D. Coppersmith, and A. L. Rosenberg. 1983. Exhaustive generation of bit patterns with applications to VLSI self-testing. *IEEE Trans. Comput.* C-32 (2): 190–194.

Bennetts, R. G., C. M. Maunder, and G. D. Robinson. 1981. CAMELOT: A computer-aided measure for logic testability. *IEE Proc.* 128 (5): 177–189.

Benowitz, N., D. F. Calhoun, G. E. Alderson, J. E. Bauer, and C. T. Joeckel. 1975. An advanced fault isolation system for digital logic. *IEEE Trans. Comput.* C-24 (5): 489–497.

Berg, W. C., and R. D. Hess. 1982. COMET: A testability analysis and design modification package. *Proc. 1982 IEEE Test Conf.*, pp. 364–378.

Betancourt, R. 1973. Derivation of minimum test sets for unate logical circuits. *IEEE Trans. Comput.* C-20 (11): 1264–1269.

Bhattacharya, B. B., and B. Gupta. 1983. Syndrome testable design of combinational networks for detecting stuck-at and bridging faults. *Proc. 1983 Int. Test Conf.*, pp. 446–452.

Bhavsar, D. K., and R. W. Heckelman. 1981. Self-testing by polynomial division. *Proc. 1981 IEEE Test Conf.*, pp. 208–216.

Bossen, D. C., and S. J. Hong. 1971. Cause and effect analysis for multiple fault detection in combinational networks. *IEEE Trans. Comput.* C-20 (11): 1252–1257.

Bozorgui-Nesbat, S., and E. J. McCluskey. 1980. Structured design for testability to eliminate test pattern generation. *Proc. 10th Int. Symp. Fault-Tolerant Computing*, pp. 158–163.

Breuer, M. A. 1972. Generation of fault tests for linear logic networks. *IEEE Trans. Comput.* C-21 (1): 79–83.

Breuer, M. A., and A. D. Friedman. 1979. TEST/80—A proposal for an advanced automatic test generation system. *Proc. IEEE Autotestcon*, pp. 305–312.

Brglez, F. 1984. On testability analysis of combinational networks. *Proc. Int. Symp. Circuits and Systems*, pp. 221–225.

Carter, J. L. 1982. The theory of signature testing for VLSI. *Proc. 14th Ann. ACM Symp. Theory of Computing*, pp. 66–76.

Carter, W. C. 1982. Signature testing with guaranteed bound for fault coverage. *Proc. 1982 IEEE Test Conf.*, pp. 75–82.

Cha, C. W., W. Donath, and F. Ozguner. 1978. 9-V algorithm for test pattern generation of combinational digital circuits. *IEEE Trans. Comput.* C-27 (3): 193–200.

Chang, H. Y., S. G. Chappell, C. H. Elmensdorf, and L. D. Schmidt. 1974. Comparison of parallel and deductive fault simulation methods. *IEEE Trans. Comput.* C-23 (11): 1132–1138.

Chappell, S. G., C. H. Elmensdorf, and L. D. Schmidt. 1974. LAMP: Logic circuit simulation. *Bell System Tech. J.* 53: 1451–1476.

Clegg, F. W. 1973. Use of SPOOFs in the analysis of faulty logic networks. *IEEE Trans. Comput.* C-22 (3): 229–234.

Cook, S. A. 1971. The complexity of theorem proving procedures. *Proc. 3rd ACM Symp. Theory of Computing*, pp. 151–158.

Coy, W., and A. Vogel. 1981. Inserting test points for simple test generation. *Proc. 4th Int. Conf. Fault-Tolerant Systems and Diagnostics*, pp. 180–186.

Daehn, W., and J. Mucha. 1981a. Hardware test pattern generation for built-in testing. *Proc. 1981 IEEE Test Conf.*, pp. 110–113.

Daehn, W., and J. Mucha. 1981b. A hardware approach to self-testing of large programmable logic arrays. *IEEE Trans. Comput.* C-30 (11): 829–833.

DasGupta, S., C. R. P. Hartmann, and L. D. Rudolph. 1980. Dual-mode logic for function-independent fault testing. *IEEE Trans. Comput.* C-29 (11): 1025–1029.

DasGupta, S., R. G. Walther, T. W. Williams, and E. B. Eichelberger. 1981. An enhancement to LSSD and some applications of LSSD in reliability, availability, and serviceability. *Proc. 11th Symp. Fault-Tolerant Computing*, pp. 32–34.

DasGupta, S., P. Goel, R. G. Walther, and T. W. Williams. 1982. A variation of LSSD and its implications on design and test pattern generation in VLSI. *Proc. 1982 IEEE Test Conf.*, pp. 63–66.

Dejka, W. J. 1977. Measure of testability in device and system design. *20th Midwest Symp. Circuits and Systems*, pp. 39–52.

Denneau, M. M. 1982. The Yorktown simulation engine. *Proc. 19th Design Automation Conf.*, pp. 55–59.

Dussault, J. A. 1978. A testability measure. *Proc. IEEE Semiconductor Test Conf.*, pp. 113–116.

Eichelberger, E. B. 1965. Hazard detection in combinational and sequential switching circuits. *IBM J. Res. Dev.* 9: 90–99.

Eichelberger, E. B., and T. W. Williams. 1977. A logic design structure for LSI testability. *Proc. 14th Design Automation Conf.*, pp. 462–468.

Eichelberger, E. B., and T. W. Williams. 1978. A logic design structure for LSI testability. *J. Design Automation and Fault-Tolerant Computing* 2 (2): 165–178.

El-ziq, Y. M., and H. H. Butt. 1983. A mixed-mode built-in self-test technique using scan path and signature analysis. *Proc. 1983 Test Conf.*, pp. 269–274.

Fantauzzi, G. 1974. An algebraic model for the analysis of logical circuits. *IEEE Trans. Comput.* C-23 (6): 576–581.

Fasang, P. P. 1982. A fault detection and isolation technique for microprocessors. *Proc. 1982 IEEE Test Conf.*, pp. 214–219.

Frohwerk, R. A. 1977. Signature analysis: A new digital field service method. *Hewlett-Packard J.* (May): 2–8.

Fujiwara, E. 1983. A self-testing group-parity prediction checker and its use for built-in testing. *Proc. 13th Int. Symp. Fault-Tolerant Computing*, pp. 146–153.

Fujiwara, H. 1981. On closedness and test complexity of logic circuits. *IEEE Trans. Comput.* C-30 (8): 556–562.

Fujiwara, H. 1984. A new PLA design for universal testability. *IEEE Trans. Comput.* C-33 (8): 745–750.

Fujiwara, H., and K. Kinoshita. 1978. Testing logic circuits with compressed data. *Proc. 8th Int. Conf. Fault-Tolerant Computing*, pp. 108–113.

Fujiwara, H., and K. Kinoshita. 1981. A design of programmable logic arrays with universal tests. *IEEE Trans. Comput.* C-30 (11): 823–838.

Fujiwara, H., and T. Shimono. 1983a. On the acceleration of test generation algorithms. *Proc. 13th Int. Symp. Fault-Tolerant Computing*, pp. 98–105.

Fujiwara, H., and T. Shimono. 1983b. On the acceleration of test generation algorithms. *IEEE Trans. Comput.* C-32 (12): 1137–1144.

Fujiwara, H., and S. Toida. 1981. The complexity of fault detection problems for combinational circuits. Techincal report 78-P-HW-150681, Dept. of System Design, University of Waterloo, Canada.

Fujiwara, H., and S. Toida. 1982a. The complexity of fault detection: An approach to design for testability. *Proc. 12th Int. Symp. Fault-Tolerant Computing*, pp. 101–108.

Fujiwara, H., and S. Toida. 1982b. The complexity of fault detection problems for combinational logic circuits. *IEEE Trans. Comput.* C-31 (6): 555–560.

Fujiwara, H., Y. Nagao, T. Sasao, and K. Kinoshita. 1975. Easily testable sequential machines with extra inputs. *IEEE Trans. Comput.* C-24 (8): 821–826.

Fujiwara, H., K. Kinoshita, and H. Ozaki. 1980. Universal test sets for programmable logic arrays. *Proc. 10th Int. Conf. Fault-Tolerant Computing*, pp. 137–142.

Funatsu, S., N. Wakatsuki, and T. Arima. 1975. Test generation systems in Japan. *Proc. 12th Design Automation Symp.*, vol. 6, pp. 114–122.

Garey, M. R. and D. S. Johnson. 1979. *Computers and Intractability: A Guide to the Theory of NP-Completeness.* W. H. Freeman and Company.

Godoy, H. C., G. B. Franklin, and P. S. Bottoroff. 1977. Automatic checking of logic design structure for compliance with testability groundrules. *Proc. 14th Design Automation Conf.*, pp. 460–478.

Goel, P. 1980. Test generation costs analysis and projections. *Proc. 17th Design Automation Conf.*, pp. 77–84.

Goel, P. 1981a. An implicit enumeration algorithm to generate tests for combinational logic circuits. *IEEE Trans. Comput.* C-30 (3): 215–222.

Goel, P. 1981b. PODEM-X: An automatic test generation system for VLSI logic structures. *Proc. 18th Design Automation Conf.*, pp. 260–268.

Gold, E. M. 1974. Complexity of automaton identification from given data, Unpublished.

Goldstein, L. H. 1979. Controllability/observability analysis of digital circuits. *IEEE Trans. Circuits and Systems* CAS-26 (9): 685–693.

Hardie, F. H., and R. J. Suhocki. 1967. Design and use of fault simulation for Saturn computer design. *IEEE Trans. Elec. Comput.* EC-16 (8): 412–429.

Hayes, J. P. 1971a. A NAND model for fault diagnosis in combinational logic networks. *IEEE Trans. Comput.* C-20 (12): 1496–1506.

Hayes, J. P. 1971b. On realizations of Boolean functions requiring a minimal or near-minimal number of tests. *IEEE Trans. Comput.* C-20 (12): 1506–1513.

Hayes, J. P. 1974. On modifying logic networks to improve their diagnosability. *IEEE Trans. Comput.* C-23 (1): 56–62.

Hayes, J. P. 1975. The fanout structure of switching functions. *J. ACM* 22 (4): 551–571.

Hayes, J. P., and A. D. Friedman. 1974. Test point placement to simplify fault detection. *IEEE Trans. Comput.* C-23 (7): 727–735.

Hong, S. J., and D. L. Ostapko. 1980. FITPLA: A programmable logic array for function independent testing. *Proc. 10th Int. Symp. Fault-Tolerant Computing*, pp. 131–136.

Hsiao, T. C., and S. C. Seth. 1982. The use of Rademacher-Walsh spectrum in testing and design of digital circuits. *Proc. ICCC*, pp. 202–205.

Ibarra, O. H., and S. K. Sahni. 1975. Polynomially complete fault detection problems. *IEEE Trans. Comput.* C-24 (3): 242–249.

Inose, H. and M. Sakauchi. 1972. Synthesis of automatic fault diagnosable logical circuits by function conversion method. *Proc. First USA-Japan Computer Conf.*, pp. 426–430.

Kautz, W. H. 1971. Testing faults in combinational cellular logic arrays. *Proc. 8th Ann. Symp. Switching and Automata Theory*, pp. 161–174.

Keiner, W., and R. West. 1977. Testability measures. *Proc. IEEE Autotestcon*, pp. 49–55.

Khakbaz, J. 1983. A testable PLA design with low overhead and high fault coverage. *Proc. 13th Int. Symp. Fault-Tolerant Computing*, pp. 426–429.

Khakbaz, J., and E. J. McCluskey. 1982. Concurrent error detection and testing for large PLAs. *IEEE J. Solid-State Circuits* SC-17 (2): 386–394.

Kinoshita, K., Y. Takamatsu, and M. Shibata. 1980. Test generation for combinational circuits by structure description functions. *Proc. 10th Int. Symp. Fault-Tolerant Computing*, pp. 152–154.

Kobayashi, T., T. Matsue, and H. Shiba. 1968. Flip-flop circuit with FLT capability. *Proc. IECEO Conf.*, p. 692. In Japanese.

Kodandapani, K. L. 1974. A note on easily testable realizations for logic functions. *IEEE Trans. Comput.* C-23 (3): 332–333.

Koenemann, B., J. Mucha, and G. Zwiehoff. 1979. Built-in logic block observation techniques. *Proc. 1979 IEEE Test Conf.*, pp. 37–41.

Komonytsky, D. 1982. LSI self-test using level sensitive scan design and signature analysis. *Proc. 1982 IEEE Test Conf.*, pp. 414–424.

Kovijanic, P. G. 1979. Testability analysis. *Proc. 1979 IEEE Test Conf.*, pp. 310–316.

Kronstadt, E. K., and G. Pfister. 1982. Software support for the Yorktown simulation engine. *Proc. 19th Design Automation Conf.*, pp. 60–64.

Ku, C. T., and G. M. Masson. 1975. The Boolean difference and multiple fault analysis. *IEEE Trans. Comput.* C-24 (1): 62–71.

Kuban, J., and B. Bruce. 1983. The MC6804P2 built-in self-test. *Proc. 1983 Int. Test Conf.*, pp. 295–300.

Kubo, H. 1968. A procedure for generating test sequences to detect sequential circuit failures. *NEC Res. Dev.* 12: 69–78.

Kuhl, J. G., and S. M. Reddy. 1978. On the detection of terminal stuck faults. *IEEE Trans. Comput.* C-27 (5): 467–469.

Kuntzmann, J. 1968. *Algebre de Boole.* Paris: Dunod.

Lai, H. C. and S. Muroga. 1979. Minimum parallel binary adders with NOR (NAND) gates. *IEEE Trans. Comput.*, C-28 (9): 648–659.

Lineback, J. R. 1982. Logic simulation speeded with new special hardware. *Electronics* (June 16): 45–46.

McCluskey, E. J., and S. Bozorgui-Nesbat. 1980. Design for autonomous test. *Proc. 1980 IEEE Test Conf.*, pp. 15–21.

McCluskey, E. J., and S. Bozorgui-Nesbat. 1981. Design for autonomous test. *IEEE Trans. Comput.* C-30 (11): 866–875.

Markowsky, G. 1981. Syndrome-testability can be achieved by circuit modification. *IEEE Trans. Comput.* C-30 (8): 604–606.

Menon, P. R., and S. Chappell. 1978. Deductive fault simulation with functional blocks. *IEEE Trans. Comput.* C-27 (8): 689–695.

Mercer, M. R., V. D. Agrawal, and C. M. Roman. 1981. Test generation for highly sequential scan-testable circuits through logic transformation. *Proc. IEEE Test Conf.*, pp. 561–565.

Muth, P. 1976. A nine-valued circuit model for test generation. *IEEE Trans. Comput.* C-25 (6): 630–636.

Oklobdzija, V. G., and M. D. Ercegovac. 1982. Testability enhancement of VLSI using circuit structures. *Proc. IEEE ICCC '82*, pp. 198–201.

Page, E. W. 1980. Minimally testable Reed-Muller canonical forms. *IEEE Trans. Comput.* C-29 (8): 746–750.

Peterson, W. W., and E. J. Weldon. 1972. *Error-Correcting Codes.* Cambridge, Mass.: MIT Press.

Pfister, G. F. 1982. The Yorktown simulation engine: Introduction. *Proc. 19th Design Automation Conf.*, pp. 51–54.

Poage, J. F. 1963. Derivation of optimum tests to detect faults in combinational circuits. *Mathematical Theory and Automation.* New York: Polytechnic Press.

Pradhan, D. K. 1978. Universal test sets for multiple fault detection in AND-EXOR arrays. *IEEE Trans. Comput.* C-27 (2): 181–187.

Pradhan, D. K., and K. Son. 1980. The effect of untestable faults in PLAs and a design for testability. *Proc. 1980 IEEE Test Conf.*, pp. 359–367.

Putzolu, G. R., and J. P. Roth. 1971. A heuristic algorithm for testing of asynchronous circuits. *IEEE Trans. Comput.* C-20 (6): 639–647.

Ramanatha, K. S., and N. N. Biswas. 1982. A design for complete testability of programmable logic array. *Proc. 1982 IEEE Test Conf.*, pp. 67–74.

Ramanatha, K. S., and N. N. Biswas. 1983. A design for testability of undetectable crosspoint faults in programmable logic arrays. *IEEE Trans. Comput.* C-32 (6): 551–557.

Reddy, S. M. 1972. Easily testable realizations for logic functions. *IEEE Trans. Comput.* C-21 (11): 1183–1188.

Reddy, S. M. 1973. Complete test sets for logic functions. *IEEE Trans. Comput.* C-22 (11): 1016–1020.

Roth, J. P. 1966. Diagnosis of automata failures: A calculus and a method. *IBM J. Res. Dev.* 10: 278–281.

Roth, J. P. 1980. *Computer Logic, Testing and Verification.* Rockville, Md.: Computer Science Press.

Roth, J. P., W. G. Bouricius, and P. R. Schneider. 1967. Programmed algorithms to compute tests to detect and distinguish between failures in logic circuits. *IEEE Trans. Electron. Comput.* EC-16 (10): 567–580.

Sakauchi, M., K. Hawiuke, and H. Inose. 1975. Synthesis and realization of diagnosable processor with necessary hardware redundancy for locating faulty packages. *Proc. 2nd USA-Japan Comput. Conf.*, pp. 122–125.

Saluja, K. K. 1982. An enhancement of SSD to reduce test pattern generation effort and increase fault coverage. *Proc. 19th Design Automation Conf.*, pp. 489–494.

Saluja, K. K., and M. Karpovsky. 1983. Testing computer hardare through data compression in space and time. *Proc. 1983 Int. Test Conf.*, pp. 83–88.

Saluja, K. K., and S. M. Reddy. 1974. On minimally testable logic networks. *IEEE Trans. Comput.* C-23 (1): 552–554.

Saluja, K. K., and S. M. Reddy. 1975. Fault detecting test sets for Reed-Muller canonic networks. *IEEE Trans. Comput.* C-24 (10): 995–998.

Saluja, K. K., K. Kinoshita, and H. Fujiwara. 1981. A multiple fault testable design of programmable logic arrays. *Proc. 11th Symp. Fault-Tolerant Computing*, pp. 137–142.

Saluja, K. K., K. Kinoshita, and H. Fujiwara. 1983. An easily testable design of programmable logic arrays for multiple faults. *IEEE Trans. Comput.* C-32 (11): 1038–1046.

Sasaki, T., N. Koike, K. Ohmori, and K. Tomita. 1983. HAL: A block level hardware logic simulator. *Proc. 20th Design Automation Conf.*, pp. 150–156.

Savir, J. 1980. Syndrome-testable design of combinational circuits. *IEEE Trans. Comput.* C-29 (6): 442–451. Corrections: November 1980.

Savir, J. 1981. Syndrome testing of syndrome-untestable combinational circuits. *IEEE Trans. Comput.* C-30 (8): 606–608.

Sedmak, R. M. 1979. Design for self-verification: An approach for dealing with testability problems in VLSI-based designs. *Proc. 1980 IEEE Test Conf.*, pp. 112–120.

Segers, M. T. M. 1981. A self-test method for digital circuits. *Proc. 1981 IEEE Test Conf.*, pp. 79–85.

Sellers, E. F., M. Y. Hsiao, and L. W. Bearnson. 1968a. Analyzing errors with the Boolean difference. *IEEE Trans. Comput.* C-17 (7): 676–683.

Sellers, E. F., M. Y. Hsiao, and L. W. Bearnson. 1968b. *Error Detecting Logic for Digital Computers.* New York: McGraw-Hill.

Seshu, S. 1965. On an improved diagnosis program. *IEEE Trans. Electron. Comput.* EC-12 (2): 76–79.

Seth, S. C., and K. L. Kodandapani. 1977. Diagnosis of faults in linear tree networks. *IEEE Trans. Comput.* C-26 (1): 29–33.

Smith, J. E. 1980. Measures of the effectiveness of fault signature analysis. *IEEE Trans. Comput.* C-29 (6): 510–514.

Son, K., and D. K. Pradhan. 1980. Design of programmable logic arrays for testability. *Proc. 1980 IEEE Test Conf.*, pp. 163–166.

Sridhar, T., D. S. Ho, T. J. Powell, and S. M. Thatte. 1982. Analysis and simulation of parallel signature analysis. *Proc. 1982 IEEE Test Conf.*, pp. 656–661.

Stephenson, J. E. and J. Grason. 1976. A testability measure for register transfer level digital circuits. *Proc. 6th Int. Symp. Fault-Tolerant Computing*, pp. 101–107.

Stewart, J. H. 1977. Future testing of large LSI circuit cards. *Proc. 1977 Semiconductor Test Symp.*, pp. 6–17.

Susskind, A. K. 1981. Testing by verifying Walsh coefficients. *Proc. 11th Int. Symp. Fault-Tolerant Computing*, pp. 206–208.

Susskind, A. K. 1983. Testing by verifying Walsh coefficients. *IEEE Trans. Comput.* C-32 (2): 198–201.

Szygenda, S. A., D. M. Rouse, and E. W. Thompson. 1970. A model for implementation of a universal time delay simulation for large digital networks. *Proc. AFIPS Conf.*, pp. 207–216.

Takamatsu, Y., M. Hiraishi, and K. Kinoshita. 1983. Test generation for combinational circuits by a ten-valued calculus. *Trans. of Information Processing Society of Japan*, 24 (4): 542–548. In Japanese.

Thatte, S. M., D. S. Ho, H.-T. Yuan, T. Sridhar, and T. J. Powell. 1982. An architecture for testable VLSI processors. *Proc. 1982 IEEE Test Conf.*, pp. 484–492.

Toth, A., and C. Holt. 1974. Automated database-driven digital testing. *Computer* 1: 13–19.

Trischler, E. 1980. Incomplete scan path with an automatic test-generation methodology. *Proc. 1980 IEEE Test Conf.*, pp. 153–162.

Ulrich, E. G., and T. Baker. 1973. The concurrent simulation of nearly identical digital networks. *Proc. 10th Design Automation Workship*, vol. 6, pp. 145–150.

Williams, M. J. Y., and J. B. Angell. 1973. Enhancing testability of large scale integrated circuits via test points and additional logic. *IEEE Trans. Comput.* C-22 (1): 46–60.

Williams, T. W., and K. P. Parker. 1982. Design for testability—A survey. *IEEE Trans. Comput.* C-31 (1): 2–15.

Wood, C. T. 1979. The quantitative measure of testability. *Proc. IEEE Autotestcon*, pp. 286–291.

Yajima, S., and T. Aramaki. 1981. Autonomously testable programmable logic arrays. *Proc. 11th Symp. Fault-Tolerant Computing*, pp. 41–43.

Yamada, T. 1983. Syndrome-testable design of programmable logic arrays. *Proc. Int. Test Conf.*, pp. 53–458.

Index

§7.4 PLA

$Q_{2i-1} = \bar{X}_i \cdot \bar{C}_1$ → odd numbered lines will be 0

$Q_{2i} = x_i C_2$ → all even lines will be zero

to make all rows low

x_1	x_2	x_i	--	x_n	C_1	C_2
0	0	0	----	0	1	0
1	1	1	---	1	0	1
0	0	1	---	0	1	0

same effect

$x_i = 1$
others 0's

Q_{2i} = high others zeros

we can always sensitize one row in

we should sensitize a single path

hence

we take

odd numbered row will be 1

		x_i			C_1	C_2
0	0	1	----	0	1	0
1	1	0	------	1	0	1

Enter

The purpose of the control array is just to sensitize one row & purpose of Q_1 registers $S_1 - S_n$ is to sensitize one column

Sensitize single column & detect faults. Then we ~~sensitize~~ & sensitize only change the row & change the column.

columns go or extra column

detects that any of the row is high

purpose of extra end column & extra bottom row. To make sure that you sensitized one specific column & one specific row we 2 is low